Infidelity
and
LOYALTY

A Devotional Study
of Ezekiel and Daniel

Warren Henderson

Infidelity and Loyalty – A Devotional Study of Ezekiel and Daniel
By Warren Henderson
Copyright © 2017

Cover Design by Benjamin Bredeweg

Published by Warren A. Henderson
3769 Indiana Road
Pomona, KS 66076

Editing/Proofreading: Mike Attwood, Mark Kolchin,
    Robert Sullivan, Marilyn MacMullen,
    Dan Macy, and David Lindstrom

Perfect Bound ISBN 978-1-939770-40-0
eBook ISBN 978-1-939770-41-7

ORDERING INFORMATION:
Gospel Folio Press
Phone 1-905-835-9166
E-mail: order@gospelfolio.com

Also available through many online retailers.

Table of Contents

Other Books by the Author

Afterlife – What Will It Be Like?
Answer the Call – Finding Life's Purpose
Be Holy and Come Near– A Devotional Study of Leviticus
Behold the Saviour
Be Angry and Sin Not
Conquest and the Life of Rest – A Devotional Study of Joshua
Exploring the Pauline Epistles
Forsaken, Forgotten, and Forgiven – A Devotional Study of
   Jeremiah
Glories Seen & Unseen
Hallowed Be Thy Name – Revering Christ in a Casual World
Hiding God – The Ambition of World Religion
In Search of God – A Quest for Truth
Knowing the All-Knowing
Managing Anger God's Way
Mind Frames – Where Life's Battle Is Won or Lost
Out of Egypt – A Devotional Study of Exodus
Overcoming Your Bully
Passing the Torch – Mentoring the Next Generation For Christ
Relativity and Redemption – A Devotional Study of Judges and
   Ruth
Revive Us Again – A Devotional Study of Ezra and Nehemiah
Seeds of Destiny – A Devotional Study of Genesis
The Beginning of Wisdom – A Devotional Study of Job, Psalms,
   Proverbs, Ecclesiastes, and Song of Solomon
The Bible: Myth or Divine Truth?
The Evil Nexus – Are You Aiding the Enemy?
The Fruitful Bough – Affirming Biblical Manhood
The Fruitful Vine – Celebrating Biblical Womanhood
The Hope of Glory – A Preview of Things to Come
The Olive Plants – Raising Spiritual Children
Your Home the Birthing Place of Heaven

Preface

The whole Bible is an expression of divine truth. Our understanding of that truth is not gained by the private interpretation of any one particular Scripture (2 Pet. 1:20), but rather through the guidance of the Holy Spirit in comparing Scripture with Scripture (1 Cor. 2:13). Though portions of Ezekiel are difficult to understand because of its extensive visionary content, the overall book is a prophetic answer to such questions as: Does God have a future plan to bless the Jewish nation of Israel? How does His agenda for the Jewish people differ from His future plans for the Church? A literal interpretation of Scripture naturally leads to a literal fulfillment of Bible prophecy. Accordingly, many yet unfulfilled Bible prophecies simply call our attention to a future day in which God will honor His Word. Consequently, there is no need to spiritualize or allegorize Scripture to help God out – He is fully capable of doing exactly what He says, when He says, without man diluting the meaning of what He says.

The book of Ezekiel conveys God's jealous anger over Israel's idolatry, His righteous judgments to purify her of spiritual harlotry, and His future intentions of restoring the Jewish nation to Himself and fulfilling all His covenants to her. Ezekiel contrasts God's loyalty with Israel's infidelity as an adulterous wife. God has not abandoned His covenant people of old; He has an agenda for restoring them to a position of honor and blessing. Hosea refers to this latter event as *"a door of hope"* for Israel (Hos. 2:15), a future reality which Ezekiel explains in more detail than any other book in the Bible.

The latter portion of the book exclusively foretells Christ's Millennial Kingdom and how the laws of nature and the topology of earth will be radically changed at that time. Ezekiel's prophecies pertaining to the Kingdom Age include: the splendor of Jerusalem with its glorious temple, the esteem of the Jewish people, phenomenal worldwide blessings, and the universal exaltation of Christ by the nations.

1

Infidelity and Loyalty

The book of Daniel highlights the personal dedication of a Jewish man named Daniel and his righteous example to other Jewish captives in Babylon for about seventy years. About half of Daniel's book is prophetic in nature; this shows that God alone governs the rise and fall of kingdoms. Like Ezekiel, Daniel acknowledges that the Lord knows how to best chasten and restore His covenant people in order to accomplish all His covenantal promises to them.

Infidelity and Loyalty is a "commentary style" devotional which upholds the glories of Christ while exploring the books of Ezekiel and Daniel within the context of the whole of Scripture. I have endeavored to include in this book some principal gleanings from other writers. The short devotional format allows the reader to use the book either as a daily devotional or as a reference source for deeper study.

— Warren Henderson

Ezekiel

Overview of Ezekiel

Just prior to the Babylonian captivity, Habakkuk, Zephaniah, and Jeremiah had crucial prophetic ministries to God's covenant people. Although Jeremiah continued serving the Lord in Jerusalem after the fall of the city, rebuking Judah's apostasy and calling for their repentance no longer marked his messages. Israel had failed to heed God's threats of disciplinary judgment and the time for His retribution had come. About seven years prior to this, God called Ezekiel to prophesy to a despondent and spiritually-hardened group of Jewish captives in Babylon, he himself also being exiled. Hence, the stark contrast between the ministries of Jeremiah and Ezekiel is evident from their commencement.

Jeremiah announces himself immediately to his countrymen and for forty years faithfully calls them to repentance with the sorrowing passion of a bruised and bleeding heart. In contrast, Ezekiel's ministry is more aloof and he, more emotionally detached. He does not immediately reveal himself to his audience, nor does he zealously plead with the Jewish elders. In fact, until the fall of Jerusalem he is physically prohibited from speaking unless God had an explanatory prophecy for the necessity of their judgment. God exhibits patience and resolve through Jeremiah while there is yet some pliability remaining in the heart of His people, but Ezekiel is sent to hardened and embittered captives.

Like Elijah, Jeremiah, Hosea, and many other prophets, Ezekiel drank from his own ministry. For several years he was called on to act out or suffer through the messages he delivered. His ministry was physically limiting (often stressful), spiritually distasteful, and emotionally painful. Yet, God sustained him during these difficult days and indeed throughout his twenty plus years of prophetic ministry.

The Author

The exile of those Jews who surrendered prior to the fall of Jerusalem and those who survived its destruction was foretold by Jeremiah on many occasions. The first Jewish deportation was in 605 B.C. when Nebuchadnezzar first invaded Jerusalem; the prophet Daniel and his three young companions were among these early exiles (Dan. 1). The second deportation of Jewish captives occurred in 597 B.C. after Nebuchadnezzar put down Jehoiachin's rebellion. Ten thousand Jews were taken to Babylon at that time, among whom was the prophet Ezekiel and his wife (2 Kgs. 24:14).

The Lord summoned Ezekiel, the son of Buzi, to prophetic ministry about four years after his capture and six to seven years before Jerusalem's destruction. His first vision was in 593 B.C. and his last in 571 B.C. We are not informed of anything more about Ezekiel after he completed his lengthy prophetic assignment. We know nothing of his fate. Ezekiel's name means, "God strengthens," and would be evident reality during his arduous ministry among the Jewish captives in Babylon. Ezekiel's name reminds us that when God calls, He amply enables. The Lord does not expect us to accomplish what He does not empower us to do; otherwise we would get the glory, not Him.

Although initially Ezekiel was not too keen on his calling, he does accept what God desires him to do. This is evident by his frequent use of "among" or "in the midst" terminology, which is found 116 times in the book to describe his service to his fellow-captives.

Like the books of Jeremiah and Hosea, the book of Ezekiel is autobiographical in nature. The entire book, except for 1:2-3 and 24:24, is written in first-person format. As a priest, his knowledge of Scripture distinctly marks the text, but he supplies much more than just frequent Old Testament quotations. One senses progressively that the Spirit of God is more deeply explaining the Law's intended purpose and is enlarging an expectation of its fulfilment in the work and blessings of Christ.

The visionary content of Ezekiel's written ministry is rivaled only by the writings of Daniel and Zechariah, but as P. C. Craigie notes, Ezekiel's sustained inspiring contact with the Spirit of God is unique in Scripture: "For no other prophet is there a record of such sustained contact with the divine word, the very essence of prophecy."[1] The book is written mainly in prose, but poetic expressions mark key portions of the text, especially in the various dirges (chps. 19, 27, 28, 31, 32). Like Hosea and Jeremiah before him, the daily affairs of God's prophets were themselves a message to the people. Even the death of Ezekiel's wife will be used to convey a somber message to the dispersed Jewish nation.

Theme

The overall theme of the book is *God's glory*. His glory is first revealed to Ezekiel, then is removed from the earth before the Babylonians destroy the temple, and then returns to Jerusalem in the Kingdom Age. Why did God's glory depart from the temple in Jerusalem? The content of Ezekiel 16 answers this question and summarizes Israel's failure. In that chapter, the nation of Israel is likened to a discarded newborn girl whom God rescues from certain death. After gently retrieving her from a field, the Lord washes her, nurtures her, and protects her from harm (16:3-7). After she reaches maturity, He confirms a marriage covenant with her to initiate the special relationship that He desired to have with Israel (16:8). The once abandoned orphan became the betrothed virgin – the wife of Jehovah. Unfortunately, Israel later forsook the Lord and devoted herself to false gods. This spiritual adultery provoked Jehovah to jealousy; He responded by writing Israel a bill of divorcement and put her away to be punished among the nations (16:38; Jer. 3:8). But that is not the end of the story!

Despite Israel's unfaithfulness to Jehovah, the Lord is moved with compassion and mercy to restore her to a place of special intimacy, likened to marital companionship, which is protected by a covenant. Jehovah moved several prophets to announce His promise to restore the Jewish nation as His faithful wife in a future day (e.g., 16:60-63). Ezekiel chapters 36 through 48 describe how God will accomplish this marvelous feat. Thus, Ezekiel shows us the authority of divine government despite human failure and the devil's attempts to thwart God's purposes, says H. A. Ironside:

> Throughout his book, Ezekiel dwells upon the fact that God is over all, working out His plans and carrying out His own decision, in spite of Satanic efforts to thwart His purposes. The devil may be, and is, the god and prince of the present world system, but over and above all is the throne of the Eternal Majesty, whose ways are past finding out,

but who controls the destinies of Israel and the nations, "working all things according to the counsel of His own will."[2]

Like an adulterous wife who violated her marriage vow, the Jews had broken their covenant with God by worshipping other gods (Deut. 28). Rather than expressing love for Jehovah, they crafted images to honor false gods, and burned incense and even their own children before them. The sin of misplaced affection is a grievous offense against the Lord. The Jews were about to learn of God's righteous jealousy in a very painful way (16:32; Jer. 3:8). Although God's glory had departed from Israel, He was still devoted to His wayward people. Through Ezekiel, God promises to be glorified among them again and forever!

Prophetic Content

Unlike the book of Jeremiah, Ezekiel's prophecies are generally arranged in chronological order, beginning in the fifth year of his exile (1:2) and ending in the twenty-fifth year of his exile (40:1). The only exception to this observation is the prophecy concerning the judgment of Egypt (29:17) and possibly the prophecy spoken against Tyre, which is not clearly dated (26:1). Apparently, the last message against Egypt was organized with the earlier ones to preserve topical uniformity: reasons for Egypt's judgment and how divine retribution would be rendered. The following table summarizes the chronology of Ezekiel's prophetic ministry:

Passage	Event	Ezekiel's Date			Julian Calendar
		M	D	Y	
1:1-2	Ezekiel's prophetic call	4	5	30[1]	July 593 B.C.
3:16	Ezekiel's commission in exile	4	12	30[1]	Aug. 593 B.C.
8:1	Visions of the polluted temple	6	5	6	Sept. 592 B.C.
20:1	The inquiry of the elders	5	10	7	Aug. 591 B.C.
24:1	Siege of Jerusalem commences	10	10	9	Jan. 588 B.C.
26:1	Prophecy against Tyre	?[2]	1	11	586/587 B.C.?
29:1	Prophecy against Egypt	10	12	10	Jan. 587 B.C.
29:17	Prophecies against Tyre & Egypt	1	1	27	March 571 B.C.
30:20	Prophecies against Pharaoh	1	7	11	April 587 B.C.

8

31:1	More prophecies against Pharaoh	3	1	11	June 587 B.C.
32:1	Lamentation for Pharaoh	12	1	12	March 585 B.C.
32:17	Pharaoh in Sheol	12	15	12	March 571 B.C.
33:21	Lamentation for fallen Jerusalem	10	5	12	Jan. 585 B.C.
40:1	Visions of new temple/Jerusalem	1[3]	10	25	Apr/Oct 73 B.C.

[1] The "thirtieth year" has no specific reference point and may be Ezekiel's age.
[2] The specific month is not stated, but was likely just prior to Jerusalem's destruction in July 586 B.C.
[3] "The beginning of the year" of Jewish calendar: April or October, depending if the reference is to Jubilee.

Outline

There are three major movements in the book. In the first section, Ezekiel rehearses the sins of Judah (e.g., their unabashed idolatry) and repeatedly warns his countrymen of imminent divine judgment which will destroy Jerusalem, including the temple, and will result in the death or captivity of most of the Jewish population. In the middle portion of the book, Ezekiel warns Israel's proud and idolatrous neighbors who had often oppressed God's covenant people. In the final section, the prophet foretells Israel's restoration to the land and spiritual renewal with God. Much of this section remains unfulfilled as it relates to a future day when the Jewish Messiah will return to the earth, crush Israel's enemies, and establish His earthly kingdom of righteousness, blessing, and peace.

The following is a general outline of the book:

I.   Ezekiel called and commissioned (chps. 1-3)

II.   Warnings of Judgment on Judah (chps. 4-24)

III. Judgment on Gentile Nations (chps. 25-32)

IV. Ezekiel the Watchman (chp. 33)

V.   The Future Restoration of Israel (chps. 34-39)

VI. The Millennial Temple (chps. 40-46)

VII. Divisions of Tribal Land in Millennial Kingdom (chps. 47-48)

Key Dates

The following are estimated dates relating to Ezekiel's ministry:

Event	Date (B.C.)
The book of the Law is found in temple – initiates Josiah's reforms	622/623
Fall of Assyria to Babylon	612
Josiah dies; Pharaoh Neco replaces Jehoahaz with his brother Jehoiakim	608
Nebuchadnezzar's first attack on Jerusalem – 1st Jewish captives exiled	605
Jehoiakim again sides with Egypt and rebels against Nebuchadnezzar	601
Jehoiakim dies in Jerusalem; son Jehoiachin reigns 3 months before Nebuchadnezzar takes Jerusalem; king & 2nd group of captives exiled	597
Zedekiah breaks agreement with Babylon and sides with Egypt	589
Siege of Jerusalem begins	589/588[1]
Jerusalem falls and 3rd group of Jewish captives taken to Babylon	587[2]
Jerusalem and temple destroyed; Gedaliah appointed governor of Judah	586
Babylon falls to Medo-Persian Empire	539
Decree of Cyrus permitting Jewish captives to return to Israel	538
Altar erected in Jerusalem and work on rebuilding temple begins	536

[1] Scholars disagree on the length of the Jerusalem siege and on the date it actually began. Jeremiah states that the siege of Jerusalem began in the tenth month of the ninth year of Zedekiah's reign and ended in the ninth day of the fourth month of the eleventh year of Zedekiah (Jer. 39:1-7). Using our Western calculator, that would be about eighteen months. The problem however, is that it was normal for Judah's vassal kings under Babylonian rule to acknowledge years of rule from Tishri (September/October) to Tishri. Yet, the Jews used their own reckoning for months with Nisan (March/April) being the first month of the year. Some think the siege began late in 589 B.C., but many prefer January 588. There was at least an 18-month siege of Jerusalem (i.e., January 588 to July 587 B.C.) that was briefly interrupted by a failed Egyptian attack against Nebuchadnezzar (Jer. 34:11-12). The city of Jerusalem was destroyed the following summer (586 B.C.) and the siege may have lasted up to that time (i.e., about two and a half years).

[2] While we know that Jerusalem fell in the fourth month of the eleventh year of Zedekiah's reign (2 Kgs. 25:1-3), scholars are divided as to whether that occurred in 586 or 587 B.C. The date of Jerusalem's destruction is widely agreed to be in July 586 B.C.

Devotions in Ezekiel

The Likeness of Glory
Ezekiel 1

What the number "thirty" refers to in verse 1 is unclear, but it is generally understood to denote Ezekiel's age when he began to see visions of God. Some believe Ezekiel was referring to the thirtieth year after Nebuchadnezzar's father Nabopolassar, an Assyrian general, rebelled and ascended to power in 625 B.C. This was the beginning of the end for the Assyrian Empire. This is a favorable explanation in that Ezekiel acknowledges the political authority that is in power at the time he begins to see visions. Others believe it refers to the thirtieth year after the priest Hilkiah discovered the book of the Law in the temple (i.e., the eighteenth year of Josiah's reign; 622/623 B.C.), that supposedly being the year of Jubilee according to rabbinic interpretation. These latter explanations would indicate a date between 594 and 592 B.C. for the commencement of Ezekiel's ministry. Ezekiel does not reckon time from Nabopolassar's rebellion or from the year of Jubilee anywhere else in the book. In one sense, it does not really matter which of the three explanations is correct, as all originate at approximately the same year (593 B.C. being most accepted based on verse 2) and Ezekiel does not use this reference to reckon time again.

We do know that a priest could not enter into the priesthood until he was thirty years of age (Num. 4:3). If Ezekiel was now thirty years old, he would previously have been prohibited from performing priestly duties in the temple. Instead of representing the people to God as a priest, God had a special calling for Ezekiel; he would represent the Lord to the people through prophetic ministry. This would be a good reason for accepting that the number thirty in verse 1 likely represents the prophet's age at his calling.

Infidelity and Loyalty

What is known is that Ezekiel was among the Jewish captives who had been transported to Babylon when he received his prophetic commission. Ezekiel notes the location in which the Spirit of God began to show him visions, near the Chebar (modern Khabour), which flows into the Euphrates River about 200 miles north of Babylon (v. 1). Perhaps he had ventured to this serene location for a time of prayer and meditation.

The timing mentioned in verse 2 does provide us with a chronological footing. Jehoiakim's eighteen-year-old son, Jehoiachin, ascended the throne of Judah only three months before he surrendered himself and the city to Nebuchadnezzar in March 597 B.C. (2 Kgs. 24:8-9). This capture date of Jehoiachin is confirmed by the Babylonian Chronicle as Adar 2, 597 B.C. He was an evil king, and Nebuchadnezzar took him, his servants, and the queen royal as prisoners to Babylon. Nebuchadnezzar also despoiled the temple of its precious vessels and treasure, and then enslaved the princes, the craftsmen, the blacksmiths, and the mighty men of valor in the land (2 Kgs. 24:11-16). In all, he took some ten thousand captives back to Babylon, the prophet Ezekiel being among them. By Jewish reckoning, the fifth year of Jehoiachin's captivity would be 593 B.C.

In the Old Testament, great significance is attached to personal names, for a name indicated not just the identity of a person but also their features, nature, or character. For example, Jacob lived up to his name "supplanter" – he was a trickster and a schemer. Esau's name related to the hairy appearance of his body at birth. Ezekiel was God's prophet to the discouraged Jews exiled in Babylon; his name, only mentioned twice in the entire book, means "God strengthens" (v. 3). The meaning of his name indeed characterized the dependent nature of his ministry and the divine power enabling it.

Furthermore, we learn that, like the prophets Jeremiah (Jer. 1:1) and Zechariah (Zech. 1:1), Ezekiel was a priest (the son of Buzi; v. 3). Although Ezekiel had been forcibly removed from the temple, God still identifies him as a priest with an important ministry among His estranged covenant people. Ezekiel was not acting on his own, as the narrative bears out, but *"the hand of the Lord"* was commencing and directing every aspect of his ministry. This is a good reminder that our spiritual calling in Christ is not determined by selfish desire, our secular circumstances, our location, or even our past failures – how we are to serve the Lord was determined before the foundation of the

12

world. Paul reminds us that *"we are His workmanship, created in Christ Jesus for good works, which God prepared beforehand that we should walk in them"* (Eph. 2:10). Let us all be faithful to walk in the good of our calling, for, as we will observe in Ezekiel, the Lord is quite able to overcome life's harsh circumstances to accomplish His glorious purposes.

We are immortal till our work is done.

— George Whitefield

Ezekiel's First Vision

Years later, Ezekiel will summarize the context of what he is about to describe to us this way: *"The vision I saw was just like the vision that I had seen when He came to destroy the city"* (43:3; ESV). As Ezekiel gazes northward, he notices an approaching thunderstorm (v. 4). At first, the ominous dark clouds, the spectacular lightning and the raging wind capture his attention. However, his gaze soon shifts to the brilliant light with the hue of molten metal, which emanates from the center of the storm, the approaching whirlwind. As the strange spectacle converges on his location, he is able to discern four angelic beings, with human-like features, at the corners of what he comes to realize is the lower part of God's throne-chariot (v. 5; 1 Chron. 28:18). These beings are later identified as cherubim (10:20).

In Moses' day, two craftsmen were guided by the Holy Spirit to sculpt and create the tabernacle furnishings, which were patterned after heavenly realities (Heb. 9:23-24). This included depicting two beautiful cherubim above the Mercy Seat of the Ark of the Covenant (Ex. 31:1-7). In the tabernacle, God's presence dwelt over the Mercy Seat between the cherubim, which depicts God's heavenly throne. Though previously mentioned in Scripture, it is in Ezekiel 1 that we first find a description of these extraordinary spiritual beings.

The post-exilic prophet informs us that cherubim have four wings, but use only two for flying; the other two cover their intrinsic glories in God's presence (vv. 6, 8, 11, 23-24). Later we will learn that Lucifer, before his fall, was a beautiful cherub, sheathed with precious stones and inherently equipped with musical ability (28:11-16). Apparently, cherubim are protectors of God's holiness; this is not to say that God needs protection, but they keep that which is sinful from coming into

13

His presence and being consumed by His glory. For example, cherubim guarded Eden after the fall of man to ensure that any return route would be met with swift judgment (Gen. 3:24).

The cherubim were standing upright (legs straight), each having four faces, bronze feet resembling calves' feet, and human hands under their wings (vv. 6-8). Perhaps their hands were visible because each extended two wings outward to touch the wings of two other cherubim to provide a covering barrier into God's intimate presence and glory (v. 9). Their appearance was like burning coals of fire and they moved quickly as flashes of lightning, to illustrate their immediate obedience to God's direction (vv. 13-14). When in motion they did not turn their heads or bodies, but operated in complete unison to maneuver God's mobile throne (v. 12).

All creation, visible and invisible, provides a wonderful testimony of God's greatness. Included in this chorus of praise are the spiritual beings in heavenly realms who continually declare the glory of God and praise His name (Ps. 103:20). The Bible informs us that classes of spiritual beings do indeed exist in heaven for this very purpose. Besides Michael the archangel, there are cherubim as we have just seen, seraphim, the four living creatures, and a host of innumerable angels with various functions and roles. Furthermore, God describes to us what many of these spiritual beings do and how they appear before God's throne in heaven. All things recorded in Scripture have a divine purpose, so why did God document all these details? What is it He wants us to learn from these angelic descriptions?

God the Father calls our attention to His Son through the appearance of these created beings. When the cherubim and seraphim cover themselves, it is for the purpose of concealing potential competing glories in God's presence – only God's glory may shine forth, for He alone is to be adored and worshipped in heaven. However, when the faces, eyes, or feet of these creatures are described, it is because they are not covered and, in fact, should not be, for some emulated glory of Christ is being proclaimed through them. This exercise of revealing and concealing glories is something that the Church is to remember and practice now; in so doing, we pattern the holy scene in heaven (1 Cor. 11:2-16).

Interestingly, the cherubim who bear up God's mobile throne (v. 6), the seraphim who praise God in Isaiah 6, and the four living creatures who do the same in Revelation 4 all have the same faces – four kinds of faces, to be more exact. Apparently, each cherub has all four: the face of a lion, the face of an ox, the face of a man, and the face of an eagle (vv. 10, 15). The faces of these beings reflect the various glorious themes of the Lord Jesus presented in the four Gospel accounts. The *lion* is the king of the beasts, which reflects Matthew's perspective of Christ being the King of the Jews. The *ox*, as a beast of burden, is harnessed for the rigors of serving, and pictures Mark's presentation of Christ as the lowly Servant of Jehovah. The face of the *man* clearly agrees with Luke's theme of the Lord's humanity. Lastly, the *eagle* flies high above all the other creatures – in view is the divine essence of the Savior declared in John's Gospel. So, in heaven right now and upon the Mercy Seat in Moses' day, the various glories of Christ, as revealed in the Gospels, are declared. God uses illustrations from creation to teach humanity about the wonders of His Son. We wholeheartedly agree with the words of the psalmist, *"Bless the Lord, all His works in all places of His dominion: bless the Lord, O my soul"* (Ps. 103:22).

Ezekiel then notices four beryl-glowing wheels at the base of each corner of God's throne – positioned by each cherub (v. 16). Beryl, beryllium aluminium cyclosilicate, may have a variety of colors, but in Scripture it general refers to a yellow-greenish tone. Emerald, for example, is a greenish color. Each wheel also had a rim full of eyes, and another wheel within it, thus permitting the throne to instantly roll any direction without steering changes to the wheels' orientation (vv. 17-19). The description of the wheels expresses functionality rather than mechanical design, as the laws of nature do not apply to this chariot. The wheels connected the throne of God to the earth and hence the rims being full of eyes symbolize God's omniscience in the affairs of men:

> *For the eyes of the Lord run to and fro throughout the whole earth, to show Himself strong on behalf of those whose heart is loyal to Him. In this you have done foolishly; therefore from now on you shall have wars* (2 Chron. 16:9).

> *The eyes of the Lord are in every place, keeping watch on the evil and the good* (Prov. 15:3).

God is intimately aware of all that happens on the earth and governs all the affairs of men to accomplish His purposes, especially for His own people. There is nothing left to chance, nothing that catches God by surprise – He sees all, knows all, and controls all things. God's homogenous sovereign agenda is evident in the actions of the cherubim, whose cooperative spirit was in the wheels to move Jehovah's chariot-throne as He directed (vv. 20-21). The firmament directly above the heads of the cherubim was brightly illuminated; it reminded Ezekiel of ice crystals sparkling in sunlight (v. 22). This is William MacDonald's concept of God's mobile throne:[3]

Ezekiel 1: God's Mobile Throne

This drawing portrays William MacDonald's understanding of God's throne-chariot, with the exception that each creature has four faces.

The sound associated with the movement of the cherubim's wings was like the crashing of an enormous waterfall (v. 24). Thus far, Ezekiel's attention had been focused on the lower portion of the spectacle before him, but that all changed when he heard the majestic sound of God's voice, like a deafening clap of thunder from above. The cherubim immediately let down their wings and Ezekiel's gaze was drawn upward to the brilliant expanse above the cherubim (v. 25). He saw the throne of God gleaming like sapphire (a translucent heavenly-blue stone) and a dazzling array of colors emanating from the throne like the full hues of a rainbow (v. 28). As first demonstrated to Noah after the deluge, the rainbow symbolizes God's unchanging promises – God always keeps His Word. The existence of the Jewish nation today is just one example of this timeless truth.

Ezekiel then describes the One who was sitting in the midst of the throne – He was in the form of a man but His "appearance" was that of an intense inferno. What Ezekiel saw was a theophany, the outshining glory of the preincarnate Christ on the throne of God. John would later see a vision of Him, the Lord Jesus Christ, walking among the lampstands (the churches) and later standing on God's heavenly throne while being worshipped by the throngs of heaven (Rev. 1, 5). Through the appearance of Christ, God declared His glory to Ezekiel in a way that would not extinguish His servant through direct exposure to the outshining brilliance of His Shekinah glory. Throughout his book, Ezekiel refers to God's glory sixteen times; only the books of Psalms and Isaiah have more occurrences.

Likewise on Mount Sinai, God visibly manifested His purity and majesty to the elders of Israel in a way that was not lethal to sinful flesh. He permitted them to view only the sapphire base of His glorious throne and not His outshining glory (Ex. 33:20). Neither did Ezekiel personally see the full glory of God, but rather *the likeness of the glory of the Lord"* in vision form (v. 28). What was Ezekiel's response to this revelation? Even witnessing a limited representation of God's intense holiness was more than flesh and blood could take in; Ezekiel immediately fell to the ground in reverential and fearful awe.

What Ezekiel saw that day would mark him for life in the same way the spectacular sight of God's throne overwhelmed the prophet Isaiah nearly two centuries earlier. Above a rumbling, smoked-filled temple Isaiah saw seraphim flying overhead, crying out to each other, *"Holy, holy, holy is the Lord of Hosts; the whole earth is full of His glory!"*

(Isa. 6:3). Six centuries after Ezekiel's time, John was caught up in the Spirit to witness a heavenly scene, similar to the one we have in this chapter. John saw four living creatures flying above God's throne, and these declared a similar message to those Isaiah observed: *"Holy, holy, holy, Lord God Almighty, Who was and is and is to come!"* (Rev. 4:8). These spiritual beings continue to declare God's holiness as a warning of His unapproachable nature. He is the almighty, holy God; His character, attributes, and ways are unique. This is what "holy" means, "to be set apart." His very essence and attributes of holiness set God apart from all He has created.

Thankfully, souls redeemed by grace and elect angels are declared positionally holy and are thus *set apart* for His glory. God is pure and alone in majesty; there is absolutely no sin or evil in God (1 Jn. 1:6). Because God is holy, He cannot approve of anything within us which is less than His own perfect nature.

> One great hindrance to holiness in the ministry of the word is that we are prone to preach and write without pressing into the things we say and making them real to our own souls. Over the years words begin to come easy, and we find we can speak of mysteries without standing in awe; we can speak of purity without feeling pure; we can speak of zeal without spiritual passion; we can speak of God's holiness without trembling; we can speak of sin without sorrow; we can speak of heaven without eagerness. And the result is a terrible hardening of the spiritual life.
>
> — John Owen

The holiness of God is a serious matter. When man loses sight of God's holiness, he exalts himself and minimizes the putrid nature of sin.

Recalling God's Words concerning His holiness to Moses on Mount Sinai, Peter reminds believers in the Church Age that God remains holy, and desires His people to reflect His moral nature: *"As obedient children, not conforming yourselves to the former lusts, as in your ignorance; but as He who called you is holy, you also be holy in all your conduct, because it is written, 'Be holy, for I am holy'"* (1 Pet. 1:14-16). Paul reminds the believers at Corinth that their bodies had become the temple of the Lord and that they should not desecrate God's dwelling place (1 Cor. 6:19). To be mindful of God's holiness is a strong defense against engaging in sin. God will not tolerate filthiness or wickedness in His presence. God is holy and He will not settle for anything less than holiness in us. There are no degrees of righteousness and holiness with God, so His people should not be satisfied with conduct of which God does not approve. No matter the dispensation God's people are in, one inescapable truth remains the same: when God's holiness is disregarded or forgotten, humanized religion and sin will abound among His people.

Meditation

There is a danger of forgetting that the Bible reveals, not first the love of God, but the intense, blazing holiness of God, with his love as the center of that holiness.

— Oswald Chambers

Sent to a Rebel Nation
Ezekiel 2

Overwhelmed by what he had seen, Ezekiel fell prostrate on the ground. The Lord spoke to him, *"Son of man, stand on your feet, and I will speak to you"* (v. 1). God's initial address to Ezekiel is in keeping with the awesome vision of God's glory that he, a mere man, had just been permitted to see. The expression "son of man" is also used in reference to Daniel (8:17), the other major post-exile prophet. "Son of man" is found ninety-three times in Ezekiel's book and affirms his scant human essence before the almighty, majestic Creator. After contemplating God's greatness and humanity's insignificance, David was prompted to inquire of God, *"What is man that You are mindful of him, And the son of man that You visit him?"* (Ps. 8:4). Yet, God is mindful of mankind and of His covenant people; He has plans for both that center in the work of Christ. Hence, Ezekiel's lowly title is fitting for his book, says J. N. Darby:

> God speaks to Ezekiel as to a "son of man" – a title that suited the testimony of a God who spoke outside of His people, as being no longer in their midst, but on the contrary was judging them from the throne of His sovereignty. It is Christ's own title, looked at as rejected and outside of Israel, although He never ceases to think of the blessing of the people in grace. This puts the prophet in connection with the position of Christ Himself. He would not, thus rejected, allow His disciples to announce Him as the Christ (Luke 9), for the Son of Man was to suffer.[4]

The tenor of Ezekiel's entire ministry would be characterized by this humble title – a title that expresses God's displeasure with humanity during this time, but especially with His covenant people.

After the Lord commanded his prophet to stand, the Holy Spirit promptly entered Ezekiel and enabled him to obey the Lord, and also to hear and understand God's Words to him (v. 2). In Old Testament days, the Holy Spirit did not regenerate and eternally indwell believers as in the Church Age, for Christ had not yet died and been resurrected. Believers today are baptized into Christ's resurrection life by the Holy Spirit and are thereby empowered to obey the Lord and to discern God's Word accurately (John 16:13-14; 1 Jn. 2:20-21). If God is directing and enabling our service, we never need to worry about being able to stand on our own two feet!

> The will of God will not take us where the grace of God cannot sustain us.
>
> — Billy Graham

Previously, the Holy Spirit suddenly and temporarily indwelt believers to powerfully enable them to accomplish some feat or to declare the Word of God. Let us remember that God does not command the believer to do anything beyond the measure of grace He extends to do His will. An example of this is before us. God commanded fearful Ezekiel to stand on his feet. The spirit of God entered him and equipped him to do so; then he received his divine commission.

> *Son of man, I am sending you to the children of Israel, to a rebellious nation that has rebelled against Me; they and their fathers have transgressed against Me to this very day. For they are impudent and stubborn children. I am sending you to them, and you shall say to them, "Thus says the Lord God." As for them, whether they hear or whether they refuse – for they are a rebellious house – yet they will know that a prophet has been among them. And you, son of man, do not be afraid of them nor be afraid of their words, though briers and thorns are with you and you dwell among scorpions; do not be afraid of their words or dismayed by their looks, though they are a rebellious house. You shall speak My words to them, whether they hear or whether they refuse, for they are rebellious. But you, son of man, hear what I say to you. Do not be rebellious like that rebellious house; open your mouth and eat what I give you* (2:3-8).

As previously mentioned, Ezekiel's name is mentioned only twice in the entire book; in fact, the Lord never addresses him by his given name, but always as "son of man" (some ninety-three times). The Lord does refer to Ezekiel once while giving him a message to deliver to Israel (24:24). Being frequently addressed by the Lord as "son of man"

21

would remind Ezekiel of his own frail humanity, during a time he was interacting frequently with the Most High God.

This title "son of man" is used widely to express human association in the Old Testament; thus, it also links Christ with earth and humanity (Dan. 7:13). Luke applies the title to the Lord Jesus twenty-five times in his Gospel, in contrast to John, whose theme being the deity of Christ, refers to the Lord as the Son of Man only twelve times. The Lord Jesus spoke of Himself as "the Son of Man" more often than as "the Son of God," for the divine title identified His mission and not His divine essence. It is noted that only the Lord Jesus spoke of Himself as "the Son of Man" in the Gospels, some eighty-four times; yet, fourteen references speak of "others" identifying the Lord Jesus as the "Son of God," a title He applied to Himself only five times. (All of these occurrences are rightly placed in John.) The Lord normally spoke of His humble station and ministry, while others were privileged to acknowledge His divine rule and essence.

One of the early biblical references to the "Son of Man" is found in Psalm 8. This psalm is then quoted in the Epistle to the Hebrews and is applied to the incarnation of Christ. The title "Son of Man" is not found in any New Testament epistle except for the one reference in Hebrew 2:6-9, which refers to Psalm 8. The Epistles inform the Church of her heavenly, not earthly, calling in Christ. The Lord Jesus will always be a glorified man, but He is now highly exalted and at the right hand of His Father in heaven. This is the proper place for the victorious and faithful Son of God.

Returning to the narrative, seven times in seven verses the Lord speaks of Judah's rebellion against him; they were "a rebellious house" (vv. 5, 6, 8) within "a rebellious nation" (v. 3). They were impudent and stubborn, and had willfully transgressed God's law from the beginning until that present time (vv. 3-4). But God still loved His people, though they were defiant. He would not have them destitute of revelation and guidance. Hence, He sent Ezekiel among them as His spokesman (v. 5). He was not to be afraid of his unruly countrymen, but to bravely declare God's message to them – *"Thus says the Lord God"* (vv. 4, 6). The Lord conveys a similar message to young Jeremiah at his commissioning (Jer. 1). Ezekiel was not responsible for how others responded to God's message; he was merely God's messenger (vv. 5, 7). However, God did warn him not to be rebellious like his countrymen: Ezekiel was to speak only His words – no more, and no less. It would be natural for Ezekiel to become discouraged by the poor response to his preaching, but he was not to lose heart – he was to remain faithful to the Lord (vv. 7-8).

The Lord then stretched out His hand, which held a scroll, and unrolled it so Ezekiel could read its writing (v. 9). In ancient times, books were written on animal skins and rolled up to preserve the information. Usually, these were written only on one side, but in this case both sides of the vellum were inscribed. This added detail likely expresses God's deep remorse over His people's wickedness and the abundance of calamities they would suffer because of it. Ezekiel then confirms the content of the scroll: God's lamentations, mourning, and judgments on His wayward people (v. 10). In the next chapter, Ezekiel will open his mouth and God will cause him to eat the scroll. Afterwards, God's very words would abide in Ezekiel's mouth and would guide his heart in their needful proclamation!

Meditation

My talents, gifts, and graces, Lord,
Into Thy blessed hands receive;
And let me live to preach Thy Word,
And let me to Thy glory live;
My every sacred moment spend
In publishing the sinner's Friend.

Enlarge, inflame, and fill my heart
With boundless charity divine;
So shall I all strength exert,
And love them with a zeal like Thine,
And lead them to Thy open side,
The sheep for whom the Shepherd died.

— Charles Wesley

23

God's Watchman
Ezekiel 3

The Jewish nation had been like an obstinate horse rejecting the bit and bridle of its master. Ezekiel, however, was to willingly open his mouth and eat (i.e., receive) from the Lord whatever He put there (2:8). Chapter 3 commences with the Lord repeating the command: His prophet was to eat the scroll that was in His hand. By doing so, Ezekiel was internalizing the divine message he was to passionately communicate to His rebellious people (vv. 1-2).

In application, this scene is a good reminder: Before we can convey truth to others, we first must know it and live it ourselves. This will require us to read, to meditate on, to rightly divide, and to memorize Scripture (2 Tim. 2:15). By comparing Scripture with Scripture, the Holy Spirit enables us to understand the mind of God and to get right with God.

When a man is right with God, God will freely use him.

— F. B. Meyer

Doctrine is not just head knowledge; it is to be lived out (Tit. 2:1). By adhering to sound doctrine, a man or woman of God is prepared for divine service and kept from sin:

All Scripture is given by inspiration of God, and is profitable for doctrine, for reproof, for correction, for instruction in righteousness, that the man of God may be complete, thoroughly equipped for every good work (2 Tim. 3:16-17).

Your word I have hidden in my heart, that I might not sin against You (Ps. 119:11).

Ezekiel did eat the scroll and it tasted as sweet as honey in his mouth. Though the message pertained to devastating judgment, it nonetheless was God's Word, and Ezekiel was reminded that its source (God) was sweet, though the content of His message was bitter.

A few centuries later, John would also eat a scroll containing God's Word, which then equipped him to reveal the deep things of God to the Church of Jesus Christ (Rev. 10:8-10). Likewise, a few years before Ezekiel's commissioning, the prophet Jeremiah had also joyfully eaten God's Word, which sustained and delighted his soul (Jer. 15:16). This divine provision empowered him to shun the company of evildoers and fools in order to sit alone with the Lord and be guided by Him (v. 17). Because Jeremiah was in such close communion with God, he too felt indignation against Judah (i.e. he could identify with God's righteous anger over their sin). These benefits are available to all those who joyfully internalize God's Word and willingly submit to it. Preachers today cannot expect to have any divine power unless they have first fed upon God's Word and permitted the Spirit of God to have His way. What God reveals must be lived out before it can be spoken out in power.

David puts the matter poetically this way: *"The judgments of the Lord are true and righteous altogether. More to be desired are they than gold, yea, than much fine gold: sweeter also than honey and the honeycomb"* (Ps. 19:9-10). God's Word and His work are a direct reflection of His character; that is, they are what He is: perfect, sure, right, pure, clean, true, and righteous. God's statutes were more precious than gold, sweeter than honey, and ensured a prodigious reward if obeyed. David considered it a joy and a privilege to know and keep God's commandments; doing so revives the soul and makes one wise in righteous living (Ps. 19:8).

Having now received God's message, Ezekiel was to deliver it to *"the house of Israel."* His main audience would be the captive Jews that he sojourned with (v. 4). Ezekiel was not being sent to a remote people with an unknown tongue, but to God's own people who understood Hebrew (v. 5). This is an important distinction, in that the sign of the unknown tongue is used throughout Scripture as a warning to the Jewish people of imminent judgment. Moses told the people that if they rebelled against the Lord, He would punish them through a nation whose language they would not understand (Deut. 28:49). This meant that God would use an army from a distant land instead of a

25

neighboring nation. Isaiah warned idolatrous Israel by employing this sign just prior to the Assyrian invasion (Isa. 28:11-12). Jeremiah referenced it as a final warning to Judah of imminent judgment for the same deeply-rooted sin (Jer. 5:15). But the Jews ignored the warnings of Moses, Isaiah, and Jeremiah; the sign of the unknown tongue was issued and severe judgment ultimately came.

Ezekiel's message delivered in their language meant that there was still time to repent and to be restored to the Lord. At a personal level, the fullness of God's wrath could be avoided if there was true repentance. Yet, the Lord informed Ezekiel that the house of Israel (emphasizing the nation as a whole) would not receive his message, because they were actively rejecting Him (vv. 6-7).

They were a coldhearted and stiff-necked people, meaning that both their thinking and affections towards the things of God were controlled by an impudent disposition (v. 8). But Ezekiel was not to fear their threatening glares or jeering rejection, for God would ensure that his own forehead was harder than flint (v. 9). F. C. Cook suggests the reference to the *"adamant stone, harder than flint"* means a diamond which was used to cut flint, implying that Ezekiel's robust diamond-like disposition would permit God's message to cut deeply into the hardened hearts of God's rebellious people.[5] The Spirit of God would infuse Ezekiel with tenacious determination to both proclaim God's Word and confront those who rejected it. Given the strenuous situation, Ezekiel might be tempted to soften the message, but God reminded him again that he was directly accountable to Him to speak exactly those words he had divinely received (vv. 10-11). God's spokesman must declare God's Word; Ezekiel was not responsible for the results of doing so, nor was he to be concerned about the consequences to those who ignored God's message.

This is an introduction to what it means to be God's watchman, a topic more fully developed later in this chapter. Gospel preaching today is similar. All believers are to be witnesses for the Lord in day-to-day life (Acts 1:8). Believers who live out the gospel will have opportunities to share its message with the lost. Only God can save lost sinners – that is His work (John 6:44). As believers, we are to accurately convey God's Word with a spirit of love and urgency that reflects the gracious character of Christ Himself. If we hold back from living for and declaring Christ's words of life to those dead in trespasses and sins, then He will hold us accountable. Like Ezekiel, believers today are to be faithful watchmen who warn the ignorant and the rebellious of impending doom.

Having provided Ezekiel with the message he was to deliver, the Spirit of God then directs the prophet to his place of ministry (vv. 12-15). The Holy Spirit, who first entered Ezekiel in the previous chapter, transported the prophet back to Tel Aviv (Tel Abib), the location of his previous vision (v. 15). He begins to describe the event, but is interrupted by the loud rushing sound of the cherubim's wings brushing together, the thunderous noise from the wheels and a great booming voice behind him saying, *"Blessed is the glory of the Lord from His place"* (v. 12). Although the entire experience was spectacular, we sense that Ezekiel is not happy about being uprooted nor the nature of his new ministry:

> *I went in bitterness, in the heat of my spirit; but the hand of the Lord was strong upon me. Then I came to the captives at Tel Abib, who dwelt by the River Chebar; and I sat where they sat, and remained there astonished among them seven days* (vv. 14-15).

Ezekiel seems less startled by the Lord's second appearance seven days later (v. 16). This encounter was a natural development in his commissioning; Ezekiel had already been made aware of his calling, but apparently was not too motivated to fulfill it. We are not told what the source of Ezekiel's bitterness was. Perhaps it related to being called to proclaim a message of judgment against his own people, whom he loved, but who had exasperated him by their conduct. However, after being permitted to observe the spiritual condition of his fellow countrymen for seven days, Ezekiel's calling as God's watchman on their behalf seems to have more importance. Kyle Yates suggests that the seven-day interim enabled embittered Ezekiel to better connect with those God had called him to serve:

> Ezekiel felt the hand of God upon him and realized a divine compulsion that could not be resisted, but he went in bitterness of spirit to a distasteful task. Fortunately for him and for the people, he did not begin preaching immediately but sat among the distraught people for the whole week. That experience gave him a clear understanding of their problems, their miseries and their crying needs. The preacher who is able to see life through the window of his people will be able to help them and provide the leadership so sorely needed.[6]

Infidelity and Loyalty

Beside spending time with those God had called him to serve, spending quiet time before the Lord provided Ezekiel the opportunity to better align his own emotions with God's own hurt concerning Israel's sin. He found that he now possessed a fierce indignation towards the sin of his countrymen. Likewise, as we sit in the presence of the Lord and commune with Him in meditating on His Word and in prayer, we learn to think as He does about the necessity of holy living. Real fellowship with the Lord compels us to feel the abhorrence of sin as He does and to love the sinner as only He can. If we learn to hate what God hates and value what He values, we will be more willing to accept His calling for us, despite its unpleasantness.

> God does not give us everything we want, but He does fulfill His promises, leading us along the best and straightest paths to Himself.
>
> — Dietrich Bonhoeffer

> God first works in us to will and then works in us to work for His good pleasure.
> — Watchman Nee

After days of sitting in silence, Ezekiel had a fresh, less self-focused motivation for ministry, the holiness of God. He also acknowledges the source of power and direction for his prophetic ministry, *"the hand of the Lord"* (v. 14). These two complementary aspects of service cannot be separated. Our zeal for holiness and truth must be accompanied by God's authority and power or we will not be able to serve Him, and worse, we will likely bring disdain upon His name. Each believer must submit to God's ongoing work of sanctification to be led by the hand of the Lord into His purposes. Without the work of sanctification, ministry for God is impossible. Fancy words and good intentions do not define a missionary. His or her character is the message and without Christ-likeness, he or she will fail miserably in representing Christ to the lost.

God is not concerned with saving lost souls only; He also wants those who respond to His salvation call to be made completely conformed to the character of His Son (Rom. 8:29). Though believers will not obtain sinless perfection until they experience glorification (1 Cor. 15:51-52), the present desire of every believer should be to be like Christ, who is sinless (1 Pet. 2:22). Through Christ's blood, provision is made for the believer to be cleansed of sin and to be restored into happy fellowship with God (1 Jn. 1:9). God's desire for us then is that we do not sin at all (1 Jn. 2:1, 3:9), but rather, we are to expose and confront sin (Eph. 5:11). Likewise, in personal holiness and in the power of the Holy Spirit, Ezekiel was to steadfastly rebuke Israel for what God hated – their deep-seated idolatry and their stubborn, rebellious nature.

Seven days after the first vision, the word of the Lord came to Ezekiel (v. 16). He was formally commissioned as God's watchman over the house of Israel (v. 17). As God's watchman, Ezekiel was responsible only to deliver God's warning; he was not accountable for the response of those hearing it (vv. 18-21). This is why Paul, God's apostle to the Gentiles, could say with a clear conscience: *"I am innocent of the blood of all men"* (Acts 20:26). He understood his accountability to God and had been faithful to sound the alarm: *"Him* [Christ] *we preach, warning every man and teaching every man in all wisdom, that we may present every man perfect in Christ Jesus"* (Col. 1:28). You and I are not called to Paul's ministry, but we are to be faithful witnesses for the Lord in a world that desperately needs to know what we know (Acts 1:8). Christians are witnesses for Christ when they live the gospel and share what they know with others as opportunities arise through God's providence.

Yes, let God be the Judge. Your job today is to be a witness.

— Warren Wiersbe

Ezekiel's ministry was important to the Lord: the righteous needed to be strengthened in their commitment to abide in God's Law, and the wicked must be warned of impending doom if they did not repent. Jehovah was not speaking to the Jewish nation as a whole through Ezekiel, for Israel's testimony was ruined and the nation was under judgment. Ezekiel was speaking to consciences of individuals. Those who heeded his message would be delivered personally, but those rejecting it would die in their iniquities when the Babylonian armies arrived. But woe to Ezekiel if he did not warn the people!

The Lord then directed Ezekiel to journey from his location out into the plain; there the Lord promised to speak with him (v. 22). Ezekiel did so and the glory of the Lord, which he had witnessed by the River

Chebar, appeared to him again (v. 23). Once more, Ezekiel is overwhelmed by the spectacular sight and falls to the ground in fearful awe. Being conscious of God's presence should always produce utter humility and a sense of worthlessness in the child of God; only from such a genuine position can reverence for God be counted as true worship.

The Spirit of God then entered Ezekiel and enabled him to stand on his feet (v. 24). The Lord commanded His prophet to remain in seclusion in his house unless summoned to speak to His people (v. 25). Did this mean that Ezekiel could never leave his home to accomplish personal affairs? The text does not expressly say. Indeed, Ezekiel had to venture from his home to dramatize certain divine messages (5:2, 12:3). Regardless, he was not to mingle openly with the people who would, on the whole, be resistant to Ezekiel's message. Perhaps he was not quite a prisoner in his own home, but he probably felt like one.

Was Ezekiel bound with ropes the entire time he was in his home? Not likely, as this would be an undue hardship for Ezekiel resulting in many practical problems and health issues. It seems more likely that for a few hours each day, he was bound with ropes while lying on his side (as discussed in the next chapter). This ensured that he could not change positions or have any freedom while performing the daily drama. The day-to-day message could thereby be conveyed without harming the prophet, though no doubt the routine would be physically taxing and uncomfortable.

From a human perspective we might wonder, Lord, why all this? What did Ezekiel do to deserve such a degrading ministry? Yet, these are selfish questions, when we consider what little a redeemed soul has to offer the Lord in thankfulness for His gift of eternal life. Is not any difficulty, any task, and any oppression much better than death and hell? Is there anything that God would ask us to do or suffer which would not have value to Him? Can we waste anything on the Lord? Perhaps Ezekiel pondered the previous two questions in his heart, but he did not audibly contest his assigned hardship, except in the one matter that offended his conscience, and God relented. Ezekiel's spiritual maturity in this matter is a good example for us to follow.

I used to ask God to help me. Then I asked if I might help Him. I ended up by asking God to do His work through me.

— Hudson Taylor

A good many are kept out of the service of Christ, deprived of the luxury of working for God, because they are trying to do some great thing. Let us be willing to do little things. And let us remember that nothing is small in which God is the source.

— D. L. Moody

Ezekiel was also informed that he would be temporarily dumb, except for such times that he was to speak for the Lord (vv. 26-27, 33:22). This lasted about six years – to the fall of Jerusalem. Hence, when Ezekiel suddenly appeared in public, everyone would unequivocally know that the Lord had a message for them to hear. This audible restriction led Jewish leaders to visit Ezekiel's home often in an attempt to gain private information from the Lord (8:1, 14:1, 20:1).

God's people were in sin, and Ezekiel, enjoying communion with a holy God, could not have close association with them. He was to live separate from sinners, but be willing to come among them to declare God's message of life and of death. Ezekiel, God's watchman for the nation, was to hate sin as God did and to love the sinner as God does.

As in Ezekiel's day, the Lord still hates sin and worldliness, and so should His followers (Jas. 4:4). The Bible says, *"Abhor that which is evil; cleave to that which is good"* (Rom. 12:9) and *"Abstain from all appearance of evil"* (1 Thess. 5:22). The believer should not ask, "How much sin and worldliness can I get away with?" but rather, "How can I demonstrate love for the Lord Jesus by obeying His revealed Word, and remain separate from what He hates?" (John 14:15). A believer can pursue spiritual sanctification only by devaluing the world's ideologies and religion, and then submitting to God.

"Are we prepared for what sanctification will do?" Oswald Chambers asks. "It will cost an intense narrowing of all our interests on earth and an immense broadening of our interest in God."[7] This is Paul's message to the Church at Colosse; may every child of God heed its exhortation:

Infidelity and Loyalty

> *If then you were raised with Christ, seek those things which are above, where Christ is, sitting at the right hand of God. Set your mind on things above, not on things on the earth.* **For you died, and your life is hidden with Christ in God.** *When Christ who is our life appears, then you also will appear with Him in glory* (Col. 3:1-4).

It may be hard for us to understand why God placed such constraining physical limitations on Ezekiel. Yet, these illustrated the detached nature of his ministry among God's rebellious people. Given the believer's position in Christ in heavenly places, Paul reminds us that such separation should also characterize our interaction in the world during this present age. A dead body has no personal ambitions, no thought of enjoying the world's pleasure, no wherewithal to make a fair show of its flesh. A corpse is not offended by the world's insults, nor is it able to strike back when attacked. A corpse has no rights. Positionally speaking, all believers died with Christ some 2000 years ago (Rom. 6:1-10); thus, we have no personal rights anymore to live the way we naturally would apart from Christ. Understanding this truth will better enable us to understand the hardships that God placed on His own prophet, for indeed there are more to come.

Meditation

> There was a day I died, utterly died, died to George Muller, his opinions, preferences, tastes, and will – died to the world, its approval or blame – even of my brethren and friends. Since then I have studied only to show myself approved unto God.
>
> — George Muller

> I think I never felt more resigned to God, not so dead to the world, its every respect as now; I am dead to all desire of reputation and greatness, either in life, or after death; all I long for is to be holy, humble and crucified to the world.
>
> — David Brainerd

The Clay Tablet and Defiled Bread
Ezekiel 4

Ezekiel's prophetic ministry commences with the issuance of four signs to symbolize Jerusalem's impending siege and destruction. The signs of the clay tablet, lying on one's side, and the defiled bread in Ezekiel 4 pertain to the siege. The sign of the razor and the cut hair in Ezekiel 5 relate to the decimation of Jerusalem and the catastrophic loss of life throughout Israel.

The Clay Tablet

The tablet in verse 1 may refer to a soft-clay writing pad on which Ezekiel could sketch Jerusalem's city boundaries, or perhaps, it was a hard-baked clay brick fashioned in the shape of Jerusalem. The later application better captures the robust fortifications of the city, but in either case the people would understand what was being depicted. Ezekiel in his elaborate model was then to erect siege walls around the brick and portray the armies of Babylon positioned about the city (v. 2). A siege ramp was added to the mockup to illustrate how the Babylonians would be able to pound the city's gates with battering rams.

Lastly, Ezekiel was to place an iron cooking pan between himself and his replica to represent the impenetrable barrier of isolation existing between the Jews and Jehovah because of their sin (v. 3). During Nebuchadnezzar's siege and after Jerusalem fell, the Jews would desperately plead for His assistance, but He was determined not to respond to their petitions.

Lying on Sides

Where the clay tablet signified the forthcoming horrific siege, the sign of Ezekiel lying on different sides conveyed the reason – persistent idolatry in Israel and Judah. God's watchman was to lie on his left side for 390 days to symbolize 390 years of reproach for Israel's iniquities –

one day for each year (vv. 4-5). The exercise was to be repeated on his right side for forty days to represent the forty years that God had to suffer Judah's rebellious behavior. But judgment was coming (vv. 6-7). To illustrate the confinement during the siege that the inhabitants of Jerusalem would suffer, Ezekiel was bound with ropes to ensure that he did not turn from one side to the other (i.e., while he performed this daily routine) until the allotted days had been served (v. 8). L. E. Cooper describes Ezekiel's orientation during this daily symbolic gesture:

> His left side would have been towards the north. Directions usually were calculated by facing east, which placed north to the left, south to the right, and west to the rear. Israel after the division of the kingdom in 931 B.C., was the Northern Kingdom while Judah was the Southern Kingdom. The right and left sides symbolically pointed to Israel and Judah.[8]

Whether Ezekiel had to lie on one side all day, or only while he slept or for a brief time each day is not specifically stated. In fact, as Charles Dyer surmises, the entire matter is hard to determine: "This is the most difficult sign in the book to interpret, partly because of the ambiguity of the text and partly because of the textual problem."[9] As Ezekiel had to be vertical to accomplish his daily cooking task (vv. 9-17), it seems mostly likely that he had to lie on one side for a few hours each day. But what exactly the 390 years signify is difficult to ascertain. The matter is further complicated by the Septuagint's attempt to resolve the difficulty by stating it was only 190 years, in lieu of 390 years. This change has no Hebrew textual support. One of the fundamental rules of biblical hermeneutics is to interpret a passage literally unless the context of the passage or other Scripture necessitates a figurative understanding. As Scripture poses no reason to assume the number 390 is anything but literal, and the context equates a day for a year of iniquity, a literal interpretation is warranted. It is the author's opinion that, because the number forty has a figurative meaning in Scripture, a literal interpretation with the figurative overtone is reasonable (this will be explained momentarily).

The Northern Kingdom of Israel came into existence in 931 B.C. with the rule of evil King Jeroboam. In 721 B.C. (i.e., after 210 years of paganism, not 390 years) God used the Assyrians to chasten and scatter the ten northern tribes. In actuality, the northern kingdom would not have even existed for 390 years to the siege of Jerusalem, which began in 588 B.C. After considering a host of explanations (some quite bizarre) and searching Scripture, this author *prefers* the following explanation: The years of iniquity for the northern kingdom refer to the years they were estranged from proper worship in the temple because of their idolatry and the repercussions of it (exile).

It is suggested that the 390 days Ezekiel had to bear would relate to the 390 years Israel was hindered from offering atoning sacrifices on the altar in Jerusalem. The edict of Cyrus, which permitted all Jews (including those exiled by the Assyrians) to return to their homeland, was issued in 538 B.C., the year after Babylon's defeat. The Jews returned to Israel sometime afterwards in several groups, mostly arriving in their homeland during the first half of 536 B.C. A few months after reoccupying various cities throughout Judah, the Jewish returnees *"gathered together as one man to Jerusalem"* to set up an altar on the first day of the seventh month of the same year (Ezra 3:1). This would be early September 536 B.C. The altar was erected among the ruins of the previous temple that had been destroyed 50 years earlier by Nebuchadnezzar.

It would have taken King Jeroboam some time to establish his throne, to create an economy, to erect pagan altars in Dan and Bethel, to form a pagan priesthood, and to put in place a complete religious and economic system that would prevent Jews in the Northern Kingdom from venturing to Jerusalem as per Levitical Law. Hence, 390 years after 931 B.C. (less two to four years) aligns well with either the end-of-captivity edict (538 B.C.) or the active-altar date (536 B.C.).

The matter of Judah's iniquity is different than Israel's, for Judah continued sacrificing at the temple, less periods of apostasy, until it was destroyed. Certainly, Judah logged more than forty years of idolatry, as wicked Manasseh's reign alone was more than forty years. In fact, Ezekiel will later mention that the Jews had been idolatrous to some degree from their Egyptian exodus, except during the reigns of a handful of godly kings such as David, Hezekiah, and Josiah. As Jeremiah explains (Jer. 3), Judah's sin was different than Israel's, because Israel was blatantly idolatrous, but Judah was two-timing Jehovah by secretly worshipping false gods. Consequently, God is marking out Judah's time differently than Israel's. It is the writer's opinion that the number forty in relationship to Judah follows the figurative way that number is used throughout Scripture.

The number forty is used to symbolize a time of trial or a probationary period of testing in the Bible. For example, after Israel doubted God's Word at Kadesh-barnea, Moses, a teacher of the Law, continued forty years with God's people in the wilderness before they were again permitted to enter the Promised Land. Furthermore, the prophet Jeremiah faithfully preached to Judah for forty years before the nation's probation ended and judgment was executed. His ministry began in the thirteenth year of Josiah's reign (627 B.C.), the same year the book of the Law was found in the temple.

God's people rejected Jeremiah's message and subjected him to much hostility, including physical brutality. Now, God was marking that period of obstinacy in a special way – Ezekiel would lie on his right side facing Jerusalem and with his arm uncovered for forty days. The Lord taught His people for forty years to suitably prepare them to enter the Promised Land by faith, and He worked with them for the same duration of time to properly usher them out of the land because of their stubborn disobedience. In summary, the 390 years represents the duration Israel was away from the Lord with no hope of recovery, while the 40 years represents the probationary time Judah was offered mercy while there was still hope of recovery.

F. C. Cook notes that 390 plus 40 years is a total of 430 years, which was the original duration assigned to the affliction of Abraham's descendants before they would come into communion with Jehovah in the Promised Land (Gen. 15:13). The 390 years was the time Abraham's descendants were apart from the Lord (mainly in Egypt), and the forty years was the probationary time the Israelites were with Jehovah in the wilderness.[10] With this understanding, God's promise to Abraham seems to form a prophetic blueprint of various aspects of Israel's future. Obviously the Lord knows exactly what these numbers relate to, for He has keenly felt the pain of His people's rebellion year after year.

Defiled Bread

The third sign, defiled bread, related to the severity of the looming siege. To symbolize the scarcity of food and water during the upcoming siege, Ezekiel's daily diet during the 390 days on his left side would be restricted to about eight ounces of mixed grain and two-thirds of a quart of water (vv. 10-11). Ezekiel was to gather wheat, barley, beans, lentils, millet, and spelt and place the grain in a container (v. 9). When ground together, this combination produced a lower grade of flour as compared to wheat or barley flour – meaning that the resulting cake would not tickle one's palate. The point of the illustration was to emphasize that Jews under siege in Jerusalem would be glad to get even such an insufficient and undesirable ration of food.

Furthermore, Ezekiel was to publicly weigh out the grain and then bake the cake over human excrement. Ezekiel, an undefiled priest from his youth, was repulsed by the idea (vv. 12, 14). Godly Ezekiel did not complain about the plain diet or the diurnal food ration, but his conscience was offended by the putrid fuel that he was to use to cook his food. The Law specifically mandated how human waste was to be disposed of, hence the social stigma of using human feces for fuel (Deut. 23:9-14). God granted his request and permitted His prophet to cook his bread over burning cow manure (v. 15).

We might wonder, Why was the meal illustration incomplete without cooking it over dung? Additionally, Why subject a godly man like Ezekiel to such a meager daily portion for fourteen months? Obviously, the famine and siege-induced starvation of Jerusalem's inhabitants was only part of the full message God wanted the Jews to comprehend. William Kelly concisely explains the remaining point of the illustration: "The prophet must set forth in his own person the degradation as well as the judgment impending because of the iniquity of the people."[11] This was the point of the entire illustration, which only slightly conveyed the utter disgust God had suffered because of Israel's willful degeneracy.

> Does God ask us to do what is beneath us? This question will never trouble us again if we consider the Lord of heaven taking a towel and washing feet.
>
> — Elisabeth Elliot

Dried dung burns evenly, but releases a foul oder which degrades the quality of the food cooking over it. Accordingly, the Lord referred to Ezekiel's barley cakes as "defiled bread" (v. 13). Ezekiel's limited diet and detestable cooking fuel was to foretell the pollution and starvation that the Jews would experience during the Babylonian siege, a matter both foretold and lamented by Jeremiah as well (vv. 16-17; Jer. 5:17, 15:2; Lam. 4:3-4).

Given Ezekiel's peculiar doings each day, there can be little doubt that some thought Ezekiel was demented. Like Elijah and other prophets before him, Ezekiel drank from his own ministry. Yet, there was a day approaching when all laughter and ridicule would cease, but then it would be too late to remedy the situation. Perhaps then the Jews would understand how gracious Ezekiel had been to suffer so much personal discomfort in order to vividly warn them of their eventual calamity. We should not be surprised, then, when the Lord asks us to do what is unconventional, costly, uncomfortable, and perhaps even painful, to express His love to those whom He longs to spare from searing wrath. Ezekiel had seen God's glory and he was willing to expend himself for others to see it too.

Meditation

Use me then, my Savior, for whatever purpose and in whatever way Thou may require. Here is my poor heart an empty vessel; fill it with Thy grace.

— Dwight L. Moody

People who do not know the Lord ask why in the world we waste our lives as missionaries. They forget that they too are expending their lives ... and when the bubble has burst, they will have nothing of eternal significance to show for the years they have wasted.

— Nate Saint (martyred in Ecuador)

The Shorn and Divided Hair
Ezekiel 5

The three signs of the previous chapter pertained to the terrible Babylonian siege that would soon beset Jerusalem. The sign of the shorn and divided hair of Ezekiel 5 relates to the ensuing slaughter and deportation of the Jews after Jerusalem was conquered. The sign of the divided hair is detailed in the first four verses; the reason for the sign and its meaning is explained in the remainder of the chapter.

After the completion of the previous three signs, Ezekiel was to take a sharp sword and use it as a razor to shave the hair off his head and to remove his beard (v. 1). The Hebrew word rendered "sword" speaks of a military-type weapon used for battle, which the prophet refers to eighty-three times in his book to speak of judgment. A sword makes a poor barber's razor and doubtless emaciated Ezekiel was by this time quite a disheveled and loathsome spectacle of a man. However, the unevenly cut hair and the prophet's general appearance were to denote the pitiful condition of the people after living through the long siege. Yet, the worst was still to come – most survivors would then be slaughtered by the Babylonians.

The shorn hair was to be carefully weighed and divided into three parts, with the exception of a few strands that were to be preserved by tucking them away in the fold of his robe. An inner fold was created when long tunics were girded by a belt. After dividing the hair, Ezekiel was to venture into Jerusalem and publicly burn one-third of his hair. This symbolized that one-third of people would die by starvation or pestilence during the siege (v. 12). Conditions would be so horrific that family members would feed on each other to survive (v. 10). The fact that cannibalism did occur is affirmed later by the prophet Jeremiah (Lam. 2:20, 4:10).

After burning the first portion of hair, Ezekiel went through the city dispersing the second-third of his cropped hair. This act showed that another third of the Jews, who did survive the siege, would be slaughtered after the Babylonians broke through Jerusalem's defenses (v. 12). The final portion of hair was to be scattered in the wind to indicate that the final third of the population, who had survived the siege and conquest, would live in constant fear as an exiled people.

The few hairs tucked away in Ezekiel's garment represent a remnant of the people that God would refine and later restore to Himself. Yet, these also would go through immense hardship, as represented by the burning of a few of these hair strands (vv. 3-4). God's judgment was against the entire house of Israel for the nation's persistent idolatry, so not even the remnant to be restored could escape God's justice.

Ezekiel explained to the people that God had created Israel to be a light and testimony of Himself among the nations, but they had behaved worse than the nations (vv. 5-7). The Jews had rebelled against God's Law and embraced false gods, so God would now make them a reproach among the nations to further add to their shame (v. 8). They had been a people of unique privilege and had received God's favor in ways no other nation had. Now they would be held accountable in an exceptional way, more than the nations.

When God graciously bestows revelation and extends privilege, there is also an equal measure of responsibility and accountability to Him. This is why James warns, *"My brethren, let not many of you become teachers, knowing that we shall receive a stricter judgment"* (Jas. 3:1). Jehovah had favored the Jewish people in comparison to Gentile nations (Rom. 9:4-5); they were about to learn that when privilege despises its Giver, there are consequences.

Once commencing, His jealous anger would not be quenched until His wrath had been fully measured out (vv. 11, 13). Jerusalem had never before witnessed the chastening hand of God to the extent they soon would, nor would He ever do so again (v. 9). Given all the bleak times that Jerusalem had faced during the previous four centuries, this prophecy should have had a significant impact on Ezekiel's audience, but apparently it did not. History shows that after the days of Nebuchadnezzar, God has never utterly destroyed Jerusalem again to punish His people. For rejecting and crucifying their Messiah, God's Son, God permitted the destruction of the temple and the ransacking of Jerusalem in 70 A.D. by Titus, but this demolition was minor in comparison to the devastation that the Babylonians caused. Furthermore, the destruction of the temple was used to signify that the system governed by the Law had served its purpose and had been replaced by a New Covenant sealed by Christ's own blood (2 Cor. 3).

Paganism originated in Babylon (Gen. 10), and had spread into Judah. Now God was leading His people to Babylon as captives. In Babylon, they would be refined, and when Jehovah called His people back home, after seventy years of exile, they would leave their idols in Babylon forever. Zechariah prophetically depicts this wonderful outcome in his book. His seventh vision illustrated that paganism originated in Babylon and that God was removing it from Israel and sending it back to Babylon in a basket carried by two winged women (Zech. 5:5-11). The meaning of that vision aligns with Ezekiel's statement in verse 9: When the Jews departed from Babylon to return to their homeland, their idols remained in that land from which they originated. Hence, God did not need to punish them for that offense again.

Ezekiel then explains that the utter devastation of Jerusalem and the humiliation of the Jews would also serve as a warning to the Gentiles that Jehovah would fiercely judge any nation that resisted Him (vv. 14-15). Ezekiel will prophecy against the nations later, but presently his primary focus is to rebuke God's covenant people.

Ezekiel concludes the explanation of the fourth sign by describing God, the divine Archer, and His quiver of judicial arrows (i.e., calamities): famine, plagues, wild beasts, and the sword (vv. 16-17). The house of Israel was His target and no one could thwart His penetrating arrows – the fletching and flinging of arrows was imminent. God's covenant people were corrupt through and through. So far, God's prophetic messages had not been heeded by His stubborn and wayward people. God wanted a purified people for Himself, but His people were so full of impurities, that He must utterly reject them.

Unrefined silver has no value; it must either be cast away or exposed to intense heat to remove its dross. Because Jehovah is a covenant-keeping God, He could not discard His people. His only option was to turn up the judicial heat and to remove the wicked dross from them. Babylon would be the flame, Jerusalem the chaff, and God's prophetic word the catalyst for the Refiner's fire. Any living soul emerging from that great conflagration would assuredly be genuine silver.

Meditation

Perhaps someday we may see clearly how unattractive, how loathsome, how useless sinful men are in the sight of a holy God. How we need to look objectively at ourselves to see the miserable emptiness that is so clearly visible to God! There is no point in keeping refuse silver. It has no worth. Can it be that God has already marked off as valueless many who consider themselves useful?

— Kyle Yates

High Places to Fall
Ezekiel 6

It had taken over fourteen months to convey the four signs pertaining to the siege and destruction of Jerusalem (chps. 4 and 5). In this chapter, Ezekiel receives a new assignment from the Lord – he was to pronounce judgment on all the high places of pagan worship throughout the land of Israel (vv. 1-2).

Ezekiel was to prophesy against the mountains, hills, ravines, and the valleys of Israel, as these were the locations in which the Jews were worshipping idols and burning incense on pagan altars (v. 3). This was often done in secret, so as not to interfere with their public worship at the temple and the commemoration of various feasts.

As previously mentioned, Jeremiah explained early in his ministry why God was angrier with Judah than with Israel who had already suffered Jehovah's chastening rod – the Assyrian invasion and subsequent deportation. Jeremiah likens the houses of Israel and Judah to two sisters (Jer. 3). Both had pledged their loyalty to Jehovah through a marriage covenant. Israel was the first of the sisters to commit fornication. She embraced false gods and worshipped their idols in various high places throughout the northern kingdom. The cover of every green tree became a canopy over her bed of adultery. God called Israel to repentance, but she would not forsake her idols and return to Him. God responded by writing her a bill of divorcement and sending her away to Assyria in 722 B.C.

Even though the other sister, Judah, had witnessed firsthand God's harsh judgment of Israel, she also committed spiritual adultery by worshipping images of stone and wood. But, as Jeremiah explains, God was more furious with Judah than He had been with Israel:

"So it came to pass, through her [Israel's] *casual harlotry, that she defiled the land and committed adultery with stones and trees. And yet for all this her treacherous sister Judah has not turned to Me with*

her whole heart, but in pretense," says the Lord. Then the Lord said to me, "Backsliding Israel has shown herself more righteous than treacherous Judah" (Jer. 3:9-11).

Judah would experience greater judgment than Israel did, for two reasons. First, Judah, having seen the harsh consequences of the sin of adultery, deliberately chose to be unfaithful to God despite this understanding. Second, although Israel was blatantly idolatrous, two-faced Judah embraced other lovers while still sweet-talking the Lord with vain pleasantries. The people of Judah acted religious, but their hearts were not with God. They pretended to be devout, but embraced pagan gods whenever they thought they could get away with it. Israel did not try to hide her adultery, but Judah disguised her treachery in order to appear righteous; thus, she deserved greater judgment.

Ezekiel then promised that the bodies of those worshipping false gods would be spread out to rot before their broken-down altars (vv. 4-5). Furthermore, Judah's cities would all be destroyed and most of the inhabitants would be slaughtered (vv. 6-7). Jehovah would wake up His sword to destroy people throughout the land. Indeed, Jehovah's punishment of Judah far exceeded that of Israel, for His jealous anger burned hotter against them. Yet, His wrath was tempered with mercy; hence, He promised to preserve a remnant through the holocaust. This remnant would be scattered among the nations until the period of chastening had ended. Then God would call them home again (v. 8).

At that time, the returning captives would recognize that Jehovah was Lord, and that He had brought this calamity upon them and for their good (v. 10). The refined captives would then comprehend how they had broken the heart of their God through unfaithfulness:

I was crushed by their adulterous heart which has departed from Me, and by their eyes which play the harlot after their idols; they will loathe themselves for the evils which they committed in all their abominations (v. 9).

Scripture employs a variety of allegories so that we can better understand how wearisome willful sin, rebellion, and misplaced devotions are to God. On behalf of the Lord, the prophet Amos informs idolatrous Israel (the northern kingdom): *"Behold, I am pressed under you, as a cart is pressed that is full of sheaves"* (Amos 2:13). Amos describes it in terms with which we can identify – it is like God's heart being smashed under a cart fully loaded with grain. Isaiah says that human sin *wearies* God (Isa. 43:24), and the psalmist writes that God is *grieved* by sin (Ps. 95:10). The wonder of the gospel is that a heavy-hearted God caused the object of His love – His sinless Son – to be sin for us, that we might have our burden of sin removed (2 Cor. 5:21). Thankfully, in a coming day, God will no longer be wearied and grieved by our sin, nor shall we!

Returning to Ezekiel's day, God's jealous anger could no longer be held back. The prophet was commanded to pound his fists and stamp his feet to visually convey Jehovah's hot disposition towards His covenant people (v. 11). In His forthcoming wrath most of them would die by the sword, famine, and pestilence and the entire region would be made more desolate than the wilderness of Diblah (vv. 12, 14). As there is no Hebrew city by that name, some scholars believe that Diblah refers to the Syrian town of Riblah in the far north. Riblah was where Zedekiah was captured by Nebuchadnezzar, who slew Zedekiah's son and then put out his eyes (2 Kgs. 25:5-7; Jer. 39:6-7). If that is the case, then Ezekiel was simply saying that the entire land, from the desert in the south to the far north would be affected by the impending invasion.

Why was the Lord permitting all this to happen to His people? The reason is stated three times in this chapter: *"They shall know that I am the Lord"* (vv. 7, 10, 14). After suffering such extreme punishment, the Jews would understand just how much the Lord loved them and wanted to enjoy communing with them.

Verse 13 shows us how deeply entrenched paganism was in the Jewish culture at this time – the hillsides were full of pagan altars. Jeremiah says that even the children worshipped at these altars and before the Asherah poles on high places (Jer. 17). Asherah was the Canaanite goddess of fertility. During Manasseh's reign an image of Asherah had been placed in the temple (2 Kgs. 21:7). Although he later removed it (2 Chron. 33:13-15), the image found its way back to the temple, because King Josiah had to remove it again (2 Kgs. 23:6). The stony hearts of the people prevailed, and, despite Josiah's sweeping reforms, idolatry returned to Judah. Idols were worshipped by propping up green trees and branches (Asherah poles) before them on the high hills surrounding Jerusalem. It was likely the image of Asherah that Ezekiel speaks of as "the idol of jealousy" being worshipped in the temple (8:3-5).

Infidelity and Loyalty

Judah was an adulterous wife and now she would pay for her treachery. Which of us would have any compassion for an unfaithful wife who continually and willfully broke the heart of her husband? "She deserves whatever she gets!" would be the response of most of us. Yet, before rebuking Judah's infidelity too loudly, we should examine ourselves to ensure that we are not making the same mistake. On this matter, H. A. Ironside provides the Church with something to think about:

> Backsliding was not so much [Judah's] continual sin as was her treachery. A strict attention to the outward ordinances of the temple worship, but the heart going after the filthiness of the nations, was generally her course; as it had been even in the days of Solomon – who built the house of Jehovah, and erected altars to the gods of his heathen wives! This is what markedly characterizes much of what is called Christendom today. There is talk of devotedness to the Lord, a prating of loyalty to Christ; but alas, how little is known of separation from that which dishonors Him. In fact, the position of Jeremiah in this book must be very much that of the man today who would stand for Christ and walk in the truth.[12]

Is not dissatisfaction with the Lord the essence of idolatry? May the Church learn from Israel's mistakes and follow David's example of an adoring and satisfied heart: *"Oh, taste and see that the Lord is good; blessed is the man who trusts in Him! Oh, fear the Lord, you His saints! There is no want to those who fear Him"* (Ps. 34:8-9).

Meditation

How fast their guilt and sorrows rise
Who haste to seek some idol-god!
I will not taste their sacrifice,
Their offerings of forbidden blood.

My God provides a richer cup,
And nobler food to live upon:
He for my life has offered up
Jesus, His best-beloved Son.

— Isaac Watts

The End Has Come
Ezekiel 7

Ezekiel received a second message from the Lord (v. 1). This poetic dissertation may be summarized as follows: the Babylonian invasion was imminent, would decimate the entire land, would result in a terrible holocaust, and God would not intervene to stop it. The time had come for God to fully judge His people for their evil ways – He would repay all their abominations (vv. 1-14). Ezekiel repeatedly announces that God's revenge for Judah's treachery was imminent: *"The end has come"* (vv. 3, 6, 10), *"Doom has come"* (v. 7), *"Trouble is near"* (v. 7), *"Destruction comes"* (v. 25), and *"Disaster will come"* (v. 25). The Jews would be devoured by sword, pestilence, and famine (v. 15). Many of those who did escape the slaughter would be captured and enslaved (v. 16).

Normal life within Jewish society would end with the Babylonian invasion. There would be no more buying and selling of goods or property because these would be confiscated by their invaders (vv. 12-13). Furthermore, there would be no Hebrew army to offer protection (v. 14). William Kelly suggests that God's overwhelming judgments and their ruin will awaken the Jews to their own shame and the futility of idolatry:

> They are thus seen shut up within concentric circles of devouring ruin (vv. 15-18). God's prophet announces terrible things to think on, stroke upon stroke, from God against His people, enfeebled by the sense of guilt. In the day of their calamity they are forced to feel that their gods are vanity, nothing but "silver and gold," and "they shall cast their silver in the streets, and their gold shall be as uncleanness."[13]

After being made feeble by the Babylonians, Ezekiel notes that the Jews will humble themselves by shaving their heads and wearing sackcloth (vv. 17-18). The cutting off of one's hair was a sign of deep mourning (Isa. 15:2-3). To illustrate that the time of pleading for repentance was now over and that judgment loomed over Judah, the prophet Jeremiah was to cut off his hair (Jer. 7:29). However, Ezekiel foretells that though shame covered them, neither the Babylonians nor the Lord would regard their self-effacing gestures. Additionally, their silver and gold would not deliver them from God's wrath, nor fill their stomachs with food (v. 19). Previously, the Jews had used their precious metals and fine jewelry to fashion idols, but they would come to realize the utter futility of their wealth and even loathe it, but this lesson would be learned too late.

The temple, God's secret place, had been erected to honor Him, but the Jews had robbed it to create images of abomination. Now God would permit the Babylonians to profane, plunder, and destroy the temple, which the Jews at this time considered to be the guarantee of their protection (vv. 20-22). The prophet Jeremiah tells us that this Jewish notion (i.e., that they believed they were invincible because they had the temple) was particularly offensive to God (Jer. 7:4). The temple, which had stood for four centuries, was viewed as a "good luck charm" which would protect the nation. The structure, having been disassociated from Jehovah, was itself regarded as a bastion of safety (i.e. the people trusted in a man-made building to protect them rather than the One it honored). Jeremiah set the matter straight: God valued obedience more than the temple, a fact He would soon demonstrate by demolishing it.

May believers in the Church Age learn a lesson from God's dealings with the Jews, and not ascribe spiritual value to any material object that God does not recognize as being profitable for us (e.g., the bread and the wine used in the Lord's Supper are appreciated by the Lord). Sophisticated buildings, stained-glass windows, altars, crosses, and other furnishings, burning candles, incense, and religious attire mean nothing to God; rather, they draw us away from the one true God and distract us from honoring His Son. If these things, the works of our own hands, gain spiritual significance in our thinking, have we not committed the same sin as Jeremiah and Ezekiel confronted in their day? May the Church keep Christ enthroned in her thinking and not allow dumb idols to rob Him of our adoration. If we worship our worship or where we worship, we are no better off than the foolish hypocrites that Ezekiel was speaking to – we are idolaters also!

The land was filled with blood and violence. Therefore God was bringing the worst of the Gentiles to punish His people; those surviving would be bound with chains and led into captivity (vv. 23-24). The reference to "blood" likely refers to the innocent blood of their children whom they had been sacrificing to pagan deities. Jeremiah informs us that the Jews had built the high places of Topheth, located just southwest of Jerusalem in the Hinnom Valley (Jer. 7:31-33). God vowed that He would change the name of this place to "The Valley of Slaughter." The very place that they had sacrificed their own children would become the slaughtering ground for countless Jews during the Babylonian invasion. Jeremiah told the Jews that the fowls of the air and the wild beasts would feed upon their carcasses in that place. There would be so many dead and so few survivors that it would not be possible to keep the birds and beasts from devouring their rotting flesh.

Scripture states, *"Behold, children are a heritage from the Lord, the fruit of the womb is a reward"* (Ps. 127:3). Yet they had chosen to sacrifice the children He had given them for a heritage to Himself to false gods: to Baal (Jer. 19:6), and perhaps others (2 Chron. 33:6). The Law forbids the shedding of innocent blood (Deut. 19:10-13) and there was to be no idolatry in the land; the Jews were to worship God alone (Ex. 20:3-4). Instead of raising up their children for the Lord (Mal. 2:15), the Jews were dedicating them to false gods. For God's people to offer their own children in sacrifice to the god of this age is perhaps the greatest insult that can be committed against the Lord. Unfortunately, the offense continues this day when Christian parents permit the lives of their children to be consumed by secular activities and godless philosophies. What may be morally permissible can still skew a child's heavenly focus and diminish their love for the Lord.

Consequently, God's anger burned hot against His people, who would soon know Him as *Jehovah the Smiter* (v. 9)! Once His disciplinary rod was invoked (i.e., the Babylonians; v. 11), Israel would cease to have an active priesthood, a judicial ruling body, and a governing king (vv. 26-27). Ezekiel concludes his poetic discourse by announcing that Jehovah would fully punish Israel with the judgment they deserved, so that they might know that He is the Lord!

Infidelity and Loyalty

Meditation

Lord, we would never forget Thy love, who hast redeemed us by Thy blood;
And now, as our High Priest above, dost intercede for us with God.

We would remember we are one with every saint that loves Thy name;
United to Thee on the throne – our life, our hope, our Lord the same.

Lord, we are Thine, we praise Thy love, one with Thy saints, all one in Thee;
We would, until we meet above, in all our ways remember Thee.

— James G. Deck

Abominations Galore
Ezekiel 8

So far, Ezekiel has delivered four signs (chps. 4-5) and two messages (chps. 6-7) to indict the Jews as a rebellious and idolatrous people, who deserve Jehovah's immediate chastening. In chapters 8-11, Jehovah will provide specific evidence to His prophet as to why His people must be punished. This required Ezekiel to be brought back to Jerusalem in a vision to witness the wickedness of God's people.

This second vision occurred fourteen months after his initial vision (chps. 1-3) which was in the sixth year, sixth month, and fifth day of Jehoiachin's Babylonian exile (i.e., September 17, 592 B.C.; v. 1). The vision has four components: idolatry in the temple (chp. 8), the slaughter of idolaters in Jerusalem (chp. 9), God's departing glory from Jerusalem (chp. 10), and judgment pronounced on Israel's rulers (chp. 11).

Ezekiel's public interaction was still limited, so the visionary drama commenced while the elders of Israel were sitting with Ezekiel in his own house (v. 1). They were likely seeking the prophet's counsel; perhaps they had asked him specific questions about the forthcoming destruction of Jerusalem. In any case, Ezekiel's vision was God's response to their inquiries (11:24-25). It must have been a strange incident for the elders to be with the prophet as he had this *out-of-body* type of experience. Was Ezekiel unresponsive during this time or coherent? We are not told. What we do know is what he reported to the elders, which he later wrote down for our benefit.

While sitting with the elders, *"a figure like that of a man"* whose appearance was as bright as glowing molten metal suddenly stood before the prophet. The vague form was not a man, per se, but human-like. This dazzling figure was a manifestation of God or perhaps an actual theophany as Ezekiel had seen in his first vision (vv. 2, 4). Something that looked like a hand stretched out from the human-like figure and caught Ezekiel by his hair and lifted him up, transporting him hundreds of miles back to Jerusalem, though his physical body remained in Babylon (v. 3). Ezekiel suddenly found himself at the northern gate between the inner and outer courts of the temple (this gate being one of three permitting access to the inner court; v. 3).

Now in the temple, Ezekiel affirms that the glory of the Lord still resided there, but he also noticed an image of jealousy – an idol before him (vv. 3, 5). Jehovah told the Israelites at Sinai that He was their God and He was jealous over them (Ex. 20:5); hence, the profane image in the temple was properly identified from God's perspective. For the first time in this vision, the blazing form speaks to Ezekiel and in doing so confirms his identity – Jehovah Himself:

> *"Son of man, lift your eyes now toward the north." So I lifted my eyes toward the north, and there, north of the altar gate, was this image of jealousy in the entrance. Furthermore He said to me, "Son of man, do you see what they are doing, the great abominations that the house of Israel commits here, to make Me go far away from My sanctuary? Now turn again, you will see greater abominations"* (vv. 5-6).

Next, the Lord brought Ezekiel to the door of the court where he found a small hole in the wall (v. 7). He was instructed to dig out the cavity in the wall (v. 8). In doing so he found a hidden door, which he was commanded to open and enter, thus gaining access to the inner court. From that vantage point Ezekiel witnessed all sorts of wicked abominations occurring within (v. 9). What he saw was appalling: *"every kind of creeping thing, abominable beasts, and all the idols of the house of Israel, portrayed all around on the walls"* (v. 10). The Jews were secretly engaging in the cultic worship of animals.

> There is nothing so abominable in the eyes of God and of men as idolatry, whereby men render to the creature that honor which is due only to the Creator.
> — Blaise Pascal

Ezekiel then saw Jaazaniah, the son of Shaphan, with the seventy elders of Israel, each having a censor of burning incense in their hands (v. 11). To ensure that Ezekiel rightly understood what he saw, the Lord said to him, *"Son of man, have you seen what the elders of the house of Israel do in the dark, every man in the room of his idols? For*

52

they say, 'The Lord does not see us, the Lord has forsaken the land'" (v. 12). Devout Ezekiel would have been stunned to learn that these esteemed men in Israel were secret idolaters. Even more troubling to the prophet was that these supposed Jehovah-worshippers thought they could conceal their gross sin from Jehovah and not be punished. Continued rebellion sears the conscience and blinds the mind from perceiving the truth. Such spiritual depravity requires stern corrective measures and Israel was about to learn just how much God loved them – too much to permit them to stay the way they were.

Although we do not know much about Jaazaniah, his father Shaphan was an honorable man who served godly King Josiah. The family of Shaphan, as Charles H. Dyer explains, had a significant role in the public affairs of Judah in years just prior to the Babylonian invasion:

> Shaphan was King Josiah's secretary who reported the findings of the Law to Josiah (2 Kgs. 22:3-13). Shaphan had at least four sons – three of which were mentioned in a positive way by Jeremiah (Ahikam, Gemariah, and Elasah). The fourth son, Jaazaniah, was the "black sheep" of the family; his presence among the idol-worshippers in the temple caught Ezekiel by surprise (Ezek. 8:11). Ahikam's son, Gedaliah, was appointed governor of Judah by Nebuchadnezzar after the fall of Jerusalem in 586 B.C.[14]

Even during these troubling times, God had His people in positions of authority to accomplish His will. Ahikam, the son of Shaphan, for example, was determined not to allow the people to murder Jeremiah and, though he risked a social backlash, used his political clout to gain Jeremiah's release (Jer. 26:24). It is also noted that Shaphan's son Gemariah, along with Elnathan, urged Jehoiakim not to burn Jeremiah's scroll (Jer. 36:12, 25). Shaphan's son Elasah hand-carried Jeremiah's letter to the exiled Jews in Babylon (Jer. 29:1-3). Though his son Jaazaniah was a rebel, Shaphan reared up three fine sons who lived for God and, indeed, raised their sons to do the same. The grandson of Shaphan through Ahikam was Gedaliah, a just and righteous governor over Judah. Micaiah, the grandson of Shaphan through Gemariah, convinced the princes of the importance of Jeremiah's scroll after hearing it read by Baruch (Jer. 36:11-26). It has been observed that the value of parenting is witnessed in one's grandchildren. To this end, Shaphan was a father who obtained a good heritage from the Lord; happy is the man who has a quiver full of such children (Ps. 127:3-5). God used Shaphan's legacy to confront wickedness and to preserve and refresh His servants. May God grant each of us the same heritage.

So far the Lord had shown Ezekiel a prominent idol situated at the northern entrance of the inner court, a conglomeration of images associated with the animal worship that was infesting Israel, and that many prominent people in Jewish society were secret idolaters. Yet, there was much more that the Lord wanted Ezekiel to see. *"Turn again, and you will see greater abominations that they are doing"* (v. 13). The Lord brought Ezekiel to the door of the north gate of the temple and there Ezekiel was astonished to see a group of women sitting and weeping for Tammuz (v. 14). A brief review of the biblical narrative and secular history is necessary to understand who Tammuz actually is and what he represents.

The tenth chapter of Genesis identifies Babylon [Babel] as the fountainhead of all pagan worship. The human founder of this city was Nimrod, whose name means "rebel." First-century Jewish historian Josephus regarded Nimrod as the father of the pagan Babylonian and Assyrian cultures. The Babylonians called their rising kingdom *Babel*; in their own estimation, they were "the gate of God" (Gen. 10:10). Through human achievement, they believed they could obtain divinity. Nimrod's quest for deity would hinge upon his success in constructing an enormous tower intended to bridge earth to heaven and close the immense gap between man and God. Obviously, such a tower would be an affront against God, who is holy and separate from sinful man. Any attempt to bridge the distance between a holy God and fallen mankind must be righteous in nature and God-ordained. Only the cross of Christ can bridge the spiritual chasm between fallen humanity and a holy God. Accordingly, God brought the construction of Babel's tower to an abrupt halt by diversifying the language of the people.

Babylonian history records that Nimrod met with a sudden and violent death. After this, his beautiful wife, Semiramis, who had ascended by marriage from a common social class to the throne, gave birth to what she claimed was the essence of Nimrod (she said that this was accomplished through soul transference). The Chaldean story that developed states that Nimrod willingly gave up his life in order to further bless the Babylonian kingdom. In any case, Semiramis' son,

Bacchus, meaning "the lamented one," was said to be her deified husband.[15] Classical history refers to him as Nimus, meaning "the son," while Scripture calls him "Tammuz" (v. 14).[16] The Lord God is addressed as *Adonai* in the Old Testament; worshippers of Tammuz would later refer to their false deity as *Adon* or *Adonis*, a clear effort to affirm the son as deity. Under the name *Mithras*, he was worshipped as the "Mediator."[17] As Zoroashta, he was worshipped as "the seed of the woman."[18]

Semiramis was licentious and gave birth to several children, though she had no husband.[19] The story concocted around Nimus' birth not only secured her throne, but in time the people reverenced her as *Rhea*, "the great goddess Mother," or *Beltis*, "the Queen of Heaven," which is how Jeremiah refers to her (Jer. 7).[20] She derived all her glory and claim to deification through the very son she held in her arms. Ancient art of the mother and son has the glow of the sun positioned behind each of their heads to indicate sun divinity, but the glory of Semiramis was accentuated even above that of her son.[21] Ancient idols have been excavated showing a mother-god and child-god that bear a strikingly resemblance to modern-day images of Mary and Jesus.[22] The Roman Catholic Church refers to Mary as "the Queen of Heaven" and the "Mother of God." Many have ascribed glory to Mary in the same way Semiramis was deified in the eyes of her people – through the glory of her son. The veneration of Mary has its roots in Babylon; indeed, it is simply a repackaged pagan lie.

The Lord stopped the work on the tower of Babel and spread mankind throughout the region by confounding their speech (Gen. 11:7-8). When the people dispersed, they also carried their developed pagan traditions with them. Consequently, the story of the death (or sacrifice) of the father, to be reincarnated as deity in the womb of a mother goddess, is found in many ancient cultures, but with different names:

Babylon: Semiramis and Nimrod (Nimus, or Yule, as son)

Assyria: Ishtar and Tammuz

Egypt: Isis and Osiris (Horus as son)

India: Iswara, or Isa, and Isani, or Isisi

Asia: Cybele and Deoius

Syria: Astarte and Bel, or Baal (Marduk, or Adonis, as son)

Infidelity and Loyalty

> Greece: Aphrodite and Adonis
>
> Rome: Kybele, or Venus, and Attis, or Adonis

In the pagan myths of all these ancient cultures runs a central theme: a goddess gives birth to a deified son, the essence of her dead husband. This early Babylonian legend has propagated all over the world! For example, in Jeremiah's day, families throughout Judah were uniting for a festive celebration in honor of the goddess Ishtar, the so-called "Queen of Heaven." The event included preparing special cakes that bore her image and were offered to her in a sacrificial rite (Jer. 7:18). This brief history highlights the main rudiments of paganism, which were eventually incorporated into the Roman papal system and, thus, infiltrated and perverted much of the professing Church.

Roman Catholicism was forged in paganism and through the centuries has culminated in blatant goddess worship of Mary, worshipped and adored as the Queen of Heaven. The Roman Catholic Catechism proudly proclaims that Mary "was exalted by the Lord as Queen over all things" (1994; line 966), a position gained after her supposed assumption into heaven. It is further taught that it is through Mary that all divine blessings, and even salvation, are obtained. The motive for *earning* heaven becomes obvious: it is to join Mary, not to be with the Lord Jesus Christ. Goddess worship has replaced the reverence of the Lord of glory, and ancient Babylon is where it began. It was the influence of Babylon that enticed the Jews to depart from the Law and the Lord in Ezekiel's day, and the same effect can be witnessed in Christendom.

Yet, the Lord had an even greater abomination for Ezekiel to witness. The prophet is escorted to a location in the inner courtyard of the temple that was between the porch leading into the temple and the Bronze Altar. There Ezekiel saw about twenty-five men facing east and worshipping the rising sun (v. 16). These men are later identified as "elders" (9:6). In Jewish society, "elder" is a general term often applied to both religious and civil leaders. Both the number of them and their access to the Bronze Altar indicate that these men were priests. Albert Barnes explains: "This was the number of the heads of the 24 courses (shifts) with the high priest presiding over them. These then were the representatives of the priests, as the seventy were of the people."[23] The entrance to the temple was eastward. Hence, to face east meant that the priests had turned their backs on the Lord and had forsaken their ministry of effecting worship on behalf of the Jewish nation. Though the Lord was physically near to them (His glorious presence being less than a hundred feet away in the most holy place), they were spiritually far from Him.

To summarize, the scenes of idolatry in this vision are: the image of jealousy (vv. 5-6), the cultic worship of animals (7-13), the weeping for Tammuz (vv. 14-15), and sun worship (vv. 16-18). This corruption was not a localized phenomenon; rulers, priests, and the common people throughout Israel were equally guilty. It is observed that all the paganism in this visionary scene happily coexist with each other: Whether the idols, the various forms of heathen worship, or the idolaters themselves, all cohabit the temple peacefully. As D. L. Moody surmises, this shows the common source of all that demeans God – the devil:

> False gods patiently endure the existence of other false gods. Dagon can stand with Bel, and Bel with Ashtaroth; how should stone, and wood, and silver, be moved to indignation; but because God is the only living and true God, Dagon must fall before His ark; Bel must be broken, and Ashtaroth must be consumed with fire.[24]

The Jews obviously did not understand God's immense love for them, nor did they realize the consequences of prompting the jealousy of the all-powerful God (v. 17). God is long-suffering, slow to anger and quick to forgive, but the time for repentance and restoration was now past. His wife (His covenant people) had continued in persistent spiritual adultery and His anger burned hot against them.

The phrase *"indeed they put the branch to their nose"* is obscure (v. 17). It is possible that this refers to some ancient obscene act to express contempt for God, but the Hebrew phrase is better translated, "Indeed they put a stench in my nose." This reflects the understanding of early Hebrew scholars and the context of the passage. His people had filled the land with violence and heathen practices which rose up to heaven as a stench in God's nostrils and had to be removed. In His righteous indignation, God would have no pity for His people, despite their urgent pleadings for mercy (v. 18).

Some 2,600 years ago, Jeremiah and Ezekiel warned the Jews of God's anger towards them because of their unrepentant idolatry (v. 18).

Their warning against worshipping the Queen of Heaven and her son Tammuz could never be more appropriate for mankind to consider than now. Love, especially for the supposed Queen of Heaven, has supplanted proper allegiance to the declared Head of the Church – Christ (Eph. 1:22; Col. 1:18). Babylon is alive and well in the Church, and God hates it! We wonder how the Jews were so blind to their social paganism, yet the Church has been entrusted with much more divine revelation, and is committing the same sin. What will be God's wrath against those who invoke the name of Christ in superficial rituals, but will not receive Him as Lord and Savior? At the Judgment Seat of Christ, what excuses will believers offer to the Lord for dabbling in pagan rituals which honored fictitious protagonists, but not Him?

Meditation

> Praise, my soul, the King of Heaven; to His feet thy tribute bring.
> Ransomed, healed, restored, forgiven, evermore His praises sing:
> Alleluia! Alleluia! Praise the everlasting King.
>
> Praise Him for His grace and favor to our fathers in distress.
> Praise Him still the same as ever, slow to chide, and swift to bless.
> Alleluia! Alleluia! Glorious in His faithfulness.
>
> — Henry Lyte

Slaughter in Jerusalem
Ezekiel 9

In this somber chapter, Ezekiel is permitted to witness in a vision the marking of the just in Jerusalem and the slaughter of the remaining population. With a thunderous voice, the Lord summoned seven men (who were really angels) for this grisly task. The men approached the Lord from the north (to indicate the direction from which the Babylonian invaders would come), and then stood by the Bronze Altar to wait for instructions. Six of the men were carrying battle-axes, but the seventh was clothed in white linen and possessed only a writer's inkhorn (v. 2). The RSV and NASB translate the Hebrew word *'iysh*, meaning "masculine attendant," as *executioners*, the implication obvious.

The glory of the Lord which had been above God's throne in the most holy place moved to the threshold of the temple (v. 3). From this location the Lord commanded the man clothed with linen to go throughout Jerusalem and *"put a mark on the foreheads of the men who sigh and cry over all the abominations that are done within it"* (v. 4). Notice that the man in linen was not to mark those who were merely innocent of idolatry (neutral parties), but rather those who were deeply grieved over the disdain the Jews had levied on Jehovah's name.

We pause to consider two applications related to God's explicit instructions about the marking of the faithful. First, the command affirms that, from God's standpoint, neutrality in matters of sin is sin. God's people should never be disinterested in things that are important to Him. We either stand with the Lord in faith or our testimony for Him becomes rancid to Him and deplorable to onlookers. When evil rules over God's people, grief is the evidence of those in genuine communion with God; unfortunately, as in Ezekiel's day, few weep with God over the prevailing wickedness of our day.

Second, those few Jews who felt hallowed sorrow are expressly and conclusively exempt from the destroyer's ax – death! In every age, God preserves a faithful remnant for a testimony of Himself among the nations. Scripture shows us that in moral and spiritual matters, the human majority is seldom in the right. In secular movements, numbers are everything, but rarely do vast hordes of people represent God's will. This anomaly is quite evident in the modern Church movement, which equates church attendance with church success. The mindset is that big church meetings are obviously evidence of divine blessing. However, it is making disciples of Christ that is the key to Church growth and vitality (Matt. 28:19-20). The Great Supper parable of Luke 14 teaches that the Lord is much more interested in the commitment of His disciples to Him than in the crowd of people merely following Him. The Lord longs for genuine numbers – quality, not quantity. In summary, God's character and testimony to the lost will not be upheld by a moral majority, but rather by the despised minority.

The "mark" on the forehead of the righteous would distinguished the guilty (those to be executed) from those who would survive the Babylonian holocaust (although many of these survivors would be exiled to Babylon). The mark that was used for this purpose then has special significance to Christians for today, says L. E. Copper:

> The word "mark" is the Hebrew word *taw*, which is the name of the last letter in the Hebrew alphabet. It may have been understood as an abbreviation for *tam*, "blameless." In the seventh and sixth centuries B.C. the *taw* of Paleo-Hebrew script was written like an X or sloped cross. Its use here was to identify the righteous and exempt them from judgment. The "man" in white linen was to place the *taw* on the forehead of every righteous person. The significance of this sign to Christian interpreters obviously goes beyond what Ezekiel understood. As H. L. Ellison observed, the prophets often spoke more than they understood. God's judgment always was tempered with mercy. The "man" in white linen marked those who were grieved over the sins of Judah. These were spared and became a small remnant of hope for future restoration. They were spared by receiving the sign of the cross (X), as would be those sealed for deliverance in Revelation 7:3-4 and 14:1.[25]

The Lord then instructed the six executioners to begin at His sanctuary and then go through the entire city and smite everyone (young and old) who had not received the *taw* by the man with the inkhorn (vv. 5-6). They were commanded to show no mercy and to begin by executing the seventy elders of Israel whom Ezekiel had seen profaning the temple's inner court in the previous chapter. Since the Jews were already secretly defiling the temple, the Lord wanted the matter to be obvious – the dead bodies of idolaters would litter His house. After defiling the temple with blood and corpses, the executioners were to go throughout the city and invoke God's justice (v. 7).

Ezekiel, still standing by the Bronze Altar, was now left alone in the temple. Heartbroken by the sight, he fell on his face and cried out to the Lord, *"Ah, Lord God! Will You destroy all the remnant of Israel in pouring out Your fury on Jerusalem?"* (v. 8). No doubt the Lord appreciated his intercession, but in this situation there would be no relenting – God's vengeance must be satisfied: *"For because of the anger of the Lord this happened in Jerusalem and Judah, that He finally cast them out from His presence"* (2 Kgs. 24:20). However, the Lord did pause to explain to His servant why mercy would not be extended:

> *"The iniquity of the house of Israel and Judah is exceedingly great, and the land is full of bloodshed, and the city full of perversity; for they say, 'The Lord has forsaken the land, and the Lord does not see!' And as for Me also, My eye will neither spare, nor will I have pity, but I will recompense their deeds on their own head"* (vv. 9-10).

With these words, the man clothed in linen returned to report that he had done all that was commanded of him, that is, he had marked all the righteous in Jerusalem to preserve them from slaughter. This somber chapter reminds us that what God opposes is what we must reject, and what God approves of is what we should desire. A mature believer wants what God wants. Today, we might hear a Christian say, "I will pray about that" in order to shun his or her responsibility for confronting obvious sin. But silent neutrality condones sin – it is a sin not to reprove what one knows is morally wrong, especially when God's name is being scorned (Eph. 5:11)! In Ezekiel's vision, only those who thought as God did about wickedness were spared death.

Meditation

On the matter of being a silent spectator of unrighteousness, William MacDonald writes:

> When innocent people are being led off to gas chambers, ovens, and other modes of execution – when unborn babies are destroyed in abortion clinics – it is inexcusable to stand by and not seek to rescue them. It is also useless to plead ignorance. As Dante said, "The hottest places in hell are reserved for those who in a time of great moral crisis maintain their neutrality."[26]

God's Glory Departs
Ezekiel 10

Though God's glory was at the entrance of the sanctuary (to the east of Ezekiel), His brilliant sapphire throne-chariot (which Ezekiel saw previously in his first vision) was positioned on the south side of the temple (vv. 1, 3). Jehovah was preparing to leave His seat of glory in Jerusalem; morally speaking, He was being driven away by the iniquities and apostasy of His own people. The scene before us is one of the most heart-wrenching episodes of Israel's history. God has had enough; He was departing from His adulterous wife.

The Lord told the man clothed in linen: *"Go in among the wheels, under the cherub, fill your hands with coals of fire from among the cherubim, and scatter them over the city"* (v. 2). Interestingly, there was no mention of burning coals between the cherubim in chapter 1. This suggests that Ezekiel had to be called to his prophetic ministry first, before he could announce God's fiery indignation towards His people. As the man walked towards the throne-chariot, Ezekiel noted that because God's presence was at the threshold of the temple and not in the Most Holy Place, a cloud had filled the inner courtyard which was now wondrously illuminated by God's glory (vv. 3-4). The shimmering hues of color and the reflecting brilliance of God's glory filled the entire courtyard with dazzling awe.

When the man arrived beneath the chariot portion of God's mobile throne (i.e., between the wheels), the wings of the cherubim became incredibly loud – like the voice of the Lord (v. 5). When the Lord commanded the man in linen to *"take fire from among the wheels, from among the cherubim,"* he moved directly behind the wheels (v. 6). One of the cherubs took fire from the altar above the wheels and placed it in the hands of the man in linen who immediately departed from the temple to disperse it upon Jerusalem, to purge and purify God's holy city (v. 7). Ezekiel notes that the cherub who transferred the fire did so with what appeared to be a hand, though not specifically of human form (v. 8). In this sense, the burning coals, associated with the glory of

God in verse 2, bring about what God's presence demands – purity and holiness. The writer of Hebrews poses the same connection:

> *He who speaks from heaven, whose voice then shook the earth [speaking of Mount Sinai]; but now He has promised, saying, "Yet once more I shake not only the earth, but also heaven." Now this, "Yet once more," indicates the removal of those things that are being shaken, as of things that are made, that the things which cannot be shaken may remain. Therefore, since we are receiving a kingdom which cannot be shaken, let us have grace, by which we may serve God acceptably with reverence and godly fear. For our God is a consuming fire* (Heb. 12:25-29).

There is a day coming when God's awesome presence on earth will demand wholesale purging and purification; all that is not honoring to Him will be removed, as it was in Ezekiel's vision. The admonition for Christians in the Church Age is to remember that this same holy God has taken up residence in every believer, and He demands nothing less than extreme purity. *"Be holy, for I am holy"* was as applicable to Israel then as it is for the Church today (1 Pet. 1:13).

In verses 9-17, Ezekiel repeated the description from chapter 1 of the cherubim, the wheels of the chariot, and how it moved. This account is interrupted by the glory of the Lord moving from the threshold of the temple to His mobile throne above the cherubim (v. 18). The cherubim immediately lifted up the throne-chariot and moved eastward, pausing momentarily at the East Gate of the temple before moving farther eastward to hover over the Mount of Olives (v. 19, 11:23). The Lord was leaving Jerusalem and His people and glory would not return from heaven for a very long time. Ezekiel resumes his description of the cherubim to ensure the explicit tie to the before-mentioned vision at the River Chebar (vv. 20-22).

During Old Testament times, Jehovah dwelt in a tabernacle or temple among His covenant people. Hence, His visible glory is identified with His favor and blessing toward His people. Because of national idolatry, God's glory and available blessing departed from Israel just prior to the Babylonian invasion. His people were immoral, idolatrous, and wicked; He could no longer reside among them.

A similar situation existed centuries earlier when God dwelt among His people in a tabernacle pitched at Shiloh. At that time, God's covenant people did whatever was right in their own eyes and the Levitical priesthood had morally digressed into an abomination. Eli, the old priest who raised young Samuel, had two perverse sons, Phinehas and Hophni, who died while escorting the Ark of the Covenant into a battle with the Philistines (1 Sam. 2-4). The Philistines captured the Ark of the Covenant from Israel. Upon hearing this tragic news, heavy Eli fell backwards off his chair and broke his neck. At the time of his death, Phinehas's pregnant wife also went into labor and gave birth to a son. She named the child Ichabod, saying, *The glory has departed from Israel!"* (1 Sam. 4:21). "Ichabod" literally means "there is no glory" and that described Israel's situation then and also in Ezekiel's day; the Lord no longer dwelt among His people. They knew that the absence of His glory meant the lack of His favor – a realization that greatly grieved Ezekiel.

Interestingly, for this reason, Jehovah is often referred to in the post-exile books of the Bible by a less familiar title, "the Lord God of heaven" or "the God of heaven." Even the Persian King Cyrus refers to him by that name in the opening verses of Ezra's book. H. A. Ironside summarizes why Ezra, Nehemiah, and Daniel often referred to the Lord as "the God of heaven":

> It was a title He took when His throne was removed from the earth, and He gave His people into the hands of the Gentiles. He went and *"returned to His place,"* as Hosea puts it. He forsook the temple at Jerusalem, dissolved the theocracy and became *"the God of heaven."* Such He is still to His ancient people, and so He will remain till He returns to Jerusalem to establish His throne again as *"the Lord of the whole earth."*[27]

God would relate to His covenant people in a more obscure sense for centuries to come. Though returning Jewish captives would rebuild a temple of less grandeur in Jerusalem, God would not dwell among them again, in that way, until the Millennial Kingdom of Christ. However, Jesus, God manifest in flesh, did tabernacle among them as *Immanuel*, God with us, although most of Israel did not realize it! After the "time of the Gentiles" is past, this same Jewish monarch will then rule over them once again. The Lord Jesus Christ is the rightful heir to David's throne.

Infidelity and Loyalty

The Jews were distraught by the destruction of the temple – the house of God. They were less grieved about the glory of the Lord departing from it. Their focus had shifted from what was spiritually vital to what was traditionally important. Unfortunately, the same superficial attitudes plague the Church today.

After Christ's death and resurrection, the entire Levitical system was put away to ensure that it, the type, did not compete with the antitype, the New Covenant seal in Christ's blood (Heb. 8:13). Yet, many Christians today still place an emphasis on an earthly sanctuary that does not exist. This results in using wrong terminology which introduces an alternative and unbiblical idea of what the Church is or where the real sanctuary is. The Church is not a lifeless building; it is a living spiritual body (Eph. 2:19-22). "The house of God" is not a building in which Christians gather; rather, it is the Church itself (1 Tim. 3:15). The only door of entrance into the true Church is the Lord Jesus (John 10:1, 14:6). Thus, there is a stark difference in the use of the term "house of God" in the Old Testament, which referred to the tabernacle or a physical temple, and how it is used in the New Testament after Pentecost to designate the Church – the spiritual body of Christ. Let us not lose sight of these scriptural distinctions in the Church Age, or we too might find God's communion far from us.

Meditation

Lord, Thy glory fills the heaven;
Earth is with its fullness stored;
Unto Thee be glory given,
Holy, holy, holy Lord!
Thus Thy glorious Name confessing,
We adopt the angels' cry,
"Holy, holy, holy" blessing
Thee, the Lord of Hosts Most High!

— Richard Mant

Wicked Leaders Judged
Ezekiel 11

The Spirit of God then lifted Ezekiel up and brought him to the East Gate of the temple which overlooked the Kidron Valley below and the Mount of Olives eastward. From this location he saw twenty-five elders of Israel, probably a group from the seventy identified in Ezekiel 8. This is not the same group of sun-worshipping priests (8:16), as Jaazaniah is among them and he was previously connected with Israel's corrupt political leadership (i.e., the seventy pagan elders; 8:11). The two groups indicate the rampant infidelity of the nation; both civil and religious leaders were apostate. The gate of a city was where Jewish elders presided over legal matters and executed judgments.

Besides Jaazaniah, the son of Azzur, Ezekiel also recognized Pelatiah, the son of Benaiah. We should be thankful that these men are not mentioned elsewhere in Scripture, for the Lord informed Ezekiel that they and the entire group were wicked. They devised iniquity and rendered perverse counsel to the people: *"The time is not near to build houses; this city is the caldron, and we are the meat"* (vv. 2-3). In other words, they were encouraging the people to ignore Ezekiel's prophecies of doom; they were as safe in Jerusalem as meat was in a cooking pot. These wicked leaders proposed that they should be building up the city, not waiting for its destruction. They had turned Jeremiah's prophetic figure of the cooking pot (Jer. 1:13) into mockery in order to promote themselves.

However, God informed Ezekiel that He knew what they were really thinking; they feared a Babylonian invasion and wanted to bolster their defenses against such an attack by building up Jerusalem (v. 5). For rejecting God's Word and trying to strengthen themselves against His chastening rod, Ezekiel was commanded to prophesy against them (v. 4). Verse 5 affirms the omniscience of the Lord: He knows all our thoughts, the quality of our thoughts, whether conscious or unconscious, and He does not forget them, though we usually do in time.

David fully understood this attribute of God and welcomed His examination: *"O Lord, You have searched me and known me. You know my sitting down and my rising up; You understand my thought afar off"* (Ps. 139:1-2). Because David realized every aspect of his life was searched out, planned, and meticulously controlled by the Lord, he could praise the Lord for His wondrous works and invite further inspection and refinement of his inner man (Ps. 139:23-24). Hamilton Smith reminds us that godly saints desire this type of spiritual scrutiny and enhancement:

> The godly man welcomes the searchings of God into the inmost recesses of his heart, desiring that he may be delivered from every evil way and led "in the way everlasting." In the experience of the psalmist, the consciousness of the omniscience of God at first plunges his soul into the deepest distress as he thinks of his own broken responsibilities towards God. When, at length, he realizes that God's "works" and God's "thoughts" are toward him in grace, the omniscience of God becomes the source of his deepest comfort.[28]

Divine inspection of David's heart would both prove his loyal devotion to the Lord and permit God to further test and enrich David's character. He knew he could not hide his thoughts and doings from the Lord, so he desired to transform all his contemplations and deeds to those that would please Him. This is the proper response to the omnipresent, omniscient, omnipotent God. Concerning one's devotion to the Lord, David shows us that there is no middle ground; we should loathe what the Lord disapproves of and long for what pleases Him. This practical mindset is the greatest heritage that believing parents can pass down to their children; unfortunately, the Jewish generation before us did not do so.

What one generation tolerates, the next will embrace.

— John Wesley

Returning to the narrative, these prominent rulers had slain righteous men and filled the streets with their bodies (v. 6). In fact, it was the righteous dead who could have saved the city from judgment, but their murders now ensured God's wrath (v. 7). From God's perspective the meat in the pot (the city) was their dead bodies and He would ensure that the pot was purged of innocent blood. The leaders were not safe in the city, for it would be destroyed by foreigners and those surviving the initial attack would be dragged to the borders of Israel and judged by the sword (vv. 8-12). This was fulfilled when Jewish captives were later transported from Jerusalem to Riblah in Syria and executed (2 Kgs. 25:18-21).

Jeremiah also prophesied the same event would occur. Jeremiah had repeatedly told the people that if they did not surrender to Nebuchadnezzar and live as captives under his rule, they would die in Jerusalem by the sword, pestilence, or famine. The Jews had rejected Jeremiah's prophecy and stiffened their necks against the Babylonians. After suffering through a drought and a siege that lasted either eighteen months or two and a half years, many in Jerusalem died before the Babylonians even took the city. Most of the inhabitants of Jerusalem at the time of its fall were slaughtered.

To confirm that Jeremiah's declaration had come true, the writer provides a partial roster of influential Jews who were beaten and then executed in Riblah by Nebuzaradan, the captain of the guard: Seraiah (the chief priest), Zephaniah (the priest next in rank), the three temple doorkeepers, the officer in charge of the soldiers, seven royal advisers, and the chief officer in charge of conscripting the people and sixty of his men (Jer. 52:24-26). Less than five years after Ezekiel delivered this message, the word of the Lord as spoken by Jeremiah and Ezekiel would be fulfilled, thus proving that they were God's true prophets.

Ezekiel obeyed the Lord and prophesied against Israel's leadership, but after witnessing Pelatiah drop dead at his feet (i.e., in his vision), the son of man fell on his face and cried out to the Lord, *"Ah, Lord God! Will You make a complete end of the remnant of Israel?"* (v. 13). The Lord answered this intercessory plea in two ways (vv. 14-15). First, He informed Ezekiel that his fellow-exiled brethren would be preserved as a remnant and not destroyed. Second, those in Jerusalem had rejected Jeremiah's edict to surrender and live, and therefore had a stubborn disposition toward those Jews in exile: *"Get far away from the Lord; this land has been given to us as a possession"* (vv. 14-15). In their view, it was the captives who were far from the Lord, whereas they were the ones remaining in the Promised Land, their possession from Jehovah. These two complimentary principles summarize how

Infidelity and Loyalty

God deals with humanity in general: Those who boast in their crimes, successes, and autonomy are ripe for wrath; however, those who decry sin, surrender to revealed truth, and humbly acknowledge their frailty will be prepared for glory; God will be their sanctuary. Paul puts the matter this way:

> *What if God, wanting to show His wrath and to make His power known, endured with much longsuffering the vessels of wrath prepared for destruction, and that He might make known the riches of His glory on the vessels of mercy, which He had prepared beforehand for glory, even us whom He called, not of the Jews only, but also of the Gentiles?* (Rom. 9:22-24).

In God's patient sovereignty, the proud prepare themselves for His wrath, but through His mercy, He predestines the humble for glory! Because of their hypocritical devotion, Israel's leaders had brought about their own destruction.

The greatness of a man's power is the measure of his surrender.

— William Booth

It is utter folly to think self-propitiating religiosity could ever be a safeguard against divine wrath, especially when one winks at sin and deliberately affronts God's character. A true profession of faith is much more than an escape from hellfire; it is an entry visa to the presence of the holy, eternal Creator. Like the Jewish leaders before us, many today profess Christ as their Savior, but know nothing of His lordship and the necessity of personal consecration.

The Lord told His disciples that *knowing* about the Him and *doing* works in His name were not the same as *trusting* Him for salvation and *following* after Him. Those who know Christ as Savior do works of righteousness for Him (Matt. 7:21), while those who do not, work to be seen by others (Matt. 7:22). Many professing Christians have religious knowledge and activities galore, but yet have not personally experienced God. They really do not know Him, and more importantly He does not know them, a matter He will confirm on judgment day: *"I never knew you; depart from Me, you who practice lawlessness"* (Matt. 7:23)! To practice sin without regard to how it injures the heart of God is the distinct behavior of an unregenerate soul. Humility, faithfulness, obedience, and purity are marks of a believer. A true profession of faith is evident, in time, by good and consistent fruit-bearing (2 Cor. 7:10).

> There's a difference between knowing God and knowing about God. When you truly know God, you have energy to serve Him, boldness to share Him, and contentment in Him.
>
> — J. I. Packer

True believers may indeed fall from time to time, but there is a consistent testimony of God's life within them which cannot be hidden; a good tree bears good fruit (Matt. 7:17-20).

But how would God purge idolaters and religious fakes from Israel and at the same time preserve a genuine remnant of faithful believers in Israel? Ezekiel explains the answer to this question:

> *Although I have cast them far off among the Gentiles, and although I have scattered them among the countries, yet I shall be a little sanctuary for them in the countries where they have gone. Therefore say, "Thus says the Lord God: 'I will gather you from the peoples, assemble you from the countries where you have been scattered, and I will give you the land of Israel.'" And they will go there, and they will take away all its detestable things and all its abominations from there. Then I will give them one heart, and I will put a new spirit within them, and take the stony heart out of their flesh, and give them a heart of flesh, that they may walk in My statutes and keep My judgments and do them; and they shall be My people, and I will be their God. But as for those whose hearts follow the desire for their detestable things and their abominations, I will recompense their deeds on their own heads* (vv. 16-21).

First, God will purify the exiled Jews of their idols. Second, He will preserve them in foreign lands. Third, He will gather them back to the land of Israel, their possession. Fourth, He will bestow on them a new heart through His indwelling Spirit. The complete fulfillment of the latter two aspects is yet future.

In the near term, the wicked rebels in Jerusalem would be destroyed and the exiled Jews would be kept safe in Babylon where God would once and for all purge them of idolatry before bringing them home (v.

17). While these Jews would lose their sanctuary in Jerusalem, the Lord Himself promised to be their sanctuary, their solace and resting place, in Babylon (v. 16).

Ezekiel uses the example of the returning exiled Jews who have been purged of their idols to foretell of a similar future event when the entire nation would receive the Holy Spirit and never rebel against the Lord again. This will occur in the Millennial Kingdom. Israel's difficulties in Ezekiel's day resulted from a heart problem – their love for Jehovah had grown cold and they were no longer in awe of Him. God promised to fix that problem so His people could always enjoy His presence and communion. So while the returning Jews from Babylon had a change of heart concerning their idols and other detestable things, this transformation was only partial. God's ultimate solution of spiritual regeneration would occur later and nationally through the New Covenant (vv. 18-19). Only then will His covenant people have the wherewithal to walk in His statutes and commandments forever (v. 20). Those not experiencing this transformation will be judged for their rebellious ways (v. 21).

The Cherubim then lifted up God's throne-chariot from Jerusalem further eastward to the Mount of Olives (vv. 22-23). Originally, the Lord had been in the Most Holy Place (8:4), then the temple threshold (9:3), then above this threshold (10:4), to the East Gate of the outer court (10:19) and now He moved to the Mount of Olives east of the temple mount. God had deserted His temple, the city of His habitation, and most importantly His people, save a remnant that He would preserve (vv. 22-23). William Kelly suggests that this small faithful remnant engulfed in the fallout of Jewish rebellion is reminiscent of the scene which draws Matthew's gospel to a close.

> It reminds one of Matthew 28 where the risen Jesus is seen on a mountain of Galilee, giving His great commission to the disciples as to all the nations, without saying a word about His ascension to heaven. Jerusalem is left aside indeed, a remnant sent out by the Lord resuming His Galilean place in resurrection, the beautiful pledge of His return spite of present rejection. The curtain drops over the Shekinah when it reaches Olivet, till we hear of its reappearance in the last chapters for the latter day.[29]

Thankfully, Ezekiel later explains that God's glory will return to the Mount of Olives in a future day and God would again dwell with His people (43:1-3). The departing glory of God signaled the city's doom. This same declaration is pictured in the glorious ascension of the Lord Jesus from the Mount of Olives six centuries later (Acts 1:9-12). Jehovah permitted the Jews several years to repent and receive His Son, their Messiah whom they had crucified, but they would not, and in 70 A.D. the temple and portions of Jerusalem were destroyed.

Foreknowing this travesty, God sent two angels to convey a message of hope to the Jewish nation, as the disciples observed the Lord ascending into heaven: *"This same Jesus, who was taken up from you into heaven, will so come in like manner as you saw Him go into heaven"* (Acts 1:11). When will the Lord return to the Mount of Olives to restore the glory of God to Jerusalem? The prophet Zechariah informs us that this event will occur at the battle of Armageddon at the end of the Tribulation Period (Zech. 14:4). The nations will have gathered against Jerusalem under the authority of the Antichrist and half the city will be conquered when He appears from heaven and descends upon and splits the Mount of Olives.

Psalm 118 is sung at the Jewish Passover, and its lyrics would have been on the minds of the people when Christ entered Jerusalem from the Mount of Olives on what is commonly referred to as Palm Sunday. In the closing verses of the hymn, the Jews request continued salvation and prosperity by the hand of the one who *"comes in the name of the Lord"* (Ps. 118:25-29). Thus, it was no accident that it was openly proclaimed by the people when the Lord descended the Mount of Olives into Jerusalem a few days before Passover and His crucifixion: *"Blessed is He who comes in the name of the Lord"* (Ps. 118:26). Jesus Christ is the one who comes in the name of the Lord, offering life and blessing.

Psalm 118:22 is quoted several times in the New Testament, where it is evident the reference to the rejected cornerstone relates to Israel's refusal of Jesus Christ as their Messiah. The psalmist says, *"this is the day which the Lord has made"* (Ps. 118:24). The Lord Jesus Himself acknowledged that this verse spoke of Him (Matt. 21:42; Luke 20:17), and so did the apostles (Eph. 2:20; 1 Pet. 2:6-7). After being rejected by the Jewish nation, the Lord suffered and died at Calvary and was resurrected to the highest station in heaven. In a future day He will return to earth to establish His throne as Israel's King – then they will know that the glory of God has returned to Jerusalem!

At the moment God's glory moved above the Mount of Olives, Ezekiel was transported back to Babylon and his vision ended (v. 24). He then informed the Jewish elders still residing in his home what the Lord had shown him (v. 25). One can only imagine the raised eyebrows, wide-open eyes, and gasps as Ezekiel recounted the details of the vision to his fellow captives. Yet, however dismal the near-term prophecies concerning Jerusalem were, there was the exciting hope of restoration looming in the not-too-distant future; God loved His people too much to leave them in pagan Babylon.

The Lord's return to the Mount of Olives is not the Church's hope of glory, though we will certain rejoice in Christ's vindication and His glorious reign on earth over the nations. Christians, through the gospel message, can rejoice that their souls are saved from the penalty of sin, and through the Holy Spirit they have power over sin. But they are to continue to anticipate a future day when they will be saved from the presence of sin. At that moment a believer's body will be transformed into holy humanity, nothing of the flesh nature inherited from Adam will remain, and he or she will be removed from the presence of sin (i.e., from the corruption of the world).

Because of spiritual regeneration, Christ is present with us on earth; in the future, we shall be with Him in heaven. His forever abiding presence with us is certain, though our intimacy with Him now depends on our desire for it. With His exaltation looming, we are to live each and every day with the anticipation of Christ's coming (2 Tim. 4:6-8). There is a reward for those who do, and our lives will be more joyful and fruitful in light of the imminent expectation.

In a twinkling of an eye, what was corruptible will be incorruptible, and what was mortal will be immortal (1 Cor. 15:51-52) and we will be caught up into the air to be ever with the Lord (1 Thess. 4:13-18). At this event, often referred to as "the Rapture of the Church," sin and pain will cease to exist within all believers in Christ. The believer's glorified body will be enabled to worship and to please God without any hindrance from the flesh or any ills of its previously fallen state.

Paul had one hope (Eph. 4:4), one earnest expectation, the *blessed hope*: "*Looking for the blessed hope and glorious appearing of our great God and Savior Jesus Christ*" (Titus 2:13). While this may include aspects of Christ's future kingdom as well, it is noted that the believer's faith and hope finish their course at Christ's coming for the Church (the rapture), yet love, as previously mentioned, continues forever (1 Cor. 13:8, 13). The Church is not to be waiting for the Antichrist to appear (his coming is a sign to the nation of Israel; Dan. 9:27), but for Christ Himself to translate them from the earth into heaven. The Church is not waiting for the inhabitants of earth to be slaughtered during the Tribulation Period, but rather longs to be removed from this wicked world to be with Christ.

While the Church is to be evangelical until the Lord's return, it is understood that He alone will cleanse wickedness from the world and establish His throne in Jerusalem. We are not preparing the Kingdom for Him. Israel was given hope of future restoration and fulfillment of the Abrahamic Covenant, but the Church's hope will be realized before that occurs – our hope is to be with the Lord in heaven.

Meditation

I'm abiding in Canaan land!
Since He washed my sin away,
It is glory all the way.

I'm abiding in Canaan land!
All my sins have been forgiven,
And I'm on my way to Heaven.

Tis a foretaste of coming glory yonder
In that land beyond the sky,
Where in bliss untold I shall ever wander
In the blessed homeland by and by.

— Avis Christiansen

I Am a Sign
Ezekiel 12

Since being commissioned as God's watchman in chapter 3, Ezekiel has provided four signs, two messages, and the details of a complex vision to show the Jewish people the necessity of Jerusalem's judgment and how it would come about. They were wicked and God must chasten them. Yet, the Jewish people were still not willing to accept Jerusalem's fate. In response to this false optimism, *"the word of the Lord"* (v. 1) will prompt Ezekiel to deliver fresh signs, proverbs, and messages in chapters 12-19. This ministry would better prepare the Jewish survivors for their inescapable and long captivity.

The preface for this entire section is found in verse 2: *"Son of man, you dwell in the midst of a rebellious house, which has eyes to see but does not see, and ears to hear but does not hear; for they are a rebellious house."* As during the Lord's earthly sojourn centuries later, Israel's problem was not that they could not perceive and understand what God wanted, but rather their willful rejection of it – they were a rebellious people. Ezekiel then performed two skits to symbolize the massive deportation of Jews from Israel that would occur and their futile attempts to escape their Babylonian captors.

The first sign was performed during the day. Ezekiel packed up his belongings and moved to a different location to symbolize the inevitable Jewish deportation (vv. 3-4). L. E. Cooper summarizes the types of things that Ezekiel might have packed for this drama: An exile's baggage probably included only the barest essentials – a skin for water, a mat for sleeping, and a bowl for food.[30] Onlookers could easily understand the meaning of this skit, as they had personally experienced this reality about six years earlier. Under the cover of darkness that same evening, Ezekiel acted out the second dramatic message. He dug a hole in the wall of his home, pulled out his bundled belongings and placed them on his shoulder, but since he was also blindfolded, he could not see where he was going (vv. 5-7). The meaning of these pantomimes would be explained on the following day.

Having aroused the people's curiosity by the performance of the previous day, the Lord sent Ezekiel the next morning to explain the prophetic meaning of what they had witnessed (vv. 8-9). The messages pertained to *"the prince in Jerusalem"* (King Zedekiah) and *"the whole house of Israel"* who dwelled with him there (v. 10). Many of those surviving the fall of Jerusalem would be taken to Babylon as captives; their only belongings would be what they could carry on their shoulders (v. 11). This illustrated that any attempt to escape God's chastening was futile; there was nowhere for the Jews to go to find peace and safety. In God's mercy He would permit a remnant of Israel to survive the holocaust (v. 16).

The second skit pertained to King Zedekiah. Though he would attempt to secretly escape the Babylonians encamped around Jerusalem under the cover of darkness, he would be caught, blinded, taken captive to Babylon and he would die there (vv. 12-16). This prophecy was exactly fulfilled about six years after it was pronounced. The prophet Jeremiah, like Ezekiel, also prophesied that King Zedekiah would be captured and taken to Babylon as a prisoner (Jer. 21:5-7).

Jeremiah later records the details of how this prophecy was actually fulfilled (Jer. 39:1-7). He was in Jerusalem at the time and notes when the siege of Jerusalem began (in the tenth month of the ninth year of Zedekiah's reign), and when it ended (the ninth day of the fourth month of the eleventh year of Zedekiah). The reigns of Hebrew vassal kings under Babylonian rule were reckoned from Tishri (September/October) to Tishri; however, the Hebrews used their own calendar which began on Nisan (March/April) in reference to months. Accordingly, the siege of Jerusalem may have lasted about two and a half years, beginning in January of 588 B.C. and ending in July of 586 B.C. If, however, only the Babylonian calendar was used, the siege would have lasted about nineteen months.

When Zedekiah saw that the city was falling into Babylonian hands, he marshalled the soldiers he had left and fled eastward from the city. He did not escape, but was captured on the plains of Jericho and brought before the Babylonian king. With Zedekiah watching, Nebuchadnezzar had the nobles of Judah executed and then he slew all of Zedekiah's sons. This horrific scene would be the last thing Zedekiah would witness, for his eyes were then put out. Then he was chained and taken to Babylon. What both Jeremiah and Ezekiel predicted, came true.

Ezekiel was then called on to deliver a third sign in conjunction with the previous two, the sign of "trembling." He was to tremble as he ate bread and shudder while drinking water (vv. 17-18). His actions represented the fear and trepidation that the besieged inhabitants of Jerusalem would experience while the Babylonians plundered and devastated the entire land (vv. 19-20).

After acting out these three signs and explaining their meaning, Ezekiel launched into preaching. He delivered five separate sermons in quick succession (12:21-14:23). Chapter 12 concludes with the first two of these messages. Interestingly, both messages commence with a divine exposé of common proverbs the Jews were frequently quoting at this time.

The proverb confronted in the first message was, *"The days are prolonged, and every vision fails"* (vv. 21-22). In application, this terse saying had the social impact of labeling prophets like Jeremiah and Ezekiel as doomsayers, who should be ignored. Jeremiah especially suffered the assault of false prophets who both confronted and countered his prophetic admonitions with optimistic messages of hope (Jer. 28:1-4, 29:1-9). Ezekiel's warnings were not like the distant rumblings of a thunderstorm that never arrived; rather, God's judgment was coming. When God's judicial tempest did arrive, then all the false visions and flattering divinations of the false prophets would be silenced by the unfolding of God's prophetic word (vv. 23-25). In the next chapter Ezekiel pronounces judgment on these lying prophets.

The second popular saying being bandied about was, *"The vision that he sees is for many days from now, and he prophesies of times far off"* (v. 27). The first proverb implied that God's judgment was not coming at all; however, the second suggested that though God's judgment was unavoidable, it would not be soon (i.e., not in their lifetime). Ezekiel's second message then confirms the imminence of God's wrath; not one detail of God's Word would go unfulfilled (v. 28).

This same lethargic attitude plagues carnal Christians today. Pseudo-faith will inevitably doubt God's Word and negate the repercussions of ignoring it: "That warning applies to someone else, probably a later generation, which means I am free to live my life the way I want to." The apostles warned that the general populace would be thinking that there was "peace and safety" immediately before the Lord would return to judge them; He would come like an unexpected thief in the night (2 Thess. 5:2-3; 2 Pet. 3:10). This was the general attitude of the Jews at this time. Even though many of them were already captives in Babylon, they still doubted God's admonitions. In their carnal imaginations they had created a different god with an altered agenda, which is nothing less than idolatry in the mind!

The second of the Ten Commandments says: *"You shall not make for yourself a carved image – any likeness of anything that is in heaven above, or that is in the Earth beneath, or that is in the water under the Earth; you shall not bow down to them nor serve them. For I, the Lord your God, am a jealous God"* (Ex. 20:4-5). Have you ever heard someone say, "God to me is …." The individual is revealing his or her self-concocted god, an imaginary image of a god which fits his or her liking and, therefore, will readily condone that person's moral standard of behavior. In this way, holiness becomes relative; a self-manufactured god will not judge sin. This idol may not be a golden calf, but neither is it the Lord revealed in the Bible.

God does not have varying degrees of holiness and righteousness; His very character defines moral integrity, and all that does not measure up to it will be judged. When an individual replaces the true God of Scripture with a created image (whether visible or imaginary), he or she has violated the second of the Ten Commandments.

To have a faith, therefore, or a trust in anything, where God hath not promised, is plain idolatry, and a worshipping of thine own imagination instead of God.

— William Tyndale

The essence of idolatry is the entertainment of thoughts about God that are unworthy of Him.

— A. W. Tozer

Creating an imaginary god that approves of sin and endorses the future that we want is never a good idea. Through these three signs and two messages, Ezekiel was preparing the people for a long captivity and teaching them that it was best to suffer in the revealed will of God, than be out of His will and reap His displeasure. We choose our sin, but God chooses the consequences of our sin. It is best to accept God's chastening as an expression of His parental love, rather than further stiffening our necks against Him and going our own way (Heb. 12:6).

Both Jeremiah and Ezekiel realized that to properly walk with the Lord, we must welcome His correction of our missteps. This disciplinary principle should have been no surprise to the Jews, as Moses informed them of it shortly after their deliverance from Egypt (Ex. 15:26). It is the same principle that parents must teach their children early in life: obedience brings blessing, but disobedience results in punishment. Accordingly, our children have a choice as to whether they will receive our warm embrace or the rod of reproof. Every child of God has the same choice: *"Be you therefore followers of God, as dear children"* (Eph. 5:1); *"As obedient children, not fashioning yourselves according to the former lusts in your ignorance"* (1 Pet. 1:14); *"For whom the Lord loves He chastens"* (Heb. 12:6). There truly is only one way for a child of God to be happy in the Lord Jesus – to trust and obey!

If one loves the Lord, submitting to His precepts will be a delight. Love for the Lord is a stronger motive for obedience than the fear of consequences: *"There is no fear in love; but perfect love casts out fear, because fear involves torment. But he who fears has not been made perfect in love"* (1 Jn. 4:18). A believer motivated by the love for Christ can venture into each and every day with confidence that God has his or her best in mind; he or she need not fear eternal retribution for every misstep. God is for those who love Him and is quite capable of overruling our mistakes for our good and His glory (Rom. 8:28).

> A providence is shaping our ends; a plan is developing in our lives; a supreme and loving Being is making all things work together for good.
>
> — F. B. Meyer

Meditation

> When we walk with the Lord in the light of His Word,
> What a glory He sheds on our way!
> While we do His good will, He abides with us still,
> And with all who will trust and obey.

Then in fellowship sweet we will sit at His feet,
Or we'll walk by His side in the way.
What He says we will do, where He sends we will go;
Never fear, only trust and obey.

— John H. Sammis

Nonsense and Lies
Ezekiel 13

Ezekiel's third message in his *certainty of divine judgment* series is recorded in this chapter. The central theme of this sermon is a pronouncement of judgment on the false Jewish prophets (vv. 1-16) and prophetesses (vv. 17-23). These spiritual frauds were deceiving the Jewish nation by promoting a false sense of hope.

Addressing the false prophets first, Ezekiel declares that they had seen no visions from God; rather, their propaganda was derived from their own imaginations; they were not conveying God's will (vv. 1-3). Because of the dangerous effect these lying prophets had on the people, Ezekiel likened them to jackals hiding among ruins, meaning that these soothsayers were particularly dangerous when a society was disintegrating into ruin (v. 4). These deceitful seers had done nothing to repair the crumbling moral walls of Israel, a society on the brink of total collapse; consequently, they would receive God's full retribution in *"the day of the Lord"* (v. 5).

False prophets have plagued the Jews throughout their history, and they still infest Christendom today, surmises H. A. Ironside:

> In every age when God has been dealing with His professed people because of their sins and apostasy, there have been such false prophets who have sought to lull the offenders to sleep in a false confidence, assuring them that all is well and there need be no fear of judgment falling upon them. How these prophets abound in Christendom today! With the Judge standing at the door, they continue to cry, "Peace, peace, when there is no peace!"[31]

This problem is compounded by the fact that God's Old Testament prophets always seemed to be greatly outnumbered by their counterparts. The ministries of Elijah (1 Kings 18), Micaiah (1 Kings 22), and Jeremiah (Jer. 20) serve as good examples. Time and again,

God's prophets have suffered greatly for their faithfulness to be a voice for God among a throng of dissident and often hostile people.

Paul warned the Corinthians that Satan often transforms himself into an angel of light and his servants into ministers of righteousness because he knows it is easier to deceive God's people in their work than it is to deter them from their purpose:

For such are false apostles, deceitful workers, transforming themselves into apostles of Christ. And no wonder! For Satan himself transforms himself into an angel of light. Therefore it is no great thing if his ministers also transform themselves into ministers of righteousness, whose end will be according to their works (2 Cor. 11:13-15).

Because the Jews throughout their history have looked for signs and wonders to substantiate their faith, they have invariably fallen into the trap of ignoring God's immutable Word. False prophets can powerfully represent a virtual reality of the truth, as they did in Ezekiel's day. Sadly, false brethren and self-ordained prophets, with their overbearing, self-promoting evil practices, continue to plague God's people today.

Discernment is not a matter of simply telling the difference between right and wrong; rather it is telling the difference between right and almost right.
— Charles Spurgeon

In verse 5, we find the first of two references in the book to "the Day of the Lord" (the other being 30:3). "The Day of the Lord" is an Old Testament term that speaks of those times when Jehovah intervened in a visible and powerful way to judge the wicked on earth. This meaning continues into the New Testament and speaks specially of the Tribulation Period and the Millennial Kingdom of Christ. (Many of the Old Testament usages also speak of these future events.) The Day of the Lord concludes with the destruction of the earth and the subsequent Great White Throne judgment.

The Day of the Lord should not be confused with the Day of Christ. In Paul's first epistle to the Thessalonians, he spoke of Christ's imminent coming for His Church – the Day of Christ (1 Thess. 4:13-18) and also of the Day of the Lord which would follow (1 Thess. 5:1-

5). Peter also speaks of the Day of the Lord (2 Pet. 3:10), and then introduces us to the Day of God (2 Pet. 3:12). Peter states that the Day of the Lord ends when the heavens and the earth pass away with a great noise and their elements shall melt with fervent heat and are burned up (2 Pet. 3:10). John tells us that this occurs directly after Christ's Millennial Kingdom and after the Great White Throne judgment of the wicked is complete (Rev. 20). Isaiah states that *"all the host of heaven shall be dissolved, and the heavens shall be rolled up like a scroll"* (Isa. 34:4). Like John, Isaiah foretells that after the Millennial Kingdom, God will create a new heaven and new earth (Isa. 65:17; Rev. 21:1). Whenever God invokes the term "the Day of the Lord," His judgment is sure, and Ezekiel was declaring that no lying prophet would escape His wrath in the day of His wrath.

When God's judgment fell on Jerusalem, the people would know that the self-proclaimed prophets (those who failed to confront sin and spoke nonsense) were not sent by Him; furthermore, God was against them (vv. 6-7). When their fellow countrymen learned who they really were, they would lose their prominent status in Jewish society and their names would be stripped from Jewish history (vv. 8-9).

Ezekiel then likens their claims of peace to constructing a block wall with untempered mortar. A wall speaks of protection and separation. Soon their make-believe wall of security would be exposed to wind and rain which would cause it to quickly crumble (vv. 10-12). Then the inhabitants of Jerusalem would realize that the prophets they had been heeding were unsafe walls that had been whitewashed to appear reliable. Time eventually verifies the truth – and in a few years when God brought His storm of vindication against Jerusalem, the words of these false prophets would quickly crumble and they would be known for what they were – liars (vv. 13-16)! While Ezekiel speaks only of how God will publicly deal with Israel's false prophets (i.e., loss of privilege, social rank, possessions, etc.), there is little doubt that their final portion will be everlasting destruction.

Ezekiel was then told to take up a similar lament and warning concerning the false prophetesses of Israel, who like their male counterparts, spoke lies from their own hearts (v. 17). These women donned pagan charms on their wrists and wore long coverings on their heads that draped down over their bodies (v. 18). The people were intrigued and even seduced by their veiled mystery and alluring custom. For a handful of barley or a scrap of bread these women were quite willing to pronounce a "good-luck charm" or to offer a promise of good fortune (v. 19). By doing so, these sorceresses had killed the righteous (those who should not have died in God's economy of justice), and spared the wicked (those who deserved to die and in time would receive God's wrath).

Ezekiel promised that God would save His gullible people from this dangerous feminine deception by ripping their charms off their wrists and removing their veils, thus exposing them as impostors (vv. 20-21). God will not tolerate false visions and divination among His people, and once these false prophetesses were publically exposed as frauds, they would be forced to confess their lies and evil ways (vv. 22-23).

After hearing conflicting evidence concerning the Lord Jesus, Pilate asked Him, *"What is truth?"* (John 18:38). Normally we speak of truth as that which conforms to fact or reality; however, some use truth to more freely infer a sincere statement. However, the words of the false prophets and prophetesses of Israel, though candidly spoken, were not truthful. We must realize that reality exists independently of our natural understanding of it. Because man is neither omniscient nor omnipresent, he cannot completely understand reality through natural means, nor through the wonderfully spoken words of intellectuals and philosophers.

A god who lets us prove his existence would be an idol.

— Dietrich Bonhoeffer

Whatever is naturally developed will tend to be imperfect, meaning we need supernatural help from the Lord to understand what truth really is and who He is. Truth is truth; it is not relative. Absolute truth cannot contradict itself. As demonstrated in this chapter, God's Word wonderfully withstands the test of time and is proven trustworthy. Let us be very careful what we accept as truth when it originates in human reasoning, for as often is the case, time proves the fallibility of such things.

Meditation

Relativism poses as humble by saying: "We are not smart enough to know what the truth is—or if there is any universal truth." It sounds humble. But look carefully at what is happening. It's like a servant saying: I am not smart enough to know which person here is my master—or if I even have a master. The result is that I don't have a master and I can be my own master. That is in reality what happens to relativists: In claiming to be too lowly to know the truth, they exalt themselves as supreme arbiter of what they can think and do. This is not humility. This is the essence of pride.

— John Piper

"These Three Men"
Ezekiel 14

The fourth of the five messages on the surety of God's wrath pertained to Israel's idolatrous leaders. Some of these men visited Ezekiel's home to inquire of the Lord (v. 1). The Lord informed Ezekiel that these elders were secret idolaters; not only did they have idols in their hearts, but they were worshipping false gods also (vv. 2-3). Consequently, they were far from Him and He was not inclined to answer them at all. Rather, Ezekiel was to rebuke them for their wickedness, to threaten them with divine retribution, and to implore them to repent (vv. 4-6).

The ache of God's wounded heart is evident in His passionate plea to His people: *"Repent, turn your faces away from all your abominations"* (v. 6). The call to repent is rare in Ezekiel's ministry; this is one of only three times the word "repent" is found in the entire book. In contrast, Jeremiah had previously implored *the nation* to repent frequently, while there was still the opportunity to do so. However, Israel rejected Jeremiah's message and now Ezekiel was preparing the nation for the full consequence of their rebellion. Yet, he still solicited *individuals* to repent in order to avoid the certainty of death.

Notice how God answered the requests of these spiritual phonies; He gave them what they needed and not what they wanted. This is how righteous love behaves and we should follow God's example: Let us not be motivated by shallow pity, but rather by a sympathy that seeks what is best for others, which may include hardship resulting from wrong or poor choices. That these hypocrites would have the gall to privately seek counsel from His prophet while they were offending God by their secret idolatry infuriated the Lord (v. 7). The Lord promised to completely cut off all those guilty of this offense from the nation and from His favor. Their example would serve a warning to others who might seek God's favor while harboring idols in their hearts (vv. 8-9).

Infidelity and Loyalty

The narrative poses a stern warning for us in the Church Age: Should God's people expect Him to answer our prayers if we have corrupt devotion? James teaches us that prayer is not an escape from moral responsibility, but rather is our response to God's holy character and ability: *"The effectual, fervent prayer of a righteous man avails much"* (Jas. 5:16). It is mockery of God's holiness to approach Him in prayer when we are only pretending to be in fellowship with Him. He knows better than we do when we are not in communion with Him, and He feels the loss much more keenly than we do (as shown by the narrative before us).

Just as the priests of old stopped at the laver to wash their hands and feet before entering the tabernacle, each believer should confess and repent of their sin before entering God's presence (1 Jn. 1:9). Since the elders of Israel were morally distant from the Lord, why should a holy God come near to them to grant their petitions? Furthermore, when we are far from the Lord, we cannot pray in the Spirit, and, therefore, we cannot be in the will of God (Eph. 6:18; 1 Jn. 5:14). God cannot walk with us in darkness; we must venture into the light of His goodness to experience Him. Hence, our sensitivity to sin is a good measure of true spiritual maturity.

> Inordinate desires commonly produce irregular endeavors. If our wishes be not kept in submission to God's providence, our pursuits will scarcely be kept under the restraints of his precepts.
>
> — Matthew Henry

David, praying with clean hands and pure heart, demonstrates the powerful reality of prayer when one is in communion with God. In Psalm 143, David is overwhelmed, desolate, and exploited. He laments his situation before the Lord. He lifts up his empty hands to the Lord to show his complete dependence and urgently begs God for help. David requests God to revive his soul and to give spiritual guidance in the way of righteousness so that he would always be walking with Him. He then concludes his prayer by requesting the Lord to cut off his enemies and deliver him from trouble. This is another example of a prayer of faith by a man of faith who desires to be in the center of God's will. When our sincere prayers rise from pure hearts, not only does God powerfully act on our behalf, but He also revives our souls.

Purity of heart means the control of the imagination and the rigorous care of the affections.

— F.B. Meyer

Unlike King David, the idolatrous leaders of Israel in Ezekiel's day would never benefit from such a meaningful prayer-life – they lacked purity of heart.

Additionally, not only would God prevent true prophets from answering Israel's idolatrous leaders, but He would also permit false prophets to do so, for the purpose of punishing those who were estranged from Him (v. 9). An illustration of this type of divine protocol is found in 1 Kings 22. In that chapter, God allowed false prophets to deceive wicked King Ahab in order to lure him into battle; his false confidence of victory would result in God's retribution – death (1 Kgs. 22:19-23). In the end, God promised to punish both the idolatrous leaders who sought His counsel, and those false prophets who spoke in His name to deceive them; this act of vindication would serve to summon His wayward people back to Him in purity (vv. 10-11).

Verses 12-20 contain Ezekiel's fifth and final message pertaining to the certainty of God's judgment: God hypothetically ponders aloud the types of judgments befitting a rebellious people. *"Persistent unfaithfulness"* suggests that a relationship has been violated; here, the Lord is not contemplating judgment of any other nation, but only His own treacherous people.

Four retributions are suggested as fitting punishments: famine and starvation (v. 13), devouring wild beasts (v. 15), military invasion (v. 17), and pestilence (v. 19). These same four devastations are connected with the four horsemen of the apocalypse who wreak death and destruction on humanity during the Tribulation Period (Rev. 6).

Perhaps Ezekiel, not wanting to see the destruction of his countrymen, wondered if such judgments could be avoided. What if there were still righteous pillars of faith among the nation of Israel? God responds to this notion: *"Even if these three men, Noah, Daniel, and Job, were in it* [the land of Israel], *they would deliver only themselves by their righteousness"* (v. 14). To underscore His point, the Lord chooses three righteous men, known for their integrity, who were delivered from the ruin and punishment that fell on others. Daniel, probably about thirty years of age at this time, was a man of sincere conviction and who enjoyed some measure of political status in Babylon. So even if the best of humanity, the most righteous saints, were living in Jerusalem, God's plan to punish the nation would not be thwarted (14, 16, 18, and 20).

Ezekiel then applies the meaning of the dialogue to Jerusalem's fate (v. 21). Jerusalem was not populated with righteous pillars of faith anyway, so there was no possibility of averting judgment. True, Jeremiah was there, but by this time, Jeremiah sought the vindication of God's honor, as well as reprisal for the harm done to him personally by Israel's wicked leadership. Therefore, the hypothetical case of esteemed righteous saints preventing God's judicial wrath from raining down on Jerusalem was not a prospect. The Lord then affirmed that He would invoke all four types of judgments to accomplish His vengeance on Israel.

The chapter does conclude on a conciliatory note (vv. 22-23). God would preserve a few of the inhabitants of Jerusalem from the forthcoming slaughter. These would be transported to Babylon as captives. When the Jews that were already in Babylon witnessed the ungodly character of those arriving from Jerusalem, they would agree that God's judgment, though agonizing, was a necessary measure of correction. All would agree that God was completely just in vindicating His name!

This realization reminds us of a future day when everyone will acknowledge the words of the Lord Jesus Christ as true: *"My judgment is just"* (John 5:30) and *"The Father judges no one, but has committed all judgment to the Son"* (John 5:22). Only a just and impartial Judge can uphold the righteousness and holiness of God in rewarding and condemning others. Paul declared that we will all answer to the just Judge: *"For it is written: 'As I live, says the Lord, every knee shall bow to Me, and every tongue shall confess to God.' So then each of us shall give account of himself to God"* (Rom. 14:11-12). The Lord will reward believers at His Judgment Seat and will also punish the wicked at His Great White Throne (Rev. 20:11-15). On that day, no one will argue with His justice or their sentence: *"Therefore God also has highly exalted Him and given Him the name which is above every name, that at the name of Jesus every knee should bow, of those in heaven, and of those on earth, and of those under the earth"* (Phil. 2:9-

10). Whether great or small, all men in a coming day will proclaim that Jesus Christ is just and Lord of all!

Meditation

I am not tired of my work, neither am I tired of the world; yet, when Christ calls me home, I shall go with gladness.

— Adoniram Judson

Let us remember, there is One who daily records all we do for Him, and sees more beauty in His servants' work than His servants do themselves... And then shall His faithful witnesses discover, to their wonder and surprise, that there never was a word spoken on their Master's behalf, which does not receive a reward.

— J. C. Ryle

The Worthless Vine
Ezekiel 15

Ezekiel concluded his five-message series on the surety of God's wrath in the previous chapter. In each of the next three chapters, God's prophet will deliver an instructive parable and then explain its allegorical meaning. The theme of Ezekiel 15 is the worthless vine – Israel. The parable commences with the Lord asking Ezekiel five questions:

> *Son of man, how is the wood of the vine better than any other wood, the vine branch which is among the trees of the forest? Is wood taken from it to make any object? Or can men make a peg from it to hang any vessel on? Instead, it is thrown into the fire for fuel; the fire devours both ends of it, and its middle is burned. Is it useful for any work? Indeed, when it was whole, no object could be made from it. How much less will it be useful for any work when the fire has devoured it, and it is burned?* (vv. 2-5).

The Lord's point was that unlike barren fruit trees, a fruitless vine has no value other than fuel for a fire. The wood of a vine is gnarled and twisted, hence unusable for building materials, even as a simple peg to hang objects on. This sad condition of the vine characterized the spiritual state of Israel. But taking the parable one step further, the Lord asked Ezekiel if a vine was worth more after being burned with fire. The obvious answer is no; the quality of the vine is diminished by fire.

The Lord then applies the parable to the Jewish nation (with a specific focus on Jerusalem) and explains its meaning. Israel was God's vine, planted by Him for His enjoyment, but she had become a fruitless wild vine spreading her foliage wherever she wanted. As indicated in the conclusion of the parable, God would now judge His spiritually fruitless people in a way that a vinedresser removes an unprofitable wild vine – he burns it (v. 6). Many had survived the first fire that He kindled against Jerusalem (the siege), but most of those remaining would not survive the second fire (the Babylonian slaughter after the fall of Jerusalem; v. 7).

In summary, the parable declares God's overwhelming disgust for the spiritual nature of His people; they had been persistently unfaithful (v. 8)! But the Lord had a remedy – purging and purification by judicial fire. This parable provided no optimism for the Jewish people, but rather a stern warning that God would finish what He promised to do: destroying Jerusalem and making the entire region desolate.

Both Jeremiah and Ezekiel employed the worthless vine imagery in their writings to convey the same meaning that we have just considered. However, Israel, as represented by foliage, has a much broader meaning in Scripture. The Jewish nation is allegorically likened to a trilogy of vegetation: the vine, the fig tree, and the olive tree. Each one represents a distinct aspect of the nation's existence. For example, the prophet Jeremiah told his fellow countrymen that God had planted a beautiful vineyard (Israel), but Israel's shepherds had made it desolate (Jer. 12:10). The nation of Israel, as a political reality, is likened to a noble vine (a grape vine; Jer. 8:13), which God planted in the world (Jer. 2:21, 12:10); Israel was God's vineyard. Jeremiah explains that the destruction of Israel in his day would be like livestock moving freely through God's vineyard and trampling the vines. Consequently, it would not be productive, bearing only the fruit of sowing to sin, that is, the thorns of affliction and a harvest of shame (Jer. 12:11-13).

When Israel is spoken of as a fig tree in Scripture, the metaphor relates to the religious element of Israel, which often was fruitless for God (Jer. 8:13; Matt. 21:19-21). This reality is known as modern Judaism and was identified during one of the events in the life of the Lord Jesus (Luke 13:6-9). After preaching three years to the lost nation of Israel, Christ cursed the fruitless fig tree just before His death at Calvary. Less than forty years later, parts of Jerusalem and the entire temple were destroyed and the Jews have not sacrificed since then. The Old Covenant was replaced by the New Covenant, sealed with Christ's blood, and God was determined not to allow the Jews to continue in what was now obsolete.

One of the signs that the Tribulation Period and the Second Advent of Christ are nearing is that the fig tree (i.e., religious Israel) will again shoot forth leaves after a long winter season of deadness (Luke 21:29-31). Leaves must precede fruit, but the fig tree will bear no fruit until the nation experiences spiritual rebirth in the latter days of the Tribulation Period. What might the new leaves speak of? This is likely a reference to the Jews reviving the old sacrificial system during, and perhaps just prior to, the Tribulation Period.

We know from various prophecies that the Antichrist will desecrate the Jewish temple and put a stop to animal sacrifices at the midpoint of the Tribulation Period (Dan. 9:27; Matt. 24:15; 2 Thess. 2:3-7). Therefore, logically speaking, a temple will have to be erected and animal sacrifices will have to be reinstituted by that point.

Therefore, during the Tribulation Period, the Jews will again offer sacrifices pictured in the Levitical system. This reality could commence just prior to the Tribulation period. The Lord Jesus said that the generation permitted to witness this event would also see His coming to the earth in glory (Luke 21:32). Today, many orthodox Jews are anticipating an imminent day when they will again perform the sacrifices as specified in the Mosaic Law.

When this does occur, leaves will become apparent on the fig tree, depicting a religious reality, but there will be no fruit. Spiritual fruit can be produced only through spiritual rebirth which coincides with the Holy Spirit being poured out upon the Jewish nation at the end of the Tribulation Period. At that time, they will know and worship Jesus Christ as Messiah (Joel 2:25-3:21; Zech. 12:10-13:1). At the end of the Tribulation Period, the refined Jewish nation will receive the Holy Spirit and obtain spiritual life in Christ. All God's covenant blessings to Israel will be spiritually realized in Christ – as Paul teaches in Romans 11. (This is what is depicted by the natural branches in the olive tree.) It is good to remember that whether cut-out natural branches (the revitalized Jewish nation) or the wild branches (believing Gentiles), all had to be grafted into the Olive Tree by divine grace to receive the blessings of the Abrahamic covenant fulfilled in Christ. The pertinent application for Israel is one that the Church must realize presently – true connection with Christ is evidenced by spiritual fruitfulness. H. A. Ironside summarizes the reality of this truth in reference to John 15:

> It is well to remember that there are no natural branches in the living Vine; all must be grafted in. Where the graft does not strike – that is, where there is only profession and not life, there will be no fruit but where there is actual union in life, there will be fruit unto God – fruit which is precious to His sight. In order that more fruit may be

94

produced, He cleanses the branches, prunes them as He sees fit, and rejoices when they bring forth much fruit.[32]

Once the Jewish nation has experienced spiritual renewal in Christ, the Lord's vineyard (i.e., the Jewish nation; Isa. 5:7) will be again planted in Israel as a testimony to the Gentile nations of God's glory (Isa. 4; 60:1-5). Only then will the worthless vine, which experienced so many centuries of fire, be rejuvenated and restored to fruitfulness again. The vine planted so long ago will once again refresh the heart of her Husbandman – Jehovah. It is the responsibility of all believers in every age to produce fruit for God's glory; otherwise our existence has no value or meaning.

Meditation

Precious Jesus, I beseech Thee,
May Thy words take root in me;
May this gift from Heaven enrich me
So that I bear fruit for Thee!

Take them never from my heart
Till I see Thee as Thou art,
When in heavenly bliss and glory
I shall greet Thee and adore Thee.

— Anna Sophia

The Adulterous Wife
Ezekiel 16

Ezekiel 16 recounts the history of the nation of Israel in the parable of the adulterous wife. In this second of three serial allegories, the Jewish nation is likened to a discarded newborn girl whom God rescues from certain death (vv. 1-2). Why was she unwanted and abandoned in a field? Israel was of a mixed pedigree: her father an Amorite and her mother a Hittite (v. 3). This reference pertains to the capital city of the Jewish nation, Jerusalem, which was inhabited for centuries by the Canaanites (the Jebusites specifically) until King David finally drove them out (1 Chron. 11). This meant that Jerusalem was composed of both Abraham's descendants through Noah's son Shem and the pagan Canaanites through Ham, Noah's third son. The mixture of the cultures brought moral and spiritual corruption – this was Jerusalem's history since the Canaan conquest in the days of Joshua.

Besides being unwanted, another facet of Israel's initial abandonment relates to her treatment after arriving in Canaan as an infant nation. The local pagans rejected the Jews' intrusion into their homeland and endeavored to push them out. Thus, the new Jewish nation did not receive the tender care ordinarily given to a newborn child. They were undesirable and oppressed from their infancy.

Returning to the allegory, the Lord was moved with compassion, because He saw that no one pitied the discarded and languishing newborn (v. 5). After gently picking her up, the Lord washed her, and then nurtured her and protected her from harm during her juvenile years (vv. 4-7). After she reached the age of maturity, He then confirmed a marriage covenant with her that spoke of the new relationship that He wanted with Israel:

> *"When I passed by you again and looked upon you, indeed your time was the time of love; so I spread My wing over you and covered your*

nakedness. Yes, I swore an oath to you and entered into a covenant with you, and you became Mine," says the Lord God (v. 8).

Jehovah's immense passion for Israel, His wife by covenant, is poetically described in this verse. The Hebrew word for "love" in this verse is *dowd*, meaning "to boil" (i.e., figuratively: "to love" and, by implication, "a lover"). This word is rendered "love" seven times in the Old Testament and always confers the sense of a boiling pot of fervent passion between a husband and his wife (not necessarily sexually). Jehovah uses wondrously intimate language to express His affection and devotion to the Jewish nation. Paul uses similar terms of real love in the New Testament when he likens the Church to the bride of Christ (2 Cor. 11:2; Eph. 5:23-32). It is difficult for us to relate to the Lord through these romantic overtones, but that suggests the very reason such profound poetic language exists in Scripture. Since God's love is so much deeper, satisfying, and more exhilarating than any natural affection that could be shared in any human relationship, why would a child of God ever snub His love? Yet, Israel did, and we have too to some extent!

Jehovah labored sacrificially on behalf of His beloved: He washed her, anointed her with oil, clothed her in fine linen, and adorned her with ornaments and jewels (vv. 9-13). As a result of His special care and gifts, Israel became a spectacle of beauty among the nations, a declaration of God's own splendor (v. 14). Unfortunately, Israel developed an ever-deepening lust for secular thrills and sensual pleasures and the gods associated with such things. In time, she forsook the Lord and embraced these false gods, even giving to them in worship the abundance that God had provided her in His love (vv. 15-19). Hosea also vividly describes this same hurtful and deceitful behavior (Hos. 2:5). So profound was Israel's treachery that she built high places and shrines to honor pagan deities, and even offered her children, which the Lord had given her, as burnt sacrifices to them (vv. 20-21, 24-26). F. C. Cook explains the literal meaning of slaying Jehovah's children and causing them to pass through the fire:

> The children of Jehovah had been devoted to Moloch. The rites of Moloch were twofold: First, the actual sacrifice of men and children as expiatory sacrifices to false gods. Second, the passing of them

through the fire by way of purification and dedication. Probably the first is alluded to in verse 20 and the two rites together in verse 21.[33]

Israel had forgotten the Lord's tender mercies that she had received in her youth and she forsook Him like an adulterous wife (vv. 22, 43).

Israel's spiritual adultery provoked Jehovah to jealousy; He responded in righteous anger by pronouncing judgments upon her (vv. 23, 27), writing her a bill of divorcement, and putting her away to be punished among the nations (v. 38; Jer. 3:8). In verses 28-34, Jehovah likens his promiscuous wife to a brazen harlot who was never satisfied by the affection of her many lovers. Normally, a prostitute is paid for her services, but Israel's depravity was so great that she was the one soliciting her lovers and paying them to defile and abuse her. Israel was blatantly worshipping any false deity that she could find and her actions were despoiling the nation and estranging her from Jehovah.

Putting aside Israel's abominations for the moment, their behavior did not even make sense – it was self-abasing. So the Lord calls their attention to the real issue – they were suffering from a "degenerate heart" and therefore were not thinking straight (v. 30). There is an insanity to sin, to which a double-minded person is oblivious. Israel, being enslaved to her own juvenile lusts, sought freedom to enjoy her licentious cravings, only to suffer spiritual bondage of the worst kind. Israel would soon learn that freedom from restraint is not liberty; it is shameful, exhausting, and destructive.

Because of Israel's unabashed lewd and wicked conduct, Jehovah was forced to take action against His unfaithful wife (vv. 35-59). The extent of Jehovah's immense love for His people would be demonstrated by the measure of their chastening. He would turn all of her previous lovers (her pagan deities and their followers) against her and they would bring destruction to Israel and despoil the nation (vv. 35-39). This retribution would be so dreadful that Israel would be aroused from her spiritual despondency, recognize her sin, and turn away from her many hired lovers (i.e., God's people would be purged of idolatry). After that occurred, the Lord promised: *"I will lay to rest My fury toward you, and My jealousy shall depart from you. I will be quiet, and be angry no more"* (v. 42). Though Israel had forgotten Him, Jehovah had not forgotten her, and He promised to restore His unfaithful wife after her purification was complete.

So far, Ezekiel has likened idolatrous Israel (with Jerusalem representing the heart of the nation) to an adulterous wife who prostituted herself by paying her lovers; however, the analogy develops to a secondary application in verses 44-59. If God was faithful to judge Jerusalem's wicked sisters of Samaria and Sodom, He certainly would judge Jerusalem whose abominations were much greater. Referring to their mixed heritage (v. 2), Ezekiel affirmed that the Jews had adopted the pagan practices and immorality of the Canaanites; thus, he gave them a new proverb, *"Like mother, like daughter"* (v. 44). Her sisters were full of abundance, but neglected the poor; yet, Jerusalem, was full of degenerative pride and had committed countless abominations against God. Surely then, if He had judged Samaria and Sodom, he would judge Jerusalem even more severely (vv. 45-50).

The prophet Ezekiel informs us that the perverse city of Sodom suffered from an *"abundance of idleness"* (v. 49). This reference serves as a good reminder that keeping busy in the Lord's work is a good defense against temptation. Solomon eloquently warns against idleness, for a body in the grave cannot serve the Lord: *"Whatever your hand finds to do, do it with your might; for there is no work or device or knowledge or wisdom in the grave where you are going"* (Eccl. 9:10). If what you desire to do is worth doing, then you must do it as unto the Lord, and if it is not worth doing, then you should do something else that is. In all things the believer's first duty and responsibility is to God Himself.

> May not a single moment of my life be spent outside the light, love and joy of God's presence and not a moment without the entire surrender of myself as a vessel for Him to fill full of His Spirit and His love.
>
> — Andrew Murray

> Employ whatever God has entrusted you with, in doing good, all possible good, in every possible kind and degree.
>
> — John Wesley

Despite all of Samaria and Sodom's odious abominations and lewdness, God said Jerusalem (representing the Jewish nation) had done much greater wickedness to provoke His wrath (v. 51).

Consequently, God must uphold His righteousness by punishing His covenant people even more severely than He did Samaria and Sodom (v. 52). However, just as God had restored Sodom and Samaria after their judgments were past, He likewise would also reinstate Jerusalem to a position of prominence and grandeur (vv. 53-59). These verses are likely referring to the Millennial Kingdom of Christ. The prophet Zechariah repeatedly mentions the coming of Messiah to rescue and restore His covenant people and to establish Jerusalem at that time as the religious capital of the world (Zech. 8:20-22).

Despite the unfaithfulness of Israel to Jehovah, the Lord will be moved with compassion and mercy to restore her to a place of special intimacy:

"Nevertheless I will remember My covenant with you in the days of your youth, and I will establish an everlasting covenant with you. Then you will remember your ways and be ashamed ... I will establish My covenant with you. Then you shall know that I am the Lord, that you may remember and be ashamed, and never open your mouth anymore because of your shame, when I provide you an atonement for all you have done," says the Lord God (vv. 60-63).

Jehovah also moved other prophets, such as Hosea and Jeremiah, to pronounce His promise to restore the Jewish nation as His faithful wife in a future day:

"I will punish her for the days of the Baals to which she burned incense. She decked herself with her earrings and jewelry, and went after her lovers; but Me she forgot," says the Lord. "Therefore, behold, I will allure her, will bring her into the wilderness, and speak comfort to her" (Hos. 2:14-15). *"I will betroth you to Me forever; yes, I will betroth you to Me in righteousness and justice, in loving kindness and mercy; I will betroth you to Me in faithfulness, and you shall know the Lord"* (Hos. 2:19-20).

"For I am with you," says the Lord, "to save you; though I make a full end of all nations where I have scattered you, yet I will not make a complete end of you. But I will correct you in justice, and will not let you go altogether unpunished" (Jer. 30:11). *"You shall be my people, and I will be your God"* (Jer. 30:22).

The prophet Hosea was allowed to experience the unfaithfulness of his wife (the allegory of this chapter) to illustrate not only the Lord's heartbreak, but also His resolve to be reconciled with His wayward people. Even after Gomer, Hosea's wife, had embraced her lovers for the provisions he had secretly provided for her, God commanded him to redeem her and take her back as his wife. He did so. After her lovers had abused and abandoned Gomer, she was sold in a common slave market (likely humiliated by being stripped bare). There Hosea bought his own adulterous wife for fifteen pieces of silver and a homer and half of barley (Hos. 3:2). Hosea then said to her: *"You shall stay with me many days; you shall not play the harlot, nor shall you have a man – so, too, will I be toward you"* (Hos. 3:3). Then the prophet immediately connected his own marital situation with the future relationship of Jehovah and His covenant people:

For the children of Israel shall abide many days without king or prince, without sacrifice or sacred pillar, without ephod or teraphim. Afterward the children of Israel shall return and seek the Lord their God and David their king. They shall fear the Lord and His goodness in the latter days (Hos. 3:4-5).

Gomer did not forsake Hosea again and neither will God's covenant people when they are restored in the latter days. The Mosaic Law did not contain a provision of forgiveness for adultery – offenders, like Gomer, were to be put to death. But Hosea's dealings with his unfaithful wife demonstrate that God would have a provision for grace which the Law could not extend. Through a new and everlasting covenant, He could forgive Israel's sin (vv. 60-62). Jehovah could righteously restore Israel to Himself because He punished His own Son in her place to fully atone (i.e., provide propitiation) for all her sins (v. 63).

This covenant was secured at Calvary and was sealed by the blood of the Lord Jesus Christ *"with the house of Israel and house of Judah"* (Heb. 8:8) as prophesied in Jeremiah 31:31-32. What would be the spiritual benefit of this New Covenant? Speaking for Jehovah, Jeremiah answers:

"But this is the covenant that I will make with the house of Israel after those days, says the Lord: I will put My law in their minds, and

> *write it on their hearts; and I will be their God, and they shall be My people. No more shall every man teach his neighbor, and every man his brother, saying, 'Know the Lord,' for they all shall know Me, from the least of them to the greatest of them, says the Lord. For I will forgive their iniquity, and their sin I will remember no more"* (Jer. 31:33-34).

Although their hearts were not with Jehovah, His heart was still with them. He promised to accompany them and sustain them through their disciplinary judgment. He loved His covenant people too much to leave them in their pagan exile, and thus sought to purify them and restore them to Himself. Both Ezekiel and Jeremiah (Jer. 3:12) employ the allegory of a marital relationship between Jehovah and the Jewish people that was broken by their unfaithfulness, but by divine grace was later restored. This story should convey hope to God's covenant people of old; they have not been cast aside forever as some teach today! God is a covenant-keeping God and He must therefore honor His promise to Abraham and restore the Jewish people to Himself.

Israel chose to pursue that which was outside of God's will (at both the spiritual and physical levels), though it made no sense to do so and the repercussions of doing so were clearly not worth it. May we learn from their mistake! The Lord has equipped all believers with His Word and His Spirit; we have all we need to live for God and to worship Him, that is, if we choose to yield to revealed truth. God has designed our bodies with various types of mechanisms to keep us healthy and to procreate, but when we lust for what is beyond the order God has put in place to guide such behaviors, we enter into sin and take the first step towards death – separation from the Lord.

Whether it is Achan lusting for a Babylonian garment he could not publicly wear, or David for another man's wife he could not have, or when God's people lust for what the world touts as satisfying and pleasurable, but is not, we can see that there is a senselessness to sin. The decision process of entering into sin (wanting what is outside of God's will) is flawed. As Israel would learn after the fact, doing what they were not supposed to had no practical benefit for them and angered the Lord. Sin has an exorbitant price tag and furthermore leaves us craving more of what can never satisfy us anyway. Full satisfaction in life is achieved only in knowing and resting in the Lord (1 Jn. 2:13).

Meditation

Take the world, but give me Jesus,
All its joys are but a name;
But His love abides forever,
Through eternal years the same.

Take the world, but give me Jesus.
In His cross my trust shall be,
Till, with clearer, brighter vision,
Face to face my Lord I see.

Oh, the height and depth of mercy!
Oh, the length and breadth of love!
Oh, the fullness of redemption,
Pledge of endless life above!

— Fanny Crosby

The Two Eagles
Ezekiel 17

Ezekiel was to publicly share the last of the three allegories, the parable of the two eagles, as a riddle which would require an explanation to understand (vv. 1-2). Ezekiel presents the riddle in verses 3-10 and then clarifies its meaning in verses 11-24. This prophecy was written between 592 B.C. (8:1) and 591 B.C. (20:1), meaning it occurred three to four years before the events described in the parable actually occurred. The following summary correlates the details of the parable with its explanation as it is being told:

There was a great eagle (Nebuchadnezzar; v. 12) that had enormous, colorful wings and long pinions that flew to Lebanon (Jerusalem) and took from a tall cedar its highest branch and cropped off its topmost tender twig and flew back to a great commercial city (vv. 3-4). Nebuchadnezzar had established control over Judah in 605 B.C., but had to return in 597 B.C. to suppress the revolt by King Jehoiachin (the twig), who was captured and transported with other Jewish nobility (the high branch) back to Babylon as prisoners (vv. 11-12).

After regaining control of Judah, the eagle took some of the seed of the land (Jews) and planted it like a willow by an abundant supply of water. The seed sprouted and become a low spreading vine (vv. 5-6). Nebuchadnezzar seriously weakened Jerusalem in 597 B.C., but mercifully did not destroy the city. Rather, he entered into a covenant with Zedekiah who became the vassal king of Jerusalem (vv. 13-14). Though the Jewish people had been humbled (they were without an army and were no longer an autonomous nation), they would thrive under Babylonian rule as long as this accord was honored.

However, in time a second eagle (Egypt) appeared and enticed the vine (Zedekiah) to rebel against the first eagle and break the treaty (vv. 7-8, 15). This rebellion began in 589 B.C. Ezekiel prophesied that the consequences to the vine would be disastrous; it would be uprooted, stripped of its fruit and cast aside to wither (vv. 9-10). Because Zedekiah did not keep his oath, he would be caught in Nebuchadnezzar's net, be brought to Babylon in shame and there he would perish; his troops would be slaughtered by the Babylonians (vv. 16-21).

Zedekiah would learn the same painful outcome that many of God's people have learned the hard way: God's people will never solve their problems by seeking help from Egypt (a symbol of the world), but only by submitting to and trusting in God's Word for direction and blessing. Looking back in Israel's history, we find that both Abraham and Isaac thought Egypt offered the best solution to preserve their lives during separate famines. God intervened to keep Isaac in the Promised Land, but Abraham was permitted to experience the personal consequences of descending into Egypt to resolve one's problems.

Jeremiah's message to King Zedekiah (at about this same time) ensured that the king knew that Babylonian rule was God's will and to rebel against it would prompt God's fury (Jer. 21:1-22:9). In fact, Jeremiah had been foretelling the destruction of Jerusalem by the Babylonians for over 35 years. His contemporary Habakkuk had also prophesied the same sorrowful message (Hab. 1:6-9). Yet, Zedekiah rejected God's Word and rebelled against Nebuchadnezzar anyway. After Jerusalem was under Babylonian siege, Zedekiah was hoping God would work a miracle of deliverance, like He did when the Assyrians threatened Jerusalem in the days of Hezekiah (2 Kgs. 18-19). God directed Jeremiah to inform Zedekiah that nothing had changed and that He would ensure every word that His prophets had spoken on His behalf would come true:

> *"I Myself will fight against you with an outstretched hand and with a strong arm, even in anger and fury and great wrath. I will strike the inhabitants of this city, both man and beast; they shall die of a great pestilence. And afterward," says the Lord, "I will deliver Zedekiah king of Judah, his servants and the people, and such as are left in this city from the pestilence and the sword and the famine, into the hand of Nebuchadnezzar king of Babylon, into the hand of their enemies, and into the hand of those who seek their life; and he shall strike them with the edge of the sword. He shall not spare them, or have pity or mercy"* (Jer. 21:5-7).

Infidelity and Loyalty

After hearing Jeremiah's edict, Zedekiah was likely wishing that he had not been enticed by Egypt to rebel against God's revealed will. It is one thing to be surrounded by an army of superior strength; it is an entirely different matter to escape the wrath of Almighty God. May God's people learn the important lesson posed in this narrative: All the world's philosophies, resources, and authorities cannot successfully contradict one word of what God decrees as truth. It is best to trust God and suffer in His will than to not do so and perish with the wicked. Zedekiah did not choose this course of action and the repercussions would be like a strong, devastating wind from the east (v. 10).

Like Jeremiah, Ezekiel likened the coming Babylonian invasion force to the strong east winds that rolled off the hot desert (Jer. 4:11). These winds (the sirocco) withered vegetation and caused severe discomfort to humans and livestock. Jeremiah relates his vision of the forthcoming destruction of the land, the cities, and the people of Judah and of the surrounding nations to the chaotic state the world must have been in during its infancy:

> I beheld the earth, and indeed it was without form, and void; and the heavens, they had no light. I beheld the mountains, and indeed they trembled, and all the hills moved back and forth. I beheld, and indeed there was no man, and all the birds of the heavens had fled. I beheld, and indeed the fruitful land was a wilderness, and all its cities were broken down at the presence of the Lord, by His fierce anger (Jer. 4:23-26).

So catastrophic would be God's actions against Israel that it would seem as if creation itself had been undone, that the commands of Genesis 1 had somehow been reversed. Imagine the effect that witnessing such a scene had upon God's prophet who was living in Jerusalem at that time! Everything that he was accustomed to would be gone, that is, except his God, who remains forever the same.

Yet, God did not want His people to be overly disheartened about the forthcoming invasion, so Ezekiel concludes the chapter by confirming that God would keep all His covenants with Israel in a future day (vv. 22-24). This promise would be a guiding light through the days of darkness directly ahead. Israel had learned experientially that neither Babylon nor Egypt could provide her with the prosperity and security she yearned for, yet Jehovah God could and would. He would take from the cedar (the Davidic line of kings) the highest twig and plant it on a prominent mountain in Israel (v. 22). This twig would grow to be a majestic cedar in which every kind of bird (representing people groups) would find peace and safety in its branches and then all the trees (nations of the world) would be drawn to it (vv. 23-24).

This pictures the establishment of the Millennial Kingdom of Christ, a descendant of King David, who will rule over all nations from Jerusalem. The One who was brought so low at Calvary will be exalted by His Father to the highest station and He will be appreciated by everyone. His rule will usher in a time of blessing and peace that the world has not known since before the fall of man in Eden, and the Jewish nation will flourish again.

Meditation

I long ago left Egypt for the promised land,
I trusted in my Savior, and to His guiding hand;
He led me out to victory through the great Red Sea,
I sang a song of triumph, and shouted, I am free!

You need not look for me, down in Egypt's sand,
For I have pitched my tent far up in Beulah land;
You need not look for me, down in Egypt's sand,
For I have pitched my tent far up in Beulah land.

— Margaret Harris

God's Righteous Justice
Ezekiel 18

In the three previous chapters, Ezekiel delivered three parables for the purpose of calling Israel's attention to their rebellious behavior. As in chapter 12, the prophet is now called on to reprove the Jews for bantering about proverbs suggesting that Jehovah would not punish them. One particular proverb implied that God was unfairly punishing them for the sins of their forefathers: *"The fathers have eaten sour grapes, and the children's teeth are set on edge"* (v. 2). God calls on Ezekiel to defend His righteous justice and to forbid those in captivity from suggesting otherwise. Interestingly, the Jews in Jerusalem were uttering the same adage, and Jeremiah was summoned to also confront the errant mentality of his countrymen (Jer. 31:29). J. B. Taylor offers two observations as to why the proverb was so popular:

> First, the idea of continuing effects of ancestral sins is found in the Ten Commandments: *"For I, the Lord your God, am a jealous God, visiting the iniquity of the fathers upon the children to the third and fourth generations of those who hate Me"* (Ex. 20:5). Second, it had been the basis of much of Ezekiel's own teaching, namely, that the sufferings of the exile could be traced back to the persistent rebellion, idolatry, and unfaithfulness to the covenant of previous generations of Israelites (e.g., 16:1-59). The exile was, in effect, the due consequence of these accumulating acts of disobedience. Furthermore, there was the element of apparent injustice in the way in which God's judgment fell indiscriminately upon both the bad and the good.[34]

In short, the maxim insinuated that children suffered for the indulgences of their parents, while their parents escaped the consequences of their own wrongdoings. However, this was not the case. Both Ezekiel and Jeremiah affirmed that everyone will be properly judged by God for his or her own sins, but as a nation, Israel deserved judgment and it was unavoidable (vv. 1-4; Jer. 31:30). Divine grace does not undermine God's governmental authority! H. A. Ironside further comments on this important distinction:

> All believers today are under the government of God the Father who, without respect of persons, judges according to every man's works (1 Pet. 1:17). It is true today, as in past ages, that whatsoever a man sows, that shall he also reap (Gal. 6:7). This is true of all men whether saints or sinners. There are temporal consequences that follow sin, which may go on all through life, even though God has forgiven the sin itself as in David's case. Nathan said by divine authority, *"The Lord also hath put away thy sin."* But he added, *"The sword shall never depart from thy house"* (2 Sam. 12:7-15). It is important to understand this order that one may not misconstrue the teaching of this chapter, as also of chapter 33, in this same book. Both have to do with the divine government in this world and not with the question of how a guilty sinner may be cleansed from his sin and saved for eternity.[35]

For decades, God's prophets had implored the Jews to consider their sin and its consequences, and then to repent. Those in Babylon who were babbling cynical proverbs had no basis for complaint: they were not innocent and had, indeed, received mercy from God in that they were still alive. Those in Jerusalem were equally guilty and deserved punishment because they had rebelled against Babylonian rule, which Jeremiah had revealed was God's rod of chastisement to reprove them of their idolatry. Ezekiel was informing his countrymen that blaming others for their troubles when they were guilty of sin and deserving God's righteous retribution was not a good idea. In fact, such an attitude would certainly prompt even more divine displeasure against them. The conclusion of the matter was clear: God, who owns all souls, will judge everyone in righteousness and *"the soul who sins shall die"* (v. 4). Everyone will be held personally responsible for their own behavior!

Ezekiel then poses three hypothetical cases to demonstrate that this principle was true. First, Ezekiel sets before the people the model righteous citizen who obeys the Law and whose conduct demonstrates integrity and compassion (vv. 5-9). Such a man was: sexually pure (i.e., did not commit adultery or have physical relations with his wife during menstruation), did not rob, cheat, or take advantage of others, but rather assisted the poor with food and clothing. "Suppose" there was such a man, would he perish for the sins of others?

The prophet's answer was "no," such a morally righteous man would live; he would not suffer death for the depravity of others. This implied that, if there were such individuals in Jerusalem when Nebuchadnezzar decimated the city, they would be spared from the slaughter. For example, Jeremiah and his personal scribe Baruch were preserved from death through the siege and fall of Jerusalem (Jer. 36:4). No doubt the point of this first case (the ideal righteous Jew) was to cause the people to examine their own morality – were there any such people still living in Jerusalem? The tragic slaughter of so many by the Babylonians would suggest that there were very few virtuous souls in Israel when the invasion occurred.

The second hypothetical case is connected with the first. Ezekiel suggests: Suppose this righteous man had a son who was a robber, who abused the poor, engaged in fraudulent business practices and was an adulterer and murderer (vv. 10-12). Could the father's righteousness preserve such a wicked man from judgment? The answer to this question was: *"He shall not live! If he has done any of these abominations, he shall surely die; his blood shall be upon him"* (v. 13). If the Jews were hoping to escape God's justice because of the good deeds of their forefathers, they were mistaken on two counts. First, their fathers had also been rebellious, and second, God holds each individual responsible for their own sins.

The third situation continues by looking at the next, the third generation. *"Suppose"* the wicked man in the second scenario had a righteous son, who, observing the sins of his father, decides to live uprightly as his grandfather did. Would such an individual be judged for the sins of his vile father (vv. 14-16)? The answer to this hypothetical quandary was, *"He shall surely live"* (v. 17). The conclusion, which directly confronted the popular proverb in verse 2, is stated in verse 18: Though the righteous grandson would be spared judgment, his wicked father would perish for his own sins.

This meant that the Jews should not be hoping to be spared judgment for their personal sins because of the righteous acts of others, nor should they be thinking that God was unjustly punishing them because of the unrighteous acts of others. Although the entire Jewish nation would be chastised for their polluted testimony for God among the nations, those Jews turning from sin to live blamelessly before the

Lord would be spared; those who did not would perish (vv. 21-22). The passage is still focusing on temporal punishment, not eternal judgment. William MacDonald clarifies this point – Ezekiel was speaking of physical death now because of sin:

> The principles stated in verses 5-24 are not dealing with eternal life; otherwise we would be forced to conclude that salvation is by works (vv. 5-9) and that the righteous may eventually be lost, two doctrines clearly refuted by our Lord in the NT (e.g., Eph. 2:8-9; John 10:28).[36]

Humble obedience meant life, but rebellion ensured death. Ezekiel will later deliver this same message again to his countrymen (33:12-20). The essence of verses 23-32 is captured in the following main points:

> *Yet you say, "The way of the Lord is not fair." O house of Israel, I will judge every one of you according to his own ways* (33:20).
> *"Therefore I will judge you, O house of Israel, every one according to his ways," says the Lord God. "Repent, and turn from all your transgressions, so that iniquity will not be your ruin. Cast away from you all the transgressions which you have committed, and get yourselves a new heart and a new spirit. For why should you die, O house of Israel? For I have no pleasure in the death of one who dies," says the Lord God. "Therefore turn and live!"* (vv. 30-32).

Ezekiel's conclusion was that everyone would be directly accountable to God for their own behavior. Israel was saying that, *the way of the Lord was not equal* (vv. 25, 29), but in reality it was their way that was unequal – not fair. W. T. P. Wolston offers this summary:

> The individual would be dealt with by God according to his own conduct. It is not a question of what their fathers had been. Their own iniquities demanded and would entail God's judgment. Long before, God had threatened to visit "the iniquities of the fathers upon the children" (see Ex. 34:7). This principle is departed from. Individually they were guilty, and as such would be judged; nevertheless, where repentance was manifest, God would pardon, for He had no pleasure in the death of the wicked (18:23).[37]

Infidelity and Loyalty

Paul echoes this same sentiment when he reminds Christians of their personal accountability to God: *"So then each of us shall give account of himself to God"* (Rom. 14:12). It is important to the Lord that His people, in every dispensation, understand that He derives no enjoyment in punishing the wayward, but rather yearns for all to repent and receive His blessing through exercising faith in His revealed will. For those in the Church Age, that means trusting Christ as Savior and submitting to His lordship while waiting for His return. When He does return for His Church, all believers will appear at His judgment seat. Given the reality of our personal accountability to Christ, Paul exhorts all believers:

> *Therefore we make it our aim, whether present or absent, to be well pleasing to Him. For we must all appear before the judgment seat of Christ, that each one may receive the things done in the body, according to what he has done, whether good or bad. Knowing, therefore, the terror of the Lord, we persuade men; but we are well known to God, and I also trust are well known in your consciences* (2 Cor. 5:9-11).

"The Judgment Seat of Christ" and "the Day of Christ" refer to the same event, which immediately follows the rapture of the Church from the earth (1 Thess. 2:19-20, 4:13-18). Christ will assess the value of each believer's works and will either burn up or reward each accordingly. Consequently, the day of Christ is always spoken of in a positive light and it is to be joyfully anticipated. In fact, those who live expectantly in light of Christ's imminent return will receive a reward, a crown of righteousness, at the Judgment Seat of Christ (2 Tim. 4:8). The Lord is very kind to not only save us from hell, but also permit believers to demonstrate their love back to Him through faithful obedience and service, which He then rewards us for! Given our direct accountability to a holy God, and the vast opportunities to explore His available grace, why would we ever want to waste time being wayward?

Meditation

Character is what you are in the dark.

— Dwight L. Moody

The measure of a man's real character is what he would do if he knew he would never be found out.

— Thomas Macaulay

Lions and Branches
Ezekiel 19

Ezekiel began a series of signs, warnings, and parables in chapter 12 to confront wrong Jewish attitudes concerning the judgment of Jerusalem, namely, that it would not happen or at least not in the near future. The Jewish people were estranged from Jehovah and could not sense how displeased God was with them. Ezekiel therefore concludes this section dealing with their false optimism with a sorrowful lament for the Davidic line of kings, which was coming to an end for a very long time. This is the first of five lamentations in the book.

The dirge-parable speaks of powerful lions which were the offspring of one lioness (vv. 1-2). The narrative relates the lions to various monarchs in Judah, but the identity of the lioness is less clear: Is she an actual woman or does she symbolize something else? Charles Dyer reasons that the lioness symbolizes the nation of Israel:

> Since the "lions" were the kings, some scholars feel that the "lioness" was Hamutal, wife of Josiah and the mother of Jehoahaz and Zedekiah (2 Kgs. 23:31, 24:18). However, this seems unlikely for two reasons. First, the "king" in Ezekiel 19:5-9 seems to be Jehoiachin; and his mother was Nehushta, another wife of Josiah (2 Kgs. 24:8). Second, the "mother" of the kings, referred to throughout Ezekiel 19 seems to depict more than a physical mother. In verse 10-14 the nation herself is the "mother" of the kings. Verse 13 seems to allude to Israel's captivity. Therefore the lioness/mother in this chapter is the nation Israel.[38]

Indeed, Israel was the one who set up her kings and also witnessed their fall, and she was the one going into captivity.

One of Israel's cubs grew to be a mighty lion, but was captured and led with hooks into Egypt (vv. 2-4). This undoubtedly speaks of King Jehoahaz who succeeded his godly father King Josiah after Josiah's untimely death fighting Pharaoh Neco at Megiddo in 609 B.C.

114

Jehoahaz reigned only three months before Pharaoh Necho removed him from the throne of Judah and took him captive to Egypt, where he later died (2 Kgs. 21:31-34).

Since Judah's next king, Jehoiakim, died in Jerusalem and did not experience Gentile captivity, Ezekiel does not refer to him; rather his lamentation skips over him to his successor, Jehoiachin (vv. 5-9). With lion-like fierceness he brought down strongholds and towns during his brief reign of three months before being deposed by Nebuchadnezzar, and brought to Babylon in chains. Jehoiachin remained in prison for most of his life, but after being incarcerated for 37 years he was released by Amel-Marduk (Evil-Merodach) after he succeeded his father Nebuchadnezzar to the throne of Babylon (2 Kgs. 24:8-17, 25:25-30). However, Jehoiachin never was permitted to return to Israel – he died in Babylon.

The remainder of Ezekiel's dirge pertains to Zedekiah, the final king of Judah until the Kingdom Age (vv. 10-14). Israel again is likened to a flourishing vine that had prospered under Jehovah's care and thus, *"She had strong branches for scepters of rulers"* (v. 11). Although God had blessed His people with strength and fortitude in past centuries and had sustained a nation fit to be ruled by David's descendants, that was not the situation now. Because of rebellion and idolatry, the vine was no longer glorious among the nations, and God was now ready to uproot it and permit it to wither on the ground (v. 12). A strong east wind (depicting the approach of the Babylonian armies) would strip the vines of their fruit, would break and burn her branches, and carry away what was left. That remnant of the vine would be planted in an arid place where it could survive, but not thrive (v. 13). This spoke of the Jews who would survive the invasion and be transported to Babylon as captives. Consequently, the vine no longer had rich foliage or strong branches (v. 14).

This prophecy undoubtedly grieved Ezekiel, for there would be no more kings to rule Israel, until a final branch appeared to hold the scepter of Israel once again. Several of the prophets, including Jeremiah, wrote of this majestic Branch and His future glorious reign:

In those days and at that time I will cause to grow up to David a Branch of righteousness; He shall execute judgment and righteousness in the earth. In those days Judah will be saved, and

115

Jerusalem will dwell safely. And this is the name by which she will be called: THE LORD OUR RIGHTEOUSNESS (Jer. 33:15-16).

The wise and righteous king to come would be a descendant of David. He would be honorable and just in every respect. He would bless His people and protect them from harm. The people would revere Him and call Him *"The Lord Our Righteousness,"* but God would refer to Him as His "Righteous Branch." God had promised that one of David's descendants would sit on his throne forever (2 Sam. 7:13-16). The fact that wicked Jehoiachin (Jeconiah) had been removed from the throne demonstrated that the Lord did not approve of him. Rather, God had pronounced a specific judgment upon him: none of his descendants would ever ascend to the throne of David (Jer. 22:30). This meant that the branch which sprouted from David would be the Messiah, but not directly in the line of Davidic kings because of this curse.

This prophecy is used to magnify the incarnation of the Lord Jesus Christ as the Messiah. Joseph, the husband of Mary (the mother of the Lord Jesus), was a descendant of Shealtiel who was the son of Jehoiachin or Jeconiah (Matt. 1:12; 1 Chron. 3:17). Therefore, no son of Joseph could sit upon David's throne. Mary, however, was also a descendant of David through Nathan (Luke 3:24-38). Thus, the son of Mary could fulfill both prophecies, if she conceived supernaturally through the power of the Holy Spirit and not by Joseph her husband. Such a child would avoid the curse of Jeconiah, would not be corrupted by the fallen nature inherited from Adam, and would be the rightful heir to the throne of David. Hence, Jeremiah and Ezekiel both foretold God's dealings with the last four wicked kings of Judah, but also laid the foundation for the future exaltation of the King of kings.

God's cutting off the branch of David through Jeconiah would serve to assist the Jews in a future day to recognize the Righteous Branch of David through the genealogies recorded in 1 Chronicles and Matthew. Indeed, the One who would rule over them in righteousness forever was in the line of David, but not a descendant of Jeconiah. Ezekiel foretold the removal of Judah's corrupt branches (their last kings), but Jeremiah's declaration of the coming "Branch of Righteousness" was good news indeed for the suffering Jews, and represents the outcome of the fuller work of God accomplished through Christ!

Meditation

Great Jehovah, mighty Lord, vast and boundless is Thy Word;
King of kings, from shore to shore Thou shalt reign forevermore.
Jew and Gentile, bond and free, all shall yet be one in Thee;
All confess Messiah's Name, all His wondrous love proclaim.

— Fanny Crosby

Reasons for Vindication
Ezekiel 20

Having reproved Israel's false optimism, in chapters 20-24 Ezekiel provides the explicit reasons why God will severely judge Judah and Jerusalem. While the latter chapters in this section contain specific prophecies of judgment, this chapter focuses mainly on Israel's long history of insubordination.

The date associated with this chapter, the seventh year and fifth month of captivity (August 591 B.C.), would be approximately eleven months after the previous date reference (8:1). Some of the elders of Israel visited Ezekiel in his home to seek counsel (v. 1). However, the question that they asked the prophet was not one God was obliged to answer; rather, He would provide the answer to the question they should have asked: Why is Jehovah going to judge His people (vv. 2-3)? The hypocritical behavior of these men reminds us that God is insulted when we do not approach Him in sincerity and with a spirit of humility. Spiritual phonies cannot fool God; otherwise He would be the phony.

> If you're sincerely seeking God, God will make His existence evident to you.
>
> — William Lane Craig

> God always answers us in the deeps, never in the shallows of our soul.
>
> — Amy Carmichael

Affronted by their behavior, the Lord asks Ezekiel, *"Will you judge them, son of man, will you judge them? Then make known to them the abominations of their fathers"* (v. 4). Israel had been indicted by heaven's court and Ezekiel would become God's prosecuting attorney to review the evidence of her long defiant past. William MacDonald suggests the attitude of these leaders and God's response to them serves as a warning for us to consider:

> The elders were quite conservative and orthodox; they did inquire of the Lord, but their hearts were far from Him. Idols keep us from getting God's answers to our questions. When God recounts our sins and shows us His grace by leading us to repentance, many of us get bored: "We've heard that so often." "The Bible is just full of dos and don'ts." "Is there nothing else but judgment in it?" Instead of reacting properly to God's Word, we are in danger of staying lukewarm.[39]

Ezekiel commences by reviewing God's sovereign promise to Moses at the burning bush to deliver the descendants of Abraham from Egypt and to bring them to a land flowing with milk and honey as a new nation (vv. 5-9). Jehovah had previously promised Abraham that He would bless his descendants, but with Moses, Jehovah solidified a covenant (i.e., He raised His hand with an oath) with a selected seed of Abraham (vv. 5-6). Yet, much of the covenant was conditional in nature. To maintain communion with Him, the Lord demanded that the Jews purge all vile images and the idols of Egypt from their company (v. 7). Regrettably, when the Jews departed from Egypt, they were a mixed company and it did not take long for idolatry to become public (e.g., the golden calf that Aaron fashioned at Mount Sinai). Newly liberated Israel failed to be a holy people separated unto God. But to uphold His holy name among the nations, God extended mercy to His covenant people and did not punish them as they fully deserved (vv. 8-9).

The second proof of Israel's waywardness relates to their history in the wilderness after their exodus from Egypt (vv. 10-17). After rescuing His people from Pharaoh through opening and closing the Red Sea, God presented His people with His Law for them to follow (vv. 10-11). If they wanted Jehovah to dwell with them and bless them, they must keep His Law, but they had not. For example, God instituted the Sabbath as a sign of His covenant with them, but they had not kept the Sabbath holy – they willfully broke His Law (v. 12). Though that generation was not permitted into the Promised Land, they were not punished in the full measure that the Law demanded, again, so as not to diminish God's testimony among the nations (vv. 13-17).

Infidelity and Loyalty

Continuing with Israel's history, Ezekiel cites the next example of spiritual failure, which related to the new generation after the forty-year wilderness experience (vv. 18-26). Jehovah reiterated His Law to the next generation of Jews, but they followed the example of their forefathers, who perished in the wilderness and disregarded God's commandments (vv. 18-21). Though they deserved destruction for their flagrant idolatry, for His name's sake among the nations, He again showed mercy and chastened His covenant people. He permitted them to suffer the repercussion of their sin and dispersed some of them among the Gentiles (vv. 22-26). Some have difficulty with the language of verse 25: *"I also gave them up to statutes that were not good."* But as William Kelly deduces, the context conveys the simple principle that God judicially chastens His guilty people, but He calls the scourge His own, even when that instrument is completely foreign to His own holiness:

> This is true even of the Holy One of God, of Christ Himself, who, when given up to utter rejection and suffering from man, is in this said to be smitten of God (Ps. 69; Zech. 13). It is a great and serious mistake that the statutes which were not good, and ordinances by which they could not live, mean God's own in which they were bound to walk obediently. This would be indeed to make scripture hopelessly obscure, and God the author of evil. Not so: whatever be the issue for the sinner, the apostle is most energetic in proving the misery even of a converted soul in his efforts after good and against his own evil under law, to vindicate that which in itself is holy, just and good. Assuredly then the Jewish prophet and St. Paul do not contradict each other, but those who apply the expression "statutes that were not good" misunderstand the matter in hand. The true reference is to the bitter bondage of His people to the corrupt and destructive regulations of the heathen, even to the demoralization of their households, and the most cruel devotion of their firstborn to Moloch, "horrid king." Thus, if they polluted God's name and Sabbaths, He polluted them in their gifts: so great was the degradation of Israel in departing from the true God.[40]

The fourth round of evidence focused on Israel's disobedience once the Canaan conquest was over and they were in the land that God had promised them (vv. 27-29). Despite God keeping His covenant, the people did not worship Him in holiness. In fact, they were sacrificing to idols under green trees and high places throughout Israel in direct rebellion against His Law.

Ezekiel then summarizes the poor spiritual fortitude of his fellow countrymen in His day (vv. 30-31). Nothing had changed since the Egyptian exodus a millennium earlier. The Jews were still blatantly idolatrous, as proven by the hideous crime of sacrificing their own children to false gods.

Hence, God had no intention of answering the elders' inquiry of Ezekiel (v. 3). Rather, He had every reason, after extending mercy to an unruly people for a thousand years, to once and for all purge idolatry from His people (v. 32). Though they wanted to be like the surrounding pagan nations, He would not permit it! His judgment would be extremely harsh, but the aftermath of it would accomplish His objective – Israel would never turn to paganism again.

Thankfully, God's wrath is tempered with some measure of mercy even when He is furious. In verses 33-44, Ezekiel provides hope to the purified remnant of Israel emerging from God's refining fire – God will restore you to Himself and you shall again bask in His love. First, they would have to pass under Jehovah's rod of correction and be scattered among the nations; this would remove those prone to idolatry from among them (vv. 38-39). Afterwards, Jehovah promised to gather them from among the nations back to the Promised Land, with the same kind of awesome power with which He opened the Red Sea and brought their forefathers out of Egypt (vv. 33-36). He would draw them to Himself again for the same reason, to commune with His people. Only those who passed under the Shepherd's rod of inspection would be permitted into His new fold of purified sheep in Israel (v. 37).

Jehovah promised to begin afresh with His spiritually cleansed people. He would again accept their sacrifices and offerings, and the Jews would hallow God's name before the Gentiles (vv. 40-41). Then His covenant people will realize that when God raised His hand centuries earlier and promised to give them a special land and to bless them in that land – He really meant what He vowed to do (v. 42). While this agenda was partially fulfilled when estranged Jews returned to Judah at the conclusion of their 70-year Babylonian exile, the nation of Israel is not yet spiritually to the point of acknowledging verses 43-44:

"And there you shall remember your ways and all your doings with which you were defiled; and you shall loathe yourselves in your own

sight because of all the evils that you have committed. Then you shall know that I am the Lord, when I have dealt with you for My name's sake, not according to your wicked ways nor according to your corrupt doings, O house of Israel," says the Lord God.

Such repentance and understanding could never be accomplished under the Law, but it could be through the New Covenant which will be accepted by the entire nation at Christ's Second Advent at the close of the Tribulation Period. The prophet Zechariah foretells this specific event:

And I will pour on the house of David and on the inhabitants of Jerusalem the Spirit of grace and supplication; then they will look on Me whom they pierced. Yes, they will mourn for Him as one mourns for his only son, and grieve for Him as one grieves for a firstborn. In that day there shall be a great mourning in Jerusalem, like the mourning at Hadad Rimmon in the plain of Megiddo (Zech. 12:10-11).

When Christ returns, the spiritual blindness of the Jewish nation will come to an end. They will trust in the Lord Jesus Christ, their Messiah, the One they pierced two thousand years earlier and they will receive the Holy Spirit. In this spiritually fruitful state, the Jews will be known as the olive tree which provides a testimony of God's goodness to the entire world (Hos. 14:6; Rom. 11:17-24). Although we see that individual Jews in the Old Testament were filled by the Holy Spirit in order to speak for the Lord or to serve Him effectively (e.g., Ex. 35:30-35; 1 Sam. 10:10), the nation as a whole has never been indwelt by the Spirit of God (Zech. 4:4-7). This will not happen until Christ's second coming to the earth (Isa. 59:21). All this to say that God is a covenant-keeping God and His marvelous plan for the Jewish nation is still unfolding and will be completed according to His sovereign plan.

Ezekiel's long message of announcing why God's patience had run out with His people and that He would now act to purge them of their stubborn idolatry once and for all ends with verse 44. The chapter concludes with a seemingly out of place parable pertaining to a prophesied forest fire. Indeed, the Hebrew Bible includes it in the next chapter, which announces four messages of judgment against Jerusalem. Regardless, God commanded Ezekiel to face southward and to prophesy against the forest lands of the Negev and in Teman (a city in Edom to the southeast; 25:13) – these would be devoured by fire (vv. 45-46). Apparently, the Negev (a region southwest of Jerusalem) was once flourishing with foliage; however, that land today is semi-arid and requires irrigation to be productive.

The fall of Jerusalem and the destruction of Judah during the Babylonian invasion is one of the darkest pages of Jewish history. The elite social class and much of the general population were massacred, the city and temple burned, wells plugged up, vineyards destroyed, and fields strewn with rocks. As Ezekiel foretold, the entire region was decimated (v. 47). Hence, Ezekiel's "fire," which would be so extensive that no one would question that the Lord had kindled it, relates to the overall judgment of Judah, but would include the actual torching of productive forest lands to the south of Jerusalem (v. 48).

After conveying this last allegory, Ezekiel mourned to the Lord: The people refuse to consider and understand my messages, because they say that I am just speaking in parables and confusing riddles. God responds to Ezekiel's complaint by causing him to utter four separate messages about Jehovah's sword in the next chapter. These would further explain the meaning of the forest fire parable: The Jews could not flourish in a land destined to be cursed by God.

The entire land was soon to be under God's sentence, so there was no reason to invest in or seek a blessing from what would be destroyed. Believers must adopt the same attitude towards the world in which they live – it has been cursed by God and is destined to be burned with fire. Why invest in that which will soon vanish? It is better to devote one's life to what will endure forever, where neither moth nor rust nor thieves can diminish its value (Matt. 5:19-20). Those who choose to invest in eternity have the promise that *"their works follow them"* (Rev. 14:13). The Lord promises that a mind properly aligned with Christ's thinking will never be self-seeking or self-exalting, for such nonsense is repulsive to His character.

Meditation

O Jesus Christ, grow Thou in me, and all things else recede!
My heart be daily nearer Thee, from sin be daily freed.
More of Thy glory let me see, Thou Holy, Wise and True!
I would Thy living image be, in joy and sorrow, too.
Make this poor self grow less and less, be Thou my life and aim;
O make me daily through Thy grace, more meet to bear Thy Name!

— Johann Lavater

God's Sword Awakes
Ezekiel 21

The parable of the burning forest in southern Judah is further explained in this chapter through four separate decrees concerning God's sword of judgment. To clarify its meaning, Ezekiel poses some substitutions: He exchanges the word "fire" for "sword" and refers to the entire region of Judah in lieu of only the southlands (e.g., the Negev). As concluded in the previous chapter, the southern forest may have been consumed by fire, but God's overall judgment would affect all of Judah and indeed the surrounding nations, as confirmed in this series of four "sword" messages.

God's Sword Is Drawn

The first message might well be entitled "God's Sword Is Drawn" (vv. 1-7). To ensure that the Jews did not think that the forest burning parable only pertained to southern Judah, God told Ezekiel to turn his face towards Jerusalem and the temple and then prophesy against both (vv. 1-2). When God would draw His sword and begin to cut down with it, nothing from north to south would remain in Judah; even the righteous would suffer hardship as the wicked perished (vv. 3-5). After conveying the message to the elders, Ezekiel was then told to sigh with deep bitterness (v. 6). When he was asked, "Why are you sighing?" Ezekiel was to respond:

> *"Because of the news; when it comes, every heart will melt, all hands will be feeble, every spirit will faint, and all knees will be weak as water. Behold, it is coming and shall be brought to pass," says the Lord God* (v. 7).

The somber meaning was obvious and no further explanation was required before Ezekiel commenced with the second "sword" sermon (vv. 8-17).

125

God's Sword Is Sharp

This message is a three-stanza poem with a similar refrain repeated between each stanza. The refrain (at the end of verse 10 and in verse 13) asserts that Israel despised God's "scepter," which most likely refers to His rod of correction – His instrument of justice. The "point" of this message was that God's sword was sharp, meaning that He was ready and able to precisely wield judgment in such a way as to ensure all His purposes were accomplished (vv. 8-11). Israel had repeatedly rejected His rod of discipline to remove idolatry from His people (the book of Judges records thirteen such attempts). Now it was time for wide sweeping and pervasive retribution – the language is graphic. The Lord was going to cut down great men, Israel's princes, and the general populace even in their own bedroom chambers.

Ezekiel likens the Lord to a soldier, who, on the eve of battle sharpens and polishes his sword – the Lord was ready to execute justice. But unlike a soldier who may not personally know his opposition, the Lord intimately knew the recipients of His wrath. The poem concludes with a solemn expression of God's stored up anger towards His own people: *"I also will beat My fists together, and I will cause My fury to rest; I, the Lord, have spoken"* (v. 17). Even the prophet was called on to pound his thigh (perhaps his chest) with his fist and also to strike his fists together to illustrate both God's fury and God's readiness to punish them (vv. 12, 14). In the first message, Ezekiel was told to sigh, but the intensity of the second message required deeper emotion; he was directed to *"cry and wail"* (v. 12).

Two Road Signs

The third sermon clarifies the sword's intended target – Jerusalem (vv. 18-27). The actions of the prophet in this message were to illustrate how God was supernaturally guiding Nebuchadnezzar and his armies to Jerusalem. Ezekiel was to post two road signs at one location to direct the sword of Babylon (vv. 18-19). This was to signify that at a certain location in his route eastward, Nebuchadnezzar would have to choose which city and region to attack first. Charles Dyer explains the geography and historical decision:

> When Jerusalem rebelled against Babylon in 588 B.C., she was one of three cities or countries seeking independence. The other two were Tyre and Ammon. Nebuchadnezzar led his forces north and west

from Babylon along the Euphrates River. When he reached Riblah (north of Damascus in Syria), he had to decide which nation he would attack first. He could head due west toward the coast and attack Tyre, or he could go south along one of two "highways" leading to Judah and Ammon. Tyre was the most difficult of three cities to attack (chp. 26, 29:17-20), so Nebuchadnezzar decided not to make it his first objective. His choice then was whether to head down the coastal highway and attack Judah and Jerusalem or to head down the Transjordanian highway and attack Ammon and Rabbah (its capital city).[41]

The two roads signs that Ezekiel posted would then have pointed to either Jerusalem or Rabbah (v. 20). Not sure which city to confront first, Nebuchadnezzar consulted his gods and sought three omens to confirm the right choice (vv. 21-22). He randomly chose one of two arrows with the name of each city written upon an arrow; he asked his pagan images questions, and his soothsayers examined the livers of sacrificed animals. Normally, these things would have no real bearing on God's providential ways, but Ezekiel told the Jews that God would control the outcome of these pagan practices to unanimously confirm that Jerusalem should be Babylon's first target (vv. 23-24).

The third message concludes by pronouncing judgment on the wicked prince (Zedekiah) who broke his covenant with Babylon and brought disaster on Judah; he would be overthrown and humbled (vv. 25-26). Yet, within this sorrowful poem is a ray of hope – God would establish the throne of David again in a future day when *"He comes whose right it is, and I will give it to Him"* (v. 27). This messianic prophecy affirmed God's intention for a glorious Israel in a future day. He had not cast off His covenant people forever. It also states that there will never be another king ruling over Israel until Christ returns from heaven to claim His throne – a fact that almost 2,600 years of history has proven to be true!

For this reason, the crown of Jacob's prophetic blessing to his sons, centuries earlier, was bestowed on Judah. Through Judah, kings would rule over Israel. One day the scepter *"would come to the one it belongs to"* (the literal meaning of *"until Shiloh come"*), and it would never depart (Gen. 49:10). This clearly speaks of the kingdom of the Lord Jesus, which will endure forever once He receives it from His Father. Then, Jacob proceeded to describe the manifold abundance of His kingdom (Gen. 49:11-12). At this very moment, in heaven's magnificent throne room, *"the Lion of the tribe of Judah, the Root of David"* (Rev. 5:5) is waiting to take the title deed of His kingdom from His Father's hand. John tells us who He is in the next verse: The Lion of the tribe of Judah is the Lamb standing amidst the throngs of heaven as though He had been slain (i.e., the Lord still bears the wounds of Calvary).

The Lord Jesus, the sacrificial Lamb that took away the sins of the world, is now a Lion ready to unleash fury and wrath upon those who had crucified Him (the Jews) and the wicked upon the earth. The Tribulation Period begins in Revelation 6:1 when He opens the first seal of the scroll handed to Him by His Father and allows the Antichrist a short dominion over the world. After seven more years, the righteous King shall appear and establish His everlasting kingdom on the earth!

God's Sword Is Coming to Ammon

The final sword sermon is directed at Ammon, the direction of the other road sign posted by Ezekiel (vv. 28-32). No doubt the Ammonites were relieved that the Babylonians attacked Judah and Jerusalem first, for this gave them several more years to prepare for the siege to come. After Jerusalem fell, Nebuchadnezzar put a godly man named Gedaliah in charge. Under his leadership, conditions in Judah improved. There was civil order, adequate food supplies, and no threat of extermination (Jer. 40:1-16). However, not everyone approved of these social advances. In fact, Gedaliah was made aware of a threat upon his life by an Ammonite named Ishmael. Such treachery seemed unlikely to Gedaliah because the Ammonites were in alliance with Judah. But indeed, King Baalis of the Ammonites had hired Ishmael to kill Gedaliah. The Ammonites believed that this would buy them more time to prepare themselves against the Babylonians. Nebuchadnezzar had moved his army away from Jerusalem in order to lay siege on the commercial metropolis of Tyre in the north (29:17-18). After the fall of Tyre, he would most assuredly attack Ammon next.

Gedaliah was murdered, which did cause Nebuchadnezzar to return to Jerusalem and reestablish order and control – a situation which added more suffering to the Jewish people (Jer. 41:1-18). While their devious scheme had delayed Nebuchadnezzar's assault on Rabbah, Ezekiel prophesied that Ammon could not prevent their ultimate slaughter. God's polished sword, which cut down Jerusalem, would also decimate Ammon. Details of this invasion and slaughter are further prophesied in chapter 25. In his four messages, Ezekiel warned the people that the Lord's sword had been sharpened and was drawn and ready to execute severe judgment, first on Jerusalem and then on Rabbah.

Should the Lord's people follow Nebuchadnezzar's example of seeking counsel by using tools of divination? The answer is emphatically "no." Such things were banned from Israel and the witches, wizards, mediums, etc. who used such pagan trappings were to be put to death (Lev. 20:27; Deut. 18:11). The Lord did provide the Urim and the Thummim, two stones in the High Priest's breastplate, to answer questions asked of Him by the High Priest (Ex. 27:21). He also used the casting of lots by the hands of a priest or recognized prophet to direct His people. For example, Joshua and the High Priest Eleazar determined land disbursements for the various tribes by drawing lots (Josh. 14:1-2). This method of distribution had been previously commanded by Moses (Num. 26:55). It was understood that Jehovah was guiding the process to confirm His will, and the proceedings left nothing to chance (Prov. 16:33).

In the dispensation of the Law, God's people were not eternally indwelt by the Holy Spirit and thus some physical means of determining the mind of the Lord was necessary where God had not already expressed His will. In the Church Age, Christians should not cast lots or draw straws (as Nebuchadnezzar did with arrows) to determine the will of God in a particular matter. Scripture does not record the casting of lots as being a practice of the early Church to obtain divine insight (although the early apostles, Jews, did seek God's mind by casting lots prior to Pentecost; Acts 1). W. Graham Scroggie affirms that this Jewish practice has been replaced by several more intimate means of distinguishing God's will:

> In our time, in place of the "lot" are the Holy Spirit, the Word of God, the Throne of Grace, and the open or closed door, that is, circumstances. By these means we may discover what God's will for us is, and if we are subject to them, these means will never fail us.[42]

"The will of God," or the related phrases, such as "the Lord's will," and "Your will" occur thirty-four times in the New Testament.

Infidelity and Loyalty

Nineteen times the sovereign plan of God to accomplish a distinct purpose is in view. There are four references to the will of God being done or that it shall be done, and seven references to believers doing God's will. Scripture further declares that the expressed will of God should be understood, and three times it is specifically declared for all believers to know. Today we know and understand God's will as the Holy Spirit illuminates our minds with truth as we examine Scripture, God's Word. We should never think that any aspect of our lives is left to chance, or that we can redirect God's sovereign affairs in our lives by seeking advice from the devil's tools of divination.

Until Genesis 31, the word "image" was exclusively used in Scripture to describe humanity's unique "God likeness" in certain aspects (having a spirit, emotions, intellect, a moral nature, communicative ability, etc.). The Hebrew word *teraphim*, which means "healer," is employed in Genesis 31:19 to describe the "images" that Rachel stole from her father Laban. These were the types of images that King Nebuchadnezzar used in an attempt to determine the best outcome of future events (v. 21). Arthur Pink explains the use of such an image:

> Scholars tell us that the word "teraphim" may be traced to a Syrian root which means "to inquire." This explains the reason why Rachel took with her their family "gods" when her husband stole away surreptitiously from her home – it was to prevent her father from "inquiring" of these idol "oracles" and thus discovering the direction in which they had gone.[43]

Whether Rachel took Laban's images to prevent her father from learning of their family's secret departure to Canaan or possibly for her own personal use is unknown. What we do know is that "teraphim" were used for consultation (Judg. 17:5, 18:6; Zech. 10:2), much in the same way Ouija boards, runes, tarot cards, crystal balls, tea leaves, dowsing rods, etc. are used today. In this chapter, we see God controlling these pagan practices to ensure that Nebuchadnezzar would do His will, which had already been revealed to Israel by Jeremiah and Ezekiel. At this time, Nebuchadnezzar was a pagan; he did not repent and become a Jehovah worshipper until the end of his life, some thirty years in the future (Dan. 4). As in this situation, God may use unseemly means (i.e., pagan superstitions) to uphold what He has already revealed, but not as a means of initially declaring His intentions. Other examples of this practice include using a pagan prophet like Balaam to bless His people (Num. 22-24), a witch to reprove King Saul (1 Sam. 28:7), and even a Midianite soldier destined for slaughter to encourage fearful Gideon (Judg. 7:13-14).

From God's perspective, there is no reason for His people to ever consult the devil for what God alone is sovereign over. God was offended that these demonic images were among His people in Jacob's day; hence, God commanded him to purge his house of them (Gen. 35:1-4). Might we heed the same warning and remove from our homes whatever would honor the devil and lead us away from the Lord. *"An idol is nothing"* concludes Paul (1 Cor. 8:4), but in Satan's hand it can lure believers away from communing with the Lord into sorrow-filled darkness:

> *The things which the Gentiles sacrifice they sacrifice to demons and not to God, and I do not want you to have fellowship with demons. You cannot drink the cup of the Lord and the cup of demons; you cannot partake of the Lord's table and of the table of demons. Or do we provoke the Lord to jealousy? Are we stronger than He?* (1 Cor. 10:20-22).

God dwelt with the nation of Israel as a whole, but in the Church Age every believer personally answers to the Lord. Let us not provoke His sharp "sword" of judicial retribution, as Israel did. We must not trust in signs, lots, or images, but rather endeavor to live *"by every word that proceeds from the mouth of God"* (Matt. 4:4). Living according to God's revealed will ensures that we never need to fear His chastening rod or smiting sword, for even in the Church Age there are sins unto death (1 Jn. 5:16-18).

Meditation

Crown, O God, Thine own endeavor;
Cleave our darkness with Thy sword;
Cleanse the body of this nation
Through the Gospel of the Lord.

— Henry Holland

131

The Sins of the People
Ezekiel 22

As in chapter 20, God calls on Ezekiel to be His prosecuting attorney. Both chapters commence in a similar fashion with God asking Ezekiel to review the evidence so that Israel will understand their guilt and why their abominations demanded severe reprisal. *"Now, son of man, will you judge, will you judge the bloody city? Yes, show her all her abominations!"* (v. 2). This chapter contains three separate messages pertaining to willful defilement and the necessity of divine retribution: The inhabitants of Jerusalem were guilty of shedding blood and idolatry (vv. 1-16), the nation as a whole was morally reprobate (vv. 17-22), and Israel's leaders were wicked (vv. 23-31).

The two chief sins imputed to Jerusalem were murdering innocent people and creating idols to worship (v. 3). Consequently, Jerusalem's days as the capital city of Israel were drawing to an end (v. 4). God was going to vanquish their pride in their infamous city and then they would become a reproach among the nations (v. 5). The Law shows sin (Rom. 3:20), but it also demonstrates how to show love to God (worship Him alone in holiness) and love to others (which was more than not stealing from others, but rather meeting their needs). However, the Jews did not love God, or others, or His Law in general (Ex. 20:1-17). Rather, they flagrantly rebelled against it. Previously, Ezekiel itemized their sins to affirm their personal accountability (18:5-17). Now he lists the social and moral sins of Jerusalem that demanded divine judgment:

- Abusing civil authority in order to murder (v. 6)
- Dishonoring parents, mistreating strangers, neglecting widows and orphans (v. 7)
- Despising God's holy things and His Sabbaths (v. 8)
- Idolatry (v. 9)
- Gross immorality (often associated with idolatry; vv. 10-11)
- Taking bribes, charging exorbitant interest, and extortion (v. 12)

Ezekiel named their greatest offense last – they, as a nation, had forgotten the Lord (v. 12). Jeremiah had told those in Jerusalem the same thing in his first message. Jeremiah used the expression "you have forsaken" four times in the first two chapters of his book (1:19, 2:13, 17, 19) before switching to the phrase "you have forgotten," which he used twice (2:32, 3:21). The progression is important to note – forsaking the Lord leads to forgetting Him. The Jews had not just recently deserted their God; the Lord bemoaned that He had been forgotten days without number (Jer. 2:32). He was now determined to jog their memory in an exceptionally painful way.

God would strike His hands together and smite Jerusalem for disregarding Him and His Law (v. 13). Their pride and courage would disappear when they were dispersed as a people unpitied among the nations (vv. 14-15). Verse 14 serves as a potent warning to all those who would willfully disregard God's Word: *"Can your heart endure, or can your hands remain strong, in the days when I shall deal with you? I, the Lord, have spoken, and will do it."* Paul similarly challenges believers, including himself, in the New Testament: *"Do we provoke the Lord to jealousy? Are we stronger than He?"* (1 Cor. 10:22). Israel would learn that it was unwise to provoke the Lord to jealousy, and that they could not stand against His righteous indignation.

> Chastisement is designed for our good, to promote our highest interests. Look beyond the rod to the All-wise hand that wields it!
>
> — A. W. Pink

> God has no pleasure in afflicting us, but He will not keep back even the most painful chastisement if He can but thereby guide His beloved child to come home and abide in the beloved Son.
>
> — Andrew Murray

What would be the prospective outcome of Israel's painful humbling? Ezekiel prophesied, *"You shall defile yourself in the sight of the nations; then you shall know that I am the Lord"* (v. 16). They had forgotten the Lord, but He had not forgotten them, and God was determined not to rest until they identified with Him again in purity.

When God's Word is not revered, when it is of little importance to those who identify with Christ, an immoral, lethargic, carnal Church is the result. As the Jews would learn, there are stringent consequences for forsaking the Lord. Regrettably, it is only those who are near to the Lord who dread this condition; the others need extreme measures to be awakened from their spiritual slumber.

Ezekiel then tells a parable of God's refining judgment for His unruly and immoral people. Like Jeremiah (Jer. 6:27-30), Ezekiel compares Judah to unrefined ore which must be put into an intensely hot furnace to separate the innumerable impurities from what was valuable – purified silver (vv. 17-22). What does the dross mean in the furnace parable?

The people of Judah were corrupt through and through; the sought after precious metal in their composition could scarcely be found (vv. 18-19). So far, God's attempts through prophetic utterance to remove the stubborn components of bronze, iron, and lead from their makeup were unsuccessful. God wanted purified silver, but His people were so full of impurities that He must utterly reject them (Jer. 6:30). Refuse silver has no value; it must either be cast away or exposed to extreme heat to remove its dross and that is what God was going to do (vv. 20-22). God knew how to remove the wicked dross from Judah: Babylon would be the flame of His wrath, Jerusalem the furnace, and God's prophetic word the catalyst for the Refiner's fire. Any living soul emerging from that great conflagration would assuredly be genuine silver.

The third segment of Ezekiel's sermon identified the recipients deserving God's judgment: civil leaders (v. 25), priests (v. 26), governing officials (v. 27), so-called prophets (v. 28), and the general populace (v. 29). This list reveals the widespread depravity that was infesting every level of Jewish society. Because of Israel's flagrant and widespread sin, she had experienced neither God's cleansing nor His blessings (vv. 23-24). Human defiance always results in corruption, which then guarantees suffering and sorrow!

> Sin is the dare of God's justice, the rape of His mercy, the jeer of His patience, the slight of His power, and the contempt of His love.
>
> — John Bunyan

134

The real tragedy before us is not that the Jews did not know Jehovah, but rather having known Him and experienced His goodness, they still insisted on going their own way.

Verse 25 recaps the sins of Israel's nobility (including Zedekiah) previously mentioned in verse 6. Israel's leaders were corrupt and greedy; they were like wild lions devouring the people's wealth and even their lives (v. 25). The religious leaders, the priests, were just as wicked as their civil counterparts. Not only had they profaned God's holy things in the temple, but they no longer taught or enforced God's Law among the people (e.g., the Sabbath was not being honored; vv. 26-27). Instead of speaking for God and warning the people about their sin, Israel's prophets (excluding men like Jeremiah, Ezekiel, Habakkuk, and Zephaniah) through false visions and lying words were offering their countrymen false hope of God's blessing (v. 28).

Lastly, Ezekiel denounces the general populace for blindly following the corrupt and immoral ways of their leaders (v. 29). Having suffered the oppression of their own greedy leaders, they should have known better than to afflict the poor and needy among them. So rampant was Israel's corruption that the Lord could not find one righteous person in any position of authority in Jerusalem (v. 30).

After Ezekiel had completed his evaluation of Israel's moral decay, Jehovah announced the only solution that would resolve this perversion: *"Therefore I have poured out My indignation on them; I have consumed them with the fire of My wrath; and I have recompensed their deeds on their own heads"* (v. 31). For centuries God's wrath was tempered by His mercy which permitted Israel ample time to repent, but the opportunity for forgiveness and restoration had passed. All that remained for God's people now was His intense fury, with a distant glimmer of hope that eventually restoration would come. They were going into the fiery furnace, the Smelter's pot of refinement, and nothing could change their punishment.

Meditation

Fear not, I am with thee, O be not dismayed,
For I am thy God and will still give thee aid;
I'll strengthen and help thee, and cause thee to stand
Upheld by My righteous, omnipotent hand.

Infidelity and Loyalty

> When through fiery trials thy pathways shall lie,
> My grace, all sufficient, shall be thy supply;
> The flame shall not hurt thee; I only design
> Thy dross to consume, and thy gold to refine.

— John Rippon

Oholah and Oholibah
Ezekiel 23

In this chapter, Ezekiel tells the story of two sisters espoused to Jehovah, the older, Oholah (representing the northern kingdom of Israel) and the younger, Oholibah (speaking of Judah in the south). Both became morally corrupt. This message closely aligns with a portion of Jeremiah's second message delivered years earlier during the early reforms of Josiah, but before the Book of the Law was found and read to the king (3:6-25). Jeremiah's message served as a call to repentance, where Ezekiel's message justifies God's jealous response for being forsaken by His beloved. In chapter 16, Ezekiel rebuked Judah for her unfaithfulness, but he goes further in this chapter to rebuke her for forging foreign alliances instead of trusting Jehovah for her peace and security.

From a spiritual perspective, these two young sisters had the same mother, meaning both had similar rearing and circumstances while in Egypt, and were mostly undistinguishable during those years (v. 2). Both lost their purity in Egypt and became harlots at an early age (speaking of their early idolatry with Egyptian gods; v. 3). The names of the sisters are given in verse 4: Oholah (Israel) and Oholibah (Judah). Charles Dyer explains that the Hebrew meaning of their names matches their character:

> These names are based on the Hebrew word for tent (*'ohel*). The first name means "her tent" and the second means "my tent is in her." Though one must be careful not to press a parable's details, probably these names have significance. The world "tent" implied a dwelling place or sanctuary. It was often used of God's sanctuary among Israel (Ex. 29:4, 10-11, 30). The name Oholah ("her tent") could imply that the sanctuary associated with this sister was of her own making. By contrast, the name Oholibah ("my tent is in her") implies that God's sanctuary was in her midst.[44]

137

This understanding seems reasonable since after the nation split, Jeroboam, Israel's new king, created a pagan religion with its own officiating priests (1 Kgs. 12:25-33), but God's temple resided in Jerusalem within Judah. Both Ezekiel and Jeremiah state that the two sisters were the Lord's, that is, they were espoused to Him. This does not suggest that God endorses polygamy as some have suggested. Some have used this marriage analogy (as recorded in Jer. 3; Ezek. 16 and 23) to declare that since God had two wives, Israel and Judah, polygamy is acceptable. However, thorough study indicates that God made a single marriage covenant with the nation of Israel (16:8), but after the kingdom split, God poetically speaks of them as two adulterous sisters, not as two wives. The distinction was necessary as Judah's spiritual adultery was more "treacherous" than Israel's blatant idolatry. So to call God a "polygamist" is insulting to Him.

Both sisters, Israel (referred to as Samaria after the Assyrian invasion) and Judah, had pledged their loyalty to Jehovah through a marriage covenant. Israel was the first of the sisters to commit fornication. She embraced false gods and worshipped their idols in various high places throughout the northern kingdom (vv. 5-8). Jeremiah tells us that the cover of every green tree became the canopy over her bed of adultery (Jer. 3:6). God called Israel to repent, but she would not forsake her idols and return to Him. Instead, she formalized an alliance with Assyria (vv. 9-10). God responded by writing her a bill of divorcement and sending her away to Assyria in 722 B.C. (Jer. 3:8). There she would be punished by God, oppressed by those with whom she committed adultery and from whom she had sought protection and security.

Even though the younger sister, Judah, had witnessed firsthand God's severe treatment of Israel, she also committed spiritual fornication by worshipping images of stone and wood (v. 11; Jer. 3:7-9). She likewise sought the influence, prestige, and security of the Assyrian Empire (vv. 12-13), but then went further to seek assistance from Babylon and embrace her gods also (vv. 14-17). This is why Ezekiel said that Judah was more corrupt than Israel in her lusting and idolatry (v. 11). Jeremiah further explains why God was more provoked by treacherous Judah than He had been with Israel:

"So it came to pass, through her [Israel's] casual harlotry, that she defiled the land and committed adultery with stones and trees. And

yet for all this her treacherous sister Judah has not turned to Me with her whole heart, but in pretense," says the Lord. Then the Lord said to me, "Backsliding Israel has shown herself more righteous than treacherous Judah" (Jer. 3:9-11).

Judah would experience greater judgment than Israel did, for two reasons. First, Judah had seen the devastating consequences of Israel's adultery, but still deliberately chose to be unfaithful. Second, Israel was blatantly idolatrous, but two-faced Judah embraced other lovers while still sweet-talking the Lord with pleasantries. The people of Judah acted religious, but their hearts were not with God. They pretended to be devout but embraced pagan gods whenever they thought they could get away with it. Israel did not try to hide her infidelity, but Judah disguised her treachery with religiosity in order to appear honorable; thus, she deserved greater judgment.

Furthermore, Judah was fickle and promiscuous; she sold herself to anyone she thought might assist her (vv. 19-21). For example, after embracing the gods of Babylon and making a political alliance with Nebuchadnezzar, Judah sided with Egypt (where she had earlier been nurtured in paganism; 29:6-7; 2 Kgs. 24:1, 25:1). However, promiscuous Judah would soon learn that her former Babylonian lover was vindictive and would leave her desolate after pillaging and slaughtering her (v. 18).

The chapter progresses to four announcements of punishment by "the Sovereign Lord" against the two immoral sisters. In the first announcement, Ezekiel prophesied that the utter devastation coming to Jerusalem would resemble the mutilation of a woman's face, meaning that when the Babylonians departed, Judah would be left so grotesque that nobody would want her whorish services again (vv. 22-27).

In the next announcement, Ezekiel repeated several points of the first, but added that because of Judah's promiscuity she would also be left naked and barren, and many survivors of the holocaust would be hauled away to Babylon (vv. 28-31). In the third oracle, Ezekiel poetically states that since Judah had participated in Israel's abominations, she would also drink from her cup of scorn, ruin, and desolations – God's judgments against her (vv. 32-34). Finally, Ezekiel reminded treacherous Jerusalem that she would suffer the consequence of casting God behind her back and forgetting Him to engage in lewd behavior (v. 35).

Infidelity and Loyalty

Ezekiel was commanded to *"declare to them their abominations"* (v. 36). He then listed seven detestable practices: desecration of the Sabbath and the temple, foreign alliances, adultery, shedding innocent blood, child sacrifices, and idolatry (vv. 37-44).

The Jews had become so coldhearted that they could offer their own children as burnt sacrifices to Baal and, later the same day, enter the temple to worship Jehovah while still having the blood of their children on their hands (vv. 36-39). Jehovah had become merely one among many deities; He was not significant in their estimation. He was not the One true God that should be feared or uniquely esteemed.

Besides their spiritual infidelity and immorality, God was disgusted with Israel's and Judah's political indiscretion – His people held more stock in the strength of pagan nations than in His ability to protect them. Additionally, the Jews were enamored with the secular aspects of Assyrian and Babylonian society (i.e., their power, fame, culture, philosophies, etc.). God hated worldliness as much then as He does today (Jas. 4:4). It is vitally important to realize that lusting in our hearts for what God hates is no less offensive to Him than actually engaging it. The Lord Jesus taught that adultery in the heart is disloyalty from God's perspective, and unfortunately, we are all guilty of this form of infidelity (Matt. 5:28)! The Jews would soon learn that, when adultery intrudes into a marriage relationship, all that is important is lost.

> Passion is the evil in adultery. If a man has no opportunity of living with another man's wife, but if it is obvious for some reason that he would like to do so, and would do so if he could, he is no less guilty than if he was caught in the act.
>
> — Augustine

> An idol of the mind is as offensive to God as an idol of the hand.
>
> — A. W. Tozer

The Jews' misplaced devotion is shown again through the analogy of the two sisters. Israel and Judah would bathe, paint their eyes, put on fine clothes and jewelry and then publicly solicit any man to come and abuse them; and the most perverse of men did (vv. 40-44). Was that behavior reasonable? The illustration was to show that the Jews were rejecting not only Jehovah, but also His way of life for them. Consequently, they did not have His blessing, but were rather being ravished by the world and left destitute of life's necessities and, more importantly, of their dignity. Because the Law decreed that an adulterer should be stoned (Lev. 20:10, 27) and an idolatrous city should be destroyed by the sword and fire (Deut. 13:12-16), death was coming to Judah. Righteous men (God's prophets) had already pronounced this just sentence on Judah, and a rioting mob of foreign invaders was gathering to execute justice (vv. 45-49).

Oholibah means "my tent is in her," and today God dwells not just in the midst of His people, as in Old Testament times, but within His people (1 Cor. 6:19-20). Would He not feel the pain of misplaced devotion and allegiance within the Church even more keenly? Having seen God's stern dealings with Israel for idolatry and with Judah for religious fraud, this author wonders how much longer the Lord will tolerate the same in Christendom today.

The Lord Jesus once encountered a group of self-righteous, religious zealots who were demanding the death of a woman caught in the act of adultery. Their demands were hypocritical; the fact that the guilty man had been set free demonstrated their lack of reverence for God's Law (Deut. 22:22-24). The Lord told them, *"He who is without sin among you, let him throw a stone at her first"* (John 8:7). He successfully appealed to their consciences, and they all departed from the guilty woman. It is relatively easy for us in the Church Age to fling a cold stone at adulterous Judah and miss the application of the illustration. Do we allow idols in our hearts to displace our love for the Lord Jesus? Do we flirt with the world and feast on immoral things, and then draw near to our Lord and pray sweet-nothings into His ear? Are we superficially pretending to be a chaste virgin awaiting her wedding day? Is our bridal attire stained with unconfessed sin and religious pride?

> Pure morality points you to the purest one of all. When impure, it points you to yourself. The purer your habits, the closer to God you will come. Moralizing from impure motives takes you away from God.
>
> — Ravi Zacharias

Infidelity and Loyalty

The marital analogy, expressed by both Jeremiah and Ezekiel, was to remind the Jews of the certainty of their relational acceptance with Him, though their sinful practices had severed their fellowship. Although their hearts were not with Jehovah, God's heart was still with them, as Isaiah informed Israel:

> *You whom I have taken from the ends of the earth, and called from its farthest regions, and said to you, "You are My servant, I have chosen you and have not cast you away: Fear not, for I am with you; be not dismayed, for I am your God. I will strengthen you, yes, I will help you, I will uphold you with My righteous right hand"* (Isa. 41:9-10).

In application, the same truth of security exists for all true Christians, though the enjoyment of our relationship with Christ is dependent on good behavior and uncontaminated thought-life. Sometimes it seems as if the Lord is far away, but when we come to our senses and turn back to Him, we find that He was right there with us all along. The abiding presence of the Lord Jesus Christ is a great defense against entering into sin. His nearness repels evil from our minds and strengthens us to overcome the lusts of our flesh. Frustration, edginess, weakness, and anxiety are warning signs that we have lost the sense of His presence, and that we need to realign our thinking with His in order to gain His peace again.

Meditation

Measure your growth in grace by your sensitivity to sin.

— Oswald Chambers

Our sense of sin is in proportion to our nearness to God.

— Thomas Bernard

A Watched Pot Does Boil
Ezekiel 24

This chapter concludes Ezekiel's prophecies against Jerusalem, which began in chapter 4. For about five years he has been diligently delivering signs, parables, messages, and warnings to the Jews dispersed in Babylon. Jeremiah had similarly been preaching in Jerusalem for nearly forty years. Ezekiel commences this chapter by recording an important date in Jewish history, which has great significance in tying several prophecies together concerning God's dealings with rebellious Judah. However, some background information is required to better understand how God fulfilled all that was predicted.

The number seventy is associated with the nation of Israel in a special way throughout Scripture. Genesis 46 provides the first roster of the nation, which included the names of those in Jacob's family who traveled with him to Egypt. In all, sixty-six sons and grandsons are named. Counting Joseph and his two sons, who were already in Egypt, and Jacob himself, the total number of males composing the nation of Israel at this time was seventy (Gen. 46:5). There were seventy elders of Israel (Num. 11:16), seventy prophetic weeks determined upon Israel before their restoration (Dan. 9:24-27), and, during New Testament times, there were seventy members of the Sanhedrin, and seventy witnesses sent out to Israel by Christ (Luke 10:1). This thread can also be seen in the book of Jeremiah; the prophet announced a twofold seventy-year prophecy concerning the nation of Israel: there would be seventy years of Babylonian captivity and seventy years of rest for the land (2 Chron. 36:21; Jer. 25:11).

The seventy years of captivity began the very year that Jeremiah spoke the prophecy, coinciding with Nebuchadnezzar's first invasion of Judah and the first deportation of Jews to Babylon in 605 B.C. The captivity portion of this prophecy was concluded seventy years later when the Babylonian empire fell to the Medes and Persians, and the

Jewish captives were freed by King Cyrus. This was an event foretold two centuries earlier by Isaiah (Isa. 44:28-45:1). The prophet Daniel, who had been in that first group of captives, understood this event to be the fulfillment of Jeremiah's prophecy (Dan. 9:2).

The second portion of the prophecy of seventy years did not begin until Nebuchadnezzar's third invasion, when he initiated a siege of Jerusalem during King Zedekiah's reign. God commanded Ezekiel to record the exact date this occurred (as relating to Jehoiachin's exile):

Again, in the ninth year, in the tenth month, on the tenth day of the month, the word of the Lord came to me, saying, "Son of man, write down the name of the day, this very day – the king of Babylon started his siege against Jerusalem this very day" (24:1-2).

There are differing opinions among scholars as to the exact date of the siege of Jerusalem, its capture, and its destruction (see "Key Dates" discussion in the *Overview* section). Although Scripture states that the city fell on the ninth day of the fourth month in the eleventh year of Zedekiah's reign, scholars are divided as to whether this refers to 586 or 587 B.C. Jeremy Hughes lists eleven scholars who preferred the first date and then eleven others who preferred the second date.[45] One's preference then affects the siege commencement date. January 15, 588 B.C. is a widely accepted date for the start of the siege, while Sir Robert Anderson prefers December 13, 589 B.C. with the fall of Jerusalem in 587 B.C.

Why did the Lord want the exact date of the beginning of the siege of Jerusalem identified? It was because it was the day that all agriculture stopped in Judah and the seventy years of desolation which was prophesied by Jeremiah began (Jer. 25:11). The Babylonian army sowed fields with rocks, filled wells with debris, destroyed vineyards and fruit groves, and confiscated food stores outside of Jerusalem. When Nebuchadnezzar surrounded Jerusalem with his army, the land began to enjoy its long overdue rest. There would be no planting or harvesting for the next seventy years.

One may wonder why the Lord would determine a seventy-year cessation from agricultural work. The Mosaic Law commanded that the Sabbath day be set aside to rest and to honor God. The Jews, their slaves, and their beasts of burden were all to rest on the Sabbath day. Likewise, the Israelites were to honor a Sabbath year. Every seventh year, the fields, the olive groves, and the vineyards were to receive a full year's rest. Whatever grew naturally during this time was to be freely gleaned by the poor, and anything left would be God's provision for the beasts of the field. Certainly, the sabbatical year would remind the Jews that God owned the land they dwelled on and that they were merely stewards of it (Lev. 25:23).

This was God's Law for the land. Unfortunately, the Jews generally ignored the Sabbath year and, ultimately, God would severely judge them by giving the land seventy years of rest. According to 2 Chronicles 35:14-21, the reason for the specific length of time was to exact the seventy years due to the Lord as His portion (i.e. one-seventh of the 490 years the Jews did not honor the Sabbath year).

Sir Robert Anderson in his book *The Coming Prince* initially placed the commencement date of the land desolation judgment to be on March 14, 589 B.C., but later revised it to December 13, 589 B.C. The seventy years of desolation ended, according to the prophet Haggai, when the foundation of the temple was laid on the base previously completed. Haggai recorded the exact day that the Lord lifted the forced agricultural rest:

> *Consider now from this day forward, from the twenty-fourth day of the ninth month, from the day that the foundation of the Lord's temple was laid – consider it: Is the seed still in the barn? As yet the vine, the fig tree, the pomegranate, and the olive tree have not yielded fruit. But from this day I will bless you* (Hag. 2:18-19).

This event occurred in the second year of Darius (Hag. 2:10). According to Anderson, the Jews who returned from Babylon began to enjoy the benefits of the land again on April 1, 520 B.C.; however, he later revised this date to be December 17, 520 B.C.:

> Now from the tenth day of Tebeth B.C. 589, to the twenty-fourth day of Chisleu B.C. 520, was a period of 25,202 days; and seventy years of 360 days contain exactly 25,200 days. We may conclude, therefore, that the era of the "desolations" was a period of seventy years of 360 days, beginning the day after the Babylonian army invaded Jerusalem, and ending the day before the foundation of the second temple was laid. The date of the Paschal new moon, by which the Jewish year is regulated, was the evening of the 14th March in B. C. 589, and about noon on 1st April B. C. 520. According to the

phases the 1st Nisan in the former year was probably the 15th or 16th March, and in the latter the 1st or 2nd April.[46]

In the tenth edition of *The Coming Prince*, Sir Robert Anderson offered a minor adjustment to his previous dates:

> Now seventy years of 360 days contains exactly 25,200 days; and as the Jewish New Year's day depended on the equinoctial moon, we can assign the 13th December as "the Julian date" of tenth Tebeth 589. And 25,200 days measured from that date ended on the 17th December 520, which was the twenty-fourth day of the ninth month in the second year of Darius of Persia – the very day on which the foundation of the second Temple was laid. (Haggai 2:18, 19.)[47]

The point is that God caused one prophet to record the exact starting date and another the precise ending date of the sabbatical period that the land would enjoy in order to prove that His Word stands sure for all time. Although today we do not know the exact date in which the seventy years of desolation began, if one uses consistent parameters the duration of the prophecy can be validated. A Jewish year is 360 days (Rev. 12:6, 14, 13:5; Dan. 12:7), meaning that there are 25,200 days in 70 Jewish years (i.e. 70 x 360 days = 25,200 days). Thus, the seventy-year period of rest that started on a date in 589 B.C. ended exactly seventy Jewish years later in 520 B.C., the exact time that God restored the land to fruitfulness according to Haggai. God kept His word to His people to the exact day. Just as Jeremiah predicted, and the writings of Ezekiel and Haggai verify, the land of Israel enjoyed seventy years of rest.

Having noted this important date, Ezekiel relates the parable of the boiling pot to illustrate Nebuchadnezzar's invasion of Judah and siege of Jerusalem (vv. 3-14). In chapter 11, some Jewish leaders were instructing the people to ignore Ezekiel's prophecies of imminent doom because they were as safe in Jerusalem as meat was in a cooking caldron. Ezekiel now uses their own analogy to foretell Jerusalem's imminent destruction; the city was not a safe haven against the Babylonian assault. The parable is presented as a poem of three stanzas, each stanza beginning with *"Thus says the Lord God."*

The first stanza describes the cooking activity of the parable: water and choice cuts of meats (God's people) were placed in a pot under which the Babylonians would soon kindle a fire, bringing it to boil (vv.

3-5). The second (vv. 6-9) and third (vv. 9-14) stanzas then explain the parable. In the process of cooking the meat, all Jerusalem's impurities (lewdness of idolatry) broke loose from the encrusted pot and floated to the top; this rank scum made the entire meal unfit for consumption, and thus it was dumped out on a rock (v. 6). The chief impurity noted was that Jerusalem had shed innocent blood and had not felt shame in doing so. They had shed blood on the rocks and did not even try to hide it by covering it with dirt (v. 7). Now God would dump them out of the putrid pot (Jerusalem) on the rocks and the Babylonians would likewise openly spill their blood (v. 8). The holy city would then be known as *"the blood city."*

Whereas the second stanza dealt with the judgment of those in Jerusalem, the third stanza addressed the destruction of the city itself. Before the contents of the pot were to be dumped out, the meat was to be cooked "well done." This illustrated the sweeping slaughter of the Jews by the Babylonians (vv. 9-10). The empty copper pot was then to be placed on hot coals to burn off its polluted deposits; hence, Jerusalem, itself had to be purified by fire to remove all its filth and impurities (vv. 11-12). This could not be accomplished unless the pot has either boiled dry or the water within has been dumped out. Only then can the pot glow (i.e., reach an extreme temperature necessary to burn off all that encrusts it). For centuries the Lord had attempted to clean the pot of its filthy scum by a prophetic scouring pad, but the pot rejected His attempts (v. 13). Consequently, the pot had become so coated with layers of impurities that the only solution was to apply intense heat to thoroughly burn away all that God deemed undesirable (v. 14).

As already observed in the book of Ezekiel, the daily life of the prophet was an illustration to his audience as much as the messages he spoke. Given the extensive judgment coming to Jerusalem, young Jeremiah was told not to marry a wife (Jer. 16:2). This command was not to punish Jeremiah in any way, but rather to save him grief later. Moreover, Jeremiah's singleness would serve as a sign to the people that the future would be catastrophic to family life; many fathers, mothers, daughters, and sons would die by the sword, famine, or disease. Such is the meaning of the painful sign given the Jews in the latter half of this chapter – Ezekiel is told by the Lord that his wife will die and that he is not to mourn for her (vv. 15-24):

Infidelity and Loyalty

> *Son of man, behold, I take away from you the desire of your eyes with*
> *one stroke; yet you shall neither mourn nor weep, nor shall your tears*
> *run down. Sigh in silence, make no mourning for the dead; bind your*
> *turban on your head, and put your sandals on your feet; do not cover*
> *your lips, and do not eat man's bread of sorrow* (vv. 15-17).

Ezekiel was not given much time to prepare himself for this loss; the next morning he told the people God's message and that same evening his wife died (v. 18). L. E. Copper speculates as to how the desire of Ezekiel's eyes was taken:

> The closeness of their relationship was heightened by the reference to
> her as the "delight" of his eyes (v. 16). She would be taken with "one
> blow." This usually described sudden death in battle (1 Sam. 4:17; 2
> Sam. 17:9, 18:7) or from plague or disease (Num. 14:37, 17:35-15,
> 25:8-9). Here it probably meant that she contracted some disease that
> was sudden and fatal.[48]

Although deeply grieved, Ezekiel did as he was commanded and showed no outward expression of mourning for his wife: he did not cry for her or remove his priestly miter. The next morning the people were aroused by these strange events and inquired of him what the passing of his wife and his lack of bereavement signified (v. 19). Because the Jews had profaned God's temple, God would now destroy the desire of their eyes, and the impure city it resided in (vv. 20-21). Additionally, with the fall of Jerusalem many of them would experience the loss of loved ones, just as Ezekiel lost his wife. Because judgment was just and deserved, the Jews were to follow Ezekiel's example and refrain from normal mourning practices for the dead (vv. 22-24). They were to grieve over their multiplied iniquities which deserved God's retribution rather than over the consequences of His judicial wrath.

As a final sign of coming doom, God confirmed that once the news of Jerusalem's fall and destruction reached the captives' ears in Babylon, Ezekiel's temporary dumbness would be ended (vv. 25-27). During his ministry of pronouncing God's judgments on Jerusalem (chps. 4-24), Ezekiel was only permitted to speak when the Lord had a message for His people (3:25-27). Now that his prophecies would be shown to be accurate, the physical restriction would be lifted. Generally speaking, he had been ignored by the people, so this final sign would confirm to the people that Ezekiel had been faithfully speaking for God throughout his ministry.

If your Christian ministry ever seems too arduous to endure, remember how the prophets of old suffered daily hardships, life-threatening rebels, and the loss of loved ones to faithfully stay the course of their God-ordained calling. Hosea was permitted to feel the pain of a lascivious wife who bore him children that were not his in order to better communicate God's pain when His people engage in worldliness and idolatry (Hos. 1). Isaiah was told to strip down and publicly proclaim God's message naked, to better demonstrate how Assyrian invaders would shamefully treat their captives (Isa. 20:1-3). As previously mentioned, Jeremiah was not permitted to take a wife because of his difficult ministry. He was estranged from his family for most of his life, put in stocks, prison often, and once was left for dead in the bottom of a cold, muddy pit. His preaching was continuously rejected for over forty years. Ezekiel was rendered partially mute for over seven years and often appeared in public a disheveled mess. He had to lay on one side or the other for fourteen months and ate a limited daily portion of defiled food throughout that time. Then, after all that, God permitted his wife to die as a final object lesson of the forthcoming sorrow that his exiled countrymen would soon feel concerning their loved ones who had been slaughtered in Jerusalem.

Many men owe the grandeur of their lives to their tremendous difficulties.

— Charles H. Spurgeon

We must learn to regard people less in light of what they do or omit to do, and more in the light of what they suffer.

— Dietrich Bonhoeffer

Our wonderful God knows that one of the best ways to reveal truth to us is through those we humanly associate with. This means that His messengers will often suffer rejection. God Himself sent His own Son from the heights of heaven to be born of a virgin, to suffer the contradiction of sinners for decades in order to personally convey His personal message of love and life. How did mankind recompense Him?

Infidelity and Loyalty

Man mocked His Son, spit on Him, beat Him, whipped Him, and then nailed Him to a tree to suffer an agonizing death. Yet, it was God's plan for Christ to be accursed and to taste death for every man (Heb. 2:9). By doing so became the sole Mediator between a holy God and sinners destined for hell (1 Tim. 2:5). God personally knows the pain and suffering which sin causes in ways we never will, and yet the Lord Jesus was faithful to stay His course, and He promises to assist us to do the same:

> *No temptation has overtaken you except such as is common to man; but God is faithful, who will not allow you to be tempted beyond what you are able, but with the temptation will also make the way of escape, that you may be able to bear it* (1 Cor. 10:13).

> *I can do all things through Christ who strengthens me* (Phil. 4:13).

> *Looking unto Jesus, the author and finisher of our faith, who for the joy that was set before Him endured the cross, despising the shame, and has sat down at the right hand of the throne of God* (Heb. 12:2).

Seeing our supreme example and boundless provision in Christ, may we all be determined to finish well by performing in His strength whatever work He asks of us. Then we too will rejoice in the grace of God and be able to say with Paul: *"I have fought the good fight, I have finished the race, I have kept the faith"* (2 Tim. 4:8).

Meditation

When silent falls the gushing tear, over cheeks grown pale with care;
And on the heart a cross is laid that seems too hard to bear,
Remember what our Lord has said, and trust, in weal or woe,
His holy Word, that changes not, though uttered years ago.

When one by one our treasured hopes like autumn leaves decay,
And they who made our life most dear are borne from us away,
O look beyond the veil of time, where springs of comfort flow,
And trust His Word, that changes not, though uttered years ago.

— Fanny Crosby

Sentencing From East to West
Ezekiel 25

Jerusalem was under siege and would soon fall; there was nothing more to prophesy against Judah. Jehovah's resolve to severely punish His own people for their wickedness meant He would more certainly rebuke those who were not His for their wrongdoings also. This pattern of warning is found in the New Testament as well: *"For the time has come for judgment to begin at the house of God; and if it begins with us first, what will be the end of those who do not obey the gospel of God?"* (1 Pet. 4:17). Because God persistently punishes His own wayward people until He achieves their obedience, what hope do those who completely reject God's authority have of escaping His judgment? None. Hence, the Lord directs Ezekiel to prophesy against the surrounding pagan nations who often afflicted the Jews and contributed to their moral downfall (chps. 25-32). Correspondingly, Jeremiah, still in Jerusalem, also turned his attention from Judah to warn the same surrounding nations of forthcoming judgment (Jer. 46-51).

In the next eight chapters, Ezekiel will deliver messages to Ammon, Moab, and Edom to the east, Philistia to the west, Egypt in the south, and the principle cities of Phoenicia, Tyre and Sidon to the north. He will first identify the specific sins each has committed against God, and then prophesy against each group. Similar decrees against these same nations and cities are found in the writings of Isaiah, Jeremiah, and Amos. Though God's wrath commenced in Jerusalem, He would use the Babylonian invasion to punish the entire region for their wickedness.

One might inquire, "Why would God bring destruction on these Gentile nations who were not under a covenant with Him?" The answer is threefold: First, there were legitimate offenses against God that angered Him. Second, God issued an unconditional promise to Abraham to punish those nations who afflicted his descendants (the future Jewish nation) from which Messiah would come:

151

> *I will make you a great nation; I will bless you and make your name great; and you shall be a blessing. I will bless those who bless you, and I will curse him who curses you; and in you all the families of the earth shall be blessed* (Gen. 12:2-3).

While the Gentiles were not God's people and were not under the Law, they had oppressed the Jews and taken advantage of them for centuries. They had certainly contributed to the corruption of God's people and would therefore receive proper retribution as promised to Abraham. Third, Jehovah wanted the nations to know that He was the one true God and that they must turn from their idolatry and trust in Him. Hence the expression *"you shall know that I am the Lord"* concludes the address to each nation (vv. 5, 7, 11, 17). In fact, the phrase *"I am the Lord"* occurs more often in the book of Ezekiel than in any other book in the Bible.

We often associate God's outpouring of love with received blessings, rather than with His rebuke and chastening, but Ezekiel teaches us that whatever God does to cause us to better understand Him and yield to Him is an expression of His grace. Hence, Ezekiel uses a three-tiered format to address the nations: "because" (to identify their offense), "therefore" (how God will respond to their offense), and then the desired outcome of God's chastening – that *"you shall know that I am the Lord."*

Prophecies Against Ammon (vv. 1-7)

The first people group to be warned was the Ammonites (vv. 1-2). This was his second prophecy against Ammon (the first is recorded in 21:28-32). The people of Ammon were descendants of Lot through his youngest daughter; hence, they were kin to the Moabites. They dwelled just to the north of Moab on the eastern side of the Jordan River. Though Ammon forged an alliance with Judah which precipitated Zedekiah's rebellion against Nebuchadnezzar, the nations had been in frequent conflict with each other since the time the Israelites entered Canaan (Judg. 10:6-11:33; 1 Sam. 11:1-11; 2 Chron. 20:1-30). Their interactions were turbulent. Recall that it was the Ammonites who conspired with the Jewish captain Ishmael to murder godly Gedaliah, even though Ishmael had previously pledged to forego such mercenary activities (Jer. 40:14).

Why was Ammon to be judged? The writings of Jeremiah and Ezekiel reveal at least three separate reasons: First, Ammon had taken possession of several cities belonging to the tribe of Gad (Jer. 49:1). God had used the Assyrians to chasten idolatrous Israel in 722 B.C. Many Jews were consequently taken captive and exiled to Assyria at that time. The Ammonites took advantage of the situation and expanded their territory by invading the troubled land of Israel. Since the Jews were no longer present to defend their inheritance, the Ammonites determined that their land was free for the taking. They were wrong – the land had been allotted to the tribe of Gad by Jehovah, and foreign intrusion would not be tolerated. Also their god, Molech, whom the Ammonites brought with them into Gad's inheritance, would be removed from the land (Jer. 49:3). God's disciplinary judgment against His people was measured for their offense; He would not allow the Ammonites to take advantage of the situation or to add further hardship to His covenant people.

The second indication for judgment was that the Ammonites were a proud people. They trusted in their vast wealth, gloried in their valleys, and believed they were invincible (Jer. 49:4). However, God would show them that they were not; indeed, their capital city of Rabbah would be reduced to rubble by the Babylonians. Additionally, the Israelites would drive the Ammonites out of the Jewish cities in which they had settled (Jer. 49:5).

The third reason God would punish the Ammonites was their proud response to the suffering of His covenant people. Ammon rejoiced that Jerusalem had been conquered and that God's sanctuary had been defiled by Gentiles; they even mocked the Jews during this terrible holocaust (vv. 3, 6). God promised that "because" of their arrogant, callous behavior, He would send the Babylonians to decimate their country (vv. 4-5, 7). Afterwards, the ruins of Rabbah would become stables for camels and folds for sheep.

Prophecies Against Moab (vv. 8-11)

Jeremiah's prophecies against the Moabites are more extensive (Jer. 48:1-47) than Ezekiel's four verses (vv. 8-11). The Moabites were also descendants of Lot (through his older daughter). They were an arrogant people with a history of conflict with the Jews reaching back to the days of Moses (the Moabites tried to impede the Israelites from entering Canaan; Num. 22-24). The Moabites greatly oppressed the Israelites under the reign of King Eglon early in the era of the judges (Judg. 3:12-30).

Ezekiel prophesied against the Moabites for one particular reason: Like the Edomites, Moab had concluded that Israel's destruction proved she was no different than any other nation: *"Look! The house of Judah is like all the nations"* (v. 8). Their envy and hatred of the Jewish people caused them to deny the validity of God's promises to the Jews. Not only did the Moabites rejoice in Israel's devastation, but they had also mocked Jehovah, suggesting that His covenant with Israel was a hoax. Since they thought that Israel was no different than any other nation, and Israel's God no different than the gods of the Gentiles, Moab too would be invaded by Babylonian armies and decimated (vv. 9-10). Then, they would know that Jehovah is Lord (v. 11).

Jeremiah's specific prophecies against Moab require some historical information to understand. With God's permission, Moses permitted the tribe of Reuben to settle on the eastern side of the Jordan River, rather than within the land of Canaan. The Reubenites settled in the cities of Nebo and Kiriathaim (Num. 32:37-38; Josh. 13:19). These cities and others in the region (like Heshbon) were later captured by the Moabites. Jeremiah pronounced judgment on these cities (Jer. 48:1-2). Just as Moab had overcome the Reubenites and occupied the region which had been assigned to them, God would now remove the Moabites from the land.

Moab had not previously experienced the cruel reality of invasion and exile, but Moab's immorality and conceit demanded God's remedy (Jer. 48:11-13). In fact, Isaiah, Jeremiah, and Ezekiel all agree as to why Moab deserved to be punished – they were proud. Moab magnified himself against the Lord (Jer. 48:26, 42). Moab was exceedingly proud, arrogant, and high-minded (Jer. 48:29). More than a century earlier, the prophet Isaiah had proclaimed the same truth, saying, *"We have heard of the pride of Moab – He is very proud"* (Isa. 16:6). Pride has been the downfall of many people. Commenting on the evidences and effects of pride, Matthew Henry writes:

> We must be clothed with humility; *for the proud in spirit* are those that cannot bear to be trampled upon, but grow outrageous, and fret themselves, when they are hardly bested. That will break a proud

man's heart, which will not break a humble man's sleep. Mortify pride, therefore, and a lowly spirit will easily be reconciled to a low condition.[49]

He that has a low opinion of his own knowledge and powers will submit to better information; such a person may be informed and improved by revelation: but the proud man, conceited of his own wisdom and understanding, will undertake to correct even divine wisdom itself, and prefer his own shallow reasonings to the revelations of infallible truth and wisdom. Note, we must abase ourselves before God if we would be either truly wise or good: *For the wisdom of this world is foolishness with God*, v. 19.[50]

True humility is selfless behavior that honors the Lord and yearns to serve others. From Genesis to Revelation, the Bible declares God's contempt for pride and His commitment to judge it. As the proverb says, *"Pride goes before destruction and a haughty spirit before a fall. Better to be of a humble spirit with the lowly, than to divide the spoil with the proud"* (Prov. 16:18-19). Both James and Peter proclaim that *"God resists the proud, but gives grace to the humble"* (Jas. 4:6; 1 Pet. 5:5). Solomon wrote, *"When pride comes, then comes shame; but with the humble is wisdom"* (Prov. 11:2). The psalmist declared, *"The sacrifices of God are a broken spirit, a broken and a contrite heart"* (Ps. 51:17). The opposite of pride is a broken spirit and a contrite heart.

None are more unjust in their judgments of others than those who have a high opinion of themselves.

— Charles H. Spurgeon

To be broken before the Lord is to be a qualified recipient of His grace. Our failures should lead to personal brokenness, which should then cause us to cast ourselves upon the Lord in a way that we were hesitant to do beforehand. Our victories, won by His grace, only prompt us to praise His name! The outcome of testing, then, is that the believer knows and trusts the Lord with a greater patience and confidence than he or she had before. This is why the Lord longs for us to come to Him with all of life's burdens.

Prophecies Against Edom (vv. 12-14)

The Edomites were the descendants of Jacob's twin brother Esau, who settled in the region south of Moab and just east of the Dead Sea. The sibling conflict that began after Esau sold Jacob his birthright for a bowl of bean soup continued among their descendants. Edom was a heathen nation that loathed the Jews, their fraternal brothers (Ezek. 35; Obad. 15-16). Like Ammon and Moab, Edom had a long history of hostility to the Jewish nation (e.g., 1 Sam. 14:47; 1 Kgs. 9:26-28; 2 Kgs. 8:20-21), which also commenced as the Israelites were journeying to Canaan. At that time, the Edomites refused to allow the Israelites to pass through their borders, which added many more miles to their route (Num. 20:14-21).

Like the Ammonites, the Edomites had assumed Israel was a nation no different from any other. Thus they undermined God's Word and His special relationship with the Jewish people (v. 8). However, Edom's sin was greater than Moab's because the Edomites had actually assisted Nebuchadnezzar in defeating Judah (v. 12). Edom had sided with Babylon in the defeat of Egypt in 605 B.C., but in 593 B.C. agreed to be part of an alliance, which included Judah and other nations, to rebel against Nebuchadnezzar (Jer. 27:1-7). However, when Babylon came against Jerusalem in 588 B.C., double-crossing Edom switched sides again and assisted Babylon in brutally conquering the Jewish nation (Jer. 49:7-22).

Jeremiah posed a logical statement for the Edomites to consider: if the Lord was determined to cause the surrounding nations, who had no fraternal ties with the Jews, to drink from His cup of wrath, how much more judgment did the Edomites deserve for oppressing their own distant kin (Jer. 49:12)? Jeremiah explains why God's wrath would be poured out on the Edomites: *"'Your fierceness has deceived you, the pride of your heart, O you who dwell in the clefts of the rock, who hold the height of the hill! Though you make your nest as high as the eagle, I will bring you down from there,' says the Lord"* (Jer. 49:16). Edom's pride had summoned God's judgment; they were high on themselves, but God would bring them low.

Pride is a barrier to all spiritual progress.

— H. A. Ironside

Ezekiel said Edom's actions were motivated by hate and revenge (v. 12). Consequently, God said He was furious and was going to stretch out His hand to execute His revenge on Edom. The capital city of Teman would be destroyed and the entire land as far south as Dedan in northern Arabia would be ravaged (vv. 13-14).

Prophecies Against Philistia (vv. 15-17)

The Philistines dwelt directly to the west of the Judean foothills and had been the enemies of Israel since Joshua led the Israelites into Canaan (Judg. 3:1-4). During the era of the Judges, the Philistines had repeatedly attempted to expand their dominion by invading Jewish territory. The conflict raged back and forth for hundreds of years until King David subdued Philistia (2 Sam. 8). King Solomon continued to hold Philistia with a firm grip, but after the Jewish kingdom split during the reign of Solomon's son Rehoboam, the wrangling for superiority began again between these two people groups.

Jeremiah informed the Philistines that the sword of the Lord was against them. He specifically prophesied against their two chief cities, Gaza and Ashkelon, which would both be devastated (Jer. 47:6). Ezekiel explained one of the reasons that Philistia deserved to be punished: *"Because the Philistines dealt vengefully and took vengeance with a spiteful heart, to destroy because of the old hatred"* (v. 15). Prompted by deep hatred and a vengeful spirit, the Philistines for centuries had opposed the Jews and had repeatedly tried to remove them from the land which Jehovah had given them.

For opposing Him and inflicting much harm to His people, God would now "cut off" the coastal people, the Cherethites (vv. 16-17). The Cherethites, or Kerethites, are mentioned ten times in Scripture and refer to the Philistine people (1 Sam. 30:14; Zeph. 2:5). Apparently the reason Ezekiel spoke of the Philistines as Cherethites here was to apply the meaning of the Hebrew root word *karath*, from which their name is derived. *Karath* means "cut off" or "destroy" and that was what God was going to do to them, that they might know for certain that He was the Lord.

The prophet Jeremiah extended to Ammon and Moab the promise of future restoration and blessing, to be realized in the Millennial Kingdom of Christ. However, proud and vengeful Edom and Philistia were not extended such hope. God hates pride and must judge it; yet,

Infidelity and Loyalty

He bestows grace and peace abundantly to all those who learn lowliness and submission through His chastening.

Meditation

> With broken heart and contrite sigh,
> A trembling sinner, Lord, I cry;
> Thy pardoning grace is rich and free:
> O God, be merciful to me.
>
> Far off I stand with tearful eyes,
> Nor dare uplift them to the skies;
> But Thou dost all my anguish see:
> O God, be merciful to me.

— Cornelius Elven

The Judgment of Tyre
Ezekiel 26-27

Jeremiah briefly prophesied against the Phoenician cities of Tyre and Sidon, when he listed all the surrounding regions that would be conquered in the Babylonian invasion (Jer. 25:15-26). He later stated that Phoenicia was going to be punished for assisting the Philistines in their assault against the Jews (Jer. 47:4). Ezekiel, on the other hand, devotes the next three chapters to the capital city of Phoenicia: to declare judgment against Tyre (chp. 26), to lament the city's destruction (chp. 27), and to condemn Tyre's king (chp. 28). This long dissertation stands in sharp contrast to the previous chapter, where Ezekiel uttered four brief prophecies, one each against the nations of Ammon, Moab, Edom, and Philistia. This extra narrative is partially required to more fully reveal the King of Tyre's wicked character and whom he represents – Lucifer himself.

Ezekiel continues to apply the "because…therefore…I am the Lord" format of the previous chapter in confronting Tyre. Besides aiding Philistia against Israel, the Lord reveals another reason for Tyre's destruction: *"Son of man, because Tyre has said against Jerusalem, 'Aha! She is broken who was the gateway of the peoples; now she is turned over to me; I shall be filled; she is laid waste'"* (26:2). The month of this prophecy is unknown, but *"the eleventh year"* of Jehoiachin's exile would place it just prior to the fall of Jerusalem in 587 to 586 B.C.

Why was God going to judge Tyre? Scripture reveals a couple of reasons: First, Tyre's future delight in hearing of Jerusalem's destruction. Second, her proud deceit in causing King Zedekiah to ignore the prophecies of Jeremiah and to rebel against Babylonian rule (Jer. 52:2-3). Tyre had sent delegates to Jerusalem to promote the idea of nations banding together to oppose Nebuchadnezzar about five years before Zedekiah actually agreed to the plan (Jer. 27:3). As a result of this rebellion, Nebuchadnezzar brought his armies westward and focused their attack on Jerusalem and Judah first. Thus, Tyre's influence on Zedekiah delayed Babylon's attack on Tyre for years.

Furthermore, the decimation of Jerusalem meant that Tyre's main competitor for trade routes in the region was no longer a threat. Situated on the Mediterranean Sea, the coastal city of Tyre dominated commerce by sea in the region, but Jerusalem was the hub for overland caravans. With their commercial rival out of the way, Tyre was gloating about the trade monopoly that would result.

Tyre had no concern for the loss of life in Jerusalem, but rather how they could profit from the situation – this angered the Lord! The Lord promised to stir up *"many nations,"* like a terrible sea tempest, to pound against the city walls of Tyre until it was plundered and then destroyed (26:3-4). Afterwards, Tyre would be nothing more than *"a barren rock"* (the meaning of Tyre's name) in which fishing nets could be laid out to dry (26:5). Tyre was a city consisting of two parts; the main trade center was located on an island about a half mile from the mainland portion of the city. The island portion of Tyre was heavily fortified. Ezekiel prophesied that those living in her "daughter villages" (i.e., those dwelling on the mainland) would be ravaged and slaughtered by the Babylonians (26:6).

Ezekiel then describes Nebuchadnezzar's confrontation with Tyre (which began in 585 B.C., a year after Jerusalem was destroyed) in more detail (26:7-14). After thirteen years of siege, the mainland portion of Tyre fell and was abandoned. Most of her inhabitants sought shelter in the island fortress, whose walls went straight down into the sea and were 150 feet high on the landward side. Tyre's island defenses held because the Babylonians could not prevent the city from being resupplied by sea. However, Tyre's commercial prosperity was shattered and their king, Ethbaal III, was captured and taken to Babylon. Tyre was now subject to Babylon.

Ezekiel then switches from "he" (Nebuchadnezzar) to "they" to speak of other nations arriving after the Babylonians to confront Tyre (26:12). One of these nations would be Greece over two centuries later. Tyre rebelled against Alexander the Great, who destroyed the mainland portion of the city and then built a causeway (a land bridge that was 200 feet wide and a half mile long) to attack the island fortress. The building materials were scavenged from the conquered mainland portion of the city. This fulfilled the first statement of Ezekiel's prophecy: *"break down your walls and destroy your pleasant houses;*

they will lay your stones, your timber, and your soil in the midst of the water" (26:12).

After the causeway, naval battering rams, and several floating catapult towers were complete, Alexander was able to hammer at the walls of the city until eventually a breech on a southern wall was achieved and his forces entered and captured the city in 332 B.C. The seven-month siege was over. Nearly ten thousand of Tyre's citizens perished in the onslaught (including 2,000 crucified on the beach); another 30,000 were sold into slavery.[51] Alexander then destroyed much of the city – the once famed commercial metropolis was no more. It was later partially rebuilt by the Romans, before being destroyed again by invading Muslims in 1291 A.D. This fulfilled the second part of Ezekiel's prophecy: those following Nebuchadnezzar would ensure that Tyre *"shall never be rebuilt"* (26:14). Although the island has been inhabited through the centuries, the ancient island fortress of Tyre was never fully rebuilt, just as Ezekiel predicted. The archeological remains of the ancient city are still observable to this day.

The destruction of Tyre, thought once to be an impenetrable city, would cause immense fear and trepidation among the coastal communities dependent on her commerce (26:15-16). Those who had previously profited from her trade would sing mournfully of Tyre's lost power, prestige, and wealth as they pondered their own financial misfortune (26:17-18). Previously, the prophet likened the battering-rams of the invaders to the sea waves pounding against Tyre's walls (26:3), but now Ezekiel prophesied that Tyre would drown in the depths of the sea and be remembered no more (26:19). In a poetic sense of finality, Tyre would descend into the pit and would never rise again (referring to the Old Testament equivalent of "the grave" or *Sheol*, the realm of disembodied spirits; 26:20). Though many in the region would long for Tyre's reemergence to financial prosperity and commercial supremacy, it was not going to happen – ever (26:21)!

Because Tyre's destruction was certain, a funeral dirge mourning her loss could commence immediately (27:1-2). To heighten the emotional effect of the lament, Ezekiel first speaks of Tyre's pride by poetically likening Tyre to the majestic sailing ship that was the master of the various seaports of the nations (27:3-4). She prided herself on being the gateway of commerce – a major seaport in the world. Hence, the vessel represents the best that the nations had to offer in trade: the ship's hull was crafted from the finest pine trees from Senir, its mast from the cedars of Lebanon, its oars from the oaks of Bashan, and its deck planking from cypress wood from Cyprus which was inlaid with ivory (27:5-6). The sails of the vessel were sown from fine embroidered Egyptian linen and the brilliant awnings of blue and purple were colored with the dyes of Elishah (27:7). The crew of the ship were veteran sailors from Sidon and Arvad, and master craftsmen from Gebal (27:8-9).

After describing her glory in former days, Ezekiel considers all of Tyre's vast trading partners and the goods that once flowed through Tyre's hub-port (27:10-25). Tyre was protected by the best soldiers money could buy: mercenaries form Persia, Lydia, and Libya (27:10). Ezekiel then provided a list of twenty-three nations (business associates) and their various articles of commerce with Tyre: silver, iron, tin, lead, bronze, slaves, horses, mules, ivory tusks, ebony, fabrics, embroidered linen, coral, rubies, wheat, olive oil, balm, honey, wine, wool, cassia, blankets, lambs, rams, goats, various spices, precious stones and gold (vv. 12-25). Tyre was greatly admired and many nations both benefitted from and contributed to her glory through trade – they were like ships anchoring alongside the flag ship of the merchant marines (27:11).

In the final section of the chapter Ezekiel poetically describes the disastrous shipwreck and sinking of Tyre (27:26-36). Thinking that she was invincible, Tyre, seeking even greater commercial exploits, sailed on the high seas even when it was unsafe to do so (27:26). Navigating the Mediterranean Sea in the fall and winter months was dangerous because the weather was unpredictable and a strong tempest might quickly emerge and last for days (Acts 27:9-26). Gale force winds from the east/northeast were particularly feared as these might blow a ship out into the Atlantic Ocean where it would be lost forever. Ezekiel prophesied that such an easterly wind (i.e., the Babylonians) would smash Tyre's hull and cause her to break up and sink; all of her commercial enterprises would be suddenly terminated (27:27).

When the news of Tyre's sinking reached her trade partners, they would be both shocked and appalled (27:28-29). They will mourn, as one who had lost a beloved family member, by shaving their heads, rolling in ashes, and wearing sackcloth (27:28-32). Their deep remorse is not for Tyre particularly, but for their own financial losses resulting from her demise. Ezekiel concludes his dirge by declaring of Tyre: *"When your wares went out by sea, you satisfied many people; you enriched the kings of the earth with your many luxury goods and your merchandise. But you are broken by the seas in the depths of the waters"* (27:33-34). All those who enjoyed prosperity through Tyre's commerce will be horrified at her loss and will hiss these words: *"You will become a horror, and be no more forever"* (27:35-36). The entire scene is a foretaste of how the entire world will bemoan the collapse of the Antichrist's lucrative financial system at the conclusion of the Tribulation Period just prior to Christ's second coming to the earth (Rev. 18).

The rich have many fair-weather friends, but once despoiled of their wealth, the selfish nature of those who benefitted from them becomes quite apparent. Both Tyre and her constituents were full of themselves. They reeked with the pride of their accomplishments; they had no fear of the One who really controlled all their assets. H. A. Ironside suggests genuine humility is evidence that one possesses God-fearing wisdom:

> Nothing is more detestable in God's sight than pride on the part of creatures who have absolutely nothing to be proud of. This was the condemnation of the devil – self-exaltation. ... Humility is an indication of true wisdom. It characterizes the man who has learned to judge himself correctly in the presence of God.[52]

Although our determination and natural abilities may secure for us fame and wealth, such high status will be short-lived if accompanied by pride and perverse doings: *"The righteousness of the blameless will direct his way aright, but the wicked will fall by his own wickedness"* (Prov. 13:5). Being wealthy is not condemned in Scripture, but God's people are to use what they have to honor the Lord; they are neither to love money, nor to trust in their riches (1 Tim. 6:9-10, 17-19). Let us, therefore, not trust in the uncertainty of riches, but rather let us put our confidence in the Lord, who freely bestows on us all good things to enjoy.

Meditation

I enjoy the luxury of few things to care for.

— Hudson Taylor

Infidelity and Loyalty

What wealth have you, if you have not got Christ? If Christ is the object before you, will all the things that fret you take Christ from you? All the things you long for, will they give you more of Christ?

— G. V. Wigram

Pride and Beauty Denounced
Ezekiel 28

Ezekiel turns his attention from pronouncing judgment on Tyre and lamenting her destruction to condemning Tyre's proud ruler, *"the Prince of Tyre"* (vv. 1-10). However, there was an evil spiritual power behind this wicked prince that was stirring up opposition to God's authority in Tyre. Ezekiel refers to him as *"the King of Tyre"* (vv. 11-19). Isaiah calls him by name, *"Lucifer"* (Isa. 14:12). The prophet first rebukes the prince, a man who wanted to be a god (vv. 1-2), and then rebukes the king, the beautiful cherub who wanted to be God (vv. 16-18).

The prince of Tyre whom Ezekiel addresses is Ethbaal III, who ruled over Tyre from 591-573 B.C. Like the pharaohs in ancient Egypt, the rulers of Tyre apparently believed they were deities. Through financial savvy and commerce, the leader of Tyre had made his city quite prosperous, but the accomplishment went to his head – he was full of himself (vv. 4-5). To confront Ethbaal's thinking that his wisdom was a proof of divinity, Ezekiel inquires of him: *"Behold, you are wiser than Daniel! There is no secret that can be hidden from you!"* (v. 3). The prophet Daniel was known throughout the Babylonian empire at this time for knowing and interpreting Nebuchadnezzar's untold dream, a feat that no other wise man in Babylon could do. Was the prince of Tyre wiser than Daniel, who openly proclaimed that his wisdom was not his own, but came from Jehovah (Dan. 2:27-28)? The answer was obviously "no," hence implying that Ethbaal was not much of a god, if a mere man like Daniel was wiser than he.

Furthermore, Babylon, the fierce and ruthless nation whom Daniel served, was about to prove that the prince of Tyre was no god (vv. 6-7). The Babylonians would be unimpressed with his wisdom and beauty and would overcome Tyre's defenses and remove the prince's splendor and wealth (vv. 8-9). Ezekiel prophesied that Ethbaal would then be cast down into the pit, and experience *"the death of the uncircumcised"*

(v. 10), a well-understood social expression among Jews to infer disgust and humiliation (1 Sam. 17:26).

Ezekiel's final lament over Tyre begins in verse 11 with the important transition from *"the prince of Tyre"* to *"the king of Tyre"*. The prophet used the Hebrew word *nagiyd* when speaking of Tyre's human leader in the first ten verses, but switches to *melek* when referring to the more majestic imperial figure actually controlling Tyre. Ezekiel invokes *melek* somewhat sparingly in his book to show the distinction between the authority of a local governor over a particular people group and someone exercising power as an emperor over a nation or nations (e.g., "the king of Babylon" and "the king of Egypt"; 17:2 and 30:22, respectively). This is why Nebuchadnezzar is referred to as *"the king of kings from the north"* (26:7). The use of *melek* in verse 12 is to make clear that the reader understands that the individual of higher authority and power than "the prince of Tyre" is now being discussed.

Like the prince, the king of Tyre was also wise and beautiful, but far more exceedingly so. Ezekiel refers to him as the anointed cherub that was created in perfection, sheathed with precious stones and equipped inherently to worship God through music and was in the Garden of Eden (v. 13). While the first mention of humanly devised music is recorded in Genesis 4:21, this was not the first occurrence of music in the history of creation. Lucifer was created with the provision of timbrels and flutes to offer music before God:

> *You were in Eden, the garden of God; every precious stone was your covering: the sardius, topaz, and diamond, beryl, onyx, and jasper, sapphire, turquoise, and emerald with gold. The workmanship of your timbrels* [tambourine] *and pipes was prepared for you on the day you were created* (Ezek. 28:13).

It is noted that many modern versions of the Bible translate "timbrels" (*toph*) and "pipes" (*neqeb*) as "settings" and "sockets," respectively. The Hebrew *neqeb* is only found here in the Old Testament, but *toph* is translated "timbrels," referring to a musical instrument, throughout the Old Testament. Context would then indicate that *neqeb* likely speaks of a flute-like instrument. Perhaps, Lucifer led the angels in worship through initiating music. Regardless, worship (accompanied by music) was being offered by spiritual beings to their Creator, even before man was created. As the anointed covering cherub, Lucifer may have had a view of God's majesty and glory that no other created being was afforded – he was with God on His holy mountain and enjoyed a state of perfection (vv. 14-15).

However, Satan became obsessed with his own beauty and wanted to be worshipped as God. In mutiny, the "light bearer," or Lucifer as Isaiah calls him, became the ruler of darkness and immersed the world in deceit, corruption, and violence (vv. 16-18). Isaiah describes Satan's pride and the consequences of it:

> *How you are fallen from heaven, O Lucifer, son of the morning! How you are cut down to the ground, you who weakened the nations! For you have said in your heart: "I will ascend into heaven, I will exalt my throne above the stars of God; I will also sit on the mount of the congregation on the farthest sides of the north; I will ascend above the heights of the clouds, I will be like the Most High." Yet you shall be brought down to Sheol, to the lowest depths of the Pit* (Isa. 14:12-15).

Lucifer was a spectacular creature that had been created to bring God glory; however, his prestigious position in creation and unique vantage point of God's preeminence led him to be dissatisfied with God's creation order. Lucifer no longer desired to cover himself and protect the sanctity of God's glory. He would no longer conceal his personal glory in God's presence. His insubordination was energized by his pride to be "lifted up" and to be like "the Most High" (Isa. 14:14). Lucifer wanted the supremacy in heaven and led a rebellion against Almighty God (Rev. 12:4), who responded by casting him off the Holy Mount (v. 16) and destining him to eternal judgment in the Lake of Fire (Matt. 25:41). Isaiah 42:8 reads, *"I am the Lord: that is My name; and My glory will I not give to another, neither My praise to carved images."* What competing glories will God tolerate in His presence? None.

In every aspect, what is described to us in Scripture about the four living creatures (Rev. 4), the seraphim (Isa. 6), and the cherubim (Ezek. 1) reflects the glory of Christ. What is not described to us is an intrinsic glory that God wants covered in His presence; the wings of these spiritual beings accomplish this. It is not that what is covered is not beautiful; rather, it is not what the Holy Spirit wants us to be occupied with. There is no description of the seraphim's wings, except in number, which provides essential information to their ministry. (They fly above the throne of God with two wings, and they conceal their own intrinsic glory with four wings.) Their wings are mentioned to highlight their use in God-ordained ministry, not to emphasize their aerodynamic abilities. The specific language ensures all glory is of and to God.

Understanding the symbolic significance of each of the revealed portions of these spiritual beings is integral to better appreciating the fuller glory of God; else why would the Holy Spirit have purposefully provided the extra revelation? The importance of the symbolic ministry of the four living creatures, the seraphim, and the cherubim before the throne of God has been acknowledged by many theologians.

Matthew Henry: [Why do the Seraphim cover themselves in God's presence?] "This bespeaks their great humility and reverence in their attendance upon God, for He is greatly feared." "... in the presence of God, they cover ... because, being conscious of an infinite distance from the divine perfections, they are ashamed to show their faces."[53]

Albert Barnes: [Why do the Seraphim cover their faces?] "This is designed, doubtless, to denote the reverence and awe inspired by the immediate presence of God." "The seraphim stood covered, or as if concealing themselves as much as possible, in token of their nothingness and unworthiness in the presence of the Holy One."[54]

William MacDonald: "The creatures symbolize those attributes of God which are seen in creation: His majesty, power, swiftness, and wisdom." Of the Seraphim he writes, "with four wings for reverence and two for service. These celebrate the holiness of God."[55]

Warren Wiersbe: "These creatures [seraphim] symbolize the glory and power of God."[56] "These creatures [the Four Living Creatures] signify the wisdom of God (full of eyes) and proclaim the holiness of God."[57]

P. P. Enns: "*Cherubim* are ... created with indescribable powers and beauty .... Their main purpose and activity might be summarized in this way: they are proclaimers and protectors of God's glorious presence, His sovereignty, and His holiness."[58]

The willingness of these powerfully created beings to cover their own intrinsic glories to ensure only God's glories are seen and appreciated in heaven serves as a personal salute to the glory and authority of God. Unfortunately, there is a similar symbol of God's authority that often receives little acknowledgement among Christians today. Paul instructs that when believers are in God's presence for the spiritual exercise of prayer or prophecy (teaching), there should be a visible salute to His authority. This salute, or sign of authority, is the covered head of the woman and the uncovered head of the man: *"For this cause ought the woman to have* [a sign of authority] *on her head"* (1 Cor. 11:10). The veil is a symbol of submission to God's authority; by wearing it, the woman shows visible agreement with divine order (1 Cor. 11:3).

The man is God's representative (God's glory) and is to remain uncovered; however, the woman, representing man's glory, is to be covered (1 Cor. 11:4-7). Long hair is a fitting covering for the woman, but this covering is also a glory in itself (1 Cor. 11:15), which must be covered so as not to compete with God's glory. When the brothers remain uncovered and the sisters covered during church meetings, all competing glories are thus concealed and only God's glory is seen. In this way, only God's glory, as represented by uncovered men, is seen by God and the angels overlooking the assembly. A visible salute to Christ's headship and God's order is thus affirmed for all to see. This pictures the scene in heaven as seraphim and cherubim cover their own glories with their wings in the presence of God, so God's glory is preeminent (Isa. 6:2; Ezek. 1:11). The angels are at present learning about submission to divine order from observing the Church's submission to it (1 Cor. 11:10; 1 Pet. 1:12). In a spectacular way, God is using the Church to testify to all creation of His manifold wisdom (Eph. 3:10).

Given this understanding, Watchman Nee, who was martyred for Christ in 1972 (after being in a Chinese labor camp for twenty years), explains why the head covering (an important sign of submission to God's authority) will always be opposed by Satan:

> Today woman has a sign of authority on her head because of the angels, that is, as a testimony to the angels. Only the sisters in the church can testify to this, for the women of the world know nothing of it. Today when the sisters have the sign of authority on their heads, they bear the testimony that, "I have covered my head so that I do not

have my own head, for I do not seek to be head. My head is veiled, and I have accepted man as head, and to accept man as head means that I have accepted Christ as head and God as head. But some of you angels have rebelled against God." This is what it meant "because of the angels."

I have on my head a sign of authority. I am a woman with my head covered. This is a most excellent testimony to the angels, to the fallen and to the unfallen ones. No wonder Satan persistently opposes the matter of head covering. It really puts him to shame. We are doing what he has failed to do. What God did not receive from the angels, He now has from the church.[59]

As part of his rebellion against God, Satan continues to beguile believers to ignore divine revelation and to forgo visibly saluting God's authority through the practice of the head covering. God knows we need a constant reminder of His authority. Seeing what happened to Lucifer, do we dare come into His presence without saluting His glory? The cherubim show us that true humility willingly displaces self and exalts God in whatever way He deems best.

This lament concludes with a prophecy that blends God's dealing with both rebels: The prince of Tyre will be cast down before his enemies (v. 17). The king of Tyre, Satan, will be cast to the earth in the Tribulation Period (Rev. 12:7-10). The city of the prince will be consumed by fire (v. 18), but Satan shall burn forever in the Lake of Fire (Rev. 20:10). *"The Lord knows how to ... reserve the unjust unto the day of judgment to be punished"* (2 Pet. 2:9) and He will be vindicated by all who rebel against Him!

Prophecies Against Sidon (vv. 20-24)

Jeremiah had previously foretold that judgment would fall on both the Phoenician cities of Tyre and Sidon because they assisted the Philistines in their assault against the Jews (Jer. 47:4). Sidon was situated only twenty miles north of Tyre and both cities had cooperated in sinning against the Lord's people, as already described in Ezekiel 26. Ezekiel is told to turn his face from Tyre and look further northward to the city of Sidon and prophesy against her (vv. 20-21). The Lord had a specific message for Sidon:

170

Behold, I am against you, O Sidon; I will be glorified in your midst;
and they shall know that I am the Lord, when I execute judgments in
her and am hallowed in her (v. 22).

The Lord would punish Sidon's arrogance with pestilence and
brutal violence (speaking of the forthcoming Babylonian invasion).
Their devastation would result in two positive outcomes: First, because
Jehovah's prophets had specifically foretold their judgment, the
inhabitants of Sidon would know that Jehovah was the Lord (v. 23).
Second, there no longer would be any nations around Israel that would
influence her not to walk with the Lord (v. 24). It is pertinent to note
that Baal worship was popularized in Israel by Jezebel, the daughter of
Ethbaal, the king of Sidon. She married wicked King Ahab some three
centuries earlier, which ushered in the darkest days of idolatry in
Israel's history. However, after the Babylonians decimated the region,
no nation encompassing Israel would be able to wrongly influence
them against the Lord.

Israel's Future Blessing (vv. 25-26)

The pronouncement of judgments on surrounding Gentile nations is
interrupted with a brief statement that God will honor His covenant
with Jacob (and Abraham before him) to settle his descendants in the
land of Israel (v. 25). After Jehovah had purged the idolatry from His
people through chastening, He would end their exile and begin again
with them. Regrettably, in the interim between the conclusion of the
Babylonian exile and the first advent of Christ, the Jewish people
became legalistic and calloused to the things of God. They even
rejected and crucified their Messiah, whom God sent to bless them.

Consequently, the Jews to this day are not dwelling safety in Israel,
nor are they esteemed among the nations. Ezekiel's prophecy will not
be fulfilled until the millennial reign of Christ on the earth. After the
nations witness God's jealousy for and faithfulness to the Jewish
people, *"then they* [the nations] *shall know that I am the Lord their
God"* (v. 26). Zechariah prophesied that, *"In those days ten men from
every language of the nations shall grasp the sleeve of a Jewish man,
saying, 'Let us go with you, for we have heard that God is with you'"*
(Zech. 8:23). In a coming day all the nations of the earth will honor and
worship the Jewish Messiah, the Lord Jesus Christ!

Meditation

The Lord, that sits above the skies, derides their rage below;
He speaks with vengeance in His eyes, and strikes their spirits
through.
"I call Him My eternal Son, and raise Him from the dead;
I make My holy hill His throne, and wide His kingdom spread.

"Ask Me, My Son, and then enjoy the utmost heathen lands:
Thy rod of iron shall destroy the rebel that withstands."
Be wise, ye rulers of the earth, obey the anointed Lord,
Adore the King of heavenly birth, and tremble at His Word.

— Isaac Watts

Despoiling Egypt and Deflating Pride
Ezekiel 29

The Lord instructed Ezekiel to turn from Sidon in the northeast and face Egypt in the southwest and prophesy against her (vv. 1-2). His first of seven prophecies against Egypt (vv. 1-16) contains three sections, each concluding with *"then they will know that I am the Lord"* (vv. 6, 9, 16). This complex message was delivered in the tenth year and tenth month of Jehoiachin's captivity (January 587 B.C.), meaning that Jerusalem was nearing the end of its long, ruthless siege. Ezekiel begins by indicting the Pharaoh of Egypt and listing Egypt's sins deserving divine retribution.

Some understanding of key historical events at this time is necessary to better understand Pharaoh's offense. Nebuchadnezzar came against Jerusalem in 605 B.C. because Pharaoh Necho II invaded Babylon. The Egyptians were soundly defeated at Carchemish, and then Nebuchadnezzar pursued their retreating army down into the Sinai Peninsula. While in the region, Nebuchadnezzar wanted to despoil and subdue Jerusalem, who had been loyal to Egypt. This desired campaign was interrupted by his father's death and Nebuchadnezzar was required to quickly return to Babylon to ensure his succession to the throne. After receiving the crown in August 605 B.C., he returned to Israel and began his attack on Jerusalem in September 605 B.C. After conquering the city, a group of Jewish captives, Daniel among them, was taken back to Babylon.

Nebuchadnezzar returned to this region again in 601 B.C. to invade Egypt. Both sides suffered heavy losses. Babylon's failed attempt in Egypt encouraged King Jehoiakim to rebel against Babylon that same year and realign with Pharaoh. Nebuchadnezzar besieged Jerusalem and captured it in 597 B.C., and then took a second group of captives to Babylon. This included Ezekiel and King Jehoiachin who had reigned only three months after Jehoiakim's death. The Babylonian Chronicles (its contents were first published in 1956) indicate that Nebuchadnezzar captured Jerusalem on March 16, 597 B.C.

At that time, Nebuchadnezzar appointed Zedekiah as a vassal king of Judah. A few years later, against Jeremiah's warning, Zedekiah aligned again with Egypt (Pharaoh Hophra) and revolted against Babylon. Nebuchadnezzar responded by invading Judah and putting Jerusalem under siege again in December 589 B.C. (perhaps January 588 B.C.), which was the tenth day of the tenth month of the ninth year of Zedekiah's reign (24:1; 2 Kgs. 25:1). Despite Hophra's promise, Egypt was unable to suppress the Babylonians and assist Jerusalem. The Babylonian Chronicles puts the fall of Jerusalem in the summer of 587 B.C. (the eleventh year of Jehoiachin's captivity), which was the eleventh year and fifth month of Zedekiah's reign (2 Kgs. 25:4-10). Tens of thousands of Jews were slaughtered and the city and the temple were destroyed the following summer (586 B.C.).

Pharaoh Hophra had promised to assist Judah, which prompted Zedekiah to rebel against Jehovah's will revealed through Jeremiah (i.e., to not resist His chastening rod – the Babylonian armies). For that reason, Egypt and its Pharaoh would receive Jehovah's retribution. Pharaoh thought he was god, that he owned Egypt, and ruled the Nile River like a powerful sea monster (v. 3). However, Pharaoh would soon learn that he was no match for his Creator. Jehovah promised metaphorically to drag Egypt from her life source, the Nile, and cast her in the desert to starve and wither away (vv. 4-5).

God hates pride and, as shown through Pharaoh's humbling, the Lord knows the best means to remove the stench of vanity from our hearts!

> The way we respond to criticism pretty much depends on the way we respond to praise. If praise humbles us, then criticism will build us up. But if praise inflates us, then criticism will crush us; and both responses lead to our defeat.
> — Warren Wiersbe

Next Ezekiel identifies the main reason for Jehovah's anger towards the Egyptians: *"Because they have been a staff of reed to the house of Israel. ... When they leaned on you, you broke and made all their backs quiver"* (vv. 6-7). Egypt was not a trustworthy ally; Pharaoh had promised to assist Judah against the Babylonians, but failed to honor that commitment when Nebuchadnezzar attacked Jerusalem. Jeremiah acknowledges that Pharaoh did make a halfhearted attempt to assist Jerusalem during its siege, but quickly backed down. In the end, the Jews bore the consequences for that failed alliance. Judah had leaned on Egypt, as one would lean on a walking stick, but Judah found out by tumbling into ruin that Egypt was just a flimsy reed. Not only had Egypt led His people astray in rebelling against Babylon, but God promised to smite Egypt with a sword and render them a desolate wasteland because of their deceitful assurance of support (vv. 8-9).

Like Ezekiel, Jeremiah also foretold that Nebuchadnezzar would invade Egypt (Jer. 43). His prophecies were an attempt to keep surviving Jews in Jerusalem from fleeing to Egypt after Governor Gedaliah's murder. Jeremiah foretold that God would use the king of Babylon to burn Egypt's temples and judge her false gods. Nebuchadnezzar's sword would destroy many, and those fortunate enough to live would be taken to Babylon as captives. Speaking for Jehovah, Ezekiel proclaims a similar judgment on Egypt:

> *I will make the land of Egypt utterly waste and desolate from Migdol to Syene, as far as the border of Ethiopia. ... it shall be uninhabited forty years. I will make the land of Egypt desolate in the midst of the countries that are desolate; and among the cities that are laid waste, her cities shall be desolate forty years; and I will scatter the Egyptians among the nations and disperse them throughout the countries* (vv. 10-12).

The pronouncement of judgment on Egypt was wide sweeping, from Migdol, situated in the Nile River delta in the north, to Syene in the far south. Much of the Old Testament's history has been affirmed through archeological evidence; however, we have only biblical references concerning Nebuchadnezzar's invasion of Egypt and the dispersion of its population. Ezekiel further foretold that God would return the Egyptian captives to their homeland after forty years (vv. 13-14), but Egypt would never recover to be the imperial force that they had been for almost two millennia (vv. 15-16).

When did this invasion occur? Since Babylon was defeated by the Medes and the Persians in late 539 B.C., and Persians then permitted many of the Babylonian captives to return to their homelands in the following years, the prophesied invasion would have likely commenced about forty years earlier (between 580 to 570 B.C.). However, information in verses 17-21 enables us to narrow the timing even further.

Ezekiel's second prophecy foretold Egypt's defeat by Babylon (vv. 17-21). This is the last prophecy in his book, dated April 571 B.C., some sixteen years after the one in the previous verses. Nebuchadnezzar had moved his army away from Jerusalem in order to lay siege to the city of Tyre in the north; Tyre surrendered in 572 B.C. after a thirteen-year siege. Ezekiel uttered this prophecy shortly after the fall of Tyre to warn Egypt that they would be Nebuchadnezzar's next target and why. The siege against Tyre had wearied the Babylonian army and Nebuchadnezzar owed his soldiers back wages (vv. 18-19). God promised to permit him to despoil Egypt's wealth to reimburse his army for their work, because in reality they were working for the Lord (v. 20). Babylon was Jehovah's chastening rod of vindication for the sins of Israel and the nations surrounding her. This invasion probably commenced shortly after Ezekiel's final prophesy (571-570 B.C.) and about seventeen years after he had first foretold Egypt's fall.

The exact meaning of the prophecy in verse 21 is difficult to ascertain. Once captives were restored to their homelands, the Lord promised to strengthen them and to lift up a horn in Israel that would speak for Him. Textually speaking, Ezekiel would be the "horn," or God's spokesman, among His people. Did this mean that Ezekiel would return from Babylon to prophesy in Jerusalem? There is no biblical evidence of that occurring and Ezekiel would have been in his mid-eighties at the time that Persia conquered Babylon. Therefore, he would likely be unable to make the 800 mile trek, an arduous journey of four months (Ezra 7:8, 8:31). It is most likely like that, after the numerous events had come to pass, that Ezekiel had been prophesying for over twenty years, the Jews would understand with clarity what God had previously revealed to them. Then, with even greater confidence, they would know that Jehovah is the Lord!

Meditation

Trials dark on every hand, and we cannot understand
All the ways that God would lead us to that blessed promised land;
But He guides us with His eye, and we'll follow till we die,
For we'll understand it better by and by.
Temptations, hidden snares often take us unawares,
And our hearts are made to bleed for a thoughtless word or deed;
And we wonder why the test when we try to do our best,
But we'll understand it better by and by.

— Charles Tindley

Egypt and Her Allies Condemned
Ezekiel 30

Ezekiel's third prophecy against Egypt is not dated. It has four sections, each commencing with the phrase, *"Thus says the Lord God"* (vv. 2, 6, 10, 13). Ezekiel warns Egypt that the day of Jehovah's vengeance was near: Gentiles would descend on Egypt like clouds and slay her inhabitants and despoil her wealth (vv. 3-4). The nations allied with Egypt (Ethiopia, Libya and Lydia) would suffer the same decimation (v. 5); their armies found anywhere within Egypt's borders would be slaughtered for helping her (vv. 6-8). The news of Egypt's destruction would spread swiftly by heralds navigating up and down the Nile River (v. 9).

There are two important terms that Ezekiel mentions in verse 3 which require further discussion: "the day of the Lord" and "the time of the Gentiles." *The Day of the Lord* is an Old Testament term that speaks of those times when Jehovah intervened in a visible and powerful way to judge the wicked on earth. This meaning continues into the New Testament and speaks of the Tribulation Period and the Millennial Kingdom of Christ (Acts 2:20; 1 Thess. 5:2). *The Day of the Lord* concludes with the destruction of the earth and the subsequent Great White Throne judgment. Then begins *the Day of God* – the eternal state (2 Pet. 3:10-12).

The Time of the Gentiles (Luke 21:24) is a period of Gentile rule and oppression of the Jewish people that commenced with the destruction of Jerusalem by the Babylonians in 586 B.C. and will continue until the battle of Armageddon at the conclusion of the Tribulation Period. *The Time of the Gentiles* is not to be confused with "the fullness of the Gentiles" (Rom. 11:25), which speaks of the conclusion of the Church Age. *The Time of the Gentiles* ends roughly seven years after the rapture of the Church.

The third section of this particular prophecy (vv. 10-12) again foretells the extent of Egypt's desolation and how it will be accomplished "by the hand of Nebuchadnezzar" (v. 10). Apparently Ezekiel is using redundancy to stress that even with Egypt's vast population, they would not be able to block the most ruthless of all nations, Babylon, from advancing and laying waste to their land. The Egyptians believed that the Nile was their source of life from their gods, so Jehovah promised to dry up Egypt's rivers so that they might know that He was the true God (vv. 11-12). While the Babylonians, *"the foreigners,"* were His visible means, three times in three verses the Lord declares *"I will"* do these things – He was the One controlling every aspect of Egypt's doom.

The final section continues the theme of the previous verses, Egypt's destruction, but Ezekiel specifically lists eight major cities that will be destroyed: Memphis, Pathros, Zoan, Thebes, Pelusium, Heliopolis, Bubastis, and Tahpanhes (vv. 13-19). Memphis (Noph) was a religious center, known for its many colossal images, and pagan temples (v. 13). Pathros refers to Upper Egypt, the far southern section of the country. Zoan, mentioned several times in Scripture, was a wealthy royal city in the Delta on the Tanitic branch of the Nile (v. 14). Thebes (No) was located in southern Egypt (v. 15). Situated a mile from the Mediterranean Sea, Pelusium (Sin) was Egypt's military garrison in the north and its main defense against invasion from the sea (v. 16). Heliopolis (Aven) and Bubastis (Pi-beseth) were religious centers (v. 17). Pharaoh's main residence at this time was on the island of Elephantie situated on the upper Nile, but Jeremiah informs us that Pharaoh also had a palace in Tahpanhes (Jer. 43:9). By naming various cities connected with royalty, prosperity, pagan worship, and military strength throughout Egypt, Ezekiel was showing how widely encompassing God's wrath on Egypt would be. Jehovah was going to break Egypt's yoke (a symbol of strength) and cover them with the clouds of smoke, dust, and debris (vv. 18-19).

Ezekiel's fourth oracle against Egypt (vv. 20-26) was spoken in April of 587 B.C., about four months after his first prophecy (29:1). This message would have been written just after Egypt's halfhearted attempted to rescue Jerusalem had failed. During this time Nebuchadnezzar briefly departed from Jerusalem to reposition his army to meet the Egyptians en route from the south. The Babylonians handily defeated Pharaoh Hophra and his army and the siege on Jerusalem resumed.

Infidelity and Loyalty

The Lord took credit for Hophra's defeat: *"I have broken the arm of Pharaoh, king of Egypt. It has not been bound up for healing or put in a splint so as to become strong enough to hold a sword"* (v. 21). Like the "yoke," the "arm" is a symbol of strength in Scripture. Egypt tried to flex its arm to assist Jerusalem, and God used Nebuchadnezzar to break it. In God's sovereign design, not even a splint to bind the arm would enable Pharaoh to hold his sword again (v. 22). Nor would there be time for it to heal because God planned to break his other arm also and mortally wound him through another Babylonian invasion (vv. 23-24).

God would strengthen Nebuchadnezzar's hand and put His own sword in it to cause Pharaoh to fall lifeless to the ground, a metaphor expressing Egypt's sudden loss of strength and defeat (v. 25). Egypt would no longer be in a position to militarily assist anyone else, for they could not even defend themselves against the Babylonians. After Egypt's defeat, the Babylonians would deport and enslave many Egyptians, just as they had done with all those who had previously sided with Egypt, including Judah: *"Then they shall know that I am the Lord."* No human or evil spiritual force can thwart God's purposes. God will have His way. May it be our way too!

Meditation

If there is one single reason why good people turn evil, it is because they fail to recognize God's ownership over their kingdom, their vocation, their resources, their abilities, and above all their lives.

— Erwin W. Lutzer

Consider Assyria
Ezekiel 31

Ezekiel's fifth prophecy against Egypt is an allegory which portrays the fall of the Assyrian Empire as a dramatic prediction of Egypt's imminent decline. The prophecy was spoken on the first day of the third month and in the eleventh year of Jehoiachin's captivity (June 587 B.C.), less than two months after the fourth prophecy in the previous chapter (v. 1).

The oracle is addressed to Pharaoh and the multitude of his people. It begins with a rhetorical question: *"Whom are you like in your greatness?"* (v. 2). Pharaoh Hophra believed that there was no nation on earth that could compare to Egypt's superior wealth and military might. Ezekiel suggests that Pharaoh had overlooked Assyria as a comparable power and that he should learn from their desolation the outcome of arrogant pride. So between His question in verse 2 and the satirical answer in verse 18, the Lord offers Pharaoh a comparative assessment. The Assyrian Empire is likened poetically to a mighty cedar in Lebanon which has just been toppled (vv. 3-12). This pictures Assyria's decline and recent defeat by the Babylonians. While it may seem out of place for Ezekiel to mention Assyria in a prophecy against Egypt, Charles Dyer warns that we should not ignore the plain meaning of the text and its application:

Some scholars thinks that "Assyria" (*'assur*) should be amended to read "cypress tree" (or "pine tree") (*tᵉ' assur*) because of the difficulty in understanding why Ezekiel would mention Assyria in his prophecies against Egypt. However, there is no need to alter the text. Assyria would have had great significance to Egypt for two reasons. First, Assyria had been the only Mesopotamian nation to invade Egypt. In 633 B.C. Assyria had entered Egypt and destroyed the capital of Thebes (Nahum 3:8-10). So the only nation that could be "compared" with Egypt was Assyria. Second, Assyria had been destroyed by Babylon; the same nation Ezekiel said would enter Egypt and destroy it.[60]

Ezekiel says, *"Indeed, Assyria was a cedar in Lebanon, with fine branches that shaded the forest, and of high stature"* (v. 3). He then describes the Assyrian Empire at the apex of its power in the Middle East as a colossal cedar whose height was above all other trees (vv. 4-9). The cedar was watered abundantly by deep springs and it blessed the other trees in the garden by sending out channels of moisture to their roots. Its full boughs provided shade for the people groups and beasts of the earth, and nesting places for all the birds of the air. Its beauty and grandeur surpassed all the other trees in God's garden (referred to as Eden in this allegory). In summary, Assyria's supremacy a few decades earlier was over all other nations (trees), including Egypt.

The point was that Egypt should observe and learn from Assyria's destruction: God had sternly dealt with wicked, proud Assyria, who was more influential than Egypt, by strengthening cruel Babylon to overcome them (vv. 10-12). In 612 B.C. Nebuchadnezzar's father, Nabopolassar, defeated Nineveh, the capital city of Assyria. Babylon felled the majestic cedar, and chopped off its branches – it no longer benefitted or controlled the people, beasts, or the birds of the earth (v. 13). Furthermore, Ezekiel promised that any other nation seeking to exalt itself among other nations, like Egypt, would suffer the same fate as Assyria; they would be cast down, even into the pit (i.e., a grave; v. 14).

Having introduced the topic of death and the grave, Ezekiel addresses the emotional response of the lesser trees to Assyria's fall (i.e., Assyria's allies and vassal kingdoms who also suffered defeat; vv. 15-17). They mourned the loss of Assyria's shade (her benefits), but they comforted themselves in death by realizing that they could have done nothing against the Babylonians, for Babylon had toppled the greatest tree in the garden. This lamentation was in a roundabout way addressed to Egypt, who became Assyria's greatest ally after Nineveh was captured by Nebopolassar, Nebuchadnezzar's father. Egypt, a lesser tree, had aligned itself with a proud nation destined for destruction because they had brutally oppressed Jehovah's covenant people. Egypt, as an overconfident ally, would suffer the same fate (v. 18).

It is somewhat ironic that God will put a similar vision of a superb tree in King Nebuchadnezzar's mind a few years later to warn him of his self-exalting pride (Dan. 4). Thankfully, after seven years of living like a wild beast in the field, his sanity and kingdom were restored to him (just as Daniel had predicted) and Nebuchadnezzar's first royal act was to laud the God of the Jews. The Lord knows how to deal with human pride and make Himself known to us!

> What were we made for? To know God. What aim should we have in life? To know God. What is the eternal life that Jesus gives? To know God. What is the best thing in life? To know God. What in humans gives God most pleasure? Knowledge of Himself.

> — J. I. Packer

Egypt arrogantly thought that no nation could be compared with her in status and might, but God supplied an example of an empire that was even more impressive, but had been brought low by Him. Acknowledging their vast conceit, the Lord sarcastically concludes the prophecy by answering His own question (v. 2) – that is, in the way Egypt would respond: *"This is Pharaoh and all his multitude"* (v. 18). Egypt would soon learn that they were nothing when acting contrary to God's sovereign purposes! However, Paul says this to humble believers who are abiding in Christ and are settled in God's will:

> *Yet in all these things we are more than conquerors through Him who loved us. For I am persuaded that neither death nor life, nor angels nor principalities nor powers, nor things present nor things to come, nor height nor depth, nor any other created thing, shall be able to separate us from the love of God which is in Christ Jesus our Lord* (Rom. 8:37-39).

Paul concludes by expressing His utter confidence in the Lord: *"What then shall we say to these things? If God is for us, who can be against us?"* The believer is not to be overcome by evil but to overcome evil with good, and God is all about that! Yet, He hates the pride in our hearts and works to remove it at all cost, that we might better know His majesty and learn to rest peacefully under the shadow of His branches.

Meditation

That eye which sees anything good in the creature is a blind eye; that eye which fancies it can discern anything in man, or anything in anything he can do to win the Divine favor, is as yet stone blind to the Truth of God, and needs to be lanced and cut, and the cataract of pride removed from it!

— Charles H. Spurgeon

You can have no greater sign of confirmed pride than when you think you are humble enough.

— William Law

Down Into the Pit
Ezekiel 32

The date of Ezekiel's sixth oracle against Egypt was the first day of the twelfth month of the twelfth year of Jehoiachin's captivity, or about two months after news of Jerusalem's fall reached the captives in Babylon (v.1, 33:21). The prophet is told to utter a lament for haughty Pharaoh (v. 2). In poetic form, Pharaoh Hophra is likened to a ferocious, young lion and a terrifying sea monster. The sea monster (likely a reference to the Nile crocodile) was guilty of churning up and muddying the river in the same way Job's terrifying leviathan did (Job 41). Thus Pharaoh had stirred up peaceful nations to revolt against the Babylonians whom God was using as His rod of discipline against Israel and the surrounding nations.

Apparently, it was not enough to foretell the demise of the Assyrian Empire as a pattern for Egypt's imminent ruin. As William Kelly summarizes, the Spirit of God adds an additional message of two parts in this chapter:

> One, in the first half of this chapter, setting forth the impending catastrophe of Pharaoh under the figures of a lion and a crocodile, once the terror of nations, now caught, slain and exposed before all, and this under the king of Babylon; the other a developed picture of that which had been more curtly sketched in the preceding chapter, the once mighty monarch with his multitude pitiably weak now in the lower parts of the earth, yea in Sheol like all that were fallen before himself, consoling him with no better solace than that he and his were sharing the inevitable doom of princes and people.[61]

Pharaoh was as bold as a lion and as troublesome as an unruly crocodile, but God had a solution: He would use a vast invasion force as a net to capture him and drag him out of the river into an open field (v. 3). The sea or "many waters" are used to symbolize the nations in Scripture (Jer. 51:13; Matt. 13:47-48; Rev. 17:1, 15) Therefore,

185

dragging Pharaoh out of the water onto land meant he would no longer have a meddling influence outside of Egypt.

Then, Ezekiel graphically describes the carnage of Pharaoh and those he represents (as pictured in the beached monster): The land will be covered with a horrific darkness when the blood of the beast drenches the entire land and unclean birds and scavengers feed on its carcass (vv. 4-8). This spectacle will unnerve other nations (all of which are lesser than Egypt); they will observe Egypt's end with horror and realize that they are completely helpless against the will of Jehovah (vv. 9-10).

To ensure the meaning of the allegory is clear, Ezekiel transitions from metaphoric to plain language in verse 11: The sword of Babylon will crush proud Egypt by slaughtering her armies and people, destroying her livestock, and despoiling her wealth (vv. 11-12). Due to the loss of life, there will not be enough humans or animals fording the rivers to muddy the water (vv. 13-14). This detail of Egypt's decimation would remind Pharaoh of his foolishness in adversely influencing the nations (churning them up in rebellion, so to speak). After the Babylonians finished with Egypt, the rivers and streams would run undisturbed; the entire region would be in a restful but ruined state as the nations mourned for Egypt (vv. 15-16).

Ezekiel's seventh and final prophecy against Egypt occurred in the same year as the previous message, but on the fifteenth day; however, the particular month is not stated (v. 17). It is generally thought to be the same month as the lament in verses 1-16, or about two weeks later. This prophecy foresees the souls of slaughtered rebel Egyptians descending into the pit, which is referred to as "hell" four times in Ezekiel 31 and 32. The Hebrew word translated "hell" in verses 21 and 27 is *sheol*, which is rendered "pit," "grave," or "hell" throughout the Old Testament (2 Sam. 22:6; Ps. 9:17, 18:5; Isa. 14:9-17). It is the equivalent of the Greek word *hades*, used in the New Testament.

In Luke 16, we learn that this spiritual domain secures disembodied spirits to one of two compartments: Abraham's Bosom, where faithful souls await resurrection unto life through Christ, and a place of torment, where the wicked continue to wait for their resurrection to stand before the Lord at the Great White Throne. Their eternal punishment in the Lake of Fire will follow. Hades is a domain of sorrow; it is the place the wicked go after death. Luke 16 is not a parable, but rather highlights the fact that souls are completely conscious of their situation (i.e. these souls are not sleeping) and are in torment; thus, the rich man pleaded that Lazarus might return from the dead to warn his five brothers about the horror of Hades. During the Church Age, the spirits of the redeemed will be with the Lord after death and not in Hades (Phil. 1:21-23; 2 Cor. 5:8). In contrast, the souls of unbelievers descend into Hades where they wait to be reunited with a resurrected body, which will afterwards be condemned to the Lake of Fire at the Great White Throne judgment (Luke 16:19-31; Rev. 20:11-15).

With this understanding, Ezekiel's lamentation for Egyptians in Sheol is quite sorrowful; there was no opportunity for them to escape their ultimate destination – the Lake of Fire (Rev. 20:11-15). The writer of Hebrews sums up the matter this way: *"It is appointed for men to die once, but after this the judgment"* (Heb. 9:27). Death seals one's eternal fate; there are no second opportunities to be saved from God's wrath, and the Egyptians took their place down in Sheol alongside other uncircumcised rebels (vv. 18-23). In the dispensation of the Law, being uncircumcised meant that these men had not become worshippers of Jehovah by trusting in His revealed word. God is no respecter of persons; only the redeemed (those who have been proclaimed righteous in Christ through faith) can avoid hell. At this present moment, all the Egyptians (and their allies) that Ezekiel is speaking of have been enduring the torment of Hades for 2,500 plus years. They are still waiting for their final judgment with all other wicked disembodied souls since the time that man became subject to death in Eden (Rev. 20).

While God's covenant with Abraham would bestow a special land to his descendants, he was also given a much broader promise: *"in you shall all families of the earth be blessed."* This covenant would have its ultimate fulfillment in the redemptive work of Christ, a descendant of Abraham. In the meantime, Uriah the Hittite, Caleb the Kenizzite, and Tamar and Rahab of the Canaanites are some of the Gentiles who received divine blessing by trusting Abraham's God. Through exercising faith in revealed truth, God is willing to declare the wonders of His grace to anyone, anywhere, and at any time. Paul puts the matter this way: *"For the grace of God that brings salvation hath appeared to all men"* (Titus 2:11) and God *"is long-suffering towards us, not willing that any should perish, but that all should come to repentance"* (2 Pet. 3:9). The Egyptians had a choice; they could either oppose

Jehovah and His people or humble themselves and worship Him alone. They chose to rebel against God.

Ezekiel closes his lamentation by naming other allies of Egypt who would also share in the same fate of the Egyptians in Sheol: Elam, Meshech, Tubal, Edom, and those from Sidon (vv. 24-30). And to eliminate any possible confusion concerning the fate of Pharaoh's soul, he too would join the uncircumcised in Sheol (v. 31). All these would experience God's terror on earth while living (the Babylonian sword), but then would realize that death's door only ushered them into an eternal horror from which they could never escape (v. 32). There are no second chances after death. Over the entrance into hell's inferno one might read this placard: "No comfort, no mercy, no love, no time, no light, no escape, and no God." God does not force people to choose Him against their will, but He will force all who do reject His love and forgiveness into a horrible abode where they will find neither – forever.

Meditation

> The lost enjoy forever the horrible freedom they have demanded.
>
> — C. S. Lewis

> Don't say that a loving God is going to send you to hell – He's not. The thing that's going to send you to hell is that you're a sinner and you don't want to admit it.
>
> — James Vernon McGee

> If sinners be damned, at least let them leap to Hell over our bodies. If they will perish, let them perish with our arms about their knees. Let no one go there unwarned and unprayed for.
>
> — Charles H. Spurgeon

The Reappointed Watchman
Ezekiel 33

Since Ezekiel's prophetic commissioning in the opening pages of this book, we have pressed through thirty chapters of warnings and lamentations. As God's appointed watchman, he first warned Judah and Jerusalem (chps. 4-24), and then the surrounding Gentile nations (chps. 25-32), of divine retribution for their wickedness. In this chapter, Ezekiel is again appointed as a watchman for the nation of Israel, but with a different ministry. Undoubtedly, the news of Jerusalem's destruction discouraged the exiled Jews dispersed throughout Babylon. Hence, the final section of Ezekiel's book affirms the faithfulness of Jehovah to both restore and wonderfully bless His covenant people in a future day. While still upholding a message of personal accountability to God, Ezekiel's ministry now centers on inspiring the Jews concerning their future.

Jehovah will restore His adulterous wife once she has been cleansed of her filthiness and sanctified for God alone. But how would that be possible? The answer to this is that Israel will receive the Holy Spirit and will experience spiritual renewal – the Jewish people will be born again as a nation. Ezekiel tells us in chapters 34-39 how God will accomplish this: The false leaders of Israel will be judged and replaced with true shepherds to guide the people (chp. 34). Gentile nations will no longer be permitted to oppress Israel (chp. 35). The Jews will be restored to the land and to their God through spiritual renewal (chps. 36-37). God will protect and secure His covenant people in the land of Israel (chps. 38-39). Ezekiel's remaining prophecies pertain mainly to when God will honor His covenant with Abraham and richly bless his descendants in the Millennial Kingdom of Christ.

The content of this chapter is similar to portions of chapters 3 and 18, which prompts us to ponder why the Lord thought it necessary to repeat Himself. H. A. Ironside suggests:

> When God repeats Himself, it is in order that His truth may be impressed upon our hearts and minds. It is so easy to forget divine principles and to let slip the teaching of any portion of God's Holy Word. ... So when we find repetition in the Holy Scriptures, we may well give the passages in question our most careful consideration, realizing that God had something very important to communicate, or He would not have duplicated it.[62]

The opening verses affirm the duties of a watchman to warn those in his care of threatening situations (e.g., the approach of an invading army; vv. 1-6). If the watchman faithfully sounds the alarm when appropriate, he is not responsible for how people respond to it (vv. 3-5). However, if the watchman chooses to save his own life and does not warn those in his care, God holds him responsible for all those slaughtered in the attack. God had seen to it that His people were duly warned before the Babylonian invasion came; in fact, Jeremiah had been faithfully blowing the trumpet in Jerusalem for forty years.

The prophet Ezekiel was chosen by God to be a watchman to the Jews in Babylon. God again warns him to be faithful to his calling or He will hold Ezekiel personally accountable for the deaths of the wicked:

> *But if the watchman sees the sword coming and does not blow the trumpet, and the people are not warned, and the sword comes and takes any person from among them, he is taken away in his iniquity; but his blood I will require at the watchman's hand. So you, son of man: I have made you a watchman for the house of Israel; therefore you shall hear a word from My mouth and warn them for Me* (vv. 6-7).

Regrettably, most of the nation of Israel and none of the surrounding nations had heeded Jeremiah's or Ezekiel's alarms and so perished at the hands of the Babylonians. However, Ezekiel was not responsible for how they had responded to his proclamation of the truth; God promised to hold each one responsible for their own choices (vv. 8-9).

The Jewish captives now knew that their temple, capital city, and entire homeland had been destroyed by Babylon. All that Ezekiel had been proclaiming for the past seven years had come to pass. This affirmed that he was a true prophet of God in the minds of the people. Perhaps they would give him more credence in the future when he spoke for the Lord. The fact that God was still speaking to them through Ezekiel meant that all was not lost, but rather that He had a plan for their future.

The Jews were likely wondering how long God would remain angry with them. Would He ever want to have communion with them again? Ezekiel was to begin His new ministry by informing the Jews that God did not enjoy punishing the wicked, but rather His holy character demanded it. God's preference was that the wicked repent and be saved: *"I have no pleasure in the death of the wicked, but that the wicked turn from his way and live"* (v. 11). The Jews should not think that the Lord derived pleasure in being wrathful; rather He longs to joyfully interact with those choosing to honor Him through obedience. No person should think that he or she has ventured too far down the wide path to destruction that he or she cannot be rescued – no one is hopelessly lost unless he or she chooses not to repent and turn to the Lord for forgiveness and mercy.

In the end, all will acknowledge Christ's lordship (Phil. 2:9-10), but we should never think that He derives pleasure from casting the wicked into the Lake of Fire. Interestingly, everlasting *hell fire* was not originally prepared for mankind but rather for Satan and the other rebellious angels (Matt. 25:41). However, God will use this abode of torment to also punish those who continue the devil's rebellion by rejecting God's offer of salvation in Christ. The Lord longs for all men to repent and to turn to Him by faith that they might be declared righteous in His sight (v. 12). However, those laboring to establish their own righteousness before God through their own doings remain unforgiven for their iniquities (vv. 13-14; Rom. 10:1-3). Conversely, if a sinner repents and seeks forgiveness from the Lord, he or she will be forgiven; such an individual would be known by their continuance in works of righteousness afterwards (vv. 15-16).

Neither the natural mind nor religious people find God's way of salvation fair (vv. 17-20). The former rejects the notion of accountability to God, for they loathe any interference in their personal affairs, while the latter delights in assisting an inadequate god to save themselves. But God states that it is their way that is not fair, for how can a righteous God forgive sinners righteously (v. 17)? Since perfection is the minimum daily requirement to enter heaven, how can doing good works ever compensate for doing one act of evil (Rom. 4:3-5)? It cannot – thus we need something beyond ourselves – God's grace! Therefore, sinners must come to God humbly on His terms to experience His forgiveness, and be declared righteous in His sight.

> *But God demonstrates His own love toward us, in that while we were still sinners, Christ died for us. Much more then, having now been justified by His blood, we shall be saved from wrath through Him. For if when we were enemies we were reconciled to God through the death of His Son, much more, having been reconciled, we shall be saved by His life* (Rom. 5:8-10).

As God judged His own Son at Calvary for all human sin (Heb. 2:9; 1 Jn. 2:2), He can righteously justify (i.e., declare righteous) those wanting to have their sin-debt forgiven through Christ (Rom. 3:24-26). Ezekiel affirms that each individual has accountability with God: *"O house of Israel, I will judge every one of you according to his own ways"* (v. 20). Given what Christ endured on the cross for each of us, to reject God's gracious offer of salvation is one of the worst offenses man can commit against a loving God. God is more than fair: He could have let us perish in our sins, or wiped humanity from the face of the planet, but instead chose, at tremendous personal cost to Himself, to intervene with grace.

In verse 21, the narrative transitions from the topic of personal responsibility to an important development in Ezekiel's ongoing ministry – he could talk again. For over seven years he had been able to speak only when God prompted him. However, the night before the news of Jerusalem's capture reached the ears of the captives in Babylon, Ezekiel's dumbness was removed (v. 22). Knowing the will of God, Ezekiel had patiently endured this hardship without one recorded complaint.

> To wait on God is to live a life of desire toward Him, delight in Him, dependence on Him, and devotedness to Him.
>
> — Matthew Henry

The timing of this release demonstrated two things: First, God was in control of all that was happening to His people. Second, Ezekiel's arduous ministry of uttering warnings and foretelling Jerusalem's fate had concluded; what he had previously foretold had occurred. The sad news pertaining to their beloved city reached the Jews in Babylon in the *"twelfth year of our captivity, in the tenth month, on the fifth day of the month"* (January 9, 585 B.C.).

In the remainder of the chapter Ezekiel delivers a twofold rebuke in retrospect, first to those Jews still residing in Israel (vv. 23-29) and then to those exiled in Babylon (vv. 30-33). Those in Israel had refused to submit to God's chastening and had resisted the Babylonian invasion. If they had surrendered, they would have lived, but sadly, most of them were slaughtered. As descendants of Abraham, they believed that they should remain in the land God gave Abraham (vv. 23-24). However, Abraham was righteous before God and they were not – the privilege of dwelling in the Promised Land was dependent upon spiritual obedience.

Ezekiel then gave some examples to prove this point: they were self-reliant and willfully broke God's Law by eating meat with the blood, worshipping idols, shedding innocent blood and committing adultery (vv. 25-26). Since they refused to be removed from the land, death by the sword, wild beasts, or pestilence would be prevalent (v. 27). There was no escaping God's wrath; the land would be made desolate because of their abominations and they would perish in the land for refusing to receive His chastening willingly (vv. 28-29).

It is evident that Ezekiel received some inside information from the Lord as to how the Jews were really responding to His preaching. Therefore, the prophet chides the Jews in Babylon for pretending to enjoy hearing God's Word, but not acting on it (vv. 30-31). They treated his oracles like enchanting love songs that tickled their fancy, but had no lasting impact on their souls (v. 32). God demanded their obedience; the reason they were suffering so much hardship was their defiance. The Jews were ignoring their spiritual deadness and sinfulness. Until they saw their problem as God did, they could not experience His solution.

Those whimpering Stateside young people will wake up on the Day of Judgment condemned to worse fates than these demon-fearing Indians, because, having a Bible, they were bored with it – while these never heard of such a thing.

— Jim Elliot

The Jews thought that they were a special people because God had given them His Law and His land. Paul, however, clarifies that it was not merely having the Law that would mark them as a peculiar people in the world, but keeping it (Rom. 2:23-25). Because they taught the tenets of the Law, but then broke the Law in practice, the testimony of God was blasphemed among the Gentiles. James summarizes the appropriate conduct of children of God: *"But be doers of the word, and not hearers only, deceiving yourselves"* (Jas. 1:22). To name Christ as Savior and then to reject His call to holy living effectively blasphemes the name of Christ in the world. This same offense is still as prevalent today as it was in the early Church, for Paul exhorts believers more than once to put away all blasphemies (Eph. 4:31; Col. 3:8). When God's people hear God's Word, but choose to ignore it, they minimize the legitimacy of the name of Christ and hence cause others to blaspheme God.

Since the exiled Jews believed Ezekiel was a prophet of God, why would they then disregard his messages spoken on God's behalf? In the future, Ezekiel was hopeful that after more of his prophecies had come true, his countrymen would really act like he was a true prophet (v. 33). Perhaps, Ezekiel was speaking of the destruction of the temple and Jerusalem, news of which had not reached Babylon yet. Or, he may have been referring to how the exiled Jews would suffer personally for their own disobedience as previously warned (vv. 12-20). In either case, Ezekiel had again preached an unpopular message to warn the people of their complacency.

Ezekiel bravely sounded the alarm warning the Jewish nation of forthcoming judgment. He was not responsible for the results, but merely to convey a message of utmost urgency on God's behalf. Six centuries later, another Jew, Saul of Tarsus, would likewise declare his unwavering allegiance to declaring God's gospel message to a lost world: *"For I am not ashamed of the gospel of Christ, for it is the power of God to salvation for everyone who believes, for the Jew first and also for the Greek"* (Rom. 1:16). Paul faithfully warned others of God's judgment for disobedience and their need to repent and receive the Lord Jesus Christ for the forgiveness of their sins. He had the joy of seeing many turn to Christ, but he also suffered in that gospel ministry (e.g., Paul was repeatedly scourged, beaten with rods, and once stoned and left for dead; 2 Cor. 11:24-25).

God forbid that I should travel with anybody a quarter of an hour without speaking of Christ to them.

— George Whitefield

Today's church wants to be raptured from responsibility.

— Leonard Ravenhill

Despite the hostility of the lost, may each watchman for the Lord stand fast in the faith of Christ and declare God's message of love and truth to those who desperately need to hear it. God will not hold us guiltless if we withhold His words of life!

Meditation

Rescue the perishing, care for the dying,
Snatch them in pity from sin and the grave;
Weep o'er the erring one, lift up the fallen,
Tell them of Jesus, the mighty to save.

Though they are slighting Him, still He is waiting,
Waiting the penitent child to receive;
Plead with them earnestly, plead with them gently;
He will forgive if they only believe.

— Fanny Crosby

Woe to Israel's Shepherds
Ezekiel 34

Ezekiel was to sharply rebuke Israel's spiritual leaders who cared for themselves and neglected God's sheep: *"Woe be to the shepherds of Israel that do feed themselves! Should not the shepherds feed the flocks?"* (vv. 1-2). God had entrusted His sheep (His people) into their care, but they had failed to fulfill that responsibility. Before passing judgment, the offenses of Israel's rulers, which would include her prophets, priests, Levites, and probably kings, are listed in verses 2-6. Israel's shepherds…

- Did not serve or care for God's people (v. 2)
- Put their own interests ahead of the flock (v. 3)
- Exploited those in their care for profit (v. 3)
- Did not care for the injured and suffering (v. 4)
- Did not search for the lost (v. 4)
- Were heavy-handed and treated God's people brutally (v. 4)
- Permitted the Lord's people to be scattered and devoured (v. 5)
- Had no concern for those aimlessly wandering in hopelessness (v. 6)

God was furious with these slothful men who called themselves shepherds, but were not. Those who have been entrusted with the care of God's people must recognize the full weight of that responsibility, says Matthew Henry:

> Those that do not do the work of shepherds are unworthy of the name. And if those that undertake to be shepherds are foolish shepherds (Zech. 11:15), if they are proud and above their business, idle and do not love their business, or faithless and unconcerned about it, the case of the flock is as bad as if it were without a shepherd. Better no shepherd than such shepherds.[63]

196

God is *against them* and they know it; for they shall be made to account for the manner in which they have discharged their trust: *"I will require my flock at their hands, and charge it upon them that so many of them are missing."* Those will have a great deal to answer for in the judgment day who take upon them the care of souls and yet take no care of them. … God will take out of men's hands that power which they have abused and that trust which they have betrayed. … Those that are enriching themselves with the spoils of the public cannot expect that they shall always be suffered to do so.[64]

If these delinquent shepherds had been God-fearing spiritual leaders, there would have been no need for God to chasten Israel by the Assyrians and then Judah by the Babylonians. For their profiteering and neglect of duty, Israel's shepherds would be removed from their positions and severely punished by the Lord (vv. 7-10). The writer of Hebrews reminds both sheep to be obedient to their shepherds and shepherds (i.e., church elders) to be faithful to the Lord, for they shall give an account to Him in a future day (Heb. 13:17).

Here lies an important principle: sheep are to follow their God-given shepherds, as the shepherds follow the Lord. As seen in the example before us, if shepherds deviate from the teaching of Scripture or fail to live it out, they will forfeit God's blessing and their flocks will suffer, and experience God's displeasure. In such situations, where God's leadership is in clear violation of scriptural truth, those whom God has placed in their care are in no way liable to follow them, but should rather submit to the higher authority of the Lord (Acts 4:15, 5:19). Unfortunately, most of Israel's history is marked by either an ignorance of or a resistance to God's Word – they truly needed faithful shepherds to guide, feed, protect, and correct them, but such were rare.

Jehovah's anger towards Israel's selfish and complacent leadership is then contrasted in the latter portion of the chapter with His utter delight in His Shepherd. This divine Shepherd will selflessly bless and care for the Jewish nation during the Kingdom Age. The Lord had permitted His flock to be scattered to minimize further damage to His sheep by Israel's pathetic shepherds (v. 10). However, in a future day, Ezekiel said that God would seek and gather His scattered sheep from among the nations through His true Shepherd; He would reestablish God's flock in the land of Israel (vv. 11-13). Phrases such as *"I will seek"* and *"so will I seek"* occur repeatedly in this chapter (e.g., vv. 12,

16). Ironically, "I will seek" reflects the implied meaning of Ezekiel's own name, "God will strengthen," and the tenor of his ministry; Ezekiel sought the lost sheep of Israel for the Lord.

Unlike Israel's shepherds, the Lord would feed, protect, heal, console, and lead His sheep in Israel (vv. 14-16). The Lord promises: *"I will feed My flock, and I will make them lie down"* (v. 15). Sadly, there are many starving and restless sheep in the world, but none such in the Lord's pasture. He knows how to care for His own much better than we ever could. As Charles H. Spurgeon said, "One would think even a poor, silly sheep would have sense enough to lie down when weary, but alas, with the sheep in Christ's flock it is often otherwise."[65] We venture where we should not, we do not rest where and when we should, and we do not feed on what we should and then we wonder why we are so weak – we need the Great Shepherd to rule and care for us! All those who know Him will agree with David: *"The Lord is my shepherd; I shall not want"* (Ps. 23:1).

When the True Shepherd does return to establish His kingdom, He will *"judge between sheep and sheep, between rams and goats"* (v. 17). The former phrase speaks of rewards and punishment for His people, while the latter relates to Him separating true believers from the lost; the goats will not be permitted into His kingdom. This verdict is referred to as the Judgment of Nations. At Christ's Second Advent, He will punish all those who followed the Antichrist and persecuted the Jews during the Tribulation Period (Matt. 13:47-50, 25:31-33). This judgment is effected suddenly and those unfit for Christ's kingdom will be abruptly removed from the earth (Matt. 24:36-44; Rev. 19:21).

When Israel's rams (older male leaders) stand before God's Shepherd, they will regret drinking first from the stream and muddying the waters so that younger sheep could not drink fresh water. They will be sorry that they ate the best pasture first and trampled it down before others could feed. Then they will wish that they had taken the low place and served others, instead of putting their interests before the needs of God's people (vv. 17-19). Because Israel's tyrants had brutalized the weak lambs by butting them away with their horns, God promised to rescue the oppressed and sternly punish the aggressors (vv. 20-21). The Lord would save His sheep from the false shepherds by sending the true Shepherd:

I will save My flock, and they shall no longer be a prey; and I will judge between sheep and sheep. I will establish one shepherd over them, and he shall feed them – My servant David. He shall feed them and be their shepherd. And I, the Lord, will be their God, and My servant David a prince among them; I, the Lord, have spoken (vv. 22-24).

Who is this true Shepherd? He is God's servant David. Does this mean David, the Old Testament patriarch, will be resurrected to again shepherd God's fold during the Kingdom Age? Some commentators, such as James Vernon McGee, think that David will be raised from the dead to serve as Messiah's vice-regent in the Kingdom Age.[66] However, we will learn later that this prince has natural children, a land inheritance, offers sacrifices for his own purification and has limitations as to where he can go in the temple – all to say that David, in a glorified body, does not fit the prophetic profile of Israel's prince discussed later.

Though David was a man after God's own heart and a faithful shepherd, he was also a man with much blood on his hands and for that reason God prohibited him from building His temple. For these reasons, there is only one person who can be the just Judge and the selfless Shepherd who is entitled to the throne of David – the Lord Jesus Christ. Although the Messiah will have a visible prince as a vice-regent who will represent Him in Jewish affairs during the Kingdom Age, the person Ezekiel is speaking of here is Messiah (also in 37:25). Jewish writer David Baron, a Christian, explains that even Jewish commentators understand that the reference to "David" refers to the coming Messiah who is from David:

Even the Jews explain the name "David" in these passages as applying to the Messiah – the great Son of David in whom all the promises to the Davidic house are centered. Thus Kimchi, in his comment on Ezekiel 34:23, says: "My servant David – that is, the Messiah who shall spring from his seed in the time of salvation" and in the 24th verse of chapter 37 he observes: "The King Messiah – His name shall be called David because He shall be of the seed of David." And so practically all the Jewish commentators."[67]

The coming, true Shepherd who would rescue God's sheep would also be *"a Plant of Renown"* (v. 29) through whom tremendous blessing will be conferred on the refined remnant of Israel. He will be a just and righteous ruler over the restored Jewish nation regathered to the land of Israel:

> *"They shall be safe in their land; and they shall know that I am the Lord, when I have broken the bands of their yoke and delivered them from the hand of those who enslaved them. And they shall no longer be a prey for the nations, nor shall beasts of the land devour them; but they shall dwell safely, and no one shall make them afraid. I will raise up for them a garden of renown, and they shall no longer be consumed with hunger in the land, nor bear the shame of the Gentiles anymore. Thus they shall know that I, the Lord their God, am with them, and they, the house of Israel, are My people," says the Lord God. "You are My flock, the flock of My pasture; you are men, and I am your God," says the Lord God* (vv. 27-31).

God moved many prophets, like Ezekiel, to speak of both the abounding ministry and fine character of the coming Jewish Messiah – the Good Shepherd. L. E. Cooper notes that Ezekiel identifies eight character traits of this promised future King (vv. 11-31)[68]:

- He has a special relationship with Yahweh.
- He will feed His sheep.
- He will gather His sheep together.
- He will reestablish His people peacefully in their land.
- He will rule with justice and compassion.
- He will personally judge His people.
- He will be the only true shepherd.
- He will mediate a covenant of peace.

While these virtues and actions were all evident to some extent during the Lord's first advent, each will be completely fulfilled in His second advent to the earth. He will gather His people from among the nations and then feed and protect them as only the true Shepherd can. As a Plant of Renown He will flourish in their presence and abundantly satisfy all their needs. Scripture prophetically describes these Messianic blessings to the Jewish people. A day is coming when the Lord Jesus Christ will watch over and care for His covenant people, His flock, as their Shepherd-King.

However, that is only part of the Lord's overall shepherding ministry. The New Testament presents His loving care of Gentiles in the Church Age also. John refers to Christ as the "Good Shepherd" who lays His life down for the sheep:

I am the Door: by Me if any man enter in, he shall be saved, and shall go in and out, and find pasture. The thief cometh not, but for to steal, and to kill, and to destroy: I am come that they might have life, and that they might have it more abundantly. I am the Good Shepherd: the good shepherd giveth His life for the sheep (John 10:9-11).

Then the writer of Hebrews highlights the sanctifying work of the Lord Jesus as the Great Shepherd (Heb. 13:20-21). Finally, Peter proclaims Christ as the Chief Shepherd who will return and gather His sheep unto Him (1 Pet. 5:4), speaking of the return of Christ to the air to "snatch away" from the earth those who have truly believed on Him.

His sacrificial love for the sheep stands in sharp contrast to the hireling shepherds of Israel, who led God's sheep astray, neglected their care, and then deserted them in times of danger. Therefore, those who have been charged with the care of God's sheep today must attend to His flock. Those who neglect this ministry should heed the Lord's decree against the base shepherds of Israel: *"I am against the shepherds and I will require My flock at their hand"* (v. 10). Peter learned a valuable lesson after he had denied the Lord – it was easier to die for the Lord than to live for Him. Later, the Lord called Peter to be one of many shepherds (church elders) of God's sheep (1 Pet. 5:1-2). Peter could be martyred only once for the Lord, but he would die a hundred times in caring for God's sheep as a demonstration of his love for the Lord: *"Simon, son of Jonah, do you love Me? ... Tend My sheep ... Feed My Sheep"* (John 21:16-17). Likewise, let us heed the warning and selflessly tend those the Lord loves immensely because we love Him.

The reason Israel's coming Shepherd would be able to gather up the lost sheep of Israel and feed, protect, and care for them is identified in verse 25: God was able to establish a *Covenant of Peace* with the Jewish nation through His Shepherd. Jeremiah says that this would be an everlasting covenant resulting in eternal blessing to the Jews (Jer. 32:40). This promise is understood to be literal, for God will erect an eternal city where the Jewish remnant will dwell (Isa. 48:2, 52:1).

Isaiah proclaimed that through this covenant, *"Israel shall be saved in the Lord with an everlasting salvation"* (Isa. 45:17). Why was the New Covenant needed and how did it secure such blessing for Israel?

The writer of Hebrews informs us that this covenant was sealed by Christ's blood and would accomplish what the Old Covenant could not – propitiation for sins (Heb. 8:8). The Old Covenant was conditional; the Jews had to keep God's Law to receive God's blessing (Ex. 19:5-8; Heb. 8:9). The New Covenant would be unconditional and would be the means by which God would honor His covenant with Abraham. It was instituted by two immutable things – God's Word and His oath (Heb. 6:13-18), neither of which can fail.

One may then wonder how the Gentiles could be brought into the goodness of the New Covenant, if it was strictly instituted between Jehovah and Israel. William Kelly addresses this question:

> I do not say we, Christians, have got the new covenant itself, but we have got the blood of the new covenant. We have that on which the new covenant is founded. The new covenant itself supposes the land of Israel blessed and the house of Israel delivered, but neither the one nor the other has become true yet. The new covenant supposes certain spiritual blessings, namely, the law of God written in the heart and our sins forgiven. These spiritual parts of the new covenant we have received now, along with other blessings peculiar to Christianity, namely, the presence of the Holy Ghost and union with Christ in heaven, which the Jews will not have. But nothing can be more evident than that this prophecy refutes the Jew when he imagines that it is a dishonor to the law for God to bring in anything better than what was enjoyed in the days of Moses.[69]

God, in His mercy, permitted the Gentiles to come into the blessing of the New Covenant as a second benefactor of His promise to bless Abraham's descendants (Eph. 2:14-3:8). Gentiles can only enter the blessing of this covenant by following Abraham's example of trusting God's Word by faith; in this way, they become spiritual descendants of Abraham and are able to partake of the spiritual blessings promised to his descendants (Rom. 4:11-17). Consequently, our claim to the Lord Jesus as our High Priest is as strong as the claim of any redeemed Jew (Heb. 4:14). The Lord Jesus Christ is the Mediator of the New Covenant. Accordingly, He is not just our Good, Great, and Chief Shepherd: He is our Great High Priest forever also!

Through the New Covenant, God is able to righteously justify sinners, if they trust Christ alone for salvation (Rom. 4:23-25). Those who do so receive the gift of the Holy Spirit (John 14:16-17; 1 Cor. 12:12-13). Thus, through the gospel of Jesus Christ, those who were not God's people (the Gentiles) can become His children (Rom. 9:25-26). It is only by the power of the Holy Spirit that believers are able to both understand the law of God and to fulfill its righteousness (1 Cor. 2:11-15; Rom. 8:4-17).

Likewise, once Israel is fully restored to God at the end of the Tribulation Period, the Holy Spirit will ensure that they will never leave Him again for false gods; instead, they will continue in His Law. As a nation, they will receive the Holy Spirit, and He will give them a new heart (vv. 23-28; Joel 2:27-29). As a result, God's Law will be deep inside them forever and they will intimately know Jehovah as *"The Lord of Hosts"* (Jer. 31:33-35).

As prophesied by Ezekiel and other Old Testament prophets, God did institute a New Covenant with His people that would give them eternal salvation, a new and clean heart, and allow the Holy Spirit to indwell them forever (v. 25; Isa. 45:17-19; Jer. 31:31-40). Christ, as High Priest, sealed this covenant with the house of Judah and the house of Israel with His own blood (Luke 22:20; Heb. 8:8). Hence, there is only one individual who can be Israel's Shepherd and King-Priest forever, the Lord Jesus Christ.

In a coming day the Jewish nation will be ecstatic to see Him and thankful to have Him rule over them. Then God will say: *"'They shall know that I, the Lord their God, am with them, and they, the house of Israel, are My people,' says the Lord God. 'You are My flock, the flock of My pasture; you are men, and I am your God,' says the Lord God"* (vv. 30-31). And we Gentile believers will also rejoice with God and utter our sincere Amen!

Meditation

> I would the precious time redeem,
> And longer live for this alone,
> To spend and to be spent for them
> Who have not yet my Savior known;
> Fully on these my mission prove,
> And only breathe, to breathe Thy love.

Infidelity and Loyalty

Enlarge, inflame, and fill my heart
With boundless charity divine,
So shall I all strength exert,
And love them with a zeal like Thine,
And lead them to Thy open side,
The sheep for whom the Shepherd died.

— Charles Wesley

Judgment Against Edom
Ezekiel 35

As mentioned in Ezekiel's first prophecy against Edom (chp. 25), the Edomites were the descendants of Jacob's twin brother Esau, who settled in the region south of Moab and east of the Dead Sea. But why does Ezekiel include a second oracle against heathen Edom, and why place this decree of judgment in the section of the book addressing Israel's future restoration and blessing?

Perhaps the answers to these questions relate to the intense and enduring conflict between both nations that began after Esau sold Jacob his birthright for a bowl of bean soup. The Edomites loathed the Jews, their fraternal brothers, from the very beginning of both nations (also see Obad. 15-16). Ezekiel refers to this as *"an ancient hatred"* (v. 5). Since Edom was first to oppose Israel and had viciously done so for centuries, it is likely that Ezekiel is using Edom as a broad metaphor to pronounce judgment on all the Gentile nations for oppressing His covenant people. Final vindication among the Gentiles is part of the Abrahamic covenant: God promised to curse all nations that would curse the promised nation – Abraham's seed (Gen. 12:3).

There is no beating around the bush; Ezekiel was commanded to set his face against Edom and pronounce God's displeasure against the nation: *"Behold, O Mount Seir, I am against you; I will stretch out My hand against you, and make you most desolate"* (v. 3). The arid region of Edom, where Mount Seir is located, is north of the Arabah desert and south of the Dead Sea, but God promised to destroy Edom's cities and make it even more of a wasteland (v. 4).

There was no promise of future restoration offered to Edom, although their cities would remain as predicted by Obadiah (v. 18). Indeed, today no descendant of the Edomites can be identified on earth. They were ruled over by the Babylonian and Medo-Persian Empires. The latter pushed them from their homeland into the southern hill country of Judah. In 126 B.C. the Jews conquered and forced the

Edomites remaining in their land to convert to Judaism. When Jerusalem was destroyed by the Romans in 70 A.D., the Jewish population was dispersed among the nations and any evidence of this once vast nation that might have still remained was lost. Edom is indeed desolate forever!

To specifically explain why God's wrath was deserved, Ezekiel twice applies the "because/therefore" format used previously to pronounce judgment on Edom and other nations. Edom's *ancient hatred* of the Jews had caused them to commit many atrocities against God's people. As the prophet Obadiah explains, even when Jehovah used Edom as a rod of reproof to correct His people, proud and overbearing Edom went too far in their brutality (v. 5; Obad. 10-14). Additionally, Edom had sought to profit from Israel's chastening. Therefore, the Lord was going to severely punish Edom (vv. 6-10).

The meaning of Edom's name, "to be red," can be traced all the way back to its founder Esau, who was hairy and red at birth (Gen. 25:25). Edom's mountains also had a reddish tint, but now God promised to make the land even redder with "blood" (i.e., by "bloodshed"). The word "blood" is mentioned four times in verse 6 for emphasis. The Lord was going to devastate both the land and the people of Edom.

The second "because/therefore" statement centers in Edom's desire to possess the land that God had given the Israelites (vv. 11-13). Edom loathed the Jewish people and envied their fertile land. This motivated them to blaspheme the mountains of Israel saying, *"They are desolate; they are given to us to consume"* (v. 12). They wanted the land of Judah and Israel for their own, but God would not permit that. Therefore, they spoke against God without constraint (v. 13). The Lord had established an enduring covenant with Jacob and his descendants that guaranteed Canaan as their inheritance – Edom was rebelling against God's expressed will on the matter.

Motivated by covetousness and hatred, the Edomites had inflicted much suffering on God's covenant people for centuries. Jehovah promised to avenge Edom's cruelty with the same measure of hatred and jealousy they had shown Israel. In this sense, Edom is an object lesson warning all Gentile nations; God will hold every nation accountable for how they treat Israel (vv. 14-15). When the Lord returns to the earth to establish His kingdom, all nations of the earth will be judged accordingly (Matt. 25:31-46). God loves His wife despite her unfaithfulness; woe to any nation that abuses her.

Jehovah prompted Moses, Jeremiah, and Zechariah to express His deep devotion to His covenant people by invoking the term *the apple of God's eye*:

> *He found him in a desert land and in the wasteland, a howling wilderness; He encircled him, He instructed him, He kept him as the apple of His eye* (Deut. 32:10).

> After Jeremiah announces that God has put Israel away as an adulterous wife he pleads: *"Their heart cried unto the Lord, O wall of the daughter of Zion, let tears run down like a river day and night: give thyself no rest; let not the apple of thine eye cease"* (Lam. 2:18; KJV).

> *For thus says the Lord of hosts: "He sent Me after glory, to the nations which plunder you; for he who touches you touches the apple of His eye"* (Zech. 2:8).

The ancient idiom, *the apple of my eye*, is an expression of endearment still commonly used today. What most do not realize is that the term originates in the Old Testament. The Oxford English Dictionary states that the phrase refers to "something or someone that one cherishes above all others."[70] The pupil, or aperture, through which light passes to the retina, is the tenderest part of the eye. Because sight is the most valued of our five senses, we treasure our eyes and diligently guard them from harm. The eye is an incredible organ to which even the slightest injury is most acutely felt and may cause loss of function. It is also an organ that is not easily repaired through surgery once damaged. For these and other reasons our eyes are dear to us! When Jehovah invokes the term *the apple of God's eye* in Scripture, He is speaking exclusively of the Jewish people that He greatly cherishes. Beware, nations of the earth: those who abuse the people that God has promised to honor, bless, and love forever, will not stand against His vindicating fury.

Meditation

If the Arabs put down their weapons today, there would be no more violence. If the Jews put down their weapons today, there would be no more Israel.

— Benjamin Netanyahu

I had faith in Israel before it was established; I have faith in it now.

— Harry Truman
(33rd US president)

When the ill winds blow, I will always stand with the Muslims.

— Barack Obama (*The Audacity of Hope,* p. 261)
(44th US president)

Israel Renewed and Restored
Ezekiel 36

Many of the prophecies against the nations listed in Ezekiel 36-39 coincide with Israel's final spiritual refinement and restoration to God as detailed in Jeremiah 46-51, Daniel 7-8, Joel 2, and Zechariah 12-14. All these prophecies preview what is to come during and after the Tribulation Period. Believers living in the Church Age should find the events leading up to the fulfillment of these prophecies of interest since the Church will be removed from the earth just prior to the Tribulation Period.

Overview
Scripture interprets Scripture, and Ezekiel's prophecies in the next four chapters are best explained by what we learn from other passages concerning the renewal and restoration of the Jewish people to Jehovah. A panoramic view is provided by the Lord Jesus in His Kingdom Parables of Matthew 13: In the fifth parable, Christ alludes to what Ezekiel speaks of in verses 16 through 38 in allegory: *"Again, the kingdom of heaven is like treasure hidden in a field, which a man found and hid; and for joy over it he goes and sells all that he has and buys that field"* (Matt. 13:44). God considers Israel *a treasure* unto Himself (Ex. 19:5; Ps. 135:4). The Jews, who had been scattered among the nations six centuries earlier for committing spiritual adultery, would be found again by Messiah for the purpose of offering Himself to them as their King. However, they rejected Him and were consequently dispersed among the nations again. As the parable states, the "treasure" was hidden again in a field. This situation will continue until the Jewish nation repents and receives Christ in the latter days of the Tribulation Period. In order to retrieve them in the future from the nations and to restore them as His people, the Lord first had to pay the debt of their sin at Calvary – He gave His life to redeem the treasure (Israel) which is still to this day buried in the field.

Infidelity and Loyalty

The fifth parable then pictures the spiritual blindness of the Jewish nation which resulted from rejecting Christ (Rom. 11:7, 25), Who then turned to woo a Gentile bride for Himself. This is the focus of the next Kingdom Parable: The Pearl of Great Price. Pearls come from the sea (which symbolizes the Gentile nations; Rev. 17:15) and a pearl has value only in its entirety, which represents the spiritual body of Christ, the Church, which cannot be divided. Like the Church, the pearl is produced through suffering. (It forms around a grain of sand trapped inside an oyster.) The Lord, who suffered and died for the Church, will continue to build it until He removes His bride from the earth. Then, the Lord will reveal Himself again to the Jewish nation (Daniel's seventieth week will commence; Dan. 9:27). When Christ returns to the earth, He will be accepted by them (Zech. 12:10), and then they will receive the Holy Spirit and be restored to God as His people. God will gather His treasure back to the land of Israel; He will not leave one Jew among the nations (39:28-29). In that day, God's *peculiar treasure* will be recovered.

Although the spiritual aspects of the Old Covenant were put away with the resurrection of Christ and the subsequent baptism of believers into His life, the visible remnants of that Testament remained for a time. Israel was given a period of time to hear the gospel of Jesus Christ and repent, but nationally speaking they rejected the terms of this covenant which required them to receive Christ as their Messiah. Three to five years after the writer of Hebrews foretold the event (Heb. 8:7-13), Israel's judgment came in 70 A.D. A large Roman army led by the future Emperor Titus besieged and conquered Jerusalem. The temple that had been built towards the end of the sixth century B.C. by the Jewish captives who returned from Babylon, and that had then been renovated by Herod the Great some five centuries later, was destroyed. There were to be no more offerings, sacrifices, Levitical priesthood, or stench of humanized religion in the nostrils of Jehovah. Even to this day, although some Jews are back in their land and are a self-governing nation, they have no temple or priesthood to reinstate what God put away.

Through the destruction of Jerusalem and the temple, God put an end to the Levitical order established by the Old Covenant, a system that the Jews had developed into their own religion (Gal. 1:13-14). No more ceremonial lip service, devoid of all spiritual value, could be offered to God. Through the New Covenant sealed by Christ's own blood, and it alone, God would forgive the sins of Israel and Judah, pour out His Spirit upon them, and restore them to Himself. During the Church Age some Jews have certainly come to faith in Christ, but the nation as a whole will not turn to Him until His Second Advent at the end of the Tribulation Period; this is the focus of Ezekiel's prophecies in this chapter. Indeed, it is a subject matter frequently addressed in Scripture (Joel 2:18-3:21; Hos. 3; Isa. 11:1-16; Zech. 12:10, 14:1-21; Rom. 11:7-25). With this overview in mind, let us consider God's wonderful promise of Israel's future spiritual renewal and restoration to Jehovah.

Ezekiel's Prophecy

Ezekiel first encourages the Jews by affirming that any nation that has scorned, persecuted, slandered or plundered them, or even rejoiced in Israel's sufferings will receive God's scorn and retribution (vv. 1-5). The Gentiles had been jealous over Israel; now God would show them His jealousy for Israel (vv. 6-7). Not only did God promise to judge Israel's enemies, but He also vowed in a future day to reverse the curses He had previously placed on the land as part of Israel's chastisement (vv. 8-9).

God, speaking to the mountains of Israel, tenderly expresses His devotion for His returning people: *"But you, O mountains of Israel, you shall shoot forth your branches and yield your fruit to My people Israel, for they are about to come."* Jehovah thus pledges His oath to these particulars as an expression of His jealous desire to bless His beloved Israel even before they had fully suffered indignity among the Gentiles. William Kelly rightly surmises that this prophecy can be fully realized only during the Millennial Kingdom:

> In vain do men apply such glowing words to the return from Babylon, which was but an earnest of what is coming for the entire people. Can anyone who respects scripture and knows the facts pretend that the Lord multiplied men on the mountains of Israel, "all the house of Israel, even all of it" (v. 10)? Such words seem expressly written to guard souls from such meagre and misleading views. Did Jehovah settle the returned remnant after their old estate, and do good more than at their beginning (v. 11)? Did the land, did the mountains, become Israel's inheritance and no more bereave them (v. 12)? Do we not know that under the fourth empire [Roman] a still worse destruction came and a longer dispersion, instead of the land

211

devouring no more, neither bereaving its own nations nor bearing the insult of the Gentiles anymore (v. 15)? No! The fulfillment of the prophecy is yet to come, but come it will as surely as Jehovah lives and has thus sworn through His prophet concerning the land of Israel. To suppose that the gospel or the church is meant by such language is very far from simplicity or intelligence.[71]

In the Kingdom Age, the Jews will no longer be plagued with drought and famine, but the land will be abundantly fruitful (vv. 29-30). Likewise, the Jews and their livestock would radically multiply at this time (vv. 10-11). Most importantly, their return to Israel will be permanent (v. 12), for God will not permit the nations to oppress His people ever again (v. 15).

Scripture foretells Israel becoming an agricultural icon in the world, which to some degree has already occurred in recent years. Isaiah not only speaks of this agricultural achievement, but also associates the timing of this realization to when Jehovah gathers His people out of the nations to worship Him in Jerusalem (Isa. 27:13). Though the Jewish nation has not fully returned to Israel, nor do they yet worship their Messiah, the process of gathering them back "one by one" has begun (Isa. 27:12). Isaiah writes:

Those who come He shall cause to take root in Jacob; Israel shall blossom and bud, and fill the face of the world with fruit (Isa. 27:6).

The wilderness and the wasteland shall be glad for them, and the desert shall rejoice and blossom as the rose (Isa. 35:1).

After 2,500 plus years of having no homeland, the Jewish people became a political reality again within their ancient homeland in May 1948. A marked increase in agricultural productivity commenced at that time. From 1950 to 1984, the amount of irrigated land in Israel increased from fifteen to fifty-four percent and agricultural production has expanded sixteen-fold (more than three times the rate of the population growth). Seventy-five years ago, Israel was full of malarial swamps and deserts. Today, there are farms in Israel that are bearing three and four bountiful crops a year and the replanted forests are thriving. After centuries of being mostly unproductive, Israel has become an agricultural marvel. However, Isaiah and Ezekiel tell us that what God will accomplish in the Millennial Kingdom will go beyond the present laws of nature – Israel will be the breadbasket of the world.

Verse 11 poses another wonderful promise to the Jewish nation. As ancient Israel was being destroyed by Babylon, Ezekiel foretold that many of these destroyed cities would, in fact, be rebuilt and resettled in the exact same locations after the Jewish exile was complete:

> *And I will multiply upon you man and beast; and they shall increase and bring fruit: and **I will settle you after your old estates**, and will do better [unto you] than at your beginnings: and ye shall know that I [am] the Lord* (v. 11).

Today, there are many cities in Israel that bear the ancient names of previous biblical cities: Cana, Nazareth, Jericho, Nain, Bethany, Bethlehem, Hebron, Gaza, etc. Ezekiel's prophecy has been fulfilled. It is also noted that the Lord Jesus put a curse on some Jewish cities such as Capernaum, Bethsaida, and Chorazin for their rejection of His message (Luke 10:13-16). Only a few ancient ruins remain of those Jewish cities today. Several cities in Israel today are called by their ancient names; however, those specifically cursed by Christ do not exist.

Ezekiel then says that not only will the Lord restore the Jews to their homeland, making it abundantly prosperous, but He will also remove the reproach of His people among the Gentile nations (vv. 13-15). The Jewish people have been hated for centuries, but during Christ's rule on earth, they will be greatly honored and appreciated by the nations (Zech. 8:20-23).

L. E. Cooper suggests that the revelation formula of verse 16 announcing a new message from Ezekiel may be divided into three parts: reasons for the coming restorations (vv. 16-23), seven elements of the coming restoration (vv. 24-32), and a summary of the benefits of the restoration (vv. 33-38).[72] Jeremiah's earlier parables of the marred belt and the wine jars in Jerusalem convey the same message that Ezekiel now delivers to the Jews in Babylon – God had scattered His people among the nations because of their idolatry and their perverse and unclean ways:

> *Moreover the word of the Lord came to me, saying: "Son of man, when the house of Israel dwelt in their own land, they defiled it by*

213

their own ways and deeds; to Me their way was like the uncleanness of a woman in her customary impurity. Therefore I poured out My fury on them for the blood they had shed on the land, and for their idols with which they had defiled it. So I scattered them among the nations, and they were dispersed throughout the countries; I judged them according to their ways and their deeds" (vv. 16-19).

Through Ezekiel, God's people learned of His anger concerning their ungodly behavior. Their insolence and idolatry had done nothing less than caused the Lord's name to be blasphemed among the nations:

*When they came to the nations, wherever they went, they profaned My holy name – when they said of them, "These are the people of the Lord, and yet they have gone out of His land." But I had concern for My holy name, which the house of Israel had profaned among the nations wherever they went. "Therefore say to the house of Israel, 'Thus says the Lord God: "I do not do this for your sake, O house of Israel, but **for My holy name's sake**, which you have profaned among the nations wherever you went. And **I will sanctify My great name**, which has been profaned among the nations, which you have profaned in their midst; and the nations shall know that I am the Lord," says the Lord God, "when I am hallowed in you before their eyes"'"* (vv. 20-23).

It is indeed a sad commentary when God's people fall so deeply that they profane the Lord's name among the nations. When the heathen exclaim, "These people are so repulsive that their God must be even worse," a terrible blasphemy of God's good name has occurred – yet this is exactly what many Moslems, Hindus, and Buddhists say of Christianity and of Christ today. The conduct of the professing church, in general, is pathetic. Yet, God's name will be sanctified one way or another – He will do it by Himself, even if we choose not to!

The subject of how God will sanctify His great name among the nations and especially by His covenant people is then addressed by Ezekiel (vv. 24-32). First, the Lord promised to honor His promise to regather His people out of the nations and back into the Promised Land: *"For I will take you from among the heathen, and gather you out of all countries, and will bring you into your own land"* (v. 24). This would certainly be an astounding feat that would amaze the world. How would a people without a land, an economic basis, and army, and without political clout suddenly become a prosperous and autonomous nation again?

Second, in a future day, God will create in His people a new heart and will pour out His Spirit upon them (vv. 24-27). *"A new heart also will I give you, and a new Spirit will I put within you"* (v. 26). The Holy Spirit will ensure that they will never leave Him again for false gods; instead, they will continue in His Law and be His people (vv. 26-27). The prophet Joel had proclaimed the same message two centuries earlier (Joel 2:27-29). Having received God's Spirit, the refined and restored nation of Israel will never bring dishonor on Jehovah's name again; therefore the nations will not blaspheme God's name because of Jewish conduct, but will honor Jehovah's name (vv. 28-29; Rom. 2:23-24). Speaking of this event, Jeremiah says that God's Law will be deep inside of His people and that all the Jews from the oldest to the youngest will intimately know Jehovah and identify Him as *"The Lord of Hosts"* (Jer. 31:33-35).

After receiving the Holy Spirit, Israel will be able to look back on their history with honest integrity and lament their past sinful ways (vv. 31-32). So deep will be Israel's remorse that she loathes herself – why would God so abundantly bless an adulterous wife? At that moment, they will realize how undeserving they are of God's forgiveness and that they were not preserved because of their own merits, but because God sought to sanctify His great name among the nations. Therefore, He will purify Israel of her impurities, return her to the land promised her, and richly prosper her in that land (vv. 33-38). Israel's cities will be rebuilt; her agricultural prosperity shall be world renowned; her flocks shall multiple, but must importantly God's name will be exalted among the nations and His people will be with and worship Him forevermore!

Ezekiel's message demonstrates God's revulsion at the pollution of His name among the nations by the very people who were called to honor it. Willful sin and rebellion draws down God's chastening hand. Paul advises that God's dealings with Israel are examples that the Church should learn from today: *"Now these things became our examples, to the intent that we should not lust after evil things as they also lusted. And do not become idolaters as were some of them. ... Now all these things happened to them as examples, and they were written for our admonition, upon whom the ends of the ages have come"* (1 Cor. 10:6, 11). Paul warned that disbelief leads to rebellion and the loss of blessing and fellowship with God. The fact that the Jews (the natural branches) could be, and indeed will be, grafted back into the covenant blessings (the olive tree) indicates that the focus of the illustration in Romans 11 is not eternal salvation per se, but rather all of the blessings in Christ that God desires to share with those who exercise faith in Him.

The Lord Jesus used a similar illustration in John 15 to convey this same truth. He likened Himself to a vine and those who believe in Him to the vine's branches. The Lord then charged His disciples, *"I am the vine, you are the branches. He who abides in Me, and I in him, bears much fruit; for without Me you can do nothing"* (John 15:5). The message is simple and profound: without Christ, a believer can do nothing (John 15:5); however, with Him a believer can do all things (Phil. 4:13)! Why then would a Christian ever want to part from the Lord's presence and provoke His chastening hand? Let us not forget that our God is jealous for our rightful attention. May we learn from Israel's mistake and choose to properly represent "His holy name" to others!

Meditation

Great God! To me the sight afford
To him of old allowed;
And let my faith behold its Lord
Descending in a cloud.

In that revealing Spirit come down,
Thine attributes proclaim,
And to my inmost soul make known
The glories of Thy Name.

— Charles Wesley

The Valley of Dry Bones
Ezekiel 37

The vision recorded in this chapter bridges the long interim between Israel's past dispersion and their physical rebirth as a nation and then their spiritual rejuvenation. It is essential to understand that physical resurrection is not the subject matter of this chapter; rather, the focus is the spiritual regeneration and restoration of the entire Jewish nation to God.

The phrases, *"The hand of the Lord came upon me,"* (v. 1) and *"Again the word of the Lord came to me,"* (v. 15) nicely divide the chapter into two main divisions: First, the vision of the valley of dry bones (vv. 1-10), followed by its interpretation (vv. 11-14). Second, the symbolic action of binding two sticks together (vv. 15-17), followed by its explanation (vv. 18-28).

There is a hint of the wonder prophesied in this chapter all the way back in Genesis, even before the nation existed: *"Abraham stood up from before his dead"* (Gen. 23:3). Through a vision, Ezekiel describes a valley of dry bones before him, which pictures the nation of Israel dead in the world (vv. 1-2). From a Jewish prophet's perspective, the sight was ghastly and hopeless – death reigned over everything. Apparently, to ensure Ezekiel comprehended the reality of the situation, the Lord asked him: *"Son of man, can these bones live?"* Although the morbid sight was appalling, Ezekiel did not answer the question from a natural point of view, but rather with supernatural confidence: *"So I answered, 'O Lord God, You know'"* (v. 3). To him it looked hopeless, but as the Lord Jesus affirmed: *"With men it is impossible, but not with God; for with God all things are possible"* (Mark 10:27).

The Lord then instructs Ezekiel to prophesy over the valley of dry bones with this message:

O dry bones, hear the word of the Lord! Thus says the Lord God to these bones: "Surely I will cause breath to enter into you, and you

217

shall live. I will put sinews on you and bring flesh upon you, cover you with skin and put breath in you; and you shall live. Then you shall know that I am the Lord" (vv. 4-6).

The location of the valley in Israel is not mentioned. (It was perhaps a location of previous slaughter.) Ezekiel does as instructed and broadcasts God's Word over the valley. Immediately the ground beneath him quivers and shakes and then he hears the thunderous noise of rattling bones as they begin to assemble into upright human skeletons. As he continued to preach, the skeletons took on flesh – this great army had the appearance of life, but in fact there was no life within them. This part of Ezekiel's prophecy was fulfilled in May 1948. After 2,500 plus years of Gentile rule, Israel became a political reality again, though the nation remains dead in the spiritual sense.

Next the Lord told Ezekiel: *"Prophesy to the breath, prophesy, son of man, and say to the breath, 'Thus says the Lord God: "Come from the four winds, O breath, and breathe on these slain, that they may live"'"* (v. 9). As Ezekiel spoke over the standing corpses, *"breath came into them, and they lived, and stood upon their feet, an exceedingly great army"* (v. 10). Although Israel is a political reality today and soon will have an awakening of religious practices, the nation will not experience rebirth by the power of the Holy Spirit until the latter days of the Tribulation Period. This is illustrated in the vision when Ezekiel prophesies to the wind (speaking of the Holy Spirit in type; John 3:8) to come and bestow life and breath to the standing, dead army. The Lord refers to these individuals as *"My people"* who were, spiritually speaking, still in *"their graves"* – locked into a hopeless reality (v. 12). This had to be a great encouragement to Ezekiel. If he was faithful to his calling and accurately preaching the word of God, the result would be new life for his people!

When the Jews receive the Holy Spirit, they will obtain spiritual life in Christ and then dwell in peace with their God in the Promised Land (vv. 11-15). Kyle Yates alludes to humanity's great need for the breath of life from God today:

With weirdness, realism and dramatic force the prophet presents the heartening news that Israel may hope to live. A revival is possible! Even dry bones, without sinew and flesh and blood, can live. The coming of God's Spirit brings life. The same thrilling truth is still needed in a world that has dry bones everywhere. What we need is to have the Holy Spirit come with His quickening power that a genuine revival may sweep the earth.[73]

> The Kingdom of God is not going to be advanced by our churches becoming filled with men, but by men in our churches becoming filled with God.
>
> — Duncan Campbell

Only the Holy Spirit can incite a great spiritual revival in the Church today and only He can draw lost souls to Christ. Yet, the same impetus for Ezekiel's spiritual miracle, is also required today – the Holy Spirit responds to the accurate preaching of God's Word and to those who will both heed it and be grieved when others do not!

> I seek the will of the Spirit of God through or in connection with the Word of God. The Spirit and the Word must be combined. If I look to the Spirit alone without the Word, I lay myself open to great delusions also.
>
> — George Mueller

> What the Church needs today is not more machinery or better, not new organizations or more and novel methods, but men whom the Holy Ghost can use, men of prayer, men mighty in prayer. The Holy Ghost does not flow through methods, but through men. He does not come on machinery, but on men. He does not anoint plans, but men, men of prayer.
>
> — E. M. Bounds

Ezekiel also prophesied that Judah (the southern kingdom) and Israel (the northern kingdom) would no longer be two nations when they come into their inheritance in Christ's Kingdom, but that they would be one (vv. 16-21). The prophet symbolized this truth by taking two sticks and making them one; the result of which He called "Israel" (v. 28). This was the name God gave to Jacob, the father of the nation (Gen. 32:28).

Isaiah and Jeremiah foretold the same event (Isa. 11:12; Jer. 3:18). However, only Ezekiel foretells that this united nation would be called "Israel." These prophecies refer to God's dealings with the Jews just prior to and then during the Millennial Kingdom, when Christ will rule over them (v. 22). Accordingly, as we approach the end of the Church Age, the initiation of these prophecies will be apparent, especially the regathering of Jews in the land of Israel after centuries of exile. Recent events seem to indicate that God has begun the process of bringing His covenant people home.

As previously mentioned, on May 14, 1948, while Egyptian fighter-bombers flew overhead and the last remaining British troops prepared to depart Palestine, Ben Gurion and his cabinet gathered at the Tel Aviv Museum where they announced the independence of the state of Israel. After more than 2,500 years of being dispersed throughout the world, the miracle birth of the Jewish nation occurred. Considering that most conquered or displaced people simply blend into the fabric of the society that is forced upon them, the fact that the Jews maintained their distinction as God's covenant people for all that time is miraculous.

The Jews formed an autonomous state called "Israel," just as the Bible had foretold. The next day, the armies of Egypt, Transjordan, Iraq, Syria, and Lebanon invaded Israel and the War of Independence began. Israel emerged victorious, but not without great cost. Thousands of Israeli and Arab soldiers died and approximately 600,000 Palestinians fled their homes, thus creating a "refugee problem" that continues to trouble the region to this day.[74] Isaiah prophesied that the nations would marvel that such a feat could happen in a day (Isa. 66:7-9). This event occurs shortly before the initiation of Christ's Millennial Kingdom (Isa. 66:10-18).

Israel's continued sin against the Lord had resulted in their confusion, shame and punishment: *"Righteousness exalts a nation, but sin is a reproach to any people"* (Prov. 14:34). They had more privilege than any nation and thus bore the reproach of their sin more than any nation. A nation that rebels against the Lord cannot expect His blessing and a nation that does so under the guise of reverence should anticipate His condemnation. Yet, once the Jewish nation receives the Holy Spirit, they will forever be with the Lord in purity of blessed communion. Then the Lord says, *"They shall be My people, and I will be their God"* (v. 23).

Why was it necessary for the Jews to be one nation and not two when they returned to the Promised Land? The answer to this question is found in the verses 24-28:

David My servant shall be king over them, and they shall all have one shepherd; they shall also walk in My judgments and observe My statutes, and do them. Then they shall dwell in the land that I have given to Jacob My servant, where your fathers dwelt; and they shall dwell there, they, their children, and their children's children, forever; and My servant David shall be their prince forever. Moreover I will make a covenant of peace with them, and it shall be an everlasting covenant with them; I will establish them and multiply them, and I will set My sanctuary in their midst forevermore. My tabernacle also shall be with them; indeed I will be their God, and they shall be My people. The nations also will know that I, the Lord, sanctify Israel, when My sanctuary is in their midst forevermore.

God would not permit two kings to reign over a divided Jewish nation again. In fact, Israel's next king will be her last, and He will be the promised Messiah from the line of David. Obviously, the Jews are not completely back in the Promised Land, worshipping their Messiah in a sanctuary set up by Him. Neither do the nations honor Christ or esteem the nation of Israel; so the fulfillment of these prophecies has not occurred yet.

All Ezekiel is foretelling will occur because the rightful heir to the throne of David has already affirmed an eternal covenant of peace between God and Israel and sealed it with His own blood (vv. 24-26). In verses 15-28, Ezekiel identified thirteen different promises of rejuvenation, renewal, and restoration made possible by this new covenant. As mentioned earlier in chapter 34, this righteous, selfless Shepherd is the Lord Jesus Christ. Through Him, the Jews will be able to offer true spiritual worship to God and they will commune with Him again in the land He promised Abraham so long ago (vv. 27-28). What effect does the spiritual conversion of the Jewish nation and their restoration to God have on the Gentile nations? *"The nations also will know that I, the Lord, sanctify Israel, when My sanctuary is in their midst forevermore"* (v. 28).

When surviving Gentiles enter Christ's kingdom and see all that He has accomplished for the Jewish people, and how He raised them up from oblivion to honor, then the Gentiles will know for certain that Jehovah is indeed the one true God!

Infidelity and Loyalty

Meditation

Great God, I own Thy sentence just,
And nature must decay;
I yield my body to the dust,
To dwell with fellow clay.

Though greedy worms devour my skin,
And gnaw my wasting flesh,
When God shall build my bones again,
He clothes them all afresh.

Then shall I see Thy lovely face
With strong immortal eyes;
And feast upon Thy unknown grace
With pleasure and surprise.

— Isaac Watts

Battle of Gog and Magog – Part I
Ezekiel 38

The Lord then commanded Ezekiel to set his face to the north and prophesy against Gog of the land of Magog (vv. 1-2). This prophecy pertains to a future time when the Jews will enjoy a state of national peace (as negotiated by the Antichrist) just before the battle of Gog and Magog around the midpoint of the Tribulation Period. Obviously, for this situation to occur, the prophecies of Jewish restoration to the land pronounced by Jeremiah and Ezekiel would have been at least partially fulfilled.

Millennial Views

Before exploring the prophecies pertaining to the battle of Gog and Magog, we pause to consider the eschatological framework necessary to properly interpret these next two chapters, and the remainder of the book. On this subject L. E. Cooper concludes that a dispensational, premillennial framework best explains these passages:

> Other millennial views are believed inadequate when applied to apocalyptic passages such as Ezekiel 38-39 and 40-48. The premillennial approach is more consistent with the biblical facts, answers more questions, and solves more problems than any of the other approaches. It views history as headed for a literal grand climax which will conclude with a literal battle between Christ and Satan. The Lord Jesus will be victorious and establish an earthly kingdom of peace for a thousand years in preparation for the eternal state.[75]

Amen and Amen! When will the Lord's Second Advent occur in relationship to the establishment of His kingdom? There are several viewpoints held by the Church and various cults, and space does not allow discussion of every view. Here are five primary millennial views held today:

Amillennialism – Good (the kingdom of God) and evil continue to grow in the world until Christ returns to the earth to defeat evil once and for all, thus beginning the eternal state. This view spiritualizes Christ's kingdom (i.e., there is no literal millennial reign of Christ on earth).

Postmillennialism – Believers are diligently working to usher in Christ's kingdom on earth through gospel outreach efforts. Once the earth is properly prepared, Christ will return; this event will be the culmination of the kingdom.

Preterism – A literal-historical view that considers all major prophetic events to have been fulfilled in the first century. Hence, there is no rapture of the Church, no Tribulation Period, and no Millennial Kingdom to come. Some moderate Preterists believe in a literal second coming of Christ to the earth to establish a state of eternal bliss.

Adventism – In 1844, Christ entered the final stage of atoning ministry to judge and cleanse the redeemed in preparation of His second coming when saints will be taken to heaven for 1000 years and wickedness infests the world. All is destroyed at the end of the millennium.

Premillennialism – Christ will return to the earth at the end of the Tribulation Period to establish His righteous kingdom and reign on the earth for one thousand years.

Amillennialism spiritualizes away most of the book of Revelation and denies Christ's glorious rule on earth during a literal thousand-year period. Clearly, the battle of Armageddon demonstrates worldwide rebellion just prior to the Lord's return; obviously believers are not purifying the world to prepare the Kingdom for Christ's return as Postmillennialism teaches. Preterism says that the book of Revelation has already been fulfilled, but nothing in human history would align with the twenty-one apocalyptic judgments or the Antichrist's activities during the Tribulation Period. Adventism suggests that the earth will be ruled by evil during the millennial reign of Christ, Who remains in heaven; this view contradicts hundreds of Old Testament verses which state that Christ will be on a greatly blessed earth during the Kingdom Age.

Premillennialism applies a literal interpretation of Scripture which views the spiritual aspects of God's kingdom today within believers as leading to a literal, earthly, and political fulfillment at Christ's return to the earth. This will be followed by His one-thousand-year peaceful and righteous reign on earth. The spiritual blessings of Christ enjoyed by believers today will benefit all who inhabit the earth in a coming day. This is the only millennial view that permits Scripture to agree with Scripture.

Jews Dwelling Safely in Israel?

At the beginning of the Tribulation Period, the Jews, having taken back their land through war (v. 8), will sign a seven-year peace treaty with the Antichrist (Dan. 9:27). Just as the false prophets in Jeremiah's day preached a false message of "peace, peace" right before their Babylonian oppressors arrived to destroy them (Jer. 4:10), the Jewish people will enjoy a short season of false peace in the last half of the Tribulation Period just before suffering a terrible holocaust. Before the Tribulation Period is over, two-thirds of the Jews in the world will be slaughtered (Zech. 13:7-8). In this sense, the events surrounding the Babylonian invasion are a precursor to the more devastating period yet to occur during the Tribulation Period.

The peace covenant will initially allow the Jews to dwell safely in unprotected villages in the land of Israel just prior to the battle of Gog and Magog (v. 11). This phenomenon has not occurred in over 2,500 years and, at this present time, it is hard to imagine how the Jewish nation could ever be at peace with all their Arab neighbors and especially radical Islamist factions intent on annihilating them. Yet, the Antichrist will accomplish this seemingly impossible feat through promoting a one-world anti-God religion. This religious reality, which originated in Babylon, is depicted as the harlot who rides the beast in Revelation 17.

The famed peace of the Antichrist is a facade which will engulf the world and allow him time to secure a political and economic system with himself at its head. Once in control, he will rid himself of the harlot, the religious system which served his worldwide agenda, and then claim to be God (Rev. 17:15-16). Anyone not pledging allegiance to him by taking his special mark (likely some technological means of economic transfer and global tracking) will be exterminated (Rev. 13:15-18; 20:4). Indeed, a great many will not bow to him and will be slaughtered (Rev. 7:9-14).

Before these events occur, the Jews must be back in the land of Israel as a political reality – that occurred in May 1948. But it should be emphasized that at no time in Israel's history have they ever possessed all the Land that was promised to Abraham and his descendants. Even during the glorious reigns of Kings David and Solomon, Israel never occupied more than about a tenth (approx. 30,000 square miles) of the land that God gave Abraham according to Genesis 15:18-21. The eastern boundary of this land is the river Euphrates, which runs through central Iraq today. So, although the nation of Israel is partially back in the Promised Land, that has been brought back by a sword (v. 8), they do not inhabit the full portion God issued Abraham. We understand the complete fulfillment of this to be future, after the Jews have turned back to Jesus Christ whom they crucified and received Him as their Messiah (Zech. 12:10; Rom. 11:26-32).

The Battle of Gog and Magog

After centuries of oppression, the supposed peace of the Antichrist will be relished by the Jewish nation. But the peace treaty will be broken by the battle of Gog and Magog (an invasion of Israel), which will likely occur just prior to the midpoint of the Tribulation Period. This battle should not be confused with the Battle of Armageddon at the end of the Tribulation Period (Rev. 19). In that confrontation the Lord descends from heaven to the earth, completely defeats all opposing armies, and every eye shall see Him (Matt. 24:30; Rev. 1:7). None of these factors are evident in the Battle of Gog and Magog.

Although these invaders from the north devised their own evil scheme for advancing against the mountains of Israel (v. 10), Ezekiel tells us that it is God who initially prompted them to attack Israel. This battle was divinely instigated to ensure His agenda for the Jewish nation would be accomplished (v. 4).This battle should not be confused with the final Battle of Gog and Magog at the end of Christ's Millennial Kingdom in which Satan gathers the nations to war, all of which are devoured by fire when the earth is destroyed (Rev. 20:7-9).

Jeremiah (chp. 31), Ezekiel (chps. 38-39), and Joel (chp. 2) provide prophetic details of the Battle of God and Magog (occurring during the Tribulation Period) discussed in this chapter. Ezekiel employs the Hebrew word *Rosh* to describe a specific people who will attack Israel during the battle of Gog and Magog:

> *Now the word of the Lord came to me, saying, "Son of man, set your face against Gog, of the land of Magog, the prince of Rosh, Meshech, and Tubal, and prophesy against him"* (vv. 1-2).

> *And you, son of man, prophesy against Gog, and say, Thus says the Lord God: "Behold, I am against you, O Gog, the prince of Rosh, Meshech, and Tubal; and I will turn you around and lead you on, bringing you up from the far north, and bring you against the mountains of Israel"* (39:1-3).

The etymology of both names *Gog* and *Magog* is uncertain. The prefix *ma* of *Magog* may indicate a land, or simply origin "from"; hence *Magog* may mean "of the land of Gog" or "from Gog." Generally speaking, Gog is thought to be the chief of the invaders and Magog, his homeland. This understanding seems to explain the listing of Japheth's sons in Genesis 10: *"The sons of Japheth were Gomer, Magog, Madai, Javan, Tubal, Meshech, and Tiras"* (Gen. 10:2). Notice that *Gog* is not cited here, probably because *Magog* means "the land of Gog." Japheth's son may have been originally known as Gog, but the nation he founded was later referred to as *Magog*. *Gog* essentially means "high peak," which may refer to a mountain in Magog or designate a dictator over the people there.

Who is the prince of Rosh? The Hebrew *rosh* may be translated as an adjective meaning "head" or "chief" as in the KJV and ESV or as a proper noun "Rosh" as rendered in the NKJV and NASV. Textually speaking, it occurs in the NKJV approximately 600 times in the Old Testament as an adjective and only four times as a proper noun (Gen. 46:21 and the three occurrences in Ezekiel 38 and 39). William Kelly presents a case for understanding *rosh* as a proper noun:

> I am aware that the Chaldean Targum of Jonathan and the Greek version of the Jew Aquila take it, like our English Bible, as "the chief prince," the Vulgate as prince of the head or chief, the Syriac as "ruler and chief," the Arabic as "prince of the princes," etc. But none of

227

these affords a tolerable or even intelligible meaning, save the latter two which desert the text. It is true that "rosh", when the context requires it to be a common appellative, means "head" or "chief"; but it is this sense which in the present instance brings in confusion. There can be no doubt therefore that it must be taken as a proper name, and here not of a man as in Genesis 46:21, if the common reading stand, but of a race. This at once furnishes a suitable sense, which is strengthened by the term which precedes it as well as by those that follow. For, as "nasi" regularly means the head of a tribe, or a prince in general, so Meshech and Tubal fix "rosh" as meaning a Gentilic name (Rosh). They were in fact three great tribes, by the ancients called Scythians.[76]

Whether *rosh* further modifies Meshech and Tubal or refers to their border social association is arguable. What we do know is that Gog from the land of Magog (which may be Rosh), with its key centers of Meshech and Tubal, will attack Israel. Meshech and Tubal may refer to two provinces of Asia Minor in the area associated with Scythians, rather than cities. Today, these people groups would reside in the most eastern region of Turkey and Armenia, just south of the Caucasus Mountains.

The Russian capital of "Moscow" may have its etymological roots in the ancient Hebrew word *Meshek* which is associated with Rosh in the above verses. It is noted that the ancient Greek derivation of this Hebrew word is *Moschoi*. Unlike many Russian cities, Moscow (*Moscva* in Russian) has not changed its name; it was called "Moscov" when founded in 1147 A.D. according to Russian chronicles.

Some have also associated Tubal with the modern city of Tobolsk in Tyumen Oblast, Russia (western Siberia), located at the confluence of the Tobol and Irtysh Rivers. While this may be possible, there is no etymological proof of the connection. In the author's opinion, Ezekiel is foretelling the actions of Gog, from the land of Magog, and he further identifies the region by naming people groups or people centers associated with it, Meshech and Tubal. Is Ezekiel prophetically speaking of two future cities in modern Russia? While it is possible, it seems more likely that he is speaking of known people centers, not future ones. If Moscow and Tobolsk did exist in some embryonic form, Ezekiel would have been unaware of Moscow, nearly seventeen hundred miles north of Jerusalem or Tobolsk, which is situated nearly twelve hundred miles east-northeast of Moscow. These cities, if they did exist in ancient times, would have been well beyond the borders of the known world at that time. Two centuries later Alexander the Great referred to these people as uncivilized barbarians whom he, like the Persians, wanted to keep bottled up in the north by erecting walls and gates in the Caucasus Mountains.

Several factors do suggest that Russia is the region from which the attack on Israel will originate. First, we know that Magog, Meshek, and Tubal were all sons of Japheth (i.e., the grandsons of Noah) who settled after the flood in a region just south of present-day Russia (Gen. 10:2). Second, the people of Rosh, Magog, Meshek, and Tubal are all situated directly north of Jerusalem (vv. 6, 15) as one passes through Turkey and Georgia (which are between the Black and Caspian Seas). The prophet Joel describes the geographic location of the inhabitants of the region (Joel 2:20). This will be the home of those who invade Israel for a spoil during the Tribulation Period (vv. 12-13). Third, many of the nations listed as co-intruders with Gog have in recent years forged strong ties with Russia (vv. 5-6).

Ezekiel identifies Togarmah, Gomer, Persia (Iran), Ethiopia, and Libya as siding with Gog. Many identify Togarmah as Turkey and Gomer as Germany; both countries are presently NATO members and clearly have no close association with Russia. However, two important clarifications are required to properly identify Togarmah and Gomer: First, the ancient reference to Togarmah recognizes a people whose ancestors now live in the far eastern portion of Turkey and Armenia. So Togarmah is not speaking of the entire country of Turkey. Second, Gomer similarly refers to an ancient people that resided in the same region called the Gimirrai or Cimmerians, who attacked Assyria in the seventh century B.C. The Gimirraian king Teushpa was defeated by Assarhadon of Assyria sometime between 681 and 668 BC.[77] Assyrian records show that the Gimirrai were known to the Assyrians as *Bit Khumri*, the "house of Omri" who held a most evil dynasty in northern Israel for about fifty years in the ninth century B.C. (which ended with the death of Athaliah). Jewish historian Josephus identified Gomer as Anatolian Galatia.[78] Early Christian writer Jerome also held this position, but Hippolytus of Rome believed Gomer to be Cappadocia just east of Galatia in old Asia Minor (Turkey today). All this to say that Gomer most likely is not modern Germany as Yoma in the Talmud indicates, but rather Gomer refers to an ancient people residing southeast of the Black Sea (in or near Armenia), which is directly north of Israel. L. M. Cooper provides this concise summary of the matter:

> Gog's army would be allied with Persia (Iran), Cush (Ethiopia), Put (Lybia), Gomer (Armenia), and Togarmah (also Armenia).[79]

It is noteworthy that a few nations oppose Gog's assault and denounce his intrusion into Israel to plunder their wealth and livestock, but they do nothing about it: *"Sheba, Dedan, the merchants of Tarshish, and all their young lions will say to you, 'Have you come to take plunder?'"* (v. 13). Diplomacy will not prevail to stop this invasion, and apparently, no nation or cooperation of nations (including NATO) is able to prevent Rosh's attack.

Biblically speaking, the actual identity of Tarshish is unknown. Scripture does speak of the ships and merchants of Tarshish to confirm its booming sea trade, especially in metals (27:4-6, 12). It may have been located in the western part of the Mediterranean Sea, such as southwestern Spain (the Iberian Peninsula is rich in metal deposits), or as some suggest, may even refer to the Isles of Britain lying north of Spain. History does record that the Phoenicians sailed to Cassiterides (the Tin Islands) in fifth century B.C. to obtain tin, as did the Greeks later. On the identification of Tarshish, H. A. Ironside writes:

> Tarshish is generally identified with the lands of the far west of Europe, including perhaps a part of Spain but very definitely Great Britain. It was from Tarshish of old that the Phoenicians obtained tin, and the word Britannia means "the land of tin."[80]

Indeed, Britain may be Tarshish of old; Cornwall in the British Isles has large deposits of tin and Tarshish in Ezekiel's day was a main supplier of tin (27:12). The amalgamation of tin and copper produces bronze, thus both metals were highly sought after during this era.

During the Tribulation Period, Ezekiel says that Sheba and Dedan (whose descendants populated the Arabian Peninsula; 25:13; Gen. 25:3; Jer. 49:8) will have strong ties with Tarshish and her young lions (i.e., nations founded by Tarshish). Today, Britain and those English-speaking countries established by her colonization have close ties with Arabia, which is not the case for Spain. Regardless of who Tarshish is, Ezekiel's prophecy declares that she and her young lions will be unable, or perhaps not divinely permitted, to impede Rosh's invasion of Israel (v. 13). The Lord Himself will defend Israel against the hordes of Gog.

The Jews will be dwelling safely in unwalled villages when Gog's armies come down from the north (vv. 8, 11, 14). They will be deceived into lowering their defenses while under the protection of the Antichrist's peace treaty (Dan. 9:27). The invading armies will be so enormous that Ezekiel likens them to a huge cloud that engulfs the entire land (vv. 9, 15, 16). Thankfully, with great fury and jealousy for His people the Lord will intervene and defeat the military incursion (Joel 2:12-20). How will He wipe out the invaders?

First, God will cause an earthquake to interrupt the invasion (v. 20). Second, He will stir up the factions within the various armies to turn on and slaughter each other (v. 21). Third, the Lord promises to use pestilence (v. 22). Fourth, He *"will rain down on him, on his troops, and on the many peoples who are with him, flooding rain, great hailstones, fire, and brimstone"* (v. 22). What will God accomplish through this specular defeat of Gog's invading armies? He says, *"I will magnify Myself and sanctify Myself, and I will be known in the eyes of many nations. Then they shall know that I am the Lord."* Not only do the nations become aware of Jehovah's existence and power in the Battle of Gog and Magog, but the victory will also awaken Israel from their long-standing spiritual blindness. So while Jerusalem itself will be saved at that time, the persecution of the Jewish people worldwide will have just begun.

Before the Kingdom Age commences, the Lord Jesus will descend to the earth to war against the Antichrist and his armies in the Megiddo Valley. This will occur about three and a half years after the Battle of Gog and Magog, just discussed. His victory will deliver Jerusalem from the Antichrist's invading armies (Zech. 14). After the Battle of Armageddon, the nations will be gathered and judged (Matt. 13:47-50, 25:31-46); all those following the Antichrist will be killed (Rev. 19:20-21). Those who did not take his mark will be allowed to enter Christ's kingdom on earth. This will conclude *"the time of the Gentiles"* (Rom. 11:25; Rev. 11:1-2).

The Bible has much to say about future events. Fulfilled prophecy is one of the evidences that the Bible is indeed God's Word to humanity. The prophecies just mentioned, as well as others, relate to the reestablishment of Israel as a nation. These are exciting times; we are seeing God's Word being fulfilled before our eyes. God is a promise-keeping God and by His everlasting love He is drawing His covenant people into His sovereign purposes for them. Their ultimate oneness with God will establish them in everlasting peace.

Thankfully, unlike the peace of the Jewish nation which is still future, the peace of God which surpasses all understanding is something that the Christian can enjoy today:

> *Be anxious for nothing, but in everything by prayer and supplication, with thanksgiving, let your requests be made known to God; and the peace of God, which surpasses all understanding, will guard your hearts and minds through Christ Jesus* (Phil. 4:6-7).

Isaiah put the matter this way, *"Thou wilt keep him in perfect peace, whose mind is stayed on thee: because he trusteth in Thee"* (Isa. 26:3; KJV). Nearness to God is the greatest defense against depression and the best means of promoting a stable mind. In a coming day the Jews will seek peace with the Antichrist and will pay dearly for that mistake. True peace is found in God alone. There is but one hiding place for the threatened, one solace for the brokenhearted, and one salve for the wounded soul – the Lord Jesus Christ. Believer, stay near Him!

Meditation

Peace, perfect peace, in this dark world of sin?
The blood of Jesus whispers peace within.
Peace, perfect peace, with sorrows surging round?
On Jesus' bosom naught but calm is found.
Peace, perfect peace, death shadowing us and ours?
Jesus has vanquished death and all its powers.
It is enough: earth's struggles soon shall cease,
And Jesus call us to Heaven's perfect peace.

— Edward H. Bickersteth, Jr.

Battle of Gog and Magog – Part II
Ezekiel 39

The prophecy against Gog and Magog continues into this chapter (38:1-39:12). Gog's multi-nation invasion force from the north will be largely destroyed in Israel; their weapons will be useless against the supernatural elements God summons against them (vv. 1-3). Birds and wild beasts will then feed on the carcasses of fallen soldiers (v. 4). Apparently, a remnant will be allowed to escape to the north between the Black and Caspian Seas (Joel 2:19-20). These will provide testimony to the nations as to what the God of the Jews did for them and then says God, *"Then they shall know that I am the Lord"* (vv. 5-6).

Not only will the nations learn of Jehovah's presence in Israel, but the defeat awakens Israel from her spiritual slumber to exalt the Lord again: *"So I will make **My holy name** known in the midst of My people Israel, and I will not let them profane **My holy name** anymore. Then the nations shall know that I am the Lord, the Holy One in Israel"* (vv. 7-8). The text proclaims that God Himself is the Holy One of Israel who shall reign over the nations from the midst of His people. Only God is perfect, self-sufficient, and self-existing – there is none like Him, for He is holy! The Lord Himself proclaims: *"For I am the Lord your God, the Holy One of Israel, your Savior"* (Isa. 43:3). *"I, even I, am the Lord, and beside Me there is no Savior"* (Isa. 43:11). *"For I am God, and there is none else; I am God, and there is none like Me"* (Isa. 46:9). The prophet Isaiah clearly teaches that the Savior of mankind is none other than the unique Holy God of the universe.

The New Testament reveals this same truth when speaking of the Lord Jesus Christ, the God-man, and the Holy One of Israel. He was acknowledged as being holy in the womb by the angel Gabriel (Luke 1:35). Demons, while fearing premature judgment, asserted: *"Let us alone! What have we to do with You, Jesus of Nazareth? Did You come to destroy us? I know who You are – the Holy One of God!"* (Mark

1:24). Peter proclaimed why Christ was holy: *"We have come to believe and know that You are the Christ, the Son of the living God"* (John 6:69). The early church recognized the intrinsic holiness of Christ (Acts 4:27, 30) and that He was the only Savior (Acts 4:12; John 14:6). Through the great victory over the armies of Gog, Israel will begin to understand that the Holy God of Israel is again making Himself known. By the end of the Tribulation Period, the Lord Jesus Christ will be fully recognized as the Holy God and the Savior of Israel and He will rule over the nations.

Gog's armies intended to despoil Israel of her wealth and livestock, but after Jehovah's intervention, it will be the Jews who seize plunder from them (v. 10). Their discarded weaponry will be so abundant that Israel will not need to cut down trees for firewood, but rather will burn the weapons of their fallen aggressors for seven years (v. 9). This will serve as a provision for the Jews through the remainder of the Tribulation Period and into the start of the Kingdom Age.

The types of weapons garnered from Gog's dead soldiers is probably more representative than literal (i.e., shields and bucklers, the bows and arrows, the javelins and spears), as Ezekiel would have had difficulty describing machine guns, rocket launchers, cruise missiles, etc. The meaning of the Hebrew words employed are flexible enough to encompass a wider range of meanings. For example, the Hebrew word *chets* rendered "arrow," means "a piercer" and the Hebrew *romach*, translated "spear," has the root meaning "to hurl." Certainly, bullets are designed to pierce and missiles go hurtling through the air. However, because of catastrophic events during the Tribulation Period, as described in the book of Revelation, it is quite possible that electronic based equipment and high-tech weaponry will be useless, meaning a return to more unsophisticated weaponry and traveling on horseback may become commonplace again. These types of archaic weapons would certainly serve well as fuel for heating homes and cooking food, better than, say, a grenade.

The armies of Gog were so quickly wiped out that there was no opportunity to bury their dead. The Jews will work diligently to cleanse their land of rotting corpses (vv. 11-16). Over a period of seven months, search parties and burial details will be dispatched to bury Gog's dead soldiers (v. 12). Local citizens will assist in this effort and will be rewarded for doing so; others will be employed to do the work (vv. 13-14). They will be buried in a valley east of the Dead Sea, perhaps the Valley of Abarim in Jordan, which is a region within the title deed of Israel's possession (Gen. 15:18). Because the valley entrance will be so clogged with dead bodies (v. 11) the burial location will be renamed "the Valley of Hamon Gog," which means "the Valley of the hordes of Gog" (vv. 15-16). The details in this section of text and the following confirm that the main location of the Battle of Gog and Magog will be in northeast Israel and just east of Israel in modern Jordan.

Normally, when a sacrifice is offered, an animal is slaughtered and a portion of it is burnt on an altar and the remainder is eaten by the offerers. However, just the opposite will be true after Gog's defeat: wild animals will be summoned to God's table set for them in Bashan (vv. 17-20). Interestingly, Jeremiah prophesied that Israel would have control of Bashan again before Christ returns to the earth to destroy the Antichrist's political and economic system referred to as Babylon (Jer. 50:19-20; Rev. 18). After being conquered by the Babylonians, Bashan (the Golan Heights in northeastern Israel) did not become a Jewish possession again until after the Six-Day War of 1967. This means that the fulfillment of Jeremiah's prophecy, the destruction of Babylon, could not have occurred before then; hence it is yet future.

The twofold outcome of Gog's defeat will draw Israel back to Jehovah and the nations will be introduced to the glory of Israel's God (vv. 21-24). God dealt with Israel's enemies according to their uncleanness and evil intentions. This miraculous defeat will be used as a catalyst to draw remaining dispersed Jews back to the land of Israel (v. 25). The remaining verses of the chapter then focus on the final days of the Tribulation Period when God will draw all His covenant people back to Israel, where they will enjoy peace and safety and the esteem of all nations (vv. 26-27). God will have forgiven their past unfaithfulness and will again choose to commune with His covenant people. Jehovah's adulterous wife will then be restored to Him.

Jews Returning to Israel

In the last chapter Ezekiel foretold that, prior to the Battle of Gog and Magog a large contingent of Jews will regain their native land through military action. In Ezekiel 39 we learn that after this battle the Lord will bring every Jew on the planet back to the land of Israel (39:28). Clearly, this prophecy does not pertain to the Jews returning from their Babylonian or Assyrian exiles, for many did not come home then.

The process of bringing Jews back to Zion started in the early twentieth century. It will be completed when all of the Jews are back in the land at the end of the Tribulation Period; the entire nation will receive the Holy Spirit at this time to complete their spiritual transformation (vv. 28-29). The following chart shows the percentage of Jews worldwide that have returned to the land of Israel in recent years. All information is derived from the *Israeli Central Bureau of Statistics*[81]:

Year	Percent of Jews Worldwide Back in Israel
1882	0
1900	1
1925	1
1939	3
1948	6
1955	13
1970	20
1980	25
1990	30
2000	37
2010	42
2014	44

The core Jewish population reached its peak just before WW2 at about 17 million, but was reduced to 11 million after Hitler's attempts to exterminate them. At the beginning of 2016, the core Jewish population was projected to be about 14.2 million worldwide, with 40 percent residing in the United States and 6,335,000 Jews (or about 44.6% of the world population) living in Israel. It is noted that Israel has the highest birth rate (an average of three children per woman) of any developed country in the world.

The land of Palestine once again became a Jewish state in May 1948, a situation that was immediately and violently challenged by surrounding Arab countries. The land belonging to the Jewish state was further expanded after their victory in the Six-Day War of 1967. As Ezekiel said, the land would only be possessed through the sword.

Prophecies predicting a Jewish regathering to the land of Israel, such as Isaiah 11:12 and Ezekiel 39:28-29, are not yet complete. Ezra and Nehemiah record that many dispersed Jews from the southern kingdom of Judah did return from Babylon to Israel in the fifth and sixth centuries B.C., exactly as Jeremiah prophesied years earlier. However, most of the northern ten nations have not returned to the land yet, nor have all the Jews from the southern kingdom returned to Israel! Accordingly, Jeremiah's prophecy pertaining to the broader event remains unrealized:

> *In those days the house of Judah shall walk with the house of Israel, and they shall come together out of the land of the north to the land that I have given as an inheritance to your fathers. But I said: "How can I put you among the children and give you a pleasant land, a beautiful heritage of the hosts of nations?" And I said: "You shall call Me, 'My Father,' and not turn away from Me. Surely, as a wife treacherously departs from her husband, so have you dealt treacherously with Me, O house of Israel," says the Lord* (Jer. 3:18-20).

The houses of Judah and Israel have not yet fully returned to the land, nor have they come together to worship the Messiah. Jeremiah's seventy-year prophecy has been fulfilled and many Jews did return from Babylon to Judah. But Ezekiel foretold that by the end of the Tribulation Period, every Jew remaining among the nations will be physically brought back to dwell in the land of Israel (vv. 28-29).

Bible prophecy is in motion; Israel has become a Jewish nation again, but God's covenant people are yet to be fully regathered to the land promised to Abraham (Gen. 15:18-21). The boundaries of this inheritance were confirmed when the Israelites entered Canaan under Joshua's leadership (Josh. 1:3-4). The Jews have yet to possess this vast region of land, which means that God is not done with the Jewish nation yet.

The seventieth week of Daniel's prophecy is rapidly approaching (Dan. 9:27). At that time, the Lord will spiritually refine His people and physically restore them to the land promised to Abraham's descendants through Jacob. However, in the process of doing so, two-thirds of the Jews will die during the Tribulation Period (Zech. 13:8-9). Only a small Jewish remnant will survive the refining fire of the Tribulation Period and be restored to God as His chosen people. There will be numerous other judgments upon the earth that will also cause death and misery. The bottom line is that earth will not be the place to be during the Tribulation Period, as perhaps eighty percent of the world's population will perish.

Throughout the Tribulation Period, God, through His judgments, will take away from man what man has ignorantly claimed as his own. For example, natural man has labored, stolen, cheated, murdered, etc. in order to gain wealth, power, prestige, and sensual gratification. However, conditions in this epic period of time will be such that death will be welcomed; even life's basic necessities of food and drinking water will be scarce (Rev. 6:6, 8:10-11). By the end of the Tribulation Period, man will have nothing. God will demonstrate His control over all things and then will purify the earth in order to usher in the Kingdom Age (Dan. 2:35, 44-45; Rom. 8:21).

Meditation

Almighty God, Thy lofty throne
Has justice for its cornerstone,
And shining bright before Thy face
Are truth and love and boundless grace.

All glory unto God we yield,
Jehovah is our Help and Shield;
All praise and honor will we bring
To Israel's Holy One, our King.

— The Psalter

The Millennial Temple
Ezekiel 40-42

The final nine chapters of the book explain the new order that will govern Jewish millennial activities: First, a new temple will be erected in Jerusalem; the detailed dimensions guiding its construction are recorded by Ezekiel (chps. 40-43). Second, a new system of worship will permit access to God (chps. 44-46). Third, there will be new divisions of land allotted to the various tribes of Israel (chps. 47-48).

While there are matters beyond our understanding in these chapters, the vast amount of detail is astounding and demands a literal, rather than a figurative, interpretation. Some suggest that the Millennial Temple is just a symbol of the Church, and the sacrifices, Sabbaths, feasts, etc. are merely pictures of the Church's spiritual access to Christ or her blessings in Him. Some would also have us believe that the 144,000 Jewish witnesses that are sealed in the Tribulation Period (12,000 from the twelve tribes of Israel, according to Rev. 7) are really Gentiles living on earth now or that have already died.

Indeed, numbers are often used in Scripture to symbolize a particular meaning which is elsewhere verified in Scripture by consistency. The number "fifty," for example, appears fourteen times in this last section of Ezekiel dealing with the Millennial Temple. The number fifty is connected with the Holy Spirit (Who came fifty days after Christ's resurrection as prefigured by the Feast of Pentecost and foretold by Christ). Fifty is also associated with Israel's return and restoration to their land (as pictured in the year of Jubilee; Lev. 25:10). Both symbolic representations are evident in chapters 40-48, so the number fifty was likely chosen to convey these meanings.

With that observation stated, it would be foolish to apply a figurative meaning to the entire text. The architectural details and layout with specific numerical measurements do have specific meaning. To conclude otherwise would in effect say: "God, You wasted Your time and our time by having Ezekiel record all this meaningless information." The only sensible conclusion is there will be a real temple built according to these exact specifications in a coming day.

This will be an exciting time for the Jewish nation! The long-barren fig tree (religious Israel) will become fruitful again; the Jewish nation will receive the Holy Spirit and have Christ as its focus. Judaism, with all its extra-biblical traditions and interpretations, will have no part in the worship of the Jewish Messiah during the Millennial Kingdom.

Replacement Theology and Amillennialism

Many Christians today believe that there are no scriptural promises remaining for the Jewish people. Consequently, Israel has no claim to the Promised Land and God's unfulfilled promises to her have been somehow transferred to the Church. This doctrine is called "Replacement Theology." Dr. Barnhouse summarized its teaching: "The amillennarians take all the promises that belong to the Jews and apply them to the Church, leaving the curses, as Satan likes to do, for the Jews."[82] Replacement Theology denies the Jews any opportunity for divine restoration as God's covenant people, a peaceful residence in the Promised Land, or a status of honor in Christ's future kingdom. This teaching coincides with that of several prominent cults.

In this respect, Replacement Theology has struck a common chord with the Muslim world – both believe that the Jewish state has no biblical reason for existing today. Most of those who hold to covenant or reformed theology frameworks believe that the Church is the Israel of today and that God has abandoned the Jewish nation forever. Proponents of this view argue that God has carefully chosen His people throughout the ages and that because of their repetitious rebellion, the Jewish people are no longer His chosen people.

Covenant theology also teaches that there is no literal, future, Millennial Kingdom of Christ, but that Christ's kingdom exists spiritually within the Church today. While it is true that the kingdom of God exists in a spiritual sense within the Church today, this cannot be equated to the literal, earthly kingdom which is foretold in numerous Scriptures. Such a conclusion is only possible by a dual hermeneutic which figuratively interprets large portions of the Bible, especially those passages which are eschatological in nature. In other words, prophecies related to Israel are treated as allegories in order to render them applicable to the Church now.

For those who hold to Replacement Theology and Amillennialism, the following chapters will be extremely difficult to explain. For example, the millennial temple described by Ezekiel has specific dimensions and is to be erected in Jerusalem so that a restored Jewish nation can offer worship to God. The various twelve tribes of Israel are also promised possessions of land with specific boundaries throughout the region as portioned to Abraham in Genesis 15. Clearly, none of these events have transpired yet, which means that if Jehovah is a covenant-keeping God, He is not finished with the nation of Israel.

The Millennial Kingdom and Beyond

During this blissful era, the earth and all its inhabitants will enjoy a thousand years of blessing under Christ's rule. It is hard to imagine a world without the divine curses that man has suffered under since sin intruded Eden. Seed casually scattered on a mountaintop will produce a great harvest. Weapons will be used as agricultural implements, and a spirit of peace and tranquility will permeate the entire planet.

Clearly, the Millennial Kingdom of Christ will be marked by strange phenomena throughout the earth. The wolf and the lamb shall dwell together, as will the kid of the goat with the leopard, and the calf with the lion (Isa. 11:6-7). Toddlers will be able to play by the hole of the asp and at the adder's den without fear of a deadly attack (Isa. 11:8). The glory of the Lord will be displayed upon the world as abundantly as *"the waters cover the sea"* (Isa. 11:9).

From Isaiah 2:1-5 and 66:20, we learn that Jerusalem shall be the religious center of the world. Christ will reign from there and all the nations will come there to praise, worship, and learn of Him. There will be no war or violence, only peace. All the earth shall see the glory of the Lord Jesus. Isaiah 4:2-4 informs us that the Jews who live through the Tribulation will gaze upon Christ (the Branch of the Lord) and appreciate His splendor, glory, fruitfulness, and beauty. So great will be the glory of the Lord upon the earth that there will be no need for the sun or moon to illuminate it (Isa. 60:18-20). These circumstances, though wonderful, should not be confused with the eternal state in which there is a new heaven and earth with no evil present (Isa. 65:17).

There are several clear distinctions between the Kingdom Age and the Eternal State, which those holding an amillennial viewpoint ignore. For example, the seas and oceans we know today will still be present during the Kingdom Age (Isa. 11:9; Ezek. 47:18; Zech. 14:8), but there will be no seas in the new earth (Rev. 21:1). Furthermore, Israel is not in the land specified and the millennial tribal allotments have not yet been delegated (47:13-23). Likewise, geographic locations on earth today will exist in the Millennial Kingdom (Joel 3:18; Zech. 14:16-21) but obviously will not in the new earth. The new heaven and earth will not be created until after the Kingdom Age is concluded, Satan's last rebellion on earth is quelled (Rev. 20:7-10), and the planet we live upon is destroyed (Rev. 20:11).

Peter further identifies the Kingdom Age as the Day of the Lord (2 Pet. 3:10), and the eternal state as the Day of God (2 Pet. 3:12). At the end of the Day of the Lord (i.e., at the end of Christ's Millennial Kingdom), the heavens and the earth shall pass away with a great noise and their elements shall melt with fervent heat and be burned up (2 Pet. 3:10). Isaiah states that *"all the host of heaven shall be dissolved, and the heavens shall be rolled up like a scroll"* (Isa. 34:4). He later foretells that after the Millennial Kingdom, God will create a new heaven and a new earth (Isa. 65:17).

Following this creative feat, Paul asserts that there will be a divine audit to confirm that Christ has completely dealt with all the negative repercussions of sin and has restored creation to perfection and to its proper association with God. All the damage caused by sin will be corrected and then God will be all in all (1 Cor. 15:26-28). It is the writer's opinion that in the eternal state, previous distinctions such as Old Testament saints, the Church, Tribulation saints, the nation of Israel, etc. will be remembered, but not emphasized. These distinctions served God's purposes in time while He was unfolding His great plan of salvation to man in various stages, but will not be significant throughout eternity (John 10:16; 1 Cor. 15:26-28; Rev. 21:24-27; 22:1-5).

The Millennial Temple

The specifications of the temple are contained within Ezekiel 40-44. Why did the prophet expend so much space to describe the Millennial Temple? We are not told the answer to this question, but from other passages of Scripture we can speculate reasons for some written detail. First, it is in keeping with the explicit directions and specifications God revealed to Moses on Mount Sinai in first erecting

God's tent of meeting in the wilderness and later a temple in Jerusalem (Ex. 25-40). Second, the temple was a visible reminder of God's presence among His people. Earlier Ezekiel recorded God's glory departing the temple because of Israel's wickedness (chp. 10); now he foretells God's presence returning to a new temple. To ensure that there was no confusion as to what temple or in what timeframe this event would occur, Ezekiel is clear. Third, as in the Levitical temple, we realize that the patterns of heavenly things are expressed in the Millennial temple to increase our appreciation of Christ's ministries, character, attributes and offices (Heb. 8:5, 9:23-24). One cannot fully appreciate the design of God's temple without realizing what is being symbolized through the intricate details.

Ezekiel's vision of the new temple occurred in the twenty-fifth year, the tenth month, and the fourteenth day of his exile, which would be April 19, 573 B.C. (v. 1). Although this is the final dated prophecy of the book, it falls chronologically before the vision of 29:17-21. It is the author's view that Ezekiel maintains the same chronological reference point (the captivity of Jehoiachin according to the Jewish calendar) throughout his book (with the exception of the first verse of the book). His dates are not tied to King Zedekiah's reign in Jerusalem, as Ezekiel never mentions Zedekiah's name, which may demonstrate his lack of esteem for the Babylonian appointee, who displaced Jehoiachin and would cause the Jews so much suffering.

However, some confusion in respect to timing has resulted from the reference to *"the beginning of the year"* in verse 1 (i.e., because it was the tenth month and not the first). Nisan is the first month in the Jewish religious calendar, but the Babylonian New Year began in the seventh month of the Jewish calendar, Tishri. Unfortunately, the Jews began widely observing the Babylonian calendar during and after their Babylonian exile. As an example, the Jews began to commemorate the Feast of Trumpets on the first day of Tishri, but as the first month of the year, instead of the first day of the seventh month as Moses commanded. Consequently, over time, the Feasts of Trumpets became *Rosh Hashanah*, which literally means "the head of the months." For this reason, Jews continue to celebrate The Feast of Trumpets as a New Year festival today.

It is possible that Ezekiel's reference to the beginning of the year was connected with the year of Jubilee, which began on the tenth day of the seventh month (Lev. 25:9). If that were the case, then the message date would be October 573 B.C. Regardless of Ezekiel's reckoning, the date of the vision would be sometime in 573 B.C., about fourteen years after the destruction of Jerusalem.

Previously, the Lord had picked Ezekiel up by his hair to initiate a vision, but this time the Lord led him by the hand to a high vantage point just south of Jerusalem. The millennial Jerusalem and its temple were quite different from what Ezekiel knew as a young man, so the Lord was going to give Ezekiel a tour. From Ezekiel's location he saw the overall structure of a city and a man looking like brilliant bronze (this individual is an angel appearing in the form of a man for Ezekiel's benefit; v. 2). He was standing at the eastern gate of the city and held a line of flax and a measuring rod in his hand (v. 3). He instructed Ezekiel to both listen and watch what he was doing and to be attentive to all the measurements and information he would be providing (v. 4).

Ezekiel then notes that there was a wall surrounding the temple and that the measuring rod in the man's hand was 6 cubits long. A regular cubit (the length of a man's forearm with his fingers extended) was approximately 18 inches. A long cubit included the addition of a hand's breadth, for a total of 21 inches. It is generally agreed that this rod was roughly ten and a half feet in length and was similar to the one John used to measure and record the dimensions of God's temple in Revelation 11:1-2. The wall about the temple was one rod high and one rod thick.

The East Gate (40:6-16)

After the height and width of the wall around the temple were known, the man went to the eastern gate of the temple. This was one of three gates leading into the outer courtyard. The man measured the gateway's threshold, its entrance, porch, alcoves, steps, and posts and the distances between various structural components (vv. 6-15). Ezekiel recorded all of the particular measurements and noted that there were beveled window frames in the gate's porch and alcoves along the gateway corridor and that a palm tree was on each gate post (v. 16). As shown below, the porch (i.e., portico or vestibule) was the most inner part of the gateway leading into the outer court.[83]

PLANS FOR TEMPLE GATES

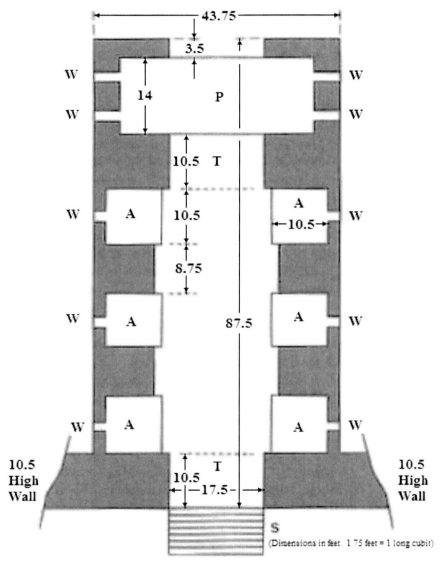

(Dimensions in feet 1.75 feet = 1 long cubit)

A = Alcoves, recesses for the guards (40:7a, 10, 12)
P = Portico, vestibule (40:8-9)
S = Steps (40:6a)
T = Thresholds (40:6b, 7b)
W = Windows (40:16)

Wall around temple area (40:5)

The gates of the temple wonderfully foreshadow man's accessibility to God through the Lord Jesus Christ. He told His disciples that, spiritually speaking, He was both the door and the only way for man to enter into God's presence:

> *I am the door. If anyone enters by Me, he will be saved, and will go in and out and find pasture* (John 10:9).

> *Jesus said to him, "I am the way, the truth, and the life. No one comes to the Father except through Me"* (John 14:6).

Furthermore, this wonderful new life and new beginning in Christ are symbolized by the eight steps before each gate entrance. When the number *eight* is used symbolically in Scripture, it speaks of "new beginnings" such as new life or a new order. We are already familiar with this concept: the eighth day begins a new week in our calendars and the eighth note in a musical scale begins a new octave. Seven is God's number of completeness (Gen. 2:3), which means eight is the start of a new series, just as the seventh day, Saturday, yields to the eighth, Sunday, to begin a new week. Accordingly, the Lord rose from the dead on Sunday to demonstrate the newness of His resurrection life.

This symbolism can be seen throughout both the Pentateuch and the history books of the Old Testament. In Noah's day, eight souls entered an ark (a picture of Christ) to escape God's judgment on the wicked through a flood (1 Pet. 3:20). The ark protected its occupants from God's wrath, lifted them off the earth to be alone with God, and safely carried them to a new life in a new world. The prophet Samuel was to anoint a new king of Israel, a man after God's own heart – that man was David, the eighth son of Jesse (1 Sam. 17:12). Through David a new and everlasting dynasty would be established – the Lord Jesus Christ will rule from the throne of David forever.

As Leviticus introduces a new era of opportunity for the Jewish nation to *come near* to Jehovah, the word "eighth" appears ten times, significantly more than in any other book in the Bible. In fact, one-fourth of all occurrences of the word "eighth" in the Bible are found in Leviticus. While Genesis is a book of initial "beginnings," Leviticus is a continuing story of "new beginnings" through blood atonement. Ezekiel is a book which repeatedly announces the eternal new beginning God has for the Jewish nation through the finished work of Christ!

The Outer Courtyard (40:17-19)

Entering the outer court through the eastern gate, Ezekiel noticed 30 rooms round about the center pavement of the courtyard. The distance from the inside edge of East Gate to the outside edge of the inner gate leading into the inner courtyard was 100 cubits (about 175 feet).

The South and North Gates (40:20-27)

Next the prophet was led across the outer court to view the north gate and then the south gate; their layout and dimensions were identical to the East Gate.

Gateways to the Inner Court (40:28-37)

Having measured the South Gate last, the bronze-gleaming man escorted Ezekiel northward to the southern gate leading into the inner courtyard. As with the outer courtyard, there were three identical gateways on the north, east, and south sides of the inner courtyard and these also were of the same dimensions as the outer gates. The only difference was that the porch orientation of the inner gateways was opposite the outer gateways (i.e., to enter into the outer court through an outer gate, one would pass through the porch last, but to enter the inner court, one would pass through the porch first).

Where Sacrifices Were Prepared (40:38-43)

Ezekiel notices four tables in the inner courtyard on either side of the gateways from the outer courtyard. Sacrifices would be prepared on these tables before being placed on the altar in the center of the inner courtyard. During the Millennial Kingdom, the Jews will perform animal sacrifices as a memorial to the propitiation for sin Christ provided at Calvary, in much the same way that the Church regularly conducts the Lord's Supper and practices believer's baptism. The former celebrates the redemptive work accomplished through Christ's death at Calvary and the latter, the new identity and life that the believer has in Christ through His resurrection. Likewise, what was typified in the Levitical offerings was fulfilled through Christ's sacrifice, and the Jews will continue to remember the goodness of God to them through various offerings. It is stressed that the animal sacrifices are not for the judicial penalty of sin, but are for a memorial of Christ's suffering and death and for the needful purification of the temple and worshippers because of the influence of sin.

In Ezekiel 45 we will learn that the Jewish nation shall be ruled by a prince in righteousness and they shall readily provide provisions to this Jewish prince, who is responsible for their continued presentation (45:16-17). The prince, by the priests, shall offer sacrifices on behalf of the nation (46:1-18). The prince is not Christ, but a vice-regent under His rule, for the prince must present sin offerings for purification purposes on behalf of himself and the people (45:22, 25). Other rationale to support this conclusion will be offered later. It suffices here to say that the prince will represent Christ in daily operations of the temple and in judging of the people. Obviously, this royal situation in a never before constructed temple has never occurred, hence must still be future.

Chambers for the Priests (40:44-46)

From the inner courtyard, Ezekiel notices two rooms, facing each other, one located on the east side of the south entrance and the other on the east side of the north entrance. The north room was for priests ministering in the temple, while the south room was for priests in charge of the altar. These utility rooms may also serve as rest areas for the priests, the descendants of Zadok, the high priest during Solomon's reign (1 Kgs. 1:26-27). Apparently, both rooms will be available for temple singers.

Inner Court and Porch (40:47-49)

Still located in the inner court, Ezekiel gazes westward on the temple structure itself. He climbs a flight of stairs to enter the porch of the eastern entrance to the temple. Ezekiel notes all pertinent details of the temple's construction and records measurements of key features of the temple as supplied by his angelic escort (the bronze-looking man). He particularly notes the existence of two pillars by the doorposts of the entrance, which would be reminiscent of Jachin and Boaz, the enormous bronze pillars at the entrance to Solomon's temple (1 Kgs. 7:21).

The Sanctuary (41:1-4)

As a priest, Ezekiel was permitted to enter the outer sanctuary (the holy place), but not the inner sanctuary (the most holy place). The man with him measured the outer sanctuary, and then ventured into the inner sanctuary alone to measure it (God's glory had not yet returned to this temple). This confirms that the man is an angelic being, as no man would have the authority to intrude into the most holy place of the temple.

The gates and doorways in the temple become more narrow when approaching the inner sanctuary. The temple entrance was 24.5 feet wide, the passageway leading into the outer sanctuary (the holy place) was 17.5 feet wide and the entrance leading into the inner sanctuary was 10.5 feet wide. The narrowing gates to enter the most holy place indicate that access would be increasingly limited as one approached the Lord.

It is also observed that the only way to advance into the temple from outside the complex is to climb stairs, enter the outer courtyard, then the inner courtyard, and finally the temple itself. The four levels of elevations provide zones of holiness to separate what is common from what is most holy – God.

The following diagram illustrates the levels of holiness depicted in the temple complex and the gate restrictions of the two eastern gates (these being dedicated to the Lord and His prince).[84]

Levels of Holiness

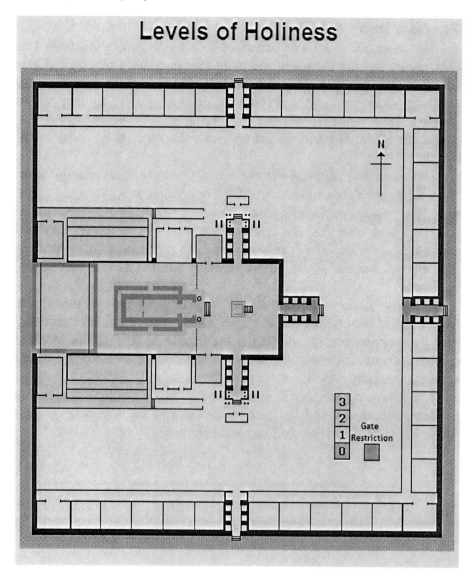

This is the law of the temple: The whole area surrounding the mountaintop is most holy. Behold, this is the law of the temple (43:12).

Though all the nations of the world will come to Jerusalem to worship God during the millennial reign of Christ, this arrangement indicates that the Jews will have a privileged position in the temple that common people will not have (42:20). Furthermore, the priests (sons of

Zadok) will have a holy ministry that permits them to come closer to the Lord than ordinary Jewish worshippers. So, although God will commune among His covenant people, there still will remain limitations in how they approach the Lord. There will be no such limitations for the Church, who will ever be with the Lord after He snatches them from the earth just prior to the Tribulation Period (1 Thess. 4:13-18). There will also be no restrictions for Old Testament saints or tribulation saints who also have experienced *the first resurrection* and are, like the Church, in glorified bodies (Isa. 26:18-21; Heb. 11:40; Rev. 20:4).

Side Chambers and Western Room (41:5-12)

The widths of the temple wall and of the storage rooms are recorded. There were three stories with thirty storage rooms per story surrounding the sanctuary on the south, west, and north sides. These rooms were freestanding (not attached to the wall of the temple) and the rooms increased slightly in dimensions with the height of each story. Access to these side chambers was possible only through a mid-level entryway in the middle of both north and south rows of rooms. The entrances were on the north side of the northern rooms and on the south side of the southern rooms with the temple between both sets of chambers. These side rooms were similar to those in Solomon's temple (1 Kgs. 6:5-10) and will likely be used for storing equipment, offering resources (i.e., spices, oil, etc.), and gifts from the people. There was also a large western room (157.5 by 122.5 feet) beyond the storage rooms, but on the same level. The wall of this room was the same thickness as the outer wall of the side chambers (5 cubits or nearly nine feet).

The Temple (41:13-26)

Next, the temple building was measured and Ezekiel recorded its measurements as 87.5 by 175 feet. He also noted that cherubim and palm trees were carved into the ornamental wood that covered the interior of the temple building. Solomon's temple had similar decorative features (1 Kgs. 6:29). The palm trees symbolize peace and long life, which only the Prince of Peace can offer humanity (Isa. 9:6). There cannot be tranquility on the earth without conquering evil, so in a practical sense, the palm trees declare the victory of the Lamb over all His foes.

The doorposts in the temple were not round but square and there were double doors that led into both the outer and inner sanctuaries. The doors entering into the outer sanctuary also had cherubim and palm trees carved into them.

No veil prohibiting access will be hanging in this temple. The entire character of the temple presents a better measure of access to God than what the Jews were accustomed to under the Law. Why did the furnishings, the layout (e.g., addition of windows), and the general decor of the temple change? The earthly Millennial Temple reflects heaven's estimation of the value of Christ's sacrifice. Jehovah was now dwelling among His people and He wanted them to come as close to Him as yet unglorified humanity could. All barriers and levels in the temple spoke of God's uninfringeable holiness and the desire for His people to be holy too.

Interestingly, Ezekiel describes only one piece of furniture in the temple: *"The altar was of wood, three cubits high, and its length two cubits. Its corners, its length, and its sides were of wood; and he said to me, 'This is the table that is before the Lord'"* (41:22). This mysterious piece of furniture is called an altar, but is referred to as *"the table that is before the Lord."* Why are the normal Levitical furnishings nowhere to be found in the Millennial Temple? Why is there but one new piece of furniture described, which seems to combine aspects of both the Table of Showbread and the Golden Altar of Incense? Scripture does not afford answers to these questions, so we can only speculate as to God's reasoning. Perhaps by reviewing the construction and purpose of the Table of Showbread and the Golden Altar of Incense we will gain a better understanding what "the table that is before the Lord" symbolizes.

From a typological perspective, the Table of Showbread with its twelve loaves identifies Christ as the Bread of Life, the One we must continually feed upon; He is the substance of our fellowship with God. The twelve loaves were a constant reminder that God desired to have such communion with the twelve tribes of Israel. The Golden Altar of Incense prefigures Christ as the Great High Priest who would offer up the believer's service and worship to God as a sweet-savor offering. As the Altar of Incense, Christ continues upon God's heavenly throne presently to intercede on the believer's behalf.

Both the Golden Altar of Incense and the Table of Showbread were constructed of acacia wood and overlaid with gold. The Table of Showbread was approximately three feet long, one foot-six inches wide, and two feet-three inches high. Each Sabbath, the priests were to exchange the twelve loaves of unleavened bread that were placed upon the Table of Showbread the previous Sabbath for new ones; they were to then eat the week-old bread while in the tabernacle (Lev. 24:5-9). The twelve loaves of unleavened bread, the *"bread of the presence,"* on the table served as a constant reminder of God's continual blessings and presence among His people.

The base of the Golden Altar of Incense was one and a half feet square and stood three feet high. Although this altar was located in the Holy Place, it was really associated with the Ark of the Covenant; thus, the altar is often spoken of as being *"before the Lord"* (Lev. 16:12-14; 1 Kgs. 6:22; Ps. 141:2). However, the Golden Altar had to be separated from the Most Holy Place by a veil so that the priests could frequently burn special incense upon it (Ex. 30:34-38) and also so they could apply sacrificial blood upon its horns to link it with the work of atonement accomplished on the Bronze Altar. It is noted that the dimensions of the Table of Presence are dissimilar to both the Table of Showbread and the Golden Altar of Incense as specified to Moses, but it does more closely resemble the Golden Altar.

In summary, both the Golden Altar and the Table of Showbread were made of wood overlaid with gold, and both were said to be before the Lord or in His presence; thus both furnishings connect well with Ezekiel's description. In the Millennial Kingdom, the Jewish nation will be before the Lord and all their worship will be made continually acceptable by the Lord. Thus, the typological meaning of the two previous furnishings is fulfilled and portrayed in the Kingdom Age as *"the table that is before the Lord."* The Church already enjoys this reality, spiritually speaking: our presence before the Lord, our acceptability before the Lord, and our offerings before the Lord are all made possible through the Lord Jesus Christ, our Great High Priest and Savior!

Ezekiel's angelic escort continued measuring the various aspects of the temple (windows, doors, etc.) including the Most Holy Place and the side gallery rooms, apparently while his human counterpart remained in the Holy Place. Ezekiel is only about halfway through his tour, but since he is presently in the heart of the temple complex, this is a good time to consider a composite view of the entire layout. The concept of the Temple complex on next page is offered by Charles Dyer.[85]

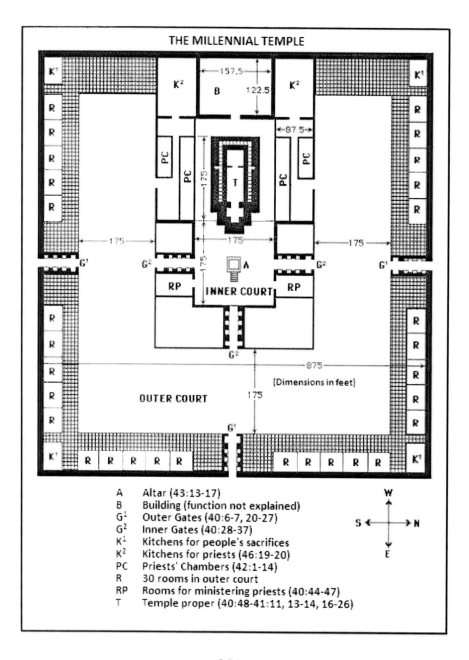

Priestly Chambers (42:1-12)

Ezekiel was then led out of the temple building into the inner court where his attention was drawn to a complex of priestly chambers on the far north and south sides of the inner court. These rooms could be entered from either the outer court or inner court and were three stories high, but their dimensions narrowed with each ascending story. The room complex was 175 feet by 87.5 feet, with a 17.5 foot corridor running east and west that divided the complex (a room on the north and south side of the corridor). The priestly chambers on the north and south sides of the temple were identical.

What was the purpose for these rooms? Just as the Levitical priests in Moses' day were able to eat the most holy things that were offered to the Lord (e.g., the showbread, and portions of meal, peace, sin and trespass offerings), priests during the Millennial Kingdom will also eat of Israel's offerings (46:20). However, there will be no sin or trespass offerings required to atone for sin during this era because Christ's sacrifice made propitiation for all human sin for all time (Heb. 10:10-18). Later, Ezekiel will inform us that the millennial priests will also store their priestly garments, which were holy, in these rooms (42:14, 44:19). Because Ezekiel noted an eastern entrance into the priestly chamber from the outer court, the two men must have walked out of the inner court into the outer court through the northern gate.

The Temple Complex (42:15-20)

The two men then walked easterly to exit the temple complex through the eastern gate through which they entered earlier. Once outside, the man with Ezekiel measured the outer dimensions of the temple complex, 875 feet square, or roughly seventeen and a half acres. The reference to "rods" or "reeds" instead of "cubits" is likely a scribal error in the Hebrew text which is completely reconciled with all the internal complex dimensions that have been previously supplied. The correct rendering should be: *"He measured the ... side with the measuring rod, five hundred cubits* [in lieu of *rods*]" (vv. 16-19). Otherwise the outside dimensions of the temple would be six times larger than the inside measurements. Furthermore, the temple complex would be about one square mile in area. The following figure summarizes the route taken in Ezekiel's tour of the Millennial Temple.[86]

255

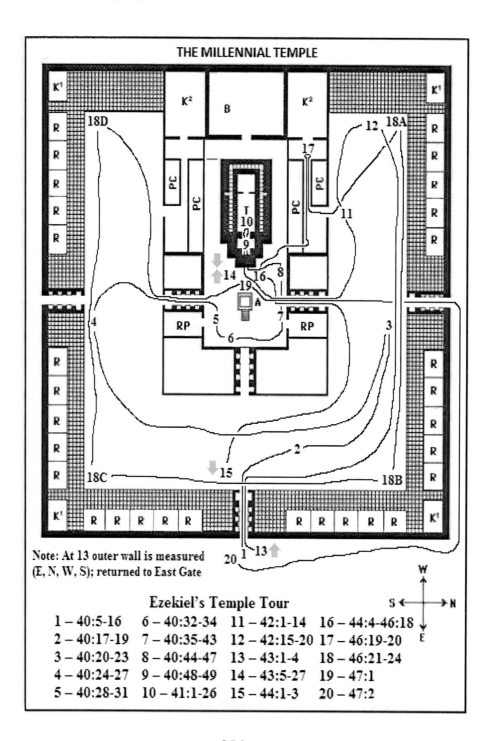

THE MILLENNIAL TEMPLE

Note: At 13 outer wall is measured (E, N, W, S); returned to East Gate

Ezekiel's Temple Tour

1 – 40:5-16	6 – 40:32-34	11 – 42:1-14	16 – 44:4-46:18
2 – 40:17-19	7 – 40:35-43	12 – 42:15-20	17 – 46:19-20
3 – 40:20-23	8 – 40:44-47	13 – 43:1-4	18 – 46:21-24
4 – 40:24-27	9 – 40:48-49	14 – 43:5-27	19 – 47:1
5 – 40:28-31	10 – 41:1-26	15 – 44:1-3	20 – 47:2

These chapters continue to define various aspects of the Kingdom Age. Paul describes the future, earthly reality of this stewardship (i.e., the final dispensation) in this way: *"That in the dispensation of the fullness of the times He* [God] *might gather together in one all things in Christ, both which are in heaven and which are on earth – in Him"* (Eph. 1:10). During this thousand-year period, Christ will reign over the nations with a rod of iron (Rev. 12:5, 20:6), His glory will fill the earth (Isa. 60:1-2; Ezek. 42:3), and the Jews will acknowledge and worship Him as their Messiah (Zech. 12:10). Amen.

Meditation

Behold the throne of grace,
The promise calls us near,
There Jesus shows a smiling face
And waits to answer prayer.

Thine image, Lord, bestow,
Thy presence and Thy love;
I ask to serve Thee here below,
And reign with Thee above.

Teach me to live by faith,
Conform my will to Thine;
Let me victorious be in death,
And then in glory shine.

— John Newton

257

God's Glory Returns
Ezekiel 43

Earlier, because of Israel's stubborn idolatry, Ezekiel witnessed the glory of the Lord departing from the temple just prior to its destruction by the Babylonians. In this chapter, Ezekiel is permitted to see a vision of the glory of God returning to the temple in Jerusalem. The events of this chapter did not occur after the Jews returned from Babylonian captivity, even though they erected a modest temple in Jerusalem. The glory of the Lord was not witnessed reentering the temple, nor was the eastern gate sealed after the Lord passed through it, nor were the Jews delivered from Gentile oppression. Nor can these prophecies be somehow spiritualized to fit Christ's incarnation, death, and resurrection. The Lord said, *"I will destroy this temple that is made with hands, and within three days I will build another made without hands"* (Mark 14:58). The Lord Jesus fulfilled that prophecy in effecting His own resurrection, but the temple before us would be made with human hands. Hence, the fulfillment of this prophesy is yet future and will inaugurate the Millennial Kingdom.

After measuring the temple complex, the bronze-appearing man (Ezekiel's angelic escort) brought Ezekiel back to the eastern entrance to the temple complex (v. 1). He suddenly saw the glory of the Lord approaching the temple from the east (v. 2). In an instant he was carried up by the Holy Spirit to the inner courtyard as the outshining brilliance of God passed through the outer eastern gate leading into the outer court (v. 5). Having a vantage point now directly in front of the temple entrance, Ezekiel saw the glory of the Lord move into and fill the temple. The sight was similar to what he had witnessed previously (chps. 10-11), but this thrilling reversal obviously would occur in a different temple and thus at a future date (v. 3).

This gate faced the rising sun, a distinct reminder that when the Lord returns to the earth, He will reign in blazing glory, power and righteousness. Years earlier the prophet had witnessed the glory of the

Lord depart from the temple by way of the East Gate (10:18-19, 11:23). He now describes the return of God's glory to the temple through the East Gate of the Millennial Temple, which coincides with Christ's Second Advent to the earth (v. 4; Zech. 14:4).

The East Gate is thus strongly connected with the glory of God. Today, the gate directly east of the old temple mount, the Golden Gate or Beautiful Gate, is sealed and has been so for nearly five centuries. Jewish tradition holds that the Messiah will come to Jerusalem through the city's eastern gate. (This assumption is based on Ezekiel 44:1-3.) Ottoman Sultan Suleiman sealed the gate in 1541, presumably to keep the Jewish Messiah from entering and reclaiming the city. Whether or not the gate will remain sealed until Jesus Christ returns to establish His kingdom is unknown, but certainly the gate directly east of the temple will be open to receive the returning King of Glory.

Romans 11 declares that God has always maintained a pure Jewish remnant to honor Him down through the centuries. Today, this remnant is a portion of the Church, but when the Church Age concludes, the blindness of the Jewish nation, which resulted from rejecting Christ, will end (Rom. 11:25). Then the entire nation will be a purified remnant that will never depart from the Lord again (Isa. 4). The Lord plainly expresses this truth to Ezekiel: *"Son of man, this is the place of My throne and the place of the soles of My feet, where I will dwell in the midst of the children of Israel forever. No more shall the house of Israel defile My holy name"* (v. 7). Accordingly, the Lord promised that His temple would be His throne on earth, His permanent dwelling place among His covenant people (vv. 6-7). Until the earth passes away, the Lord will reside with His idolatry-free people in Jerusalem (vv. 8-9). This also meant He would never punish them again, but rather always enjoy communion with them.

Next, either the Lord or perhaps the man standing next to Ezekiel told him to *"describe the temple to the house of Israel, that they may be ashamed of their iniquities; and let them measure the pattern"* (v. 10). A thorough understanding of God's plans for His future temple and that He would again dwell with His people would remind the Jews of the reason He departed from them previously and permitted His temple to be destroyed – their idolatry. God's future temple, from its mountaintop location, will be a beacon of hope and holiness to the entire world (v. 11). The law of God's house was the way of holiness, which meant that

God made Himself known to all those who would walk before Him in purity (v. 12).

Once God is enthroned in His Millennial Temple, daily worship services will commence. The material of this altar is not specified, but it was situated in the inner courtyard east of the temple, much like the Bronze Altar was in the tabernacle in Moses' day. The altar was eleven long-cubits high, but one cubit was below the ground, meaning that it stood 19.25 feet above the ground (vv. 13-17). The base was 31.5 feet square as marked by a rim about the ground. Centered on the base level was another level 3.5 feet in height and 28 feet square. On this level was another section 7 feet high and 24.5 feet square. The final level with the four horns on the corners was also 7 feet high (excluding the horns) and 21 feet square.

As depicted by Charles Dyer, the altar telescoped upward with ledges about each level and stairs on the east side of the altar to allow priest access to the top.[87]

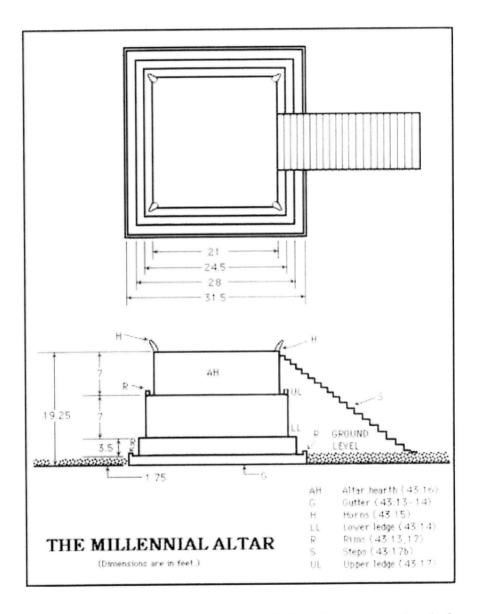

THE MILLENNIAL ALTAR

(Dimensions are in feet.)

AH	Altar hearth (43:16)
G	Gutter (43:13-14)
H	Horns (43:15)
LL	Lower ledge (43:14)
R	Rims (43:13,17)
S	Steps (43:17b)
UL	Upper ledge (43:17)

Having described the altar, the regulations for consecrating it for service are then given (vv. 18-27). A seven-day purification ceremony in which bulls, rams, and goats without blemish were to be offered on the altar was required. Afterwards, the people could present burnt offerings or fellowship offerings before the Lord. Although these are referred to as "sin offerings," the context of the passage explains that they did not atone for human sin, but rather cleansed the altar of defilement resulting from sin. Ezekiel noted that the horns of the altar, its corners and rim were to be sprinkled with blood for purification (v. 20).

Interestingly, the bulls and goats offered for sin offerings for seven days were burnt in the outer court of the temple complex (vv. 21-22, 25-26). This is a change from the Levitical system which required the portions of the animals not burnt on the Bronze Altar to be burned outside of the camp in a clean place (on top of the ashes of the burnt offering). This is a further indication that human sin is not being atoned for in these sacrifices, but rather defilement resulting from human sin is being purified. After the altar was cleansed, bulls and rams were to be offered with salt as burnt offerings to the Lord. Salt is another symbol of purification in Scripture (vv. 23-24, 27; Num. 18:19).

The salt on the offerings created white smoke when burned. Salt adds flavor to what is eaten, and also serves as a food preservative. Salt then stands in contrast with leaven, which corrupts. Accordingly, leaven was never permitted on the Bronze Altar during any of the Levitical sacrifices. This is why Paul used salt as a metaphor to speak of uncompromised truth (Col. 4:6), and why the Lord Jesus exhorted His disciples to have a "salty" testimony (Matt. 5:13). The Gospels confirm that the entire life of the Lord Jesus was marked by dedication to living and declaring truth – His testimony was thus pure (salty) and appreciated by God. Though the Jews rejected this idea at Christ's first advent, they will repeatedly acknowledge its truth by their sacrifices during the Kingdom Age.

Overall, the entire purification process that Ezekiel describes here aligns well with the initial consecration activities for the priests by Moses in Exodus 29:26-37. The purification process was to last seven days with a bullock being slaughtered each day as a sin offering. Their blood was used to purify and sanctify the Bronze Altar. Likewise, in future generations there was to be a seven-day consecration ceremony for passing down the high priest's holy garments to a successor. Only the current high priest could initiate that ceremony and the successor had to be his son. It is quite possible that the Lord, as Israel's Great High Priest, will initiate these purification rituals to allow Israel to freely worship God, and to acknowledge His redeeming work accomplished at Calvary. Through Him alone, God will gladly and righteously declare to His covenant people: *"I will accept you"* (v. 27). Wonderful words to a people that have been removed from their God for over twenty-five hundred years and counting!

Burnt offerings were an expression of one's appreciation for the Lord and were consumed by fire. That is, no part of the animal was ingested. The peace offering symbolized God's fellowship with and provision for man; it was the only offering of which God, the offering priest, and the offerer all received a portion. For centuries the peace offerings were God's provision for the priest's food. Now, God would again share with the priests what had been offered to Him. But because this meat was holy, it had to be eaten in the Priestly chambers between the inner and outer courtyards. Beforehand, Israel offered the Levitical sacrifices without understanding to Whom they pointed – Christ and His redemptive work. The purpose of these offerings in the Millennial Kingdom is to ensure that Israel never forgets what has been accomplished through Christ on their behalf. The Church repeatedly breaks bread today for a similar reason – that believers do not forget the Lord and the value of His sacrifice (1 Cor. 11:24-26).

Meditation

> Once, only once, and once for all,
> His precious life He gave;
> Before the cross in faith we fall,
> And own it strong to save.
>
> For as the priest of Aaron's line
> Within the holiest stood,
> And sprinkled all the mercy shrine
> With sacrificial blood;
>
> So He, who once atonement brought,
> Our Priest of endless power,
> Presents Himself for those He bought
> In that dark noontide hour.
>
> And so we show Thy death, O Lord,
> Till Thou again appear,
> And feel, when we approach Thy board,
> We have an altar here.

— William Bright

Access to the Temple
Ezekiel 44

The East Gate and the Prince

A few moments earlier Ezekiel had been caught up by the Spirit to the inner courtyard to witness the glory of God fill the temple. The Lord returned Ezekiel to the outer courtyard side of the East Gate entering the temple complex (v. 1). After Ezekiel observed that the gate's doors were closed, the Lord explained why they were divinely sealed:

> *This gate shall be shut; it shall not be opened, and no man shall enter by it, because the Lord God of Israel has entered by it; therefore it shall be shut. As for the prince, because he is the prince, he may sit in it to eat bread before the Lord; he shall enter by way of the vestibule of the gateway, and go out the same way* (vv. 2-3).

Because the glory of God had passed through that gate, it was sanctified for God and His earthly representative, the prince of Israel. But though the prince could eat bread (i.e., what was most holy from the sacrifices) in the vestibule of the gateway before the Lord, he could not, nor could any man, pass through the doorway of the gate. As William Kelly clarifies, the prince was given high honor, but he will be a natural man who represents the Messiah to Israel:

No high priest ever claimed this. Indeed it is not a priest but the prince, the earthly chief of Israel. We shall learn from chapters 45 and 46 a little more about the prince. Suffice it to say that he is certainly not the Messiah, for although he is thoroughly distinguished from a priest, he needs to offer a sin offering, and he may have sons. Doubtless it is a future prince of the house of David.[88]

Although the following chapters reveal more about the prince's inheritance, posterity, and ministry, we already have some idea as to his identity. First, he is a Jew with special access to God. Second, the prince is not a priest, but from the line of Judah through David (34:24, 37:24-25). This is important as only the Messiah will ever hold both offices of priest and king (2 Chron. 26:16-21; Zech. 6:13). Third, the prophet Jeremiah also referred to him as the future governor of Israel at the time that God promised to restore the Jews to their land, to spiritually heal them, and to also punish those who had abused and despoiled them (Jer. 30:16-17): *"And their governor shall come from their midst; then I will cause him to draw near, and he shall approach Me"* (Jer. 30:21). H. A. Ironside suggests that the governor identified by Jeremiah who restores peace and order to Israel is also the prince that Ezekiel speaks of in these latter chapters:

> There seems to be good reason to believe that the "governor" here spoken of is the same as the prince referred to so frequently in the last five chapters of Ezekiel. (See Ezek. 44:3; 45:7; 46:2, etc.) He will, we gather, be a direct lineal descendant of David, and will be the earthly ruler, subject in all things to the glorified Immanuel. In this day of *"the restitution of all things spoken of by the prophets,"* the hearts of the people will have been fully turned to the Lord, that is, the spared remnant, for the apostate part of the nation will be destroyed in the great tribulation which is brought to our notice once more in the closing verses of this chapter.[89]

Ezekiel speaks of a future day in which all Jews are back in Israel and each tribe will have their specific allotted territories (chp. 45). At that time, the nation shall be ruled by a prince in righteousness. The Jewish nation shall readily bring offerings to this Jewish prince (45:16-17) and the prince, acting on behalf of the people, shall offer sacrifices for the nation (46:1-18). The prince is clearly not Messiah, for he must offer purification sacrifices for himself as well as for the people (46:22). The prince does, however, represent the Messiah in Jewish affairs on earth during the Millennial Kingdom. He is a vice-regent under Christ's rule.

Who May Enter the Temple?

Ezekiel's angelic companion led him back to the inner courtyard through the northern gate between the two courts. After witnessing the spectacular glory of God streaming out of the temple, Ezekiel fell to the ground in awe (v. 4). Ezekiel is then given a message from the Lord to be relayed to the rebellious house of Israel: God is holy; what He deems holy is holy, including His people. Therefore He demands consecration from His people (v. 5). No more detestable pagan practices were to be committed in His house and no uncircumcised foreigner was to have access to His temple. Only those who were circumcised in heart (i.e., speaking of spiritual purity) and in the flesh could enter His house (vv. 6-7). Physical circumcision was never meant as a badge of Jewish entitlement, but rather it was to be an outward sign of a person wholly consecrated to the Lord.

Paul explains the deeper spiritual meaning of circumcision which the Jews did not perceive: *"For he is not a Jew who is one outwardly, nor is circumcision that which is outward in the flesh; but he is a Jew who is one inwardly; and circumcision is that of the heart, in the Spirit, not in the letter; whose praise is not from men but from God"* (Rom. 2:28-29). Symbolically speaking, circumcision speaks of a life that has no confidence in the flesh (Phil. 3:3). To have no confidence in the flesh means to have no glory in it either. All Christians have been positionally circumcised in Christ (Col. 2:11) and are thus to manifest this inner spiritual reality daily. It is a quality of life that mere physical circumcision and Law-keeping could never accomplish. After receiving the Holy Spirit, the Jews will experience this type of spiritual renewal – they will live the circumcised life that God first demanded of them at Mount Sinai and then later at Gilgal.

The Temple Servants

The Lord then explains to Ezekiel the duties of the Levites and priests in the Millennial Temple (vv. 10-31). As the tabernacle would no longer be moved and would soon be replaced by a temple in Jerusalem, David revised the original duties of the Levites before His death (1 Chron. 23). Because of their wicked pagan practices prior to the temple's destruction by Babylon, their duties would be more limited in God's Millennial Temple, for *"they shall bear their iniquities"* (vv. 10, 12). The Levites could serve as gatekeepers, slay the various sacrifices, assist worshippers coming before the Lord with their offerings, and assist in the administrative duties in temple operations (vv. 11, 14). They could not infringe on any part of the priesthood; they were not permitted to come near what God had designated as holy within His temple, nor were they permitted to venture into the temple (v. 13). Both Levites and the priests would receive a portion of land near the temple complex for a possession (45:1-6).

Then regulations were given for the priests, who could be only from the lineage of Zadok. He was a faithful priest and loyal to both King David and then to King Solomon (1 Chron. 29:33). Zadok was the first high priest to oversee Solomon's temple and now his descendants would have an honored position of authority within God's Millennial Temple. The Lord indeed rewards faithfulness. Only Zadok's ancestors could enter God's sanctuary and offer sacrifices to Him on behalf of the people (vv. 15-16). Two Levitical edicts regarding the priests' clothing were restated (vv. 17-19): First, they should wear garments of linen to minimize perspiration. Second, these linen robes were holy and must not be worn beyond the inner courtyard. Wool garments were heavier and did not breathe as well as the lighter linen. When priests were finished with their duties, they would go to the priests' chambers and change into their normal clothing.

Furthermore, the priests were to be well groomed; they were not permitted to shave their heads or allow their hair to grow long (v. 20). Shaving or uncovering one's head was a sign of mourning (Lev. 10:6), and those serving the Lord were to do so joyfully and not looking disheveled. During the Millennial Kingdom, Jerusalem will be the origin of joy for the entire earth:

> But be glad and rejoice forever in what I create; for behold, I create Jerusalem as a rejoicing, and her people a joy. I will rejoice in Jerusalem, and joy in My people; the voice of weeping shall no longer be heard in her, nor the voice of crying (Isa. 65:18-19).

Priests were to be joyful servants in the presence of the Lord, but not because of intoxication. Accordingly, priests were prohibited from drinking wine while in their holy attire, lest they become drunk and fail to perform their ministry properly (v. 21). Since this stern prohibition was stated immediately after the Lord slew Nadab and Abihu (Aaron's sons) for offering strange fire in the most Holy Place, it suggests that these young men were intoxicated (Lev. 10:9). The stipulation was to preclude a repeat offense. F. B. Hole suggests a valuable application for believers today:

> All who have come to the Lord, while He is still disallowed of men, are constituted priests, as we learn in 1 Peter 2:3-4, and all of us should be in right priestly condition. But the **position** is one thing, and the **condition** which answers to it is another. Hence that important word, "Be not drunk with wine, wherein is excess; but be filled with the Spirit" (Eph. 5:18). When thus filled we can offer the sacrifice of praise, as the next verse indicates. The contrast is between what is fleshly and what is spiritual. We are to decline what excites the flesh that we may know the power of the Spirit. The same thing, of course, is true not only of our praise but also as to our powers of spiritual discernment, and as to our ability to teach others that which we may have learned from God of His things.[90]

Whether a priest in the Millennial Temple or a believer-priest in the Church age, all who come before the Lord to worship should be controlled by God's Word and Spirit and nothing else.

The Millennial priests also were to marry only *"virgins of the descendants of the house of Israel, or widows of priests"* (v. 22). These priestly restrictions would assist the people in understanding the difference between what was holy and common; the priests were to exemplify the holy, consecrated life that they were to teach others to follow (v. 23). One cannot teach what is right if one does not do what is right. Many of the regulations in Leviticus were to assist the priests in maintaining a clear distinction between the *holy* and the *profane* and between *clean* and *unclean* (Lev. 10:10). Whether priests at Mount Sinai in Moses' day or millennial priests on Mount Zion in a future day, all were responsible to the Lord to maintain these discernable merits and instruct the people in the same.

Although the Jewish nation repeatedly strayed from God's Law, Ezekiel informs us that during the Millennial Kingdom this will not be the case. Through the power of the Holy Spirit, the Levites will once more teach their brethren God's Word and will render impartial decisions as judges; they will never abandon the Lord again (vv. 23-24). The priests were to ensure that Jehovah's feasts and His Sabbaths remained holy. This reminds us of Paul's declaration: *"For the gifts and the calling of God are irrevocable"* (Rom. 11:29); God's original calling for the Levites to establish His Word in the land of Israel will ultimately be fulfilled.

The priests were not to go near a dead body during times of mourning, unless it was for a close family member (v. 25). If a priest did come in contact with something dead, he would be considered unclean for seven days, after which time he could offer a purification sacrifice in the temple and return to service (vv. 26-27). During the Millennial Kingdom death will be a rare thing and mainly result from willful sin of those not yet in glorified bodies or controlled by the Holy Spirit (i.e., those surviving the Tribulation Period from the nations and their descendants). Isaiah foretold:

> No more shall an infant from there live but a few days, nor an old man who has not fulfilled his days; for the child shall die one hundred years old, but the sinner being one hundred years old shall be accursed (Isa. 65:20).

> They shall not hurt nor destroy in all My holy mountain (Isa. 65:25).

What a blessing it will be when the curses that were a result of man's sin are lifted in the Kingdom Age (Rom. 8:21-22). A handful of seed casually scattered on a mountaintop will produce a great harvest (Ps. 72:16), longevity will be restored to humanity, weapons will be used as agricultural implements (Mic. 4:3), and a spirit of peace and tranquility will engulf the earth (Isa. 11:9). All this and more Christ shall do!

The final restriction dealt with the priest's inheritance (vv. 28-31). The priest would not be given a possession of land other than what was allotted near the temple complex (45:1-6), for the Lord was their possession (v. 28). He would then be sure to provide amply for His priests through the offerings that the people brought to the temple (vv. 29-30). They were to eat meat only from freshly slain sacrifices at the temple, not from an animal or bird found dead or torn by a beast (v. 31).

The priests were often neglected in Old Testament times by the stinginess of God's people. But in a world full of Spirit-filled people, governed by Christ in peace and righteousness, and where the land brings forth in its full strength, joyful worshippers will gladly give their best back to the Lord. And the Lord will be glad to pass it on to His faithful servants: *"The best of all firstfruits of any kind, and every sacrifice of any kind from all your sacrifices, shall be the priest's; also you shall give to the priest the first of your ground meal, to cause a blessing to rest on your house"* (v. 30). No priest will starve in Christ's kingdom, for the goodness of the Lord shall be so bountiful that no one would want to hoard past expressions of His love and miss out on His unrelenting hand of blessing. What will it be like to be unhindered by sin and experience the fullness of God?

Meditation

An infinite God can give all of Himself to each of His children. He does not distribute Himself that each may have a part, but to each one He gives all of Himself as fully as if there were no others.

— A. W. Tozer

A Holy District
Ezekiel 45:1-12

It was necessary in Joshua's day to have the Levites and priests scattered among their countrymen in forty-eight cities to ensure the availability of God's Word to everyone (Josh. 21). By design, no one would need to travel more than a day (roughly twenty miles) to seek the mind of the Lord. This will not be necessary in the Kingdom Age, as God will be with His people and everyone is to seek Him in Jerusalem.

In the Millennial Kingdom, both the Levites and the priests will receive a land possession of 25,000 by 10,000 cubits (i.e., 8.3 by 3.3 miles to reside in near the temple complex; vv. 1, 5). The temple complex will be located within the priests' possession (vv. 3-4). As stated earlier, the temple complex will require an area of 500 by 500 cubits, but Ezekiel adds an additional open space of 50 cubits about the temple wall (v. 2).

Jerusalem proper will be located directly south of the priests' possession and the temple in an area of 5,000 cubits square (or 1.7 square miles). We will learn later that it has twelve gates, one for each tribe (48:30-34). The city will have adjoining land on both the east and west sides of the city of 10,000 by 5,000 cubits; which will be available for agricultural purposes (v. 6). The prince will receive a possession of land on either side of the holy district (being 8.3 miles wide) westward to the Mediterranean Sea and eastward to the border of Israel (v. 7). The tribes of Israel in their new inheritances (chps. 47-48) will enjoy rest under the prince's rule (v. 8).

Jerusalem in the Kingdom Age

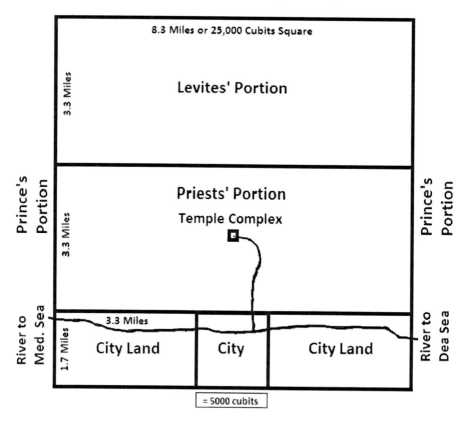

Having prophesied the future righteousness of Israel's leadership in the Kingdom Age, Ezekiel diverges from foretelling the blessings of Christ's reign on earth to admonish Israel's present leaders to mimic His example. They were to cease from their violent, oppressive, unjust, and greedy ways (v. 9). Israel's rulers were to uphold justice in the land, which meant guaranteeing accurate scales and fair money exchange in their commerce (vv. 10-12).

One of the exciting aspects of this prophecy is that Ezekiel foretold that after Israel became a political reality again they would have their own currency and it would be the same as that used in Old Testament days, the shekel: *"The shekel shall be twenty gerahs; twenty shekels, twenty-five shekels, and fifteen shekels shall be your mina"* (v. 12). Although the context of this passage refers to the Millennial Kingdom, it is quite interesting that after almost 2,000 years the shekel has been reinstated as the common monetary unit in Israel today, just as Ezekiel predicted.

During the Kingdom Age, Israel's rulers will exhibit the holiness which is becoming to a servant of God. Instead of using their position to take advantage of the people, they will humbly reflect the kindness and goodness of God to all those in their care. Their virtuous and just service will effectively draw men to worship God, instead of causing them to blaspheme His holy name, as in centuries past.

Meditation

One great hindrance to holiness in the ministry of the Word is that we are prone to preach and write without pressing into the things we say and making them real to our own souls. Over the years words begin to come easy, and we find we can speak of mysteries without standing in awe; we can speak of purity without feeling pure; we can speak of zeal without spiritual passion; we can speak of God's holiness without trembling; we can speak of sin without sorrow; we can speak of heaven without eagerness. And the result is a terrible hardening of the spiritual life.

— John Owen

Sacrifices and Feasts
Ezekiel 45:13-46:24

Having rebuked Israel's present leaders by the righteous and just example of their future prince, Ezekiel addresses the types of offerings which the Lord will accept during the Kingdom Age (45:13-46:24). The Jews will be engaging in various sacrifices and feasts during the Kingdom Age as a memorial of what God had accomplished for them through the ages (Zech. 14:16-21). This is appreciated by God in the same way that the Church today honors Christ by remembering Him and proclaiming the value of His death through the breaking of bread (1 Cor. 11:24-30). Though the Lord's sacrifice of Himself occurred two thousand years ago, believers are not to forget what God accomplished for them in Christ. The Church was created after Calvary and, thus, was not under the Jewish stewardship of the Law; however, Israel will remember the value of Christ's redemptive work through the regular sacrifices in the Millennial Kingdom.

Kingdom Sacrifices

There will be various free-will sacrifices which show appreciation for the Lord (e.g., the burnt offering) and others which prompt rejoicing and fellowship in His presence (e.g., the peace offering). There will also be *atoning* sacrifices, which refer to ceremonial purification to ensure the millennial temple and priests are not polluted by any unclean thing (e.g., Lev. 8:22-26; 14:4-7). It is important to remember that in the Old Testament, the word atonement never means "the putting away of sins," but rather to cover sin or provide ceremonial cleansing for a time.

The writer of Hebrews affirms both the purpose of Old Testament blood atonement and also what it symbolized – complete cleansing and redemption in Christ's own blood:

But Christ came as High Priest of the good things to come, with the greater and more perfect tabernacle not made with hands, that is, not of this creation. Not with the blood of goats and calves, but with His own blood He entered the Most Holy Place once for all, having obtained eternal redemption. For if the blood of bulls and goats and the ashes of a heifer, sprinkling the unclean, sanctifies for the purifying of the flesh, how much more shall the blood of Christ, who through the eternal Spirit offered Himself without spot to God, cleanse your conscience from dead works to serve the living God? (Heb. 9:11-15).*

For the law, having a shadow of the good things to come, and not the very image of the things, can never with these same sacrifices, which they offer continually year by year, make those who approach perfect. For then would they not have ceased to be offered? For the worshippers, once purified, would have had no more consciousness of sins. But in those sacrifices there is a reminder of sins every year. For it is not possible that the blood of bulls and goats could take away sins (Heb. 10:1-4).*

Then He said, "Behold, I have come to do Your will, O God." He takes away the first that He may establish the second. By that will we have been sanctified through the offering of the body of Jesus Christ once for all. And every priest stands ministering daily and offering repeatedly the same sacrifices, which can never take away sins. But this Man, after He had offered one sacrifice for sins forever, sat down at the right hand of God, from that time waiting till His enemies are made His footstool. For by one offering He has perfected forever those who are being sanctified (Heb. 10:9-14).*

Ezekiel's predictions of *atoning* sacrifices, feasts, and other Levitical-type ordinances cause many Christians consternation; they feel that these must be explained (or most likely explained away) so as to not contradict the book of Hebrews. But this assumes that there can be no change of dispensation, meaning that because we are Christians, those of whom the prophecy speaks must be in the same relationship to Christ as the Church. William Kelly further clarifies why this reasoning is flawed:

The Epistle [of Hebrews] looks at believers since redemption while Christ is on high till He comes again in glory; the prophecy of

> Ezekiel, on the contrary, is occupied with the earthly people and supposes the glory of Jehovah dwelling once again in the land of Canaan. The truth is that to bless Israel as such and the Gentiles only moderately and subordinately to the Jews, as this prophecy and almost all others suppose and definitely declare, is a state of things in distinct contrast with Christianity, where there is neither Jew nor Gentile but all are one in Christ Jesus. Hence the whole ground and position here are quite different from what we see in the Epistle to the Hebrews.[91]

In the Kingdom Age, God will be dealing with His covenant people the way He has all along, but with the realization that the completion of all that was foretold and pictured in the sacrifices and feasts has been realized. Hence, the daily animal sacrifices in the Kingdom Age will result in a constant awareness of God's holiness and the necessity of worshippers' purity throughout the Kingdom Age. (That part has not changed since Israel's days at Mount Sinai.) The blood of animals during this time is for ceremonial purification only (that aspect of the dispensation of the Law has changed), as the judicial penalty for all sin, for all time, has already been accomplished through Christ's blood (Rom. 3:25).

This assessment is derived from a literal interpretation of the passage and does not compromise a dispensational understanding of God's method of salvation declared throughout Scripture. Charles Ryrie explains:

> The basis of salvation in every age is the death of Christ: the *requirement* for salvation in every age is faith; the *object* of faith in every age is God, the *content* of faith changes in the various dispensations [i.e., with the progress of revelation].[92]

Hence, these atoning sacrifices represent the *content* of faith of those worshippers who have trusted Christ for salvation during the Kingdom Age. Their faith is evidenced by their obedience to God's Word – their sacrifices (Jas. 2:17).

The prince of Israel is to receive his portion from all the people in Israel: one-sixtieth of their harvested grain, one percent of their olive oil, and one in two hundred sheep (vv. 13-16). There is an important reason the prince must receive these supplies:

Then it shall be the prince's part to give burnt offerings, grain offerings, and drink offerings, at the feasts, the New Moons, the Sabbaths, and at all the appointed seasons of the house of Israel. He shall prepare the sin offering, the grain offering, the burnt offering, and the peace offerings to make atonement for the house of Israel (v. 17).

With the resources that the people willingly provide, the prince will maintain all the appropriate temple sacrifices and offer worship on behalf of the nation through the priests.

Kingdom Feasts

The particular feasts that will be kept in the Kingdom Age are also listed: the New Year feast (vv. 18-20), the Passover and Unleavened Bread feast (vv. 21-24), and the Feast of Tabernacles (v. 25). The New Year feast will commence on the first day of the first Jewish month to purify the sanctuary (v. 18). If someone sins unintentionally, a second purification offering would occur seven days later (vv. 19-20). Christ's sacrifice at Calvary provided complete propitiation for all human sin (1 Jn. 2:2); however, personal sin will still be a very real possibility in the Kingdom Age for those in non-glorified bodies. So while the penalty of such sins has already been righteously dealt with by God, the offending person must properly relate to God's holiness by repenting of sins committed to receive forgiveness and be restored to fellowship with Him again.

In the Church Age, this is accomplished by going, spiritually speaking, directly before the throne of grace and confessing one's sin and being cleansed of guilt by the blood of Christ (1 Jn. 1:9). In the economy of the Law, the Jews offered sin offerings and trespass offerings and the High Priest dealt with the remainder of the nation's sins on the Day of Atonement. In the Kingdom Age, the sin offerings will continue as a reminder that personal sin still grieves God and must be dealt with to permit a worshipper to come near a Holy God. The Day of Atonement apparently is replaced by the initial purification sacrifice at the start of each new year.

The Passover and Feast of Unleavened Bread will continue to commence on the fourteenth day of the first month (v. 21). During the seven days of the Feast of Unleavened Bread the prince will offer an unblemished bull and a ram as a burnt offering and an acceptable goat for a sin offering each day (v. 23). An ephah of grain and a hin of oil were to be offered with each bull and ram (v. 24). The entire procedure was to be repeated six months later during the seven days associated with the Feast of Tabernacles (i.e., on the fifteenth day of the seventh month, as commemorated in the Old Testament; v. 25).

The fact that the prince was to conduct these sin offerings on behalf of himself and the people strongly suggests that the future prince of Israel is not Christ Himself (vv. 22, 25). Rather, the prince will be a regal regent representing Christ in the daily operations of the temple as both a priest and a judge of the people.

During the Kingdom Age, only those original Feasts of Jehovah (Lev. 23) which have symbolic meaning under the blessings of the New Covenant will be observed. Under the Law, three seasons of festivals, including a total of seven feasts, were to be observed by the Israelites. Every Jewish male was required to present himself before Jehovah three times a year at the Feast of Unleavened Bread, the Feast of Weeks, and the Feast of Ingathering.

Leviticus 23 identifies all seven of the Feasts of Jehovah. These feasts provide an exceptional prophetic blueprint of God's means of reconciling the nation of Israel to Himself forever. Every aspect of this blueprint centers in the work of Christ:

Passover (14th day of 1st month) pictures Christ on the cross on Friday; this was the day the Passover lambs were slain and was also the day when the Lamb of God was slain for the sins of the world (1 Cor. 5:7).

Unleavened Bread (15th day of 1st month) speaks of Christ in the grave on Saturday; like the bread, Christ's body had no life while in the grave, nor had it been previously influenced by sin (i.e., Christ lived an unleavened life).

First Fruits (16th day of the 1st month) typifies Christ's resurrection on Sunday; He was the first fruits from the dead (1 Cor. 15:20).

Pentecost (fifty days after First Fruits) pictures the formation of the Church (Christ's body of believers) fifty days after Christ's resurrection. The events at Pentecost conveyed a final ultimatum to Israel (Acts 2).

Note: The Church Age is represented by the gap between the Spring and Autumn feasts (this also relates to the interval between Daniel's 69th and

70th weeks; Dan. 9:24-27). The Autumn feasts speak of Israel's future acknowledgement of Christ as Messiah, their restoration to Him, and the blessings of His Millennial Kingdom.

Trumpets (1ˢᵗ day of the 7ᵗʰ month) refers to the time when Christ will gather all the Jews back to Israel and under His rule (Matt. 24:29-31; Ezek. 39:28-29).

The Day of Atonement (10ᵗʰ day of the 7ᵗʰ month) pictures the future event when the Jews will repent and receive Jesus Christ as their Messiah (Heb. 9:28; Zech. 12:10).

Tabernacles (15ᵗʰ day of the 7ᵗʰ month) announces the future release of the Jews from the Antichrist's rule during the Tribulation Period, and the blessings of Christ's rule during His Millennial Kingdom.

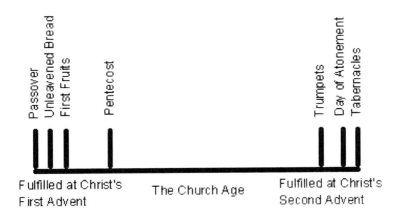

God indeed has a wonderful plan for the nation of Israel. Prophetically speaking, the spring feasts are already completed, while the fall feasts are yet to be fulfilled. When the last trumpet of the Tribulation Period is heard, every Jew will be gathered out of the nations back to the land of Israel; this refined remnant will then receive the Holy Spirit and forever be with the Lord. This will fulfill the typological meaning of the last of the seven feasts, the Feast of Tabernacles (39:28-29).

In this chapter, however, Ezekiel's view is connected exclusively to Israel in the Kingdom Age. Accordingly, only three national feasts will be necessary: The New Year Festival will be a constant reminder that sin hinders fellowship with a holy God and must be repudiated. The Feast of Passover/Unleavened Bread will celebrate how Israel was restored to God through Christ's redemptive work at Calvary. The Feast of Tabernacles will rejoice in being in God's presence again and all the blessings that result from communion with God.

Sabbath and New Moon Celebrations

Besides the three national festivals, the Jewish nation will offer sacrifices daily, on the Sabbaths, and at new moons (46:1-10). Combining these sacrifices with the festival of the New Year will mean that the Jewish nation will freshly consecrate to the Lord every new day, every new week, every new month, and every new year to the Lord.

The East Gate between the inner and outer courts will be closed except for New Moon and Sabbath day offerings (46:1). On these joyous occasions the prince will enter the porch of the gate from the outer court and stand beside the gate posts and worship while sacrifices are being offered on behalf of the nation (v. 2). The prince may leave after the offerings are presented the same way he came in, but the gate will remain open until evening (vv. 2, 8). This will permit Jewish worshippers, who have assembled at the East Gate, an unobstructed view of the temple and God's glory (v. 3). The limitation of passing through the East Gate is another indication that the prince is a vice-regent representing the Lord and not Christ Himself.

It is phenomenal to think that every believer abiding in Christ during the Church Age has access to God that not even the Jewish prince representing Christ has in the glorious Kingdom Age. J. N. Darby puts the matter this way:

> Those who are most blessed on the earth in that day of blessing will never have that access into God's presence which we have by the Spirit, through the veil. Pentecost belongs to, and links itself with, the rending of the veil; and gives us to walk in all liberty in the light, as God Himself is in the light, having entered into the holy place by the new and living way which He has consecrated for us, through the veil, that is to say, His flesh.[93]

The heavenly inheritance that believers have today in Christ far exceeds the earthly blessings God will extend to His covenant people, though we will much rejoice in their part as well, for it is all to the glory of Christ. Ezekiel records the sacrifices that were to be offered on these special days by the prince through the priests:

The burnt offering that the prince offers to the Lord on the Sabbath day shall be six lambs without blemish, and a ram without blemish; and the grain offering shall be one ephah for a ram, and the grain offering for the lambs, as much as he wants to give, as well as a hin of oil with every ephah. On the day of the New Moon it shall be a young bull without blemish, six lambs, and a ram; they shall be without blemish. He shall prepare a grain offering of an ephah for a bull, an ephah for a ram, as much as he wants to give for the lambs, and a hin of oil with every ephah (46:4-7).

During these offerings the doors of the inner eastern gate leading into the inner courtyard would be open until evening and the prince would enter the vestibule of the gateway and stand there during the sacrifices (v. 8). He would come in and go out among the people assembled in the outer courtyard (v. 10). Worshippers present for the prince's offerings were to depart in the opposite direction to which they had entered the outer court previously (i.e., if one entered through the north gate, then one departed through the south gate and vice versa; vv. 9, 11). The reason for this is not explained, but Matthew Henry suggests a practical reason for the dismissal protocol:

Some think this was to prevent thrusting and jostling one another; for God is *the God of order, and not of confusion.* We may suppose that they came in at the gate that was next to their own houses, but, when they went away, God would have them go out at that gate which would lead them *the furthest way about,* that they might have time for meditation; being thereby obliged to go a great way round the sanctuary, they might have an opportunity to consider the palaces of it, and, if they improved their time well in fetching this circuit, they would call it the nearest way home. Some observe that this may remind us, in the service of God, to be still pressing forward (Phil. 3:13) and not to look back, and, in our attendance upon ordinances, not to go back as we came, but more holy, and heavenly, and spiritual.[94]

Indeed, we often fail to appreciate the Lord as we should because we do not afford ourselves more time to mediate on Him beyond corporate times of worship. The more we muse on Christ, the more heavenly minded we will be in His earthly affairs. We cannot retrace our steps during our earthly sojourn to fix our past failures, but we can go on with the Lord in His strength. Walking in the Spirit, abiding in Christ, and enjoying fellowship with the Father are all synonymous expressions of divine communion.

The one exception for which the eastern gate of the inner courtyard might be reopened (i.e., other than Sabbath or New Moon celebrations) would be if the prince desired to offer a voluntary burnt offering or peace offering (v. 12). However, the gate was to be reclosed after he departed the porch of the gate (i.e., it did not stay open until evening).

Daily Sacrifices

Ezekiel then confirms that a daily burnt offering of an unblemished lamb and a meal offering moistened with oil was to occur each morning (vv. 13-15). The corresponding evening offering that the Jews were accustomed to under the Law is not mentioned. Perhaps in overviewing the offerings, Ezekiel did not think it was necessary to repeat himself, as the two sacrifices were inseparable in the Old Testament (Ex. 29:38-41). Or, it may be that only a morning sacrifice to celebrate each new day before the Lord will be all that is ceremonially necessary in the Kingdom Age.

The Year of Jubilee

Under the Law, land sold from one's inheritance reverted back to the original owner every fifty years to ensure tribal allotments were preserved over time. This event was called "the Year of Jubilee" (Lev. 25:10-13). During the Kingdom Age, the Jubilee mandate will be in effect; even the prince must abide by it. If he sells or gives land to a son, then that land would remain the son's in the Year of Jubilee, but if he sold or donated the land to a servant, the ownership of that land was to revert to the prince (vv. 16-17). The fact that the prince can have human offspring further proves that he is not Christ, but a descendant of David representing His righteous rule among the people. Ezekiel reminds the people how their past rulers abused their power and seized their land and oppressed them. The prince of the Kingdom Age will not behave so. In fact, he is prohibited from obtaining any land outside his portion (v. 18).

In Leviticus 25, Moses promised that if the Jews heeded God's "Laws of the Land," then He would bless them in the land: there would be neither want nor war (Lev. 25:19). To alleviate the Jews' anxiety about not sowing or harvesting crops for two years, the Lord promised an abundant harvest in the sixth year preceding the Sabbath year and the year of Jubilee to hold them over for those two years (Lev. 25:20-22). Regrettably, there is no biblical evidence that the Jews ever obeyed the year of Jubilee statute; in fact, it is not mentioned outside the Pentateuch. Because of their obvious violation of seventy straight Sabbath years prior to the Babylonian exile (2 Chron. 36:20-21), it is doubtful that the Jews ever consistently honored the year of Jubilee command. However, in the Kingdom Age, everyone, including the prince, will honor this statute and, as God promised, He will richly bless His people in the land.

Ezekiel's angelic counterpart then ushered him northward and then westward through the outer court to show him how shared offerings, such as peace offerings, were cooked (vv. 19-24). He was shown a kitchen in the far northwest corner of the outer courtyard and then three more, each in the remaining corners of the courtyard. Each common kitchen was forty by thirty cubits and should not be confused with the two kitchens designated for only the priests, located on either side of the large western room against the wall that surrounded the complex. In these common kitchens the priests cook meat that had been offered to God and enjoy portions of the food themselves as did the offerer's family and friends. This was a joyous time of fellowship among God's people as they were before the Lord.

Meditation

> Break forth in hymns of gladness,
> O wasted Jerusalem;
> Let songs instead of sadness,
> Thy jubilee proclaim;
> The Lord, in strength victorious,
> Upon thy foes has trod;
> Behold, O earth, the glorious
> Salvation of our God.

> — Benjamin Gough

Rivers of Living Water
Ezekiel 47:1-12

After touring the kitchens in the outer courtyard, Ezekiel was led by his escort into the inner courtyard and to the entrance of the temple. There he noticed water streaming out from under the threshold and flowing eastward on the south side of the altar (v. 1). After leaving the temple complex through both north gates, he ventured to the east side of the temple wall and observed that water was gushing out from under the wall just south of the East Gate (v. 2). As the two continued to follow the flowing water eastward, the stream became a broadening and deepening river (vv. 3-5).

The angelic measurer checked the depth of the river every 1,750 feet while traveling eastward and found it to increase from ankle-deep to knee-deep, to waist-deep, to over-the-head-deep. So unusual and unpredictable is the outworking of God's infinite grace as shown in this vision: The water gushes forth from God's house and deepens rapidly as it flows instead of growing shallower, yet there are no tributaries adding to its capacity. In nature, springs, brooks, streams, etc. flow into rivers to increase their volume, but in God's economy His abounding grace originates in Himself and streams forth into the world to satisfy every human need, and yet there is more.

In response to his escort's inquiry, Ezekiel affirms what he has seen. Then, Ezekiel abruptly notices the many trees that are rooted into both banks of the river (v. 7). It is not likely that the trees were there previously, for trees require time to grow. Clearly, the wonderful influence of the water promoted growth and also, as we will soon see, fruitfulness. Putting all these components together, what is being symbolized in Ezekiel's vision?

The work of the Holy Spirit is generally depicted in Scripture as an *active* component (such as fluids): flowing olive oil (Zech. 4), blowing wind (John 3), seven flames of fire (Rev. 4), and rushing water (John 7). The Holy Spirit, in these types, is not visibly seen doing the Father's will, but rather He is enabling and accomplishing the task at hand in a powerful and invisible fashion for the glory of Christ. The Lord Himself foretold that the energizing power of the Holy Spirit in His people would be like the fresh flowing water that poured from the rock that Moses struck (John 7:37-39). He was speaking of the wonderful spiritual benefits the Holy Spirit provides a believer who has trusted in Christ for salvation.

This dynamic was first prefigured in Exodus 16, when Moses, with the rod of God, struck a particular rock that God pointed out to him and an abundant flow of water gushed out from the rock to satisfy the thirsty Israelites. The rock pictures Christ at Calvary, the rod symbolizes God's authority, and the water represents the work of the Holy Spirit. Only after drinking from the rock did the Israelites have the wherewithal to enter into battle for the first time and they defeated the Amalekites (Ex. 17).

However, we learn from an episode in Samson's life that we must rely on the Holy Spirit not only to engage the enemy, but also to sustain the victor afterwards. When thirsty Samson called on Jehovah after slaying a thousand Philistines, the word of God came to him and led him to a refreshing spring of water that God had caused to flow out of a rock. Throughout Scripture, the rock speaks of Christ (e.g. Matt. 16:18; 1 Cor. 10:4) and He repeatedly extends this invitation: *"If any man thirst, let him come unto Me, and drink"* (John 7:37). It is important to remember that serving the Lord does not quench the believer's thirst; something else does that, or rather Someone else – the Holy Spirit.

If we do not want to lose the benefits of the conflict won, we must continue to seek Christ's presence in the Word of God as our refreshment and continue to rely on the Holy Spirit for wisdom and strength. No believer in communion with God will ever have a thirsty soul – He has resources that cannot be exhausted.

During the Kingdom Age the abundant, free-flowing water from the throne of God will symbolize all the blessings and refreshment available through the energizing power of the Holy Spirit. This future spiritual reality seems to be the literal fulfillment of the following psalms:

They are abundantly satisfied with the fullness of Your house, and You give them drink from the river of Your pleasures. For with You is the fountain of life; in Your light we see light (Ps. 36:8-9).

Infidelity and Loyalty

> *There is a river whose streams shall make glad the city of God, the holy place of the tabernacle of the Most High. God is in the midst of her, she shall not be moved; God shall help her, just at the break of dawn* (Ps. 46:4-5).

Fruitfulness, as depicted in the thriving fruit-laden trees lining the river, will be characteristic of the Holy Spirit's influence among the nations during the Kingdom Age:

> *Along the bank of the river, on this side and that, will grow all kinds of trees used for food; their leaves will not wither, and their fruit will not fail. They will bear fruit every month, because their water flows from the sanctuary. Their fruit will be for food, and their leaves for medicine* (v. 12).

This fruit will never drop to the ground and spoil, but will always be available to refresh the soul. Furthermore, the leaves of the trees will always be accessible to heal any ailment. There will be nothing in the Kingdom Age to stop individuals from receiving God's blessings, other than their own exercise of faith and holiness. Some will be able to get only their ankles wet, so to speak, but others will not be satisfied until they are completely submerged in God's goodness.

Before exploring Ezekiel's vision further, we will pause to consider other prophecies and visions related to the Lord's Second Coming in an attempt to gain a fuller picture of what Ezekiel is referring to in this chapter.

Zechariah writes:

> *For I will gather all the nations to battle against Jerusalem; the city shall be taken ... Then the Lord will go forth and fight against those nations, as He fights in the day of battle. And in that day His feet will stand on the Mount of Olives, which faces Jerusalem on the east. And the Mount of Olives shall be split in two, from east to west, making a very large valley; half of the mountain shall move toward the north and half of it toward the south. ... And in that day it shall be that living waters shall flow from Jerusalem, half of them toward the eastern sea and half of them toward the western sea; in both summer and winter it shall occur...All the land shall be turned into a plain from Geba to Rimmon south of Jerusalem. Jerusalem shall be raised up* (Zech. 14:2-10).

Isaiah writes:

A highway shall be there, and a road, and it shall be called the Highway of Holiness. ... But the redeemed shall walk there, and the ransomed of the Lord shall return, and come to Zion with singing, with everlasting joy on their heads. They shall obtain joy and gladness, and sorrow and sighing shall flee away (Isa. 35:8-10).

John writes:

And there were noises and thunderings and lightnings; and there was a great earthquake, such a mighty and great earthquake as had not occurred since men were on the earth.... Then every island fled away, and the mountains were not found (Rev. 16:18, 20).

John identifies five separate earthquakes during the Tribulation Period, but the last one which accompanies the bowl judgments is the mother of all earthquakes – mountains around the earth fall and islands vanish. This means that the world's geography will be quite different after the Tribulation Period. Zechariah records that Jerusalem is actually elevated at this time, while the highlands to the south become a flat plain. He also states that when Christ returns to the earth, He will cleave the Mount of Olives in two (i.e., what is remaining of it) and will create a valley running east and west. Two rivers will then originate from the mount; one will flow west to the Mediterranean Sea and the other east to the Dead Sea. The Mount of Olives is located just east of Jerusalem, and at Christ's ascension it was prophesied to be the location of His return (Acts 1).

These events all happen prior to the Kingdom Age, and before the temple complex Ezekiel has been describing exists. The source of all life is Christ (John 1:1-4). When He steps on the Mount of Olives, refreshing rivers of life appear; when He is on His throne in the temple, living water will also flow freely. It is this author's opinion that Ezekiel was following the flow of water from the temple eastward before it turned south and connected with the dual flowing rivers described by Zechariah. This seems reasonable, since both Ezekiel and Zechariah mention that the easterly flowing rivers they saw terminated in the Dead Sea. To allow easy access to the temple complex, there may be a road called "the Highway of Holiness" which will allow the redeemed to travel easily from Jerusalem over the river to the temple (Isa. 35:8).

Much death and destruction will occur during the Tribulation Period, but these rivers will have a rejuvenating effect on the ruined ecosystem. The water from the river running eastward heals the Dead Sea and transforms it into a fresh water basin having an abundance of fish. At present, the Dead Sea contains twenty-four to twenty-six percent minerals, as compared to normal sea water which ranges between four and six percent. Because of its extreme mineral content, there is no aquatic life in the Dead Sea today. This will not be the case in the Kingdom Age because the rejuvenating water from God's throne will heal the sea's deadness. Fishermen at either end of the once Dead Sea (i.e., at En Gedi or En Eglaim) will fill their nets with fish, like those caught in the Mediterranean Sea. No doubt the river flowing westward also has a healing influence on that body of water. Although the Dead Sea will be bursting with life, its stagnant marshes and swamps will remained fouled and salty; these were not blessed by the river's life. Both rivers are lined with prolific fruit-bearing trees, because their roots will draw up God's life-giving water (v. 12).

The entire scene is a prelude to John's vision of God's Garden/Throne in the New Jerusalem, that 1,500 mile tri-dimensional city of gold that hovers above the new earth in the eternal state (Rev. 21-22). In the final chapter of the Bible, John describes the vista about God's throne: *"A pure river of water of life, clear as crystal, proceeding from the throne of God and of the Lamb. In the middle of its street, and on either side of the river, was the tree of life, which bore twelve fruits, each tree yielding its fruit every month"* (Rev. 22:1-2). Besides drinking from the pure river of water, the inhabitants of heaven are also invited to eat from the tree of life connected with the river.

God calls our attention to three important trees in Scripture. The fruit from the tree of the knowledge of good and evil was forbidden, but tasted by human desire (Gen. 3:1-7). The center of Scripture calls us to kneel before the suffering Savior nailed to a tree at Golgotha. Those who do are able to freely eat of the tree of life, which will be available in Heaven forever. The only remedy for sin and its handmaiden death is to obtain eternal life in Christ. Those who do will be able to eat freely from the tree of life.

After our first parents sinned, they were cast out of the Garden of Eden and prohibited from eating from the tree of life. Cherubim and a flaming sword guarded Eden to ensure every possible return route would be met with judgment – God would prevent Adam and Eve from securing humanity's eternal doom. There is only one way to the tree of life. It is by Calvary's Road. The Lord Jesus declared, *"I am the way, the truth, and the life. No one comes to the Father except through Me"* (John 14:6). That is why there is only one street in heaven leading to the tree of life. The way to God was not man venturing in, but God coming out to man. The Son of God took on Himself the judgment of the flaming sword so that we might have access to the tree of life.

Consequently, the Bible commences and ends with the Creator in fellowship with man in a garden paradise (Rev. 22:1-6). However, the journey man travels between these two gardens is a difficult one. But thankfully this journey is bridged by a third garden – *"Now in the place where He was crucified there was a garden; and in the garden a new sepulcher"* (John 19:41; KJV). Both the first Adam and last Adam – Christ (1 Cor. 15:45) – died in a garden. The first Adam changed the first garden into a spiritual graveyard, but the Lord Jesus was resurrected from His garden tomb to offer spiritual life. Those who receive this provision will be restored to their Creator and will be returned to an eternal garden paradise. Only through the center garden of Calvary may a connection between bliss and eternity be obtained.

All that Ezekiel is describing for us is just a foretaste of the manifold blessings in Christ that God will share with all the redeemed for eternity. The Bible closes with this invitation: *"And let him who thirsts come. Whoever desires, let him take the water of life freely"* (Rev. 22:17). "Whoever will," my friend, means you; anyone desiring to satisfy his or her deep yearning to be one with God is invited to come and drink of Him. *"Oh, taste and see that the Lord is good; blessed is the man who trusts in Him!"* (Ps. 34:8).

Meditation

The soul's deepest thirst is for God Himself, who has made us so that we can never be satisfied without Him.

— F. F. Bruce

Division of Tribal Lands
Ezekiel 47:13-48:35

The remainder of the book relates to the divisions of tribal lands. More than eight centuries before the Jews were removed from Judah by the Babylonians, the Lord tasked Joshua with leading His people into the Promised Land and then distributing land after it was conquered. The land allotted to Abraham was vast (Gen. 15:19-21); Canaan was merely the first portion to be possessed for an inheritance (Josh. 1:4, 6). God would fulfill his promise to Abraham by giving his descendants the land in stages, as determined by their faithfulness and willingness to conquer and possess it in the years that followed (Deut. 19:8). But Israel's longevity and blessing in Canaan was contingent on their obedience to the Law of Moses (Deut. 28). Time would prove that the Israelites were not obedient, neither did they have sufficient faith to obtain all that God had for them.

Historically speaking, the Jewish people have never fully possessed more than about a tenth of all that was promised to Abraham. The western boundary of the land was the Mediterranean Sea and the eastern boundary was to be the Euphrates River, which runs through central Iraq today. The land was to extend from the mountains of Lebanon in the north to the southern wilderness. So, although the nation of Israel is partially back in the Promised Land after reclaiming it through military effort (38:8), they do not inhabit the full portion God issued to Abraham.

Ezekiel explains that the literal fulfillment of this promise will occur in the Kingdom Age, after the Jews have received Jesus Christ as their Messiah. At the start of the millennial reign of Christ, God will remind the nation of Israel of His previous promise to their forefathers:

These are the borders by which you shall divide the land as an inheritance among the twelve tribes of Israel. Joseph shall have two portions. You shall inherit it equally with one another; for I raised My hand in an oath to give it to your fathers, and this land shall fall to you as your inheritance (vv. 13-14).

Indeed, God will keep all His pledges, but He cannot fulfill His land promise to Israel until the "fullness of the Gentiles" (the Church Age) is complete, and the nation of Israel has been refined and restored to Him through Christ (Zech. 12:10; Rom. 11:26-32). This is one of the strongest evidences to substantiate a pre-millennial Second Advent of Christ to the earth. We learn that the land portion of the Levites, the priests, the prince, and Jerusalem is the center swath through the Promised Land with seven tribes having an inheritance to the north and five to the south. In Joshua's day, tribal allotments of land were distributed with relationship to tribal populations, but in the Millennial Kingdom the strips of land running east and west (parallel to the prince's portion) will be equal in width. F. C. Cook estimates this to be approximately 17 geographic miles across (i.e., a little less than twenty English miles).[95]

The northern boundary will be from the Mediterranean Sea, north of Sidon, through several cities north of Damascus (vv. 15-17). The eastern boundary will extend between Hauran and Damascus, but arching back from Hazar Enan below the Sea of Galilee to the Jordan River (v. 18). The southern border of Israel's land will be from Tamar (as far as the waters of Meribah Kadesh), then along the brook Wadi in Egypt northward to the Mediterranean Sea (v. 20). The western border will be the Mediterranean Sea as far north as Lebo Hamath in the north (the starting point of the description; v. 20).

This land was an inheritance for the tribes of Israel and was to be distributed by lot (vv. 21-22). However, in an astonishing reversal of Levitical Law, those born in the land of sojourning strangers would also receive an inheritance among the tribe of Israel in which they lived (vv. 23-24). Under the Law, foreigners who became worshippers of Jehovah were welcome to live among God's people; they became subject to Law (Lev. 16:29; Num. 15:29). However, they were not permitted the full privileges extended to the Jehovah's covenant people (Lev. 22:10; Num. 1:51). In the Kingdom Age, Gentiles desiring to live near Jehovah and among His covenant people will receive privileges not previously possible; all shall enjoy the blessings of God.

More detail is provided in reference to the center band of land belonging to the prince, the Levites, and the priests and the portion designated for Jerusalem previously discussed in chapter 45 (vv. 8-22). It suffices here to summarize that Jerusalem's boundary will be a 7,875-foot-wide square, with 437 feet of pastureland surrounding the city for the flocks of those dwelling in the city. The circumference of the city in Josephus' day was said to be about four miles, but in the Kingdom Age, it will be 37 miles – two days' journey on foot. It will also have designated farmland on the western and eastern sides of the city proper measuring 3.3 by 1.7 miles.

The twelve tribes of Israel will receive land allotments on either side of the central strip. (Actual widths are not mentioned, but will be evenly divided.) From the northern boundary to the center portion the tribes receiving land will be: Dan, Asher, Naphtali, Manasseh, Ephraim, Reuben, and Judah (vv. 1-7). Continuing southward from the central strip: Benjamin, Simeon, Issachar, Zebulun and Gad were to obtain inheritances (vv. 23-29). Although some of the geographical reference points mentioned in Scripture are difficult for us to identify, God knows the full area into which He is going to bring Israel. Since the boundaries of Israel's inheritance promised to Abraham (Gen. 15:18-21) extend further northward and eastward to the Euphrates River, perhaps there will be more tribal allotments during the Kingdom Age or maybe this undesignated land is considered the commonwealth of Israel.

The following diagram depicts the inheritance of the twelve tribes of Israel during the Millennial Kingdom.[96] Also shown is the central band containing the possessions of the prince, the Levites, and the priests, and the city of Jerusalem.

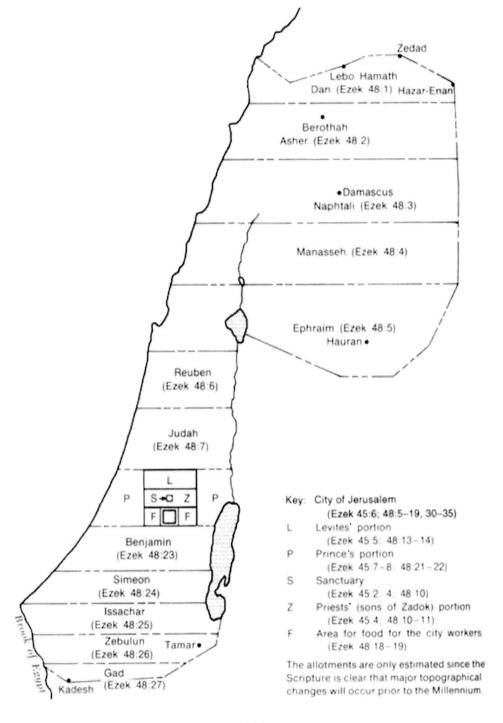

Zedad

Lebo Hamath
Dan (Ezek 48:1) Hazar-Enan

Berothah
Asher (Ezek 48:2)

•Damascus
Naphtali (Ezek 48:3)

Manasseh (Ezek 48:4)

Ephraim (Ezek 48:5)
Hauran •

Reuben
(Ezek 48:6)

Judah
(Ezek 48:7)

L

P   S ←□ Z   P

F □ F

Benjamin
(Ezek 48:23)

Simeon
(Ezek 48:24)

Issachar
(Ezek 48:25)

Zebulun   Tamar •
(Ezek 48:26)

Gad
Kadesh (Ezek 48:27)

Brook of Egypt

Key: City of Jerusalem
      (Ezek 45:6; 48:5-19, 30-35)
L   Levites' portion
      (Ezek 45:5; 48:13-14)
P   Prince's portion
      (Ezek 45:7-8; 48:21-22)
S   Sanctuary
      (Ezek 45:2, 4; 48:10)
Z   Priests' (sons of Zadok) portion
      (Ezek 45:4; 48:10-11)
F   Area for food for the city workers
      (Ezek 48:18-19)

The allotments are only estimated since the
Scripture is clear that major topographical
changes will occur prior to the Millennium.

Infidelity and Loyalty

Notice that the two tribes who held to the truth of Levitical Law by worshipping Jehovah in the temple at Jerusalem will be positioned the closest to the Lord in the Kingdom Age. Additionally, the tribe of Simeon, which was absorbed into Judah over time, is the next closest to the Lord towards the south. This serves as a good reminder that faithfulness to truth and to the Lord will be rewarded by Him later. For the Christian, the rewards that are earned during this lifetime provide the believer with a greater appreciation for the Lord, a greater capacity to worship Him throughout eternity, and, indeed, a greater capability to enjoy heaven (1 Cor. 15:41-42; Rev. 4:11).

Ezekiel then affirms that the city of Jerusalem will have twelve gates, one for each tribe, and three gates on each side of the city (vv. 30-34): Reuben, Judah, and Levi (north side); Joseph, Benjamin, and Dan (east side); Simeon, Issachar, and Zebulun (south side), and Gad, Asher, and Naphtali (west side). As the temple complex will be north of Jerusalem, the gates associated with Reuben, Judah, and Levi will be closest to the Lord. This designation may be to honor Reuben as Jacob's firstborn, Judah as the royal tribe, and Levi as the priestly tribe.

Nehemiah's wall featured ten main gates (though two additional minor gates are mentioned in Nehemiah 12:39). Modern Jerusalem has eight gates. Ezekiel prophesied that Jerusalem in the Kingdom Age will have twelve main gates, one for each tribe. Similarly, God's eternal city, the New Jerusalem, which descends out of heaven at the conclusion of Christ's Millennial Kingdom, will have twelve operational gates (Rev. 21:10-12). What practical message is being conveyed in the changing number of gates?

Twelve in Scripture is the number of *perfect administration*; thus, twelve tribes comprised the nation of Israel; the Church was founded on the teachings of the twelve apostles. Consequently, the New Jerusalem has twelve gates, one named after each tribe of Israel, and twelve foundations, one named after each apostle (Rev. 21:12-14). The number *ten* is used to represent *responsibility* in Scripture; for example, the Ten Commandments made the Jews directly accountable to God for their behavior. This partly explains why Jerusalem had only ten chief gates in Nehemiah's day, but ultimately would have twelve main gates in the Kingdom Age: since Israel had not yet reached perfection after their Babylonian exile, they were to remember that they were directly accountable to God while being guided into maturity.

There is no greater discovery than seeing God as the author of your destiny.

— Ravi Zacharias

After acknowledging Christ as their Messiah, and receiving the Holy Spirit, the nation will have achieved their spiritual destiny – full maturity and irrevocable communion with God. They will know the Lord and His faithful, abiding presence in a new way. In fact, Jerusalem itself will be referred to as *Yahweh-Shammah*, meaning "the Lord is present" or "the Lord is there" (v. 35). Here then is the complete fulfillment of what the angel told Joseph just prior to the birth of Christ: *"Behold, a virgin shall be with child, and shall bring forth a son, and they shall call His name Emmanuel, which being interpreted is, God with us"* (Matt. 1:23). God veiled in flesh offered Himself to Israel, but was rejected; however, at His Second Advent the Lord Jesus will be admired by those He came to save – this is the power of the gospel message and the majesty of God!

By the light of nature we see God as a God above us, by the light of the law we see Him as a God against us, but by the light of the gospel we see Him as Emmanuel, God with us.

— Matthew Henry

After witnessing in a vision the glory of the Lord departing the temple (chps. 10-11), it must have been thrilling for Ezekiel to now see the glory of the Lord among His people again. For the Jew, this will be the most wonderful feature of the Millennial Kingdom: God once again among them and in His temple. William Kelly summarizes the whole matter:

This then is the last and chief glory – the presence of Jehovah in the city of His choice. In this Israel shall boast above all their privileges; and justly, for it is the complement and crown of all. How bright an end of their long wanderings, and of their manifold sorrows! How worthy of His redeeming grace, who will cleanse away the guilt which shed it, when they turn to Him in faith, discerning and owning at length their self-destructive folly in the light of His love, who never wavered but died for them so many centuries before they broke down in shame and contrition before Him![97]

Infidelity and Loyalty

The Jews will never again commit spiritual adultery; therefore, God will never have a reason to depart from them. The entire planet will be filled with the knowledge, blessings, and glory of God in Christ. All Gentile nations will learn of God's holiness and just how much He loves His once adulterous wife, the nation of Israel. In the Millennial Kingdom, there will be no such questions as: "Who is the Lord?" or "Where is the Lord?" His presence will be cherished and His glory extolled by all.

Happy the soul that has been awed by a view of God's majesty.

— A. W. Pink

Ezekiel began his prophecy by describing the magnificent grandeur of God and he concludes with a description of God's glory in His millennial temple. It reminds us of John's apocalypse, which likewise commences with a description of Christ's glorious splendor and concludes with the glory of God filling the New Jerusalem, all the new earth, and indeed all the new heavens. But most importantly, the Creator is once more in full communion with the only creature that was fashioned in His image and likeness – redeemed man.

Meditation

Thy kingdom come, O God,
Thy reign, O Christ, begin;
Break with Thine iron rod
The tyrannies of sin.

Men scorn Thy sacred name,
And wolves devour Thy fold;
By many deeds of shame
We learn that love grows cold.

Over heathen lands afar
Thick darkness broodeth yet:
Arise, O morning Star,
Arise, and never set.

— Lewis Hensley

Epilogue: God Is Not Finished With Israel

The book of Ezekiel and many other Old Testament passages provide overwhelming evidence that God has not abandoned the Jewish people. When Scripture is interpreted literally, we see that God's future plan for glorifying the Church is quite different than His agenda for restoring the nation of Israel to a position of honor and blessing. Hosea refers to this latter event as *"a door of hope"* for Israel (Hos. 2:15). Such prophetic evidence not only bestows hope to the Jewish nation, but also should excite every Christian to love *"the blessed hope,"* the appearing of the Lord Jesus Christ (2 Tim. 4:8)! Consequently, both the nation of Israel and the Church have all their hopes in Christ!

The following is a sampling of the hundreds of Old Testament prophecies pertaining to the Jewish nation of Israel which have yet to be fulfilled:

1. The land given to Abraham has never been possessed by the Jews, but must be (Gen. 15:18). This land was to be possessed incrementally, based on the Jews' faithfulness to obey Jehovah and co-labor with Him in faith (Deut. 7:22; Josh. 13:1; 21:43-44). But even during the glory days of David's and Solomon's reigns, the Jews never controlled more than about ten percent of the inheritance promised to Abraham.

2. The Jews will start sacrificing again until the abomination of desolation, which occurs in the middle of the Tribulation Period (Dan. 9:27). At that time, the beast (Antichrist) will declare himself to be God and will stop the Jewish sacrifices (2 Thess. 2:4-7). While on the earth, the Lord made mention of this prophecy as still being future (Matt. 24). It has not been fulfilled since that time.

3. Jerusalem will be the worship center of the earth during the millennium. All nations will come to Jerusalem to see the glory of God (Isa. 2:1-4; 60:14; 66:10-18; Zech. 14:16-21).

4. The Jews will be highly esteemed by all Gentiles during the millennial reign of Christ (Isa. 60:12-15; Zech. 8:20-23). This worldwide favor for the Jewish people has never been realized.

5. The Jewish nation will be restored to Jehovah. Though the prophecies predicting a political rebirth have recently been fulfilled (e.g. Ezek. 37:15-20; Isa. 11:13; 66:8), the nation has yet to experience spiritual rebirth (Joel 3). This will occur at the end of the Tribulation Period.

6. As a disciplinary action, God began scattering the Jews throughout the nations in 722 B.C. with the invasion of Israel by the Assyrians. He will completely gather all Jews back to the land of Israel at the close of the Tribulation Period (Ezek. 39:28-29).

7. After the Jews regain the land of Israel by the sword (war), they will experience a period of false peace under the Antichrist (Dan. 9:27).

8. Towards the end of the first half of the Tribulation Period, the armies of Russia, Iraq, Iran, Egypt, and Turkey will attack the Jews, but God will protect Israel from this invasion by raining down large hailstones, heavy rain, pestilence, and even fire from heaven (Ezek. 38-39).

9. By the end of the Tribulation Period, the Jewish nation will receive a new heart and will be indwelt by the Holy Spirit (Ezek. 36:17-26; Joel 2:18-28; Isa. 32; Isa. 44:1-6). This will begin with the sealing of the 144,000 Jews in the early portion of the Tribulation Period (Rev. 7).

10. The battle of Armageddon is yet future, but will not happen until Israel is back in the Promised Land, including the Golan Heights (Joel 3; Zech. 12; 14).

11. Babylon will be completely destroyed by fire and made uninhabitable. This could not happen until the Jews were dwelling in Bashan (the Golan Heights), as they are today (Jer. 50).

12. Only after the adulterous nation of Israel repents and receives Jesus Christ as Messiah in the "latter days" will the kingdom of David be established (Hosea 3:1-5; Zech. 12:1-10). This was Jehovah's unconditional promise to David (1 Chron. 17:12).

13. A resurrection of faithful Jews will accompany the spiritual restoration of the Jewish nation (Isa. 26:8, 18-21).

14. God will restore Israel, the adulterous wife, and He will protect her from harm, though all nations will oppose her during the Tribulation Period (Isa. 54; Jer. 30:7; Rev. 12:13-17). Those Jews surviving this terrible holocaust will enter Christ's kingdom (Isa. 4:2).

15. During the Millennial Kingdom of Christ, the faithful from the Gentile nations will gather with the Jewish nation to honor Christ at Jerusalem (Isa. 11:1-11; Isa. 60; 65:18-25; Rev. 21).

16. During the Millennial Kingdom, a temple with specific dimensions will be built in Jerusalem (Ezek. 40-43). This temple has never existed.

17. During the Millennial Kingdom, the twelve tribes will receive specific land allotments within the region promised Abraham (Ezek. 47-48). These specific allocations have never occurred.

18. Paul declares that God has always maintained a pure Jewish remnant to honor Him (Rom. 11). Today, this remnant is a portion of the Church, but when the times of the Gentiles are over, the blindness of the Jewish nation, which resulted from rejecting Christ, will end. Then the entire nation will be a purified remnant never to depart from the Lord again (Isa. 4). The Lord plainly describes this future reality to Ezekiel (43:7-9).

Infidelity and Loyalty

Clearly Jehovah, through the prophets of old, has declared His future plans for the Jewish nation. All these unfilled prophecies indicate the Messiah is coming again and that Jehovah is not finished with His covenant people. The prophet Isaiah declares that, in a future day, once idolatrous Israel is restored to the Lord in purity, the wealth and honor of the nations will be theirs. At that time, the Jews' relation with Christ will serve as a beacon to draw all men to praise the blessed Savior (Isa. 44:12-22).

Daniel

Overview of Daniel

Historical Setting

Seven closely-linked Old Testament books describe the post-exilic circumstances of God's covenant people. Three historical books (Ezra, Nehemiah, and Esther) and four prophetic books (Daniel, Haggai, Zechariah, and Malachi) combine to provide a composite picture of the deplorable spiritual and social conditions of the Jewish nation at that time. Judah suffered from deep-seated idolatry, yet pretended to honor Jehovah by offering sacrifices and keeping His feasts. Despite these impediments, God was able to refine His people by severe chastening, and revive them through a handful of faithful Jews who had not lost hope in Him.

Isaiah, then later Habakkuk, Jeremiah, and Ezekiel, foretold that the Babylonians would invade and decimate Jerusalem, slaughtering many Jews and hauling others to Babylon. But God promised that the Jews would be permitted to return to their homeland after seventy years (Jer. 25:11).

Daniel confirmed the meaning of Jeremiah's seventy-year prophecy and lived as a captive in Babylon throughout this period to provide an eye-witness account of its fulfillment (9:2). Although Ezekiel, Daniel, and Jeremiah vividly describe the destruction of Jerusalem and the taking of Jewish captives, little is known of their actual captivity in Babylon. Other than the brief view of Jewish life in Babylon afforded by the books of Esther and Daniel, the biblical narrative is mainly silent until the Jews return home in their various groups.

The Author

The exile of those Jews who surrendered prior to Jerusalem's capture and those who survived its destruction was foretold by Jeremiah on many occasions. The first Jewish deportation was in 605 B.C. when Nebuchadnezzar initially invaded Jerusalem; the prophet Daniel and his three companions Hananiah, Mishael, and Azariah were among those exiled then (chp. 1). The second Jewish deportation occurred in 597 B.C. after Nebuchadnezzar put down Jehoiachin's rebellion. Ten thousand Jews were taken to Babylon at that time, among whom was the prophet Ezekiel and his wife (2 Kgs. 24:14).

Daniel's name means "God is my judge." He was summoned by the Lord in his teenage years (chps. 1-2) for prophetic ministry and continued as God's mouthpiece into his mid-eighties (chp. 10). We are not told anything about Daniel's Jewish lineage or his final days, though it would seem that he died in Babylon of natural causes at a good old age. He was a man devoted to the Lord his entire life.

Scripture upholds Daniel as a blameless man who was widely known for his righteous behavior (chp. 6). Various pagan rulers and the prophet Ezekiel acknowledged that Daniel had a brilliant mind and possessed wisdom beyond his years (1:19-20, 6:3; Ezek. 28:3). God Himself referred to Daniel's righteousness while speaking to Ezekiel (Ezek. 14:14, 20) and the Lord Jesus also quoted him (Matt. 24:15). All this to say that Daniel, despite what some skeptics suggest, was a real person and a devout Jew living in Babylon during the sixth century B.C.

The Date

Because Daniel is one of the most crucial prophetic books in the Old Testament, it has also been one of the most attacked by secular skeptics and scholars. Besides containing many messianic prophecies (pertaining to both advents), the tenor of the work upholds the believer's consecration from worldliness and its religions, a conviction many liberals loathe. The date of its writing is much debated: it is argued that a sixth century B.C. Daniel could not have so precisely predicted future events, such as military campaigns, marriage alliances, and the rise and fall of world empires by name; hence, the book or at least parts of it were written much later as history, not prophecy. Those holding this position would suggest that a date during the Maccabean era of the second century B.C. is more reasonable.

Indeed, the prophetic content in Daniel is so astounding that it would be natural for an unconverted skeptic to think that it must be just a historical account of previous events garnished with a personal narrative to make it interesting. This erroneous idea views the book of Daniel as historic fiction (like a G. A. Henty-type novel). If the book of Daniel were a forgery, why did the Lord Jesus quote from it to others

(Matt. 24:15)? Certainly, He would have known of the book's authenticity and would not propagate a lie to His audience!

Furthermore, let us consider the archeological evidence for an older date for the book. Presently, eight separate scrolls containing portions of the book of Daniel (found in Qumran Caves 1, 4, and 6) have been published as part of the Dead Sea Scroll collection. These scrolls are dated before the Maccabean revolt in the second century B.C.

The significance of this fact was voiced first in 1958 when Professor Frank M. Cross of Harvard University published *The Ancient Library of Qumran*, a comprehensive survey of the Dead Sea scrolls. Professor Cross refers to the fragments of the Daniel scrolls: "One copy of Daniel is inscribed in the script of the late second century B.C.".[98] Additionally, the official Greek translation of Daniel used in ancient times was that of Theodotion, an Ephesian (approximately 180 A.D.). It also dates before the Maccabean revolt in 168-165 B.C.

To date, portions of every chapter in Daniel have been translated and published, except chapters 9 and 12.[99] However, many more scrolls remain unpublished, such as a few fragments pertaining to Daniel's prayer in chapter 9 found in Cave 4.[100]

Lastly, consider all the prophetic content in Daniel that pertains to events after the second century B.C. (some of which has now been fulfilled): the fall of the Greek Empire and the Rise of the Roman Empire; Christ's first advent, His death, and His second coming; the Tribulation Period in which the Antichrist rules the world with ten kings (which was also later affirmed by John; Rev. 17). Daniel tells us that there will never be another world empire after the collapse of the Old Roman Empire until the Antichrist appears and rules the world – a reality that has been observed for over sixteen hundred years of world history. Even if the book of Daniel were written during the Maccabean era, the Roman Empire did not become a reality for more than another century.

Yet, many of Daniel's predictions are woven into the same text containing the earliest predictions, which some say is just history. This author believes that the precision of foretelling so many future events proves that the book is divinely inspired. Even if a later date of authorship were assumed, the same conclusion would be a rational one. What is to be gained then by belittling any portion of the book which Christ referred to and God has sought fit to preserve for us to learn from for over two millennia?

In summary, Daniel was a contemporary of Ezekiel (Ezekiel mentions Daniel in his own book) and is the author of the book bearing his own name; it was likely penned at the end of his life (535-530 B.C.). If the reader has any further doubts on this matter, William Kelly provides a fuller critique of authenticity and authorship in his commentary on the book of Daniel.

Theme

There are three themes that run throughout the book: First, Daniel's personal dedication to the Lord and his righteous example to other Jewish captives in Babylon. Second, God is sovereign over all the earth; He alone governs the rise and fall of kingdoms. Third, the Lord knows how to chasten and restore His covenant people in order to accomplish all His covenantal promises extended to them. As Hamilton Smith explains, these themes have their placement in a specific historical period between the loss of Israel's autonomy and its restoration by Christ in His kingdom:

> The Book of Daniel treats of the period of the world's history between these two events — the breakdown and setting aside of Israel in government, and the setting up of Christ's kingdom from Zion in the midst of restored Israel. During this time, the government of the world passes from Israel to the Gentiles, and the nation of Israel, ceasing to be the head of the nations, is brought into subjection to the Gentiles. For this reason, this period is called "the times of the Gentiles." It is obvious that Israel, as a nation, is still scattered and in subjection to the Gentiles, and that the reign of Christ is not yet come, so that the times in which we live are still "the times of the Gentiles."[101]

Daniel's narrative in the first six chapters contains historical incidences in chronological order pertaining to the loss of Israel's political autonomy and physical dispersion. The prophecies and visions in the last six chapters relate to "the times of the Gentiles" and Christ's Second Advent and while organized sequentially as they were written, there is overlapping content. The latter six chapters pertain to future world empires, the Tribulation Period and the Kingdom Age and provide telescoping detail of particular events within future kingdoms.

The apocalyptic visions of the last six chapters all occurred in Daniel's autumn years (i.e., somewhere between 65 and about 85 years of age).

Interestingly, the book was written in Hebrew, except for the mid-portion of the text relating to the Gentiles (2:4-7:28). This portion is written in Aramaic, the more commonly spoken language of that period. The two languages represent God's differing future programs for the Gentile nations and His covenant people. It is also observed that the first six chapters are written in historic form relating to Gentile rule over God's dispersed people; however, Daniel switches to first-person format in chapter 7 to shown that the revelation of the final chapters was to him specifically and not for the Jewish nation at that time. The following table summarizes the chronology of Daniel's prophetic ministry:

Chapter	Event	Approx. Year
1	Daniel's early life in Babylon	605-601 B.C.
2	Nebuchadnezzar's dream	604-603 B.C.
3	The image of gold/fiery furnace	587 B.C.
4	The king's vision/humbling	571-564 B.C.[1]
5	Belshazzar's feast/writing on wall	539 B.C.
6	Daniel and the lions	538-537 B.C.
7	Vision of four beasts	553 B.C.
8	Vison of ram, he-goat, little horn	551 B.C.
9	Prayer and seventy weeks	539-538 B.C.
10	Final vision/angelic intervention	536 B.C.
11	Prophecies: Darius to man of sin	536 B.C.
12	Prophecies: Tribulation/kingdom	536 B.C.

[1] Assumes Nebuchadnezzar died two years after his mental restoration.

Outline

There are two major movements in the book. In the first six chapters, Daniel records key events in his life and those of his three Hebrew friends as captives in Babylon. The final six chapters contain visions and prophecies focusing on the rise and fall of future world empires, including the final political system ruled by the Antichrist. The book concludes with prophecies concerning the resurrection of the just, the fall of the Antichrist, and the blessings of the Kingdom Age.

Infidelity and Loyalty

Within these two major movements in the book are the following subdivisions:

Daniel 1: Introduction. Despite Israel's failure, God reserves a faithful remnant of His covenant people during the times of the Gentiles. Jehovah always maintains a true witness of Himself on the earth, and through the testimony of this Jewish remnant, the spirit of prophecy and divine understanding are revealed.

Daniel 2-6: The prophetic history of four future Gentile empires, including their moral characteristics, distinguishing features, failures, and their final judgment; this culminates with the setting up of Christ's kingdom.

Daniel 7-11: The prophetic history of the four final Gentile empires, but with a divine focus on their relation with and treatment of God's covenant people.

Daniel 12: The conclusion and prophetic announcement of the Antichrist's destruction, the resurrection of the just to enjoy Christ's kingdom with a refined and restored Jewish nation and the resurrection of the wicked to everlasting torment.

Devotions in Daniel

Faithfulness in Captivity
Daniel 1

Daniel immediately tells us of the tragic situation that brought him to Babylon as a Jewish captive:

In the third year of the reign of Jehoiakim king of Judah, Nebuchadnezzar king of Babylon came to Jerusalem and besieged it. And the Lord gave Jehoiakim king of Judah into his hand, with some of the articles of the house of God, which he carried into the land of Shinar to the house of his god; and he brought the articles into the treasure house of his god (1:1-2).

Jehoiakim was the eldest son of King Josiah who died in battle at Carchemish in 608 B.C. while fighting the Egyptians. (Pharaoh Neco was en route to war with Babylon.) Babylonian historical records state that Nebuchadnezzar became the king of Babylon in August of 605 B.C. and then invaded Judah the following month.

Jeremiah states that Nebuchadnezzar's initial invasion of Jerusalem occurred during the fourth year of Jehoiakim and during Nebuchadnezzar's first year of ascension (Jer. 25:1). The statements of Daniel and Jeremiah can be reconciled by understanding the difference in time reckoning used during this era, a matter which has caused much confusion. Apparently, Jeremiah is referring to the Jewish calendar, which commences with the month of Nisan (March/April). If he had used the Babylonian calendar, whose first month is Tishri (September/October), Nebuchadnezzar would have just started his second numerical year of rule after only reigning a few weeks, but Jeremiah says the invasion occurred in his first year. Daniel, a captive in Babylon is most likely using the Babylonian calendar. Nebuchadnezzar's coronation and invasion would have happened within the same Jewish year, but not the same Babylonian year. Accordingly, it was the fourth year of Jehoiakim, for the reigns of vassal kings within the empire were tied to the Babylonian calendar (i.e., in reference to reigning years).

Pharaoh Neco put Jehoiakim on the throne instead of Jehoahaz. Jehoiakim was a selfish and corrupt king who oppressed the people and perverted justice for his personal gain (Jer. 22:15-17). Jehoiakim had been paying heavy tribute to Egypt, when Nebuchadnezzar surrounded Jerusalem. To prevent the city from being destroyed, Jehoiakim switched sides and paid tribute to Nebuchadnezzar. Many of the gold and silver vessels from the Jewish temple then became the possessions of the conquerors and were transported back to Babylon and stored in pagan temples (v. 2; 2 Chron. 36:7). Nebuchadnezzar also brought to Babylon a number of Jewish captives, including choice young men of nobility who were unblemished, handsome, intelligent, wise, and quick learners (vv. 3-4).

The above events explicitly fulfilled the prophecy Isaiah delivered to King Hezekiah over a hundred years previously. Hezekiah had foolishly shown the wealth of Jerusalem to the Babylonians in the hope of forming an alliance. This angered the Lord, and Isaiah was sent to deliver the follow message to Hezekiah:

> *Then Isaiah said to Hezekiah, "Hear the word of the Lord: 'Behold, the days are coming when all that is in your house, and what your fathers have accumulated until this day, shall be carried to Babylon; nothing shall be left,' says the Lord. 'And they shall take away some of your sons who will descend from you, whom you will beget; and they shall be eunuchs in the palace of the king of Babylon'"* (2 Kgs. 20:16-18).

Lest the matter be forgotten, Isaiah repeated the divine decree in chapter 39. Whether promising blessings or judgments, the Lord is always faithful to His word, as Daniel 1 confirms: the vessels of the temple, the wealth of the people, and the seed royal were carried away to Babylon.

How old was Daniel when he became a captive? The Hebrew words *ben* (v. 3) and *yeled* (v. 4), which are rendered "children" and "young men" respectively, pertain to a broad age range. Early church writer

Ignatius says that Daniel was twelve years old. Given Daniel's longevity, he and his friends were likely teenagers when exiled.

According to Isaiah's prophecy, these young men were likely made eunuchs (Isa. 20:18, 39:7), and then they were put under the supervision of Ashpenaz, the master of his eunuchs. For three years they were to reside in the king's palace, eat the king's food, and learn the customs, literature, and language of Babylon. At the end of this training period, each pupil would be examined personally by the king (v. 5). Besides bolstering the number of wise counselors in Babylon, the king was likely grooming these astute captives for administrative positions in his kingdom. Slaves without families do not have political ambitions and could be better trusted.

Scripture does not record the number of Jewish captives exiled in 605 B.C., but four individuals are named in verse 6 because of their impact on the Babylonian society and their testimony for Jehovah: Daniel, Hananiah, Mishael, and Azariah. Because each of their names honored Jehovah, they were renamed by their captors with Babylonian names which did not:

Daniel, meaning "God is my judge" became *Belteshazzar* – "Bel protects his life."

Hananiah, meaning "Jehovah is gracious" became *Shadrach* – "the command of Aku"; in the ancient Akkadian language, Aku was the Babylonian god of the moon.

Mishael, meaning "Who is like God?" became *Meshach* – "Who is what Aku is?" Again, Aku is the name of the Babylonian god of the moon.

Azariah, meaning "Jehovah has helped" became *Abednego* – "servant of Nebo" (Babylonian god of vegetation).

These four young men, who had been consecrated to Jehovah since their birth, were now unwilling subjects of a hostile pagan culture bent on driving all remembrance of their God from their existence. Babylon is a symbol of the religious world throughout Scripture. According to Genesis 10, paganism originated in Babylon with Nimrod and thus is the mother to all anti-God religions in the world (Rev. 17:5). Hence, the prince of this world, Satan, is quite eager to rid these four young men of their true Jewish identity and godly heritage in order to convert them to his secular liking.

Four satanic strategies were used on Daniel and his friends to accomplish this corrupt agenda: First, the devil wanted their natural abilities and talents for his own wicked purposes. Second, the devil desired to control their speech; he did not want them speaking Hebrew, the language of Jehovah for His people. Third, he wanted them to compromise their dietary convictions as based on God's Law; they were to eat all that the world had to offer them. Fourth, the devil attempted to strip them of their identity as a Jehovah worshipper by giving them pagan names. Satan continues this same agenda in an attempt to conform Christians to the policies and philosophies of the evil world he has manufactured through sin and rebellion.

The highest calling of a believer is to be a living sacrifice for Christ, which means separation from worldliness and full consecration to Christ. One of the ways that believers worship the Lord is to reject the world's values and attractions by renewing our minds on what is true and spiritual. Paul writes:

> *I beseech you therefore, brethren, by the mercies of God, that you present your bodies a living sacrifice, holy, acceptable to God, which is your reasonable service. And do not be conformed to this world, but be transformed by the renewing of your mind, that you may prove what is that good and acceptable and perfect will of God* (Rom. 12:1-2).

Scripture speaks of two complementary means of calling the believer's heart out of the world. The first is to set one's mind on things above (Col. 3:1-2), and the second is to come to realize that the things of the earth are temporary and shakable. As the writer of Hebrews reminds us, in a coming day, all that is not of the Lord will be removed: "... *removing of those things that are shaken, as of things that are made, that those things which cannot be shaken may remain. Wherefore, we receiving a kingdom which cannot be moved, let us have grace, whereby we may serve God acceptably with reverence and godly fear; for our God is a consuming fire*" (Heb. 12:27-29). The world is a nasty and temporal place, but heaven is wonderful and eternal. This is why believers should devote themselves and all their resources to the

Lord. All that is not dedicated to Him will ultimately burn up, without securing for us any eternal benefit.

The high moral character of Christ is exhibited and ascends to God as a living sacrifice when believer-priests are controlled by the Holy Spirit (Rom. 12:1). In this sense, every moment of every day can be a worship experience with the Lord. To want what God wants, and to say "no" to what He disapproves of is a pleasing sacrifice to Him. It is a sacrifice because it costs us something: our desires that are contrary to His will. May we be God-fearing, Christ-loving, Bible-believing, Spirit-controlled Christians who remind everyone of the Lord Jesus!

Returning to the narrative, we see that Daniel was a young man of purity and conviction:

> *Daniel purposed in his heart that he would not defile himself with the portion of the king's delicacies, nor with the wine which he drank; therefore he requested of the chief of the eunuchs that he might not defile himself* (v. 8).

The Law prohibited the Jews from eating meat derived from various animals, fowls, and fish and also any meats that had been offered to idols (Ex. 34:15; Deut. 14). It was customary for the king's meat to be offered to idols before being served. Furthermore, the fact that the king's food was prepared by Gentile hands rendered it unclean for Jewish consumption. Additionally, the King's wine would have included strong drink; in keeping with Scriptural principles and commands, Daniel wanted to avoid drunkenness (Lev. 10:9, Num. 6:3; Prov. 20:1). The Jews commonly drank wine that had been significantly diluted to ensure intoxication was avoided. Just because Daniel resided in Babylon did not mean he had to behave like the Babylonians! On this conviction, Albert Barnes writes:

> Daniel resolved, with them, to avoid at once the danger of conforming to the habits of idolaters; of "polluting" himself by customs forbidden by his religion, and of jeopardizing his own health and life by intemperate indulgence. He aimed also to secure the utmost vigor of body and the utmost clearness of mind by a course of strict and conscientious temperance.[102]

Infidelity and Loyalty

Daniel's devotion to the Lord is witnessed in his commitment to purity; he was a man of principle. However, as Hamilton Smith points out, Daniel's wisdom and courage are evident in the manner he addressed Melzar, whom Ashpenaz had put in charge of Daniel, Hananiah, Mishael, and Azariah:

> The secret of Daniel's strength was that his heart was right with God, as we read, "Daniel *purposed in his heart* that he would not defile himself with the portion of the king's meat." He acts, however, with great discretion, for he makes request to the prince that "he *might not* defile himself," without irritating and antagonizing the man by telling him that he had already purposed in his heart that "he *would not* defile himself." … *Obedience* to the word of God, *faith* in the living God, *separation* from the defilements of Babylon are the outstanding marks of these godly men. [103]

Melzar may not be a proper name, but rather a title meaning "steward." His response to Daniel's respectful quandary demonstrates two things: First, Melzar had already noticed and valued Daniel's fine character and blameless manner. Second, as we will see more clearly in chapter 10, God works within human authority to accomplish His purposes. In Exodus, we read that God hardened Pharaoh's heart ten times to bring about the most blessing to His people and the most glory to Himself. At times Pharaoh stiffened himself against the Lord's will (which God foreknew); at strategic times God worked within Pharaoh's mind to directly accomplish His sovereign purposes. Since captives could be put to death for refusing to eat the king's food, there is little doubt that God had softened Melzar's heart towards the Jewish captives. This point is more punctuated by the fact that Melzar's own life was in danger if those in his care were not thriving when examined by the king. Nebuchadnezzar, for example, might conclude that Melzar was embezzling the captives' food for profit (v. 10). Clearly, Nebuchadnezzar had big plans for these young men and would be strongly displeased if his expectations were not met.

A solution of profound faith was immediately offered by Daniel to resolve the dilemma (vv. 11-13): Permit him and his three friends to eat vegetables and to drink water for ten days and then let them be examined. There were no vegetables deemed unclean by the Law, so this would be the safest diet for them, even though several kinds of meats were permissible for them to eat per the Levitical statutes. If their countenances were favorable in comparison to those who had eaten the king's rich food during that same time period, then they would be permitted to continue that same diet. If, however, Daniel and his friends were not found to be thriving, they agreed that Melzar could deal with them as he thought best. This meant that they would willingly receive the consequences for rejecting the king's food, which could mean death.

It is evident that God was already working in this situation, for Melzar readily agreed to the conditions of the test posed by the young and inflexible slaves in his care (v. 14). The Jewish youths stood on conviction; they wanted to obey God's Word, and were trusting in the Lord to work the outcome of this trial in their favor.

> If we cannot believe God when circumstances seem to be against us, we do not believe Him at all.
> — Charles H. Spurgeon

After ten days the Jewish youths were examined and found to be more fit than other captives that had been eating the king's delicacies and drinking his wine (v. 16). Albert Barnes suggests that such an outcome is indicative of a consecrated life:

> There was no diminution of beauty, of vigor, or of the usual indications of health. One of the results of a course of temperance appears in the countenance, and it is among the wise appointments of God that it should be so. He has so made us, that while the other parts of the body may be protected from the gaze of men, it is necessary that the face should be exposed. Hence he has made the countenance the principal seat of expression, for the chief muscles which indicate expression have their location there. Hence, there are certain marks of guilt and vice which always are indicated in the countenance.[104]

Not only were Daniel, Hananiah, Mishael, and Azariah found to be physically fit, but also, because they had a clear conscience with their God, their countenance gleamed with vigor and joy. The steward then permitted the Jewish youths to continue their vegetable diet and the crisis was resolved. Melzar would not be in trouble with the king, and the Jews were able to eat that which did not offend their conscience. The text should not be used to promote vegetarianism as many biblical passages confirm the appropriateness of eating meat (e.g., Gen. 9:3; 1 Cor. 10:25-26). Daniel's diet was chosen to keep him safe from eating meats that the Law deemed would be unclean; he could have eaten beef, mutton, chevon (i.e., goat meat). However, the logistics of confirming where the meat was from, if it had been offered to idols and how it had been prepared would be cumbersome. For example, Jews could not eat meat from an animal that had been strangled or that had died from causes other than legitimate slaughter and immediate butchering.

The progress of this trial with its blessed outcome is a cycle repeated several times in the book of Daniel. The sequence begins when God's people are determined not to compromise God's revealed will. But faith that is not tested will not be trusted; therefore God permits His people to suffer the testing of their faith to prove and to refine its quality. Next, God blesses the faithfulness of His people with victory. This results in further blessings to the faithful which better equips them to serve the Lord. The overall end of the matter is that the Lord is exalted before the nations. Hence, Daniel's example is a good one to follow!

> Dare to be a Daniel,
> Dare to stand alone;
> Dare to have a purpose firm!
> Dare to make it known!

Because of their steadfast conviction, the Lord enabled Daniel, Hananiah, Mishael, and Azariah to forbear and overcome the trial. He then greatly rewarded them afterwards with knowledge in all arts and sciences, and wisdom in their application; Daniel also received the ability to understand dreams and visions (v. 17). So although Nebuchadnezzar had great expectations for these young Jewish men, God had an even higher agenda for which He was preparing them. Nebuchadnezzar would simply benefit from God's unfolding determinations to be accomplished in His people.

After finishing three years of academic training, each captive was interviewed by King Nebuchadnezzar (vv. 5, 18). It is noteworthy that this meeting occurred about two years after the extraordinary events in the subsequent chapter, which meant that Daniel and his three friends had already established their credibility. The king acknowledged that

316

the four Jews excelled over all the other captives and therefore appointed them to administrative positions within his kingdom (v. 19). Furthermore, when comparing these young men to the magicians and astrologers of Babylon (i.e., those dabbling in the occult), Nebuchadnezzar found that the Jews were ten times better in matters of wisdom and understanding (v. 20). Daniel and his friends, now likely in their late teenage years, were the "who's who" of Babylonian academia. God had seen fit to put them in key positions by which He would bring further glory to Himself in the coming years.

God revealed a principle through his prophet centuries earlier that has a timeless application, as we see here: *Those who honor Me I will honor, and those who despise Me shall be lightly esteemed"* (1 Sam. 2:30). With this promise in mind, Matthew Henry exhorts young people to deeply consider the practical ramifications of Daniel 1:

> Pious young persons should endeavor to do better than their fellows in useful things; not for the praise of man, but for the honor of the gospel, and that they may be qualified for usefulness. And it is well for a country, and for the honor of a prince, when he is able to judge who are best fitted to serve him, and prefers them on that account. Let young men steadily attend to this chapter; and let all remember that God will honor those who honor him, but those who despise him shall be lightly esteemed.[105]

The Lord Jesus put the matter this way: *"Therefore whoever confesses Me before men, him I will also confess before My Father who is in heaven. But whoever denies Me before men, him I will also deny before My Father who is in heaven"* (Matt. 10:32-33). Daniel, Hananiah, Mishael, and Azariah chose to identify with the Lord and honor His word no matter what the personal cost was to themselves. Because they chose to keep a good conscience, the Lord bestowed on them much enlightenment and honor in the coming years. From this chapter we learn that purity of heart and faithfulness to God precede enlightenment of divine mysteries. H. A. Ironside explains the application for us:

> These Hebrew young men were given spiritual enlightenment above all the men of their times. They had an understanding in divine mysteries that others failed to enter into, because it remains true in all dispensations that "spiritual things are spiritually discerned." God

does not commonly impart His secrets to careless men, but to those who are devoted to His interests. He may, in His sovereignty, use even a Balaam or a Caiaphas to utter divine truth; but cases like these are extraordinary. The rule is that *"the secret of the Lord is with them that fear Him"* (Ps. 25:14).[106]

The Lord honored Daniel and his friends because they feared Him more than Nebuchadnezzar as shown by their willing consecration. Consequently, Daniel would enjoy a long and respected tenure, not just in the Babylonian court, but he would have a position of prominence in the Persian administration some seventy years into the future (v. 21). For adhering to divine truth and trusting in their God, Daniel and his friends overcame the life-threatening trial, and obtained blessings and honor unimaginable for slaves in a foreign land.

Meditation

Faith expects from God what is beyond all expectation.

— Andrew Murray

God always gives His best to those who leave the choice with Him.

— Jim Elliot

The Terrible Dream
Daniel 2:1-30

The events in this chapter occurred in the second year of Nebuchadnezzar's reign, which means Daniel and his friends are in their second year of intense training. The king had a recurring dream that haunted his mind and deprived him of sleep (v. 1). This was no normal dream, but rather a vision from God, planted in the king's mind while he slept. Normally after we wake, our nighttime dreams quickly fade from our consciousness, yet somehow seem to be retained in the recesses of our mind in a way we cannot explain. We might remember a vague portion of a dream, but Nebuchadnezzar remembered enough detail of his recurring nightmare and that he could test his wise men's knowledge of it.

Being anxious to know the dream, Nebuchadnezzar summoned his magicians, astrologers, and sorcerers, and the wise men of the Chaldeans to tell the king his dream and its meaning (vv. 2-3). The wise men, speaking in Aramaic, requested that the king inform them of the dream first, and then they would give its interpretation (v. 4). It is noted that the language of the narrative transitions from Hebrew to Aramaic at this point. This Gentile language is related to Hebrew and was widely used in international communication, thus the language of the Gentiles.

The king suspected that his wise men had conjured up erroneous interpretations of dreams previously, and as the dream was so vivid and troubling, he wanted to know its true meaning. His decision was firm; the only way to ensure that he was not being lied to again (v. 9) was for his counselors to tell him his dream and its interpretation. Anyone who could accomplish this feat would be greatly rewarded with riches and honor, but those who could not would be cut to pieces and their homes destroyed (vv. 5-6). The wise men of Babylon were rebuffed by the king's request and again petitioned him to tell them his dream (v. 7). However, Nebuchadnezzar saw through their attempt to stall for time;

he was determined to uphold the terms of his previous decree to ensure their integrity in the matter (v. 8).

Knowing that their lives were in danger, the Chaldeans voiced their complaint and admission:

> *There is not a man on earth who can tell the king's matter; therefore no king, lord, or ruler has ever asked such things of any magician, astrologer, or Chaldean. It is a difficult thing that the king requests, and there is no other who can tell it to the king except the gods, whose dwelling is not with flesh* (vv. 10-11).

This response angered the king for two reasons: First, his wise men accused him of making an unreasonable request that no other king would make. Second, his suspicions about their past deceitfulness were confirmed, for they admitted that only the gods could know the future, not flesh and blood. The king was furious and commanded that all the wise men of Babylon be slaughtered (v. 13). Several Chaldeans had already died when Arioch, captain of the king's guard, arrived to execute Daniel and his companions (v. 14). Daniel asked Arioch what had prompted the king's urgent command (v. 15).

After learning of the situation, Daniel bravely approached the king in person to request time that he might tell the king his dream and its interpretation (v. 16). We learn from the book of Esther that approaching a Persian king without being summoned was a capital offense, which could be overlooked only if the king extended his gold scepter to the intruder (Est. 5:2, 8:4). There was likely a similar protocol in the Babylonian court, but since Daniel had been condemned to death anyway, it was worth the attempt to pacify the king, who indeed granted Daniel's request.

We pause to consider the work of a sovereign God to bring about His purposes in time. First, the Lord can interject dreams into the minds of the wicked to accomplish His will for His people. For example, Abimelech was sternly warned in a dream what the consequences would be if he did not return Sarah, Abraham's wife, to him (Gen. 20:6). Likewise, Laban was cautioned in a dream against harming Jacob and his family who were fleeing from him (Gen. 31:24). Daniel will later confirm that God had inserted this dream in Nebuchadnezzar's mind in order to reveal Himself to the king as the One who controls the events of the future (v. 28).

With their lives seemingly hanging in the balance, Daniel informed his three companions of the king's decision and they all gathered at Daniel's home to *"seek mercies from the God of heaven concerning this secret"* (vv. 17-18). This is the first of six instances in which Daniel refers to Jehovah as the *"God of Heaven."* Ezekiel describes the glory of the Lord leaving the temple and returning to heaven at the time of the Babylonian invasion, which God permitted to remove widespread idolatry from Judah (Ezek. 10). For this reason, Jehovah is often referred to in the post-exile books of the Bible by a less familiar title, "the Lord God of heaven" or "the God of heaven." Even the Persian King Cyrus refers to him by that name in the opening verses of Ezra's book. H. A. Ironside summarizes why Ezra, Nehemiah, and Daniel often referred to the Lord as "the God of heaven":

> It was a title He took when His throne was removed from the earth, and He gave His people into the hands of the Gentiles. He went and *"returned to His place,"* as Hosea puts it. He forsook the temple at Jerusalem, dissolved the theocracy and became *"the God of heaven."* Such He is still to His ancient people, and so He will remain till He returns to Jerusalem to establish His throne again as *"the Lord of the whole earth."*[107]

God chose to relate to His covenant people in a more obscure sense for centuries to come. Though returning Jewish captives would rebuild a temple of less grandeur in Jerusalem, God will not dwell among them in glory again until the Millennial Kingdom of Christ. Hence, Daniel, Hananiah, Mishael, and Azariah urgently petitioned "the God of heaven" for assistance. Daniel's actions, says Hamilton Smith, indicate the value that Daniel sets upon fellowship and specific prayers:

> Having left the presence of the king, he goes to his own company, and makes the thing known to his companions. He values the fellowship of his brethren and has confidence in their prayers, for he requires that "they would desire mercies of the God of heaven." Further, he values *definite prayer,* for their prayers are to be for mercies "concerning this secret." Herein we discover that fellowship with his brethren and dependence upon God is the secret of Daniel's calm assurance and confidence before men.[108]

To earnestly pray with likeminded believers having pure hearts and clean hands is one of the most enjoyable and powerful endeavors that mere humans on earth can ever engage in. Daniel and his friends had cast themselves upon a sovereign God and fully rested in whatever outcome he deemed would bring Him the most glory.

To be anxious for nothing, but be given to prayer is the epitome of identification with Christ and of devotion and faith in Him (Phil. 4:6). As Hudson Taylor testified, such a disposition completely liberates the soul from anxiety:

> The sweetest part, if one may speak of one part being sweeter than another, is the rest which full identification with Christ brings. I am no longer anxious about anything, as I realize this; for He, I know, is able to carry out His will, and His will is mine. It makes no matter where He places me, or how. That is rather for Him to consider than for me; for in the easiest positions He must give me grace, and in the most difficult His grace is sufficient.[109]

The Lord responds to prayers of obedient and consecrated believers. James says, *"The effective, fervent prayer of a righteous man avails much"* (Jas. 5:16). Accordingly, Daniel and his friends received an immediate answer to their prayers: Daniel received a night vision that same evening that revealed Nebuchadnezzar's dream and its explanation (v. 19). It is encouraging that Daniel's first response was not to hurry into the king's presence with the revelation that would save their lives, but rather to humbly express his gratitude to God:

> *Blessed be the name of God forever and ever, for wisdom and might are His. And He changes the times and the seasons; He removes kings and raises up kings; He gives wisdom to the wise and knowledge to those who have understanding. He reveals deep and secret things; He knows what is in the darkness, and light dwells with Him. "I thank You and praise You, O God of my fathers; You have given me wisdom and might, and have now made known to me what we asked of You, for You have made known to us the king's demand"* (vv. 20-23).

Before approaching the king, Daniel first paused to praise God for answering their prayers. Although Daniel received the revelation that would preserve their lives, he knows it was provided in response to their collective prayers: *"what we asked for"* ... *"made know to us."*

The power of believers collectively praying in unity is also witnessed in the Church Age, such as in Acts 4:

They raised their voice to God with one accord (v. 24) ... *grant to Your servants that with all boldness they may speak Your word (v. 29) ... And when they had prayed, the place where they were assembled together was shaken; and they were all filled with the Holy Spirit, and they spoke the word of God with boldness* (v. 31).

This is exactly what the Lord Jesus promised His disciples that He would do for them, if they sought Him in humble, united prayer:

Again I say to you that if two of you agree on earth concerning anything that they ask, it will be done for them by My Father in heaven. For where two or three are gathered together in My name, I am there in the midst of them (Matt. 18:19-20).

Unfortunately, effective corporate prayer is much hindered today by sin, by disunity, and because we do not pray in the Spirit (i.e., we ask for those things which are not in God's will). When God's people are walking together in holiness, united in vision, and desperate for God – the Lord shows Himself strong. May we collectively beseech the Lord in prayer with the same vigor and oneness of heart that Daniel and His friends did. Their lives were completely reliant on a direct answer to their prayers. Our Christian experience should be no less dependent on God's hand for security and assistance.

Then, Daniel went to Arioch and confirmed that he had received revelation concerning Nebuchadnezzar's dream and therefore not to destroy the wise men of Babylon (v. 24). Arioch immediately brought young Daniel to the king to tell him both his recurring dream and the interpretation of it (v. 25). After Arioch announced Daniel's arrival and intentions, the king asked Daniel if he could tell him both his dream and its meaning (v. 26).

If ever there was a situation that could suddenly catapult a Jewish captive into fame, riches, and honor, this was such a time. However, Daniel surpasses the temptation for self-promotion and glory by informing the king that only *the God of heaven*, and not all the acclaimed wise men of Babylon, could disclose the secrets that God had placed in the king's mind (v. 27). Daniel confirms that the dream relates to *"what will be in latter days"* (vv. 28-29). Daniel told Nebuchadnezzar that the interpretation of the dream was not derived by his own wisdom, but that his God had revealed the matter to him to preserve their lives (v. 30). Nebuchadnezzar must have felt honored that Daniel's God had chosen him to receive this special revelation, but the entire situation had been initiated by God to honor those who would and had honored Him and to reveal His future purposes for the nation of Israel in Christ.

Daniel shows us a wonderful pattern to follow when facing dire situations in life: First, seek the Lord in united prayer with those who are likewise committed to purity. Second, pause and praise the Lord for answers to prayer before relishing the outcome personally. Third, share what the Lord has accomplished with others who can also benefit from knowing God's will and faithfulness. Fourth, ensure that God alone is honored in the matter. Let us be careful not to rob the Lord of what is to be only His, for it is written, *"He who glories, let him glory in the Lord"* (1 Cor. 1:31).

Meditation

> The church that is not jealously protected by mighty intercession and sacrificial labors will before long become the abode of every evil bird and the hiding place for unsuspected corruption. The creeping wilderness will soon take over that church that trusts in its own strength and forgets to watch and pray.
>
> — A. W. Tozer

> We are too busy to pray, and so we are too busy to have power. We have a great deal of activity, but we accomplish little; many services but few conversions; much machinery but few results. ...Oh, men and women, pray through; pray through! Do not just begin to pray and pray a little while and throw up your hands and quit; but pray and pray and pray until God bends the heavens and comes down.
>
> — R. A. Torrey

Things to Come
Daniel 2:31-49

As Nebuchadnezzar had been disturbed by the same dream for some time, the prospect of being told its meaning and ending the recurring torment to his soul was much desired. Daniel begins by first telling the king that what he saw in his dream pertains to *"what will be in the latter days"* (v. 28). Then Daniel described the eerie image that the king had become quite familiar with and also the drama surrounding it:

> *This great image, whose splendor was excellent, stood before you; and its form was awesome. This image's head was of fine gold, its chest and arms of silver, its belly and thighs of bronze, its legs of iron, its feet partly of iron and partly of clay. You watched while a stone was cut out without hands, which struck the image on its feet of iron and clay, and broke them in pieces. Then the iron, the clay, the bronze, the silver, and the gold were crushed together, and became like chaff from the summer threshing floors; the wind carried them away so that no trace of them was found. And the stone that struck the image became a great mountain and filled the whole earth* (vv. 31-35).

One can only imagine Nebuchadnezzar's astonishment that Daniel could tell him exactly what was in his mind. But this proved that Daniel's God had put what was in the king's mind through a dream into Daniel's mind through a vision. But, that is only half of the miracle, for then Daniel provides a detailed explanation of what the various components of the image symbolized and also the meaning of its destruction.

Starting with the head of gold and moving to the ten toes forged of clay and iron, Daniel explains that the image is a blueprint of five world empires that would be permitted to rule over God's covenant people. Each of these kingdoms would exist before Christ's return to establish His own kingdom on earth: Babylon, under Nebuchadnezzar's leadership was the head of gold; the Medes and Persians were the chest and arms of silver; the bronze torso and thighs represented the Greeks; the two iron legs, the Roman empire; and the ten toes of clay and iron, the final Gentile empire rising out of the old Roman Empire and controlled by Antichrist.

The intrinsic value of each metal decreases with each subsequent world empire, but also increases in strength. This would be an accurate depiction of the moral fineness of sequential kingdoms, though each was clearly pagan. The Babylonians treated their captives well and incorporated them into their society; Nebuchadnezzar openly praised God twice during his rule and became a Jehovah worshipper during the latter years of his reign. However, the Roman Empire, from the emperor down, was marked by corruption and immorality; the Romans made bloody sport of their captives and brutalized their slaves. In fact, half of the Roman Empire at the time of Christ were slaves.

The increased robustness of the metal forecast the increasing strength of each passing empire: The Babylonians ruled for 66 years (605-539 B.C.). The Medes and Persians were in power for 205 years (539-334 B.C.). Commencing with the conquest of Alexander the Great, the Grecian Empire lasted 267 years (330-63 B.C.). The Romans, who ruled the world during Christ's first advent, held power for 476 years before Rome fell in the west (27 B.C. to 422 A.D.), but continued in the east (Constantinople being the capital) until 1,453 A.D. (330-1453 A.D.) or another 1123 years. In general, each empire was able to establish a longer hold on more territory than the previous power. Alexander moved east all the way to India; the Romans ventured west and conquered most of Europe. In fact, the final world empire, governed by the Antichrist and his ten kings, will not just rule "the known world," but rather the entire planet for a brief time (Rev. 17). Iron and clay cannot be successfully forged together and the cohesiveness of this empire apparently does not last long. In fact, Daniel will inform us in chapter 8 that the Antichrist will remove three of these kings from power. What first appeared to be a democratic world government will quickly transition into an autocratic dictatorship.

The stone that was not cut with human hands (an expression of deity) and that came down from heaven to strike the image in the feet represents Christ's Second Advent to earth. At that time He will wipe out His enemies and establish a worldwide kingdom of peace and righteousness. (This is symbolized by the mountain that rose up out of the stone.) Ezekiel's prophecy, about sixteen years after Daniel interprets Nebuchadnezzar's dream, uses two important terms which are applicable to the prophetic spectacle before us: "the day of the Lord" and "the time of the Gentiles" (Ezek. 30:3). *The Day of the Lord* is an Old Testament term that speaks of those times when Jehovah intervened in a visible and powerful way to judge the wicked on earth. This meaning continues into the New Testament and speaks of the Tribulation Period and the Millennial Kingdom of Christ (Acts 2:20; 1 Thess. 5:2). *The Day of the Lord* concludes with the destruction of the earth and the subsequent Great White Throne judgment. Then begins *the Day of God* – the eternal state (2 Pet. 3:10-12).

The Time of the Gentiles (Luke 21:24) is a period of Gentile rule and oppression of the Jewish people that commenced with the destruction of Jerusalem by the Babylonians in 586 B.C. and will continue until the battle of Armageddon at the conclusion of the Tribulation Period. *The Time of the Gentiles* is not to be confused with "the fullness of the Gentiles" (Rom. 11:25), which speaks of the conclusion of the Church Age. *The Time of the Gentiles* concludes roughly seven years after the rapture of the Church and is symbolized here by the divine stone smashing the king's image in the feet.

The Lord Jesus Christ is often likened to a stone in Scripture to portray either His character, His work, or how others respond to Him. For example, He was the Rock struck by God's rod in the wilderness, so Moses could supply life-sustaining water for the thirsty Israelites (Ex. 17:1-6; compare with John 4:6-14, 7:37-39). He was the Rock of Offense, the rejected Cornerstone, which the nation of Israel stumbled over at His first advent to earth (1 Pet. 2:6-8). He is the Rock of Strength (Deut. 32:4) and the Foundation Stone of the Church (1 Cor. 3:11). For those who will not trust in Him, He will be the Smiting Stone (vv. 44-45) and a Grinding Stone (Matt. 21:44). For those who trust Him, He will satisfy their souls in a way only God can (eternal peace and joy) – these will be gladly broken upon their divine Stone!

Notice that after the image falls and crumbles, there is a short duration in which the wind clears away all undesirable debris from the stone's presence (v. 35). Likewise, the Millennial Kingdom of Christ will begin directly after all that has defiled and devastated the earth is removed. This includes *The Judgment of Nations* (Matt. 25:40; Rev. 19:20), which will be explained more fully in chapter 7.

After the unwanted debris from the Gentile image is blown away, the stone grows to become a magnificent mountain. When referred to metaphorically in Scripture, mountains are used to symbolize kingdoms (e.g., Micah 4:1; Rev. 17:9-10). There was one instance during the latter days of the Lord's ministry in Decapolis that His divine essence was permitted to shine out of Him to picture exactly what Daniel is alluding to in verses 44-45. The event is what we commonly call the "transfiguration" of the Lord. Matthew describes it:

> *Now after six days Jesus took Peter, James, and John his brother, led them up on a high mountain by themselves; and He was transfigured before them. His face shone like the sun, and His clothes became as white as the light* (Matt. 17:1-2).

In the preceding verse, the Lord had said, *"Assuredly, I say to you, there are some standing here who shall not taste death till they see the Son of Man coming in His kingdom"* (Matt. 16:28). For a brief moment, the disciples were given a foretaste of the coming kingdom; they saw the intrinsic glory of Christ, at least in a measure.

One can only imagine how the glory of the Lord appeared from a high mountain in a remote region and apparently at night (Luke 9:32-37). The transfiguration foretells of a future day when Christ will rule the world and His intrinsic glory will be seen throughout the earth – the Smiting Stone, that was Himself smitten, will have His everlasting Kingdom! For this reason, Daniel could tell the king: *"The dream is certain, and its interpretation is sure"* (v. 45). God had greatly honored the pagan king by informing him of what God would bring about for millennia to come. Indeed, the prophetic framework for all Gentile rule had been revealed to Nebuchadnezzar.

King Nebuchadnezzar was overcome with emotion and awe after hearing Daniel tell him of his disconcerting dream and its complex meaning. He fell face down and prostrated himself before Daniel, even commanding that a sacrifice should be offered and that incense should be burned to honor him. Given the king's response in verse 47, *"Truly your God is the God of gods, the Lord of kings, and a revealer of secrets, since you could reveal this secret,"* it is suggested that Daniel may have explained again to the king that it was his God that was the revealer of secrets, and that he was only His messenger (v. 28). Daniel was very careful to ensure that God was the one obtaining the glory throughout the situation and as a result, God greatly honored him too:

> Then the king promoted Daniel and gave him many great gifts; and he made him ruler over the whole province of Babylon, and chief administrator over all the wise men of Babylon. Also Daniel petitioned the king, and he set Shadrach, Meshach, and Abed-nego over the affairs of the province of Babylon; but Daniel sat in the gate of the king (vv. 48-49).

Whether or not Daniel was to be referred to as an official satrap (governor) is unknown, but his newly appointed rank over all the wise men of Babylon and new responsibility to govern an entire province are astonishing. What emperor, in his right mind, would appoint a mere teenager from a foreign land to supervise the capital province of his kingdom? The answer is a king who had personally witnessed the glory of God through His people.

Would not it be wise to entrust all that one has to the God who knows our innermost secrets and who completely controls our future? Absolutely! Why then do so many who already know the God of heaven fail to behave as this pagan king did after first being introduced to Him? Do not we have more divine revelation than he did? Have we not personally experienced the goodness of God to a greater degree than Nebuchadnezzar? Yet we often fail to fall on our faces in reverential awe or to eagerly commit our resources from Him to Him. This pagan king teaches us not to belittle what we have in Christ, but rather to be humbly grateful that the God of heaven would choose to bless us in so many more ways than we can even comprehend.

Besides his promotion, Daniel received many great gifts from the king. However, Daniel was faithful to remember his three Jewish friends who had prayed with him during their severe trial. He commended them to the king, who also appointed Shadrach, Meshach, and Abed-nego to administrative affairs in the same province that Daniel would oversee. These young Jewish men had cast themselves completely on the Lord and now they were enjoying prestigious positions in Babylon, whereas the day before they were a hair's breadth from death. Jehovah longs to show Himself strong on behalf of those who are desperate for Him.

Meditation

Perhaps the greatest barrier to revival on a large scale is the fact that we are too interested in a great display. We want an exhibition; God is looking for a man who will throw himself entirely on God. Whenever self-effort, self-glory, self-seeking or self-promotion enters into the work of revival, then God leaves us to ourselves.

— Ted Rendall

Faithfulness Draws Fire
Daniel 3

The Septuagint records the events of this chapter occurring in 587 B.C., or about seventeen years after the dream incident in the previous chapter. If that is correct, Jerusalem was under siege and would be destroyed the following year, and Daniel and his Jewish friends would be in their mid-thirties.

It would appear that the image in Nebuchadnezzar's dream went to his head, for he had a gold image ninety feet tall and nine feet wide erected in the plain of Dura, in the province of Babylon (v. 1). Through Daniel, God had told Nebuchadnezzar, *"You are this head of gold"* (2:38). It is likely that this image was in his likeness or represented him in some way (v. 12). The elongated height in comparison with proper width further indicates Nebuchadnezzar was high on himself, a matter God deals with in the next chapter. It is noted that archeologists have located a large brick foundation, where such an image may have been fabricated about six miles east of the ancient city of Babylon.

Besides Nebuchadnezzar's pride, Hamilton Smith suggests that the gargantuan image actually served a political agenda – to promote unity in the empire by impeding religious diversity:

> History and experience show that nothing so sharply divides and breaks up nations and families as a difference in religion. On the other hand, nothing will so powerfully cement nations together as unity of religion, be it false or true. Religious unity will go far to establish a political unity. Nebuchadnezzar, apparently recognizing these facts, attempts to secure a political unity by setting up a religious unity. To this end he uses his great power to force upon all nations a state religion under penalty of death for those who will not conform.[110]

The king informed all his satraps (governors of each province) to summon all government officials (e.g., administrators, counselors, treasurers, judges, magistrates, etc.) to come to the dedication of the image he had set up (v. 2). Indeed, all the officials throughout the empire gathered for the image dedication, though for some reason, perhaps official business, Daniel was not among this who's-who entourage (v. 3). A herald explained the proceedings with a loud voice so that the entire multitude of various people groups and nations could hear (v. 4). When the people heard the Babylonian Philharmonic Orchestra playing all kinds of music with all kinds of instruments, they were to fall down and worship the gigantic idol that the king had fashioned. Anyone not doing so would be immediately thrown into a burning fiery furnace (vv. 5-6).

As then, Satan continues to use music today to stimulate emotional responses which do not uphold the truth or to ease troubled consciences of men who are disobeying the truth. Christians are more likely to accept false doctrine couched in a musical lyric than when distinctly spoken from a pulpit. As we see throughout the Psalms, music can enhance worship where truth and genuine devotion are present, or it can be used to invoke paganism as witnessed in this chapter. In the Church Age, it is the Holy Spirit who initiates and directs worshippers, not human musicians.

We pause to consider four tactics that the devil employed against Shadrach, Meshach, and Abed-Nego in an attempt to cause them to compromise what they knew to be true. First, surprise is used to stun believers and hopefully cause them to render a quick decision which they do not have time to think through. It is important for believers to remember that God is patient and wants us to understand and to confirm in our minds what is wise before acting in questionable matters (Rom. 14:23). Satan is a high-pressure salesman! If you do not know what to do in a particular situation because Scripture is silent – wait! Study the guidelines, warnings, and lessons recorded in Scripture; pray for divine guidance; and consult wise counselors. God will direct your path if you will patiently wait on Him. In this situation, the decision was not a debatable matter, but a matter of idolatry. But bombshell tactics by the devil are still effective in causing Christians to stumble in their faith (i.e., to do what they know is an offense to God).

Second, an enormous group of influential people in Babylon had gathered for the dedication of the image. Peer pressure is often an effective method to cause God's people to compromise the truth – "everyone is doing it, so should you." It took incredible courage for the three Jewish young men to remain standing when likely thousands of people fell prostrate before the ninety-foot idol. Believers must withstand the peer pressure exerted by the masses, including government agencies and educational systems which compromise biblical edicts for marriage, family order, and rearing children. Just because our neighbors adhere to secular philosophies in such things does not mean that we should conform to what compromises God's design for our home and His training for our children.

Third, Satan used the emotional effect of music in an attempt to make the situation more favorable to those whose consciences were unsettled. This is a tactic often employed today in children's movies: The devil uses a sensational song or humor to make some New Age doctrine or biblical heresy more palatable for uneasy parents, who deep down know something is not right. The scene before us is not the first example in Scripture where music was used to prompt anti-God behavior.

The first mention of "music" in the Bible is in Genesis 4:21; however, this was not the first occurrence of music in the history of creation. According to Ezekiel 28:13, Lucifer was created with every precious stone as a covering and was given timbrels and flutes to make music before God. In the celestial realms, worship (accompanied by music) was being offered by spiritual beings to their Creator, even before man was created. But Satan's inflated pride motivated a desire to be worshipped. Thus God cast him off His holy mount. The "light bearer" became the "father of darkness."

Why did the descendants of Cain, and not Seth, become musicians? There are many avenues of expressing what is in one's heart: musical composition, painting, speaking, and facial expressions are but a few. Music can settle the soul (as when David played for King Saul), or it can afflict the soul (as with David and Jeremiah; see Psalm 69:12 and Lam. 3:14, respectively). Music can be used to affect pagan worship as we see here (vv. 4-6) or to worship God (Ps. 150). If one is full of Christ, acceptable music reflecting humility on our part and adoration towards God will be enjoyed by all (see Rev. 14:2-3, 18:22). The Lord Jesus, whose heart swelled with love for His Father, sang hymns of praise unto His God (Mark 14:26).

Jubal was the originator of music on earth, *"the father of all such that handled* (literally manipulated) *the harp and pipe"* (Gen. 4:21). What kind of music do you think ascended Jubal's heart towards God? Worship, praise, or perhaps a spiritual song? Probably not. Jubal's name is derived from the Hebrew word *yuwbal*, which means "stream." His name is rooted in the word *yabal*, which means "to flow," or by implication, "to carry or bring with pomp." Jubal was the descendant of three murderers. His father, Lamech, was the third murderer recorded in the Bible; his great-great-great-grandfather, Cain, was the second, and the devil murdered (took life away from) Adam and Eve in the garden (John 8:44). Jubal's name, his ungodly ancestors, and the stimulation of demonic forces controlling the line of Cain suggest his music displayed the inherent rebellion and depraved heart of his family and his father Satan, the devil.

The reality for the believer-priest in the Church Age is that he or she can offer worship to God at any moment in time. Every time we yield to God's truth instead of pursuing our lusts and selfish will, we offer a living sacrifice to God (Rom. 12:1-2). It is the pagan who works to *induce or force* worship and usually through disordered music as witnessed in this chapter, but the Lord's people may be, and should be, prompted to worship from a joyful heart anytime, not just at one particular church meeting. So let us be careful that we worship God without worshipping our worship. Otherwise we are no different than the Babylonians!

The fourth strategy employed against the three Hebrews was the threat of death through political authority. Believers should expect that secular governments, under the control of *the god of this age*, will continually approve legislation that contradicts God's Laws. In the United States, for example, there are federal laws that are presently being enforced that undermine every one of the Ten Commandments. This means that there is a growing likelihood that Christians living in the twenty-first century will face civil prosecution for choosing behaviors that honor the Lord. This is the situation before us and Shadrach, Meshach, and Abed-Nego did not rationalize or compromise; rather they were willing to suffer the consequences of civil dissidence.

Therefore, the Hebrews refused to commit an act of idolatry. They remained standing while everyone else prostrated themselves before the image when they heard the cacophony of all sorts of music playing at once. Such a blatant act of rebellion did not go unnoticed, for certain Chaldeans brought the matter to the king to directly accuse those he had set over administrative affairs in the province (vv. 8-9). The accusers first verified that the king's command and the punishment for not heeding it had been understood by everyone (vv. 10-11). Then they provided the names of those Jews who had refused to honor the king and his gods (v. 12). The king was enraged by this information and summoned the Jewish rebels for interrogation (v. 13).

Nebuchadnezzar knew the three well, as he had previously commended them for their academic astuteness and promoted them to key positons in his administration. For this reason, he inquired of them to see if the accusation was valid. Then he offered them an opportunity to avoid death by correcting their previous offense, for what god would deliver them from his indignation in the matter?

Is it true, Shadrach, Meshach, and Abed-nego, that you do not serve my gods or worship the gold image which I have set up? Now if you are ready at the time you hear the sound of the horn, flute, harp, lyre, and psaltery, in symphony with all kinds of music, and you fall down and worship the image which I have made, good! But if you do not worship, you shall be cast immediately into the midst of a burning fiery furnace. And **who is the god who will deliver you from my hands?** *(vv. 14-15).*

The latter statement further compounded Nebuchadnezzar's sin. He had already usurped God's right to be worshipped alone when he erected the pagan image, but now he openly mocked the God of the Jews as being incapable. While God may briefly tolerate such rebellion so as to accomplish His sovereign purposes, all such pompous men prepare themselves for ultimate defeat. Initially, the contest was between Nebuchadnezzar and noncompliant Jews, but his public defiance of their God had taken the conflict to a level where Jehovah would be obliged to honor His name and defend His people.

While the king's offer of a second chance seemed gracious, it really was nothing more than a satanic overture to play on the emotions of God's people, soliciting them to compromise what they knew was right. Since this was a matter of upholding truth, Shadrach, Meshach, and Abed-Nego did not need time to contemplate their course of action; they immediately responded to the king's ultimatum (vv.16-18):

O Nebuchadnezzar, we have no need to answer you in this matter. If that is the case, our God whom we serve is able to deliver us from the burning fiery furnace, and He will deliver us from your hand, O king. But if not, let it be known to you, O king, that we do not serve your gods, nor will we worship the gold image which you have set up.

Infidelity and Loyalty

Believers can answer the enemy quickly when convinced of the truth. Under no circumstance would the three Jewish young men compromise their integrity by bowing to any false god or its image. They were Jehovah worshippers and would honor Him, even if He chose not to deliver them from the fiery furnace. They were willing to die for what they knew would honor the Lord! J. N. Darby affirms that this is really the only course of action a child of God has in such a trial:

> He does not maintain himself by leaning upon the civil power; he acts according to his conscience, and seeks only the will of God; at the same time he submits, and in so doing yields up his body; for his conscience is submissive to no one but the Lord: he cannot serve two masters. Shadrach and his friends undergo their punishment, but they refuse to do what the king, in the exercise of his power, wishes them to do. They do not seek to turn away the king from his plans; they are threatened and punished by Nebuchadnezzar, but they are faithful to their God, and He delivers them. They leave their case with Him.[111]

The courage of these three young men to confront the emperor with the imminent threat of death before them is astounding. They had received only a little Jewish training, and they were captives in a distant land standing before the most powerful official in the world. Thankfully, their faith was anchored in what truth they did know and was furthermore settled in the sovereignty of God. Accordingly, they could face death with confidence and with the expectation of being honored by the Lord no matter the outcome of the trial. Effectively, what they were telling Nebuchadnezzar was, "Our great God is worth dying for!"

About six years before being martyred with four others in an Ecuadorian jungle, Jim Elliot wrote in his journal: "He is no fool who gives what he cannot keep to gain that which he cannot lose."[112] This statement weighs the experiences of life in the balances of eternity and rightly concludes that the here and now is temporary, and it is best to invest in the hereafter.

> Only one life and 'twill soon be past; only what's done for Christ will last.
>
> — C. T. Studd

Paul explains in 1 Corinthians 15:40-42 that after the resurrection, some saints will shine forth the glory of God more brightly than others, just as some stars in the nighttime sky are more luminous than other stars. This acquired glory directly reflects the good works that are done for Christ by His strength in this present life. Eternal glory, evidently, has a weight to it (2 Cor. 4:17); in other words, its quality is measurable and can be earned by believers through selfless service for Christ now. At the judgment seat of Christ, everyone worthy of God's praise shall receive it (1 Cor. 4:5). While the church at Laodicea was spiritually naked (i.e. they had no righteous acts for clothing), the Holy Spirit does bear fruit in the life of the individual "overcomer" (Rev. 3:18, 21). Though believers will suffer varying degrees of loss at the judgment seat of Christ, all will have the praise of God and are thus guaranteed righteous attire for eternity (1 Cor. 4:5).

In heaven, the bride of Christ must have righteous attire; she is *"arrayed in fine linen, clean and bright, for the fine linen is the righteous acts of the saints"* (Rev. 19:8). Those things which are done in accordance with revealed truth and in the power of the Spirit have eternal value; these righteous acts are what the believer is adorned with throughout eternity. Matthew Henry also notes the benefit of tranquility to the believer's soul that submission to God's Word affords:

> True devotion calms the spirit, quiets and softens it, but superstition and devotion to false gods inflame men's passions. The matter is put into a little compass, Turn, or burn. Proud men are still ready to say, as Nebuchadnezzar, "Who is the Lord, that I should fear His power?" Shadrach, Meshach, and Abednego did not hesitate whether they should comply or not. Life or death were not to be considered. Those that would avoid sin must not parley with temptation when that to which we are allured or affrighted is manifestly evil. ... They did not contrive an evasive answer, when a direct answer was expected. Those who make their duty their main care need not be anxious or fearful concerning the event. The faithful servants of God find Him able to control and overrule all the powers armed against them. Lord, if Thou wilt, Thou canst. If He be for us, we need not fear what man can do unto us. God will deliver us, either from death or in death. They must obey God rather than man; they must rather suffer than sin; and must not do evil that good may come. Therefore none of these things moved them.[113]

Their respectful and courageous response infuriated the king. They had snubbed his gracious offer to avoid death; now he was determined to make an example of them before all his subjects by burning them alive. In his rage Nebuchadnezzar ordered that the furnace used for executions should be heated seven times hotter than normal and that his mightiest warriors should bind the Jewish insurrectionists and then cast them into the inferno (vv. 19-20). This was accomplished, but the heat from the furnace was so intense that it killed the king's mighty men who executed his order (vv. 21-22). Apparently, these soldiers believed that their king was worth dying for. But the king would soon learn that the God of the Jews was the one true God, meaning that Nebuchadnezzar's men threw their lives away for nothing. The devil is still enticing people to dedicate themselves to false causes and thus to waste their lives pursuing ideologies that in reality oppose the God of heaven.

Although the three Hebrews fell down bound in the midst of the inferno, it was not long before the king noticed they were loosened from their bindings and walking around in the flames with a fourth figure, who looked like *"the Son of God"* (vv. 23-25). Given the king's pagan background, the Hebrew text might be better understood as "a son of the gods" (see NKJV marginal note). This is not to say that this pagan king recognized a theophany of the second person of the Godhead, but rather he and his counselors were expressing in the best way that they could that there had been supernatural intervention by the God of the Hebrews. The entire event demonstrated that Nebuchadnezzar was not a god, but rather Shadrach, Meshach, and Abed-Nego's God was the One in authority and He had overruled the king's actions.

The now humbled king went as near to the mouth of the fiery furnace as he could and called to the three Hebrews: *"Shadrach, Meshach, and Abed-nego, servants of the Most High God, come out, and come here"* (v. 26). They obeyed the king and when examined by him and his counselors, they were found not to be harmed at all. Neither did their clothing have the stench of smoke; only the cords that bound them were burnt (v. 27). In His mercy, God did not destroy the king for mocking His name or attempting to harm His people, but rather He chose to demonstrate His power in such a way that even Nebuchadnezzar knew that Shadrach, Meshach and Abed-nego worshipped the Most High God.

Although filled with admiration for the God of the Jews, as in chapter 2, the king does not choose to worship and serve Jehovah at this time. The king's spiritual conversion is recorded in the next chapter, but here he is merely aware of God's greatness. The king commends the three for not compromising their conviction to worship only their God and promotes them to higher positions of authority in the province of Babylon (vv. 28, 30).

What happened that day stunned the entire empire: Nebuchadnezzar issued a public decree informing his kingdom what had happened and declaring that anyone who spoke against the God of the Hebrews should be cut to pieces and their houses should be made ash heaps (i.e., burned by fire). Then the king explains why his declaration was now the law of the land: *"because there is no other God who can deliver like this"* (v. 29). Because three believers would not compromise the truth and were confident that their God would honor Himself in their hostile situation, the entire empire was introduced to Jehovah. This entire scene foreshadows a future day when the Antichrist will set up an image before the entire world to be worshipped, and he will slaughter those who will not bow before it. Yet, as seen in this chapter, the Lord will preserve a faithful remnant of Jews from the devil's wrath, and as a result everyone will witness the greatness of their God to deliver them.

Furthermore, the whole Babylonian scene in this chapter displays the devil's mockery of his condemnation. The Bible teaches that the devil and all those who follow him will end up in the eternal burning fiery furnace called *hell*. Yet, Satan would pose a counterfeit reality – those who worship and live for God will experience the horror of intense flame. It is good to remember that Satan will always have his rival system to the things of God: Congregating to build a tower to heaven at Babel vs. obediently spreading out and populating the earth; idols and false gods vs. Levitical worship and obedience to the Law; Satan's harlot (false religion) vs. Christ's virgin Bride (the Church); the Antichrist vs. Christ. Satan is the counterfeit king and continually rebels and resists the things of God and causes others to do the same.

As mentioned in the first chapter, the arduous progression and blessed outcome of trials, such as this one, is a cycle repeated in Daniel. The sequence begins when God's people are determined not to compromise God's revealed will. The Lord then permits His people to suffer the testing of their faith to prove and to refine its quality. Next,

Infidelity and Loyalty

God blesses such faith with victory. This results in further blessings to the righteous which better enables them to serve the Lord. But the overall end of the matter is that the name of the Lord is exalted before the nations.

Meditation

Take your stand on the Rock of Ages. Let death, let the judgment come: the victory is Christ's and yours through Him.

— D. L. Moody

God often delays His help. He tarries ere He comes, long enough to bring us to the end of ourselves, and to show us the futility of looking for creature aid.

— F. B. Meyer

Pride Before the Fall
Daniel 4

The Septuagint is the Greek version of the Old Testament translated from the Hebrew manuscripts between the third and second century B.C. If the Septuagint's dating of chapter 3 is correct, then sixteen years silently pass between chapter 3 and 4. It seems doubtful that Nebuchadnezzar's exaltation of God in the first three verses relates to the distant happenings of the previous chapter, but rather it is connected to his conversion, as recorded in this chapter. It is a deeply inspiring story that the king personally communicates to all his subjects by royal decree and one which Daniel, as led by the Holy Spirit, preserves for us. Accordingly, the king sent out the following proclamation *to all peoples, nations, and languages that dwell in all the earth*:

Peace be multiplied to you. I thought it good to declare the signs and wonders that the Most High God has worked for me. How great are His signs, and how mighty His wonders! His kingdom is an everlasting kingdom, and His dominion is from generation to generation (vv. 1-3).

Although the king publically testified as to the greatness of the Hebrew God after witnessing the miracle at the fiery furnace, he still was not a Jehovah worshipper. The text before us demonstrates three important principles reiterated throughout Scripture pertaining to true spiritual conversion. First, the observance of signs and wonders will never produce the faith necessary to trust God's revealed Word and be saved. The king had already witnessed incredible wonders, but was still not converted. Miracles endorse divine truth, but do not beget trust in truths that must be received by faith alone to experience justification with God (Heb. 11:6).

God had demonstrated His great power to His covenant people through signs and wonders since their very conception as a nation

(Deut. 4:34). In the wilderness they observed supernatural evidences of God's presence among them daily for forty years. Later, during the prophetic ministries of Elijah and Elisha, they witnessed twenty-one incredible feats over a period of about sixty years. But as in the wilderness experience, signs and wonders did not result in building up the nation's spirituality; rather, they continued to be prone to waywardness and carnality. In fact, throughout the centuries, the Jews have demonstrated their propensity to live by sight and not by faith. We see them repeatedly lusting for signs and wonders in order to affirm God's presence and direction in the New Testament also (Luke 11:16; 1 Cor. 1:22). Trusting in signs and wonders will never result in spiritual growth; rather, spiritual deception is the likely outcome because Satan can produce spectacular signs also (2 Cor. 11:13-15; Rev. 13:11-15). One's faith is built through taking God at His Word and then being tested to prove its accuracy. Confidence in what God says when it cannot be verified by our five senses or by empirical reasoning is faith and *without faith it is impossible to please God* (Heb. 11:6).

The second principle demonstrated in the king's declaration is that it is possible to know something about the Lord and still not be saved. Just believing that some higher power exists (as Nebuchadnezzar did), or that there is one true God, will not save anyone. James warns, *"You believe that there is one God. You do well. Even the demons believe – and tremble!"* (Jas. 2:19). Clearly the demons believe in God, but are still condemned to the Lake of Fire because of their past rebellion against God (Matt. 25:41).

Lastly, the Lord Jesus also made it clear that doing good works will not earn anyone a place in His heaven:

> *Not everyone who says to Me, "Lord, Lord," shall enter the kingdom of heaven, but he who does the will of My Father in heaven. Many will say to Me in that day, "Lord, Lord, have we not prophesied in Your name, cast out demons in Your name, and done many wonders in Your name?" And then I will declare to them, "I never knew you; depart from Me, you who practice lawlessness!"* (Matt. 7:21-23).

The Lord said many will know who He is without trusting Him as Lord and Savior. He goes on to say that many who identify with Him and do things in His name are not saved. It is quite possible for people to know a lot about the Lord and to serve Him without ever being saved. The Lord knows who are truly His and who the counterfeits are. The king, who had witnessed God accomplish great wonders, did a good work by sending out this proclamation and speaking about the God he had become familiar with, but he still was not saved!

If we assume that Nebuchadnezzar lived two years after his mental restoration discussed later in this chapter, that would mean that the events in this chapter commence in 572 B.C. Daniel and his friends would be about fifty years of age. Nebuchadnezzar reigned over Babylon for forty-three years (605 B.C. to 562 B.C.).

The allegory of felling a majestic tree to represent the humbling of a proud king or nation is used several times in Scripture. For example, Ezekiel applies the imagery twice in the same chapter when speaking of the fall of the Assyrian Empire and foretelling Pharaoh's decimation (Ezek. 31). Many nations and peoples who benefitted from these towering trees then lamented their destruction. This idea is similar to the chilling daytime vision that Nebuchadnezzar received while resting on his bed in the palace (vv. 4-5). As in chapter 2 the wise men of Babylon are summoned to assist the king in understanding the meaning of his dream, but none can (vv. 6-7).

Finally, Nebuchadnezzar consulted with Daniel. The king knew Daniel was not troubled by secrets because the Spirit of the Holy God was within him (vv. 8-9). The king requested that Daniel listen to the details of his dream and tell him the meaning of it:

I was looking, and behold, a tree in the midst of the earth, and its height was great. The tree grew and became strong; its height reached to the heavens, and it could be seen to the ends of all the earth. Its leaves were lovely, its fruit abundant, and in it was food for all. The beasts of the field found shade under it, the birds of the heavens dwelt in its branches, and all flesh was fed from it. I saw in the visions of my head while on my bed, and there was a watcher, a holy one, coming down from heaven. He cried aloud and said thus: "Chop down the tree and cut off its branches, strip off its leaves and scatter its fruit. Let the beasts get out from under it, and the birds from its branches. Nevertheless leave the stump and roots in the earth, bound with a band of iron and bronze, in the tender grass of the field. Let it be wet with the dew of heaven, and let him graze with the beasts on the grass of the earth. Let his heart be changed from that of a man, let him be given the heart of a beast, and let seven times pass over him." This decision is by the decree of the watchers, and the sentence by the word of the holy ones, in order that the living may know that the Most High rules in the kingdom of men, gives it to whomever He will, and sets over it the lowest of men (vv. 10-17).

The king again pleaded for Daniel, who had the Spirit of the Holy God, to do what no one else in Babylon had been able to do – tell him the meaning of his dream (v. 18). With God's help Daniel discerned the meaning of the dream immediately, but its interpretation troubled him. Nebuchadnezzar observed Daniel's silence as an indication that the dream's meaning was not favorable; however, he pressed Daniel to tell him its meaning regardless (v. 19).

Daniel first told the king the prophetic meaning of the dream (vv. 20-26) and then sincerely warned him as to what he needed to do to keep it from coming true (v. 27). As ruler of the Babylonian Empire, Nebuchadnezzar both dominated and provided for the nations of the world; hence he is represented as the towering tree. But because of his pride, the Mighty One who rules heaven directed His angels to chop down the tree, leaving the stump and its roots, for after seven years it would again grow and become magnificent. During the seven-year interim the king would lose his sanity and be bound with a band of iron and bronze and driven from human society. He would roam in the wild like a beast. His hair would grow to be like long feathers and the morning dew would wet his back. However, after seven years his mental faculties and kingdom will be restored to him because he will have learned that *"the Most High rules in the kingdom of men"* (vv. 17, 26).

Being greatly disturbed by the dream, Daniel pleaded with the king: *"Break off your sins by being righteous, and your iniquities by showing mercy to the poor. Perhaps there may be a lengthening of your prosperity"* (v. 27). Daniel's earnest counsel suggests that God was offering Nebuchadnezzar a way of escape, if he would humble himself. Indeed, the Lord suffered the king's pride a full year before judgment fell (vv. 28-29). One day while the king was walking through the palace he was heard to say: *"Is not this great Babylon, that I have built for a royal dwelling by my mighty power and for the honor of my majesty?"* (v. 30). Just one pompous sentence, but it was the last straw; God immediately invoked the consequences of His warning from the previous year that had gone unheeded.

The king forgot that he was completely indebted to the Most High God for the riches, the glory, and the position he enjoyed in the Babylonian kingdom. Pride and conceit are sins that easily beset great men, but, as Nebuchadnezzar will soon learn, those who choose to steal God's glory will be brought low. We read that, while the king's words were still in his mouth, a voice from heaven rebuked the king:

King Nebuchadnezzar, to you it is spoken: the kingdom has departed from you! And they shall drive you from men, and your dwelling shall be with the beasts of the field. They shall make you eat grass like oxen; and seven times shall pass over you, until you know that the Most High rules in the kingdom of men, and gives it to whomever He chooses (vv. 31-32).

That same hour that God spoke from heaven, the king was driven out of the palace into nature's harsh domain. He ate grass like an ox, his nails became like the claws of birds, and his hair grew long like the feathers of an eagle (v. 33). The physical changes that beset Nebuchadnezzar were a direct reflection of his pitiful spiritual state, says William Kelly:

Reduced to the condition of a beast, he lost what characterizes a man – all recognition of God. He had a beast's heart. He had nothing of the character and glory of a man. Man is put here below as the image and glory of God. He is responsible to make God known; and he can only do it because he looks up to God. There are those that have an outward semblance of man, but *"man that is in honor and understands not, is like the beasts that perish."* This received its most remarkable confirmation in the case of Nebuchadnezzar; but the same thing is true, in principle, of every man that has got self and not God before his eyes. That was exactly true of the Babylonish king. He understood not. He attributed all to himself and not to God; and so, by a terrible retribution, he is reduced to the most abject state. Never had a Gentile possessed such glory and majesty as Nebuchadnezzar; but in a moment all is changed. In the height of his pride the sentence of God falls upon him.[114]

William Kelly also warns Christians to cherish the knowledge of God in humility and not to be stiff-necked when God graciously corrects us after straying from His path of truth:

As original uprightness was lost in the fall, even if there be a new nature by grace, soul discipline is ever needed, and blessed in the genuine humility that values knowledge from on high. Pride and vanity are alike disdainful of reproof, and therefore go from bad to worse. Those unwilling to own their faults or to submit to God's faithful dealings sink below humanity.[115]

Thankfully, God's Word in judgment is equally valid in restoration, and after seven years of living like a wild animal, Nebuchadnezzar's sanity was returned to him. His first royal act was to laud the God of the Jews, now his God, throughout his kingdom.

> *And at the end of the time I, Nebuchadnezzar, lifted my eyes to heaven, and my understanding returned to me; and I blessed the Most High and praised and honored Him who lives forever: For His dominion is an everlasting dominion, and His kingdom is from generation to generation. All the inhabitants of the earth are reputed as nothing; He does according to His will in the army of heaven and among the inhabitants of the earth. No one can restrain His hand or say to Him, "What have You done?"* (vv. 34-35).

His honor, his counselors, his nobles and the kingdom were restored to Nebuchadnezzar, who rose to greater heights of majesty after learning humility (v. 36). What lesson did he learn after being in the Lord's school for seven years? The king had learned who Daniel's God was, and he now chose to willingly praise Him and to uphold His character to others: *"Now, I, Nebuchadnezzar, praise and extol and honor the King of heaven, all of whose works are truth, and His ways justice. And those who walk in pride He is able to put down"* (v. 37). Nebuchadnezzar had come into personal contact with his Creator and he would never be the same.

The Lord knows how to deal with human pride and also how to make Himself known to us! Solomon wrote: *"The fear of the Lord is to hate evil; pride and arrogance and the evil way and the perverse mouth I hate"* (Prov. 8:13). H. A. Ironside agrees with Solomon – genuine humility is evidence that one possesses God-fearing wisdom:

> Nothing is more detestable in God's sight than pride on the part of creatures who have absolutely nothing to be proud of. This was the condemnation of the devil – self-exaltation. ... Humility is an indication

of true wisdom. It characterizes the man who has learned to judge himself correctly in the presence of God.[116]

As King Nebuchadnezzar learned the hard way, determination and natural abilities may secure for us fame and wealth, but such status will be short-lived if accompanied by pride and character that is not God-fearing: *"The righteousness of the blameless will direct his way aright, but the wicked will fall by his own wickedness"* (Prov. 11:5). This is a warning that we would do well to heed today!

Meditation

All the disunity and contention within the Church today is the result of our pride in one form or another. Nothing good can come from pride! This is why Paul admonished the believers at Philippi to follow Christ's example of selfless humility: *"Let nothing be done through strife or vainglory; but in lowliness of mind let each esteem others better than themselves"* (Phil. 2:3; KJV). As R. C. Chapman attests, this is the best defense against the pride that naturally consumes us:

> In 1 Corinthians 15:28 we read: *"Then shall the Son also Himself be subject,"* and in Revelation, *"The throne of God and of the Lamb."* Christ is forever the Shepherd and forever the Lamb, and it is the lowly or little Lamb, the diminutive being used. There is an infiniteness in the lowliness of the blessed Lamb, and He is now at the utmost of His lowliness. Satan took upon himself the form of a master, being created a servant; instead of serving in obedience he would be lord, and "the condemnation of the devil" is in his self-will; he chose to take to himself what belonged only to God. What a rebuke to the devil the exaltation of the Son of God will be to all eternity – a mirror in which to see his own folly! Acquaintance with the Cross of Christ brings me to nothing! Let any thought of self-exaltation be to me as a serpent; I have nothing to do but to kill it![117]

The Writings on the Wall
Daniel 5

The events in this chapter pertain to the conquering of the city of Babylon by Medo-Persian forces. Before contemplating the narrative of this chapter it will be helpful to review a few biblical prophecies pertaining to the fall of Babylon and information about the city and the political landscape of that time.

Background

Jeremiah had previously prophesied that Babylon would be attacked and conquered by an army from the north and that Babylon's chief deity Bel, also known as Marduk, would not be able to avert the calamity (Jer. 50-51). The city of Babylon itself would be laid waste (i.e. destroyed by fire – Jer. 50:32) and uninhabited, and the nation as a whole would be put to shame (Jer. 50:13). The Babylonians would be filled with terror and would suffer the same fate they had inflicted on so many others. God had used Babylon as an instrument of chastening, but they were a pagan nation also deserving judgment for their own wickedness and atrocities against their fellow man.

The question, then, is, Have these prophecies already been fulfilled, or do they have a future application? History records that the Medes and the Persians under the command of Cyrus, conquered the city of Babylon in 539 B.C. However, extra-biblical documentation of this conquest does not confirm the descriptions Jeremiah and Isaiah provide of Babylon's destruction or their prophecy that the city would be uninhabitable (Isa. 13:17-22; Jer. 50-51). Reviewing what we know of ancient Babylon, how it fell to the Persians, and what became of the city afterwards will be helpful in substantiating this conclusion.

The Greek historian Herodotus (fifth century B.C.) recorded the following information about ancient Babylon at the time of its conquest:[118]

348

- The city was in the form of a square (each side was fourteen miles in length).
- The outer brick wall surrounding the city was 56 miles long, 300 feet high, 25 feet thick, and had a base that extended 35 feet below the ground.
- An inner wall 75 feet high was behind the first wall.
- The city had 250 towers that were each 450 feet high.
- The Euphrates River flowed through and around the city providing it with a deep and wide moat for protection.
- Access to the city was gained either by ferryboats or across a half-mile-long bridge having drawbridges that were closed at night.
- The city had eight massive gates leading to the inner city, plus another hundred brass gates.
- The streets of Babylon were paved with stone slabs 3 feet square.
- Within the city was a great tower (a ziggurat) and fifty-three temples, including the "Great Temple of Marduk."

The famous walls of Babylon were indeed impenetrable. The only way into the city was through its gates or by the Euphrates River, which flowed through submersed passages in and out of the city. The Babylonians had built metal grids at each point where the river flowed in and out of the city to prevent underwater intrusions. However, while Babylon was under siege, Cyrus' corps of engineers devised a way of diverting the Euphrates River from Babylon and into a lake. Persian troops, placed at strategic points on the north and south sides of the city, waited until the water level dropped. The plan was executed on the evening of a Babylonian feast (v. 1). At the appropriate time, Cyrus' engineers diverted the Euphrates River upstream, which caused it to become significantly shallower. Herodotus describes what then happened in Babylon:

Hereupon the Persians who had been left for the purpose at Babylon by the riverside entered the stream, which had now sunk so as to reach about midway up a man's thigh, and thus got into the town. Had the Babylonians been apprised of what Cyrus was about, or had they noticed their danger, they would never have allowed the Persians to enter the city, but would have destroyed them utterly; for they would have made fast all the street gates which gave access to the river, and mounting upon the walls along both sides of the stream, would so have caught the enemy, as it were, in a trap. But, as it was, the

349

Persians came upon them by surprise and so took the city. Owing to the vast size of the place, the inhabitants of the central parts (as the residents at Babylon declare) long after the outer portions of the town were taken, knew nothing of what had changed, but as they were engaged in a festival, continued dancing and reveling until they learnt about the capture. Such, then, were the circumstances of the first taking of Babylon. [119]

Because the Babylonian soldiers and the general populace were intoxicated and indulging in all kinds of godless amusements the Persian army swiftly conquered the entire city unhindered. At the time Babylon fell, Nabunaid (Nabonidus) shared its kingship with his oldest son Belshazzar. The Nabonidus Chronicle provides the exact date on which Cyrus conquered Babylon:

In the month of Tashritu on the fourteenth day [October 10, 539 B.C.] the Persian forces took Sippar; on the sixteenth day [October 12] "the army of Cyrus entered Babylon without battle"; and in the month of Arahsamnu, on the third day [October 29], Cyrus himself came into the city. [120]

According to the Nabonidus Chronicle, Ugbaru (the governor of Gutium, perhaps Darius) entered the city during the time of the annual Babylonian feast on October 12, 539 B.C. Two hundred years prior to these events, the prophet Isaiah foretold by name the man whom God would use to defeat the Babylonians: Cyrus, who entered the city a little over two weeks after it fell to seal the victory. He would punish the Babylonians, end the Jewish exile, and initiate the rebuilding of the temple in Jerusalem (Isa. 44:28-45:4). But did Cyrus destroy the city of Babylon by fire? Was it uninhabited afterwards, as Jeremiah prophesied? The answer to these questions is, No. Cyrus used Babylon as a Persian outpost, but through the centuries Babylon gradually lost its political influence across the Persian Empire. The population of Babylon declined over the next two centuries and, ultimately, the city was dismantled under the Greek Empire to provide building materials for other cities.

In summary, Jeremiah's prophecies concerning the method of Babylon's destruction have not yet been fulfilled. The events related to Babylon's capture in the sixth century B.C. and its eventual demise centuries later do not conform to the specific prophecies of Isaiah and

Jeremiah. Babylon has never been destroyed by fire, remaining uninhabitable. These prophecies will be fulfilled at Christ's Second Advent (Rev. 18).

Nebuchadnezzar died twenty-three years earlier, and was succeeded by several incompetent rulers. His son Evil-Merodach (Jer. 52:31-34) ruled after his father's death, but was a poor leader. He was assassinated by his brother-in-law Neriglissar after only two years. Neriglissar (Nergal-Sharezer; Jer. 39:2) died four years later, leaving a minor son, Labashi-Marduk. Conspirators assassinated the boy after two months. Nabonidus, the first king since Nebuchadnezzar to restore some honor to the Babylonian Empire was the successor. Nabonidus married Nebuchadnezzar's daughter Nitocris and presided over Babylon for seventeen years, though absent ten of those years while engaged in military campaigns. Due to his absence, Nabonidus made his son Belshazzar, who resided in the city of Babylon, a coregent.

Archeological evidence has confirmed the accuracy of much of what is recorded in the biblical narrative. For example, The Nabonidus Cylinder confirms that Belshazzar exercised royal authority from Nabonidus' third year onwards, because Nabonidus was engaged in the conquest of Tema (Arabia).[121] The biblical account picks up in the fourteenth year of Belshazzar's rule in Babylon; the year is 539 B.C. and the city has been under siege by the Persians for some time.

The Narrative

Nabonidus had engaged and retreated from Cyrus and his Persian army at Opis, 115 miles north of Babylon. Then on October 10, 539 B.C. at a location about 50 miles north of the city, he was forced to surrender without a fight, but he escaped capture by fleeing south to Borsippa. The Medes and Persians readied their troops at the walls of Babylon. Given that the empire had virtually fallen (except for its capital city), that Nabonidus was in hiding, and with the enemy mustered around them, you might think it was a poor time for Belshazzar to celebrate the popular, annual New Year's feast.

However, because they regarded their city's walls as impregnable, the Babylonians were swollen with confidence and seemingly unconcerned with what the Persians were doing. They had plenty of stored supplies and an endless resource of fresh water and aquatic life from the Euphrates. They thought they could endure a siege indefinitely – so why not party and enjoy life? Indeed, King Belshazzar hosted a huge banquet for a thousand civil officials and their wives and mistresses (v. 1). They consumed much wine and the event became a drunken party. Either because they needed more drinking vessels for this sizeable gathering or merely to spite the gods of the people they had conquered, Belshazzar commanded that the sacred vessels Nebuchadnezzar confiscated from the temple in Jerusalem be brought to the banquet hall (v. 2). It is noted the archeologists have unearthed a plastered, walled room in the ancient city of Babylon that measures 160 by 50 feet. A room of these dimensions would be adequate to accommodate a thousand people.

The vessels were brought and the king, his officials, and their wives and concubines drank from them as they praised the gods of gold and silver (vv. 3-4). The festivities came to an abrupt halt when the fingers of a large hand appeared and began to etch a message into the plastered wall near the lampstand (v. 5). Although not an invited guest, the Lord was prompted by the blasphemous act to crash Belshazzar's party and to deliver a pungent message in writing. This is only the second time in Scripture that we read of God writing on anything, the first instance being the two tables of stone given to Moses which contained the Law.

The mysterious hand had a sobering effect on the intoxicated king. Belshazzar, who had apparently been standing, became so frightened at the sight of the hand that his legs gave out from underneath him and gravity took over – he fell to the floor (v. 6). For the third time in the book, all of Babylon's soothsayers, astrologers, and wise men were summoned by an anxious Babylonian king to understand the meaning of God's secret message and were promised great reward if they could (v. 7). Belshazzar promised royal apparel (a purple robe), a gold neck chain, and a position as third ruler of the kingdom (probably with Nabonidus and himself). However, none of these things would have any value to any Babylonian on the next day, for the kingdom was finished and all riches and honor would be transferred to the Persians.

Of course, no pagan intellectual or satanic collaborator can know the deep things of God; hence, none of the king's wise men could interpret the meaning of the message carved into the wall (v. 8). This gloomy assessment further troubled the king, astonished his lords, and threw the entire assembly into a state of babbling confusion (v. 9).

Moses affirmed mankind is not responsible to know what God has not revealed, but we are to strive to understand and obey what He has disclosed to us: *"The secret things belong to the Lord our God, but those things which are revealed belong to us and to our children forever, that we may do all the words of this law"* (Deut. 29:29). The paramount reason that a believer is to study Scripture is to learn what God reveals about Himself; He is the source of true wisdom. Man cannot gain true wisdom by his own efforts, but those who sincerely seek after God will generously receive His wisdom (Prov. 2:6). The only way that Belshazzar would learn the meaning of a message from God would be by consulting a true prophet of His. Thankfully, the queen royal remembered such a man from the days of Nebuchadnezzar, Daniel (v. 10).

The exact identity of the queen is unknown; she was not at the feast, but arrived at the hall in response to all the commotion. The king's wives were with him at the feast, so the queen was either Belshazzar's mother or grandmother. The latter is more likely as she knew of Nebuchadnezzar's dream that no one could interpret except Daniel, meaning she had likely witnessed the event sixty-five years earlier. The queen was also personally familiar with Daniel and describes him as a man of insight, intelligence, knowledge and understanding, and one who had the ability to interpret dreams (vv. 11-12).

Daniel actively served in King Belshazzar's administration eleven years previously (8:12), but is apparently unknown to the king at this time. Perhaps Daniel, now about eighty years of age, was no longer involved with the administrative affairs of the kingdom or at least had no significant role as he did during Nebuchadnezzar's reign.

The king heeded the queen's suggestion, but rather than extending Daniel the honor he deserved (given the Queen's endorsement), Belshazzar insults Daniel by inquiring if he was one of the captives Nebuchadnezzar brought from Judah (v. 13). This was a fact that he was already aware of, which meant he knew that he was requesting a favor from one whose God he had just blasphemed. The king repeats to Daniel what he has heard about him, directs his attention to the Aramaic writing on the wall that is in an unknown dialect or script. The king then promises Daniel fame and fortune if he can interpret it (vv. 14-16). Daniel agrees to inform the king of the writing's meaning, but declines to receive anything for doing so (v. 17).

Infidelity and Loyalty

The longstanding Jewish captive begins by giving the imprudent king a history lesson. It was Daniel's God, the Most High God, who had given Nebuchadnezzar a kingdom of majesty and honor which put all the people groups and nations throughout the region under his control (v. 18). The king then did as he pleased, pardoning those he determined to forgive and executing those who were rebellious or a threat to his dominion (v. 19). In time, however, Nebuchadnezzar's pride swelled beyond what God would tolerate and so He confiscated the king's sanity and he became like a wild beast and all his honor was stripped from him in a moment (vv. 20-21). Daniel told Belshazzar that God did this as a testimony that He alone is sovereign over human authorities and powers; He determines the rise and fall of kingdoms (v. 22). Yet, knowing all this history, Belshazzar still dared to raise his hand in blatant defiance against Daniel's God. He should have learned from Nebuchadnezzar's mistake and not repeated it.

> Until the will and the affections are brought under the authority of Christ, we have not begun to understand, let alone to accept, His lordship.
> — Elisabeth Elliot

Daniel continued his monologue by condemning the king's proud, blasphemous actions of desecrating the sacred temple vessels and praising the gods of gold and silver, which were only figments of human imagination (v. 23). Clearly, Daniel did not have the same respect for Belshazzar, whose doom was sealed, as he did for Nebuchadnezzar when he despairingly informed the king the meaning of his dream in chapter 4. Nebuchadnezzar, even before his conversion, honored the God of the Jews, but Belshazzar had chosen to rebel against the One who actively controls every aspect of all life. Consequently, God would reveal Himself to the king in a forthright and tangible way by writing a message on the king's banquet wall (v. 24).

God's prophet then proceeded to read the inscription and give its meaning:

> *MENE, MENE, TEKEL, UPHARSIN. This is the interpretation of each word. MENE: God has numbered your kingdom, and finished it; TEKEL: You have been weighed in the balances, and found wanting;*

PERES: Your kingdom has been divided, and given to the Medes and Persians (vv. 25-28).

UPHARSIN means "divided" and PHARSIN is the plural of PERES; the "U" is an "and." Because of the moral and spiritual corruption in the king and his kingdom, Daniel's God had determined to divide Belshazzar's kingdom and bestow it to the Medes and the Persians. Given the sternness of the message, one might think the king would have Daniel executed, but instead, he honors his word and rewards Daniel. After Daniel foretold Nebuchadnezzar's dream in chapter 2, the king promoted Daniel to a position as second ruler; however, because Belshazzar is a prince-regent with his father, Daniel is proclaimed the third ruler of the Babylonian Empire (v. 29). The king also commanded that Daniel be clothed with purple and that a chain of gold be put around his neck.

This honorary status was short-lived, however, for that evening Belshazzar was assassinated and sixty-two-year-old Darius the Mede took control of the city as previously discussed in the *Background* section. Who Darius actually is remains somewhat of a mystery, as we do not read his name on any ancient monuments. H. A. Ironside suggests that absence of Darius' name in historical records does not pose any difficulty, as ancient kings were often known by various names:

> In fact, no two lists of the later Median kings, as given by the old historians, agree with each other; and the monuments seem to differ from them all. The last king of the Medians was Cyaxares II, who formed an alliance with Cyrus his nephew, and led a part of the armies of the confederate kingdoms to battle. His age, as given by Herodotus, agrees with that of Darius, as given in this chapter. The two may therefore be identical. On the other hand, some suppose Darius to be the same as Gobryas, who according to ancient records conducted the siege of Babylon as representative of the allied kings. The discrepancy in names is no greater than that in the case of Cambyses and Atrodates, both names being applied to the same monarch; the one by Xenophon; the other, by Nicolas of Damascus; while it is a well-known fact that the lists of Median kings given by Ctesias and Herodotus differ in every instance, and the chronologies are hopelessly confusing and contradictory.[122]

Ancient records confirm that Gobryas or Gubaru was born in 601 B.C. and would have been 62 years old when the city of Babylon was captured; this agrees with the information supplied in Daniel 5:31.[123] Regardless of Darius' true identity, the Lord again shows in this chapter that He is in full control of all human endeavors. He knows how to vanquish the proud, exalt the humble, and quell man's feeble attempts to foil His predetermined purposes to bless Israel. Belshazzar was not destitute of revelation, but rather rejected it and thus was found wanting when weighed on divine balances – he perished in his sins. It is the same for all those who despise God's Word, for that is the same as rejecting the Holy Spirit who moved holy men to produce a living testimony of truth which ever guides us heavenward.

Meditation

No government is lawful or innocent that does not recognize the moral law as the only universal law, and God as the Supreme Lawgiver and Judge, to whom nations in their national capacity, as well as individuals, are amenable. ... The moral law of God is the only law of individuals and of nations, and nothing can be rightful government but such as is established and administered with a view to its support.

— Charles Finney

Faithful Despite Lions
Daniel 6

This chapter contains one of the most popular stories in Scripture: Daniel safely spends a night with hungry lions because he would not compromise his faith – a faith God was determined to honor. King Darius the Mede, who was introduced in the previous chapter, ruled the capital city of Babylon under Cyrus' authority.

Darius reorganized the new empire into 120 districts, each having its own satrap, each district leader reporting to one of three governors (v. 1). Daniel, now in his eighties, was recognized for his wisdom and intellect and was initially appointed as one of the three governors (v. 2). However, Darius was so impressed with Daniel that he thought to promote him to be the head over the other two governors, effectively making him a powerful vice-president in the kingdom (v. 3).

Darius' intentions did not set well with the other governors and satraps, who became determined to find some charge that they could accuse Daniel of before the king. However, the conspirators utterly failed; *"they could find no charge or fault, because he was faithful; nor was there any error or fault found in him"* (v. 4). Daniel was a man of high morals, and blameless in his conduct. It is interesting that the character quality first mentioned pertaining to elders in 1 Timothy 3 and Titus 1 is *blamelessness*: *"An overseer, then, must be **above reproach**"* (1 Tim. 3:2; NASV) or "blameless" as translated NKJV and KJV. *Anegkletos* is used as a negative particle to mean "above reproach or accusation in character." *"If any be **blameless**, the husband of one wife ...a bishop* [overseer] *must be **blameless**, as the steward of God"* (Tit. 1:6-7). A spiritual man is not necessarily sinless, but he does sin less. He is morally and socially above reproach – his walk with the Lord is evidenced by his observed character.

The prophet Daniel is a good example of a man who walked so closely with God that his jealous enemies could find no fault in him. Because he lived and breathed God's Word, no one could accuse him of wrongdoing. These evil men then surmised that the only way to bring Daniel down was to devise a civil law that would be contrary to Daniel's religious convictions. They believed that Daniel was a man of character who would not compromise no matter the personal cost (v. 5). Likewise, as believers yield to the Word of God today, we should also expect the enemy to wrongly accuse us; however, the truth of the matter, as we observe in this story, will be known in the end. If our lives are not yielded to God's Word, we cannot hide the fact – bad doctrine is always lived out. The enemy's just accusations will abound, and will lead to the disdaining of the name of Christ by those who do not know Him.

A plan was devised that would cater to the king's pride, would promote unity throughout the kingdom, and would also condemn Daniel as a lawbreaker: For thirty days no one in the empire was to petition any man or god for anything, except the king; anyone found guilty of violating this law would be thrown into a den of lions and devoured (vv. 6-7). The king overstepped his God-given authority by signing the statute into law and, as Hamilton Smith observes, commits what is always the final and climactic act of apostasy:

> We have seen that the moral characteristics of the governing powers during the times of the Gentiles are set forth in the historical incidents recorded in Daniel 3-6. The worst and final evil is apostasy, or man usurping the place of God upon the earth. The setting aside the rights of God, the exaltation of man, the open defiance of God, that have already passed before us, end in the awful attempt to stamp out all recognition of God on the earth by dethroning God and enthroning man in His place. This climax of all evil is forecast in the decree signed by King Darius whereby no petition is to be addressed to any God or man, save to the king, for thirty days.[124]

Nebuchadnezzar erred by erecting an idol in the place of God, but Darius's sin was worse. He set himself up in the place of God. The king would soon learn that whenever we act beyond the scope of our ascribed authority, difficulties always develop, especially when we defy the One who bestows all authority. Under the legal protocol of Medes and Persians, not even a flawed statute could be voided by an imperial decree (vv. 8-9). The trap was now set by the satraps, and no doubt the antagonists were monitoring Daniel night and day, waiting for him to violate their decree by committing the treasonous act of praying to his God.

After hearing of the edict, Daniel was determined to turn the matter over to his God. He would not abandon his normal practice of kneeling three times a day while facing Jerusalem to offer thanksgiving, praise, and supplications to his God (v. 10). Daniel had been taught this Jewish practice in his childhood (see Ps. 55:17 and 138:2) and had continued the daily routine of systematic prayer his entire life. Daniel continued his custom of praying in front of an open west-facing window, that is, towards Jerusalem (v. 11). His adversaries must have been surprised that Daniel did not even try to hide his praying. His window was already open and it would have been cowardice to close it in this situation; likewise, if it had been closed, it would have been courting needless persecution to open it. But Daniel was a praying man, and it is likely that this west-facing window was usually open.

Notice that Daniel did not shortchange his normal praying routine because of the threatening circumstances; he was careful to praise the Lord as well as to request His intervention. How often the Lord's people become rattled by circumstances and rush into the throne room of grace in a state of hopeless panic, as if God is unaware of what is happening in our lives or is somehow not in control. There is a reason, dear believer, that the sea of glass before God's throne is ripple free – God's peace resides within His sovereign control over all things. From Daniel's heavenly perspective, nothing has changed but a few details pertaining to his earthly supplications.

For their devious plot to succeed, Daniel's enemies had counted on both the vanity of the king and Daniel's conviction to hold to his habit of prayer with unwavering devotion, even if it cost him his life. Their character assessment of both men was correct. A bit of flattery promptly elevated the king's pride and upright Daniel would not compromise. After witnessing Daniel's repeated resolve to pray (apparently watching him pray more than once; v. 13), the jealous constituents immediately sought an audience with the king: First, they confirmed the edict that he had signed into law. Second, they affirmed that it could not be changed. Third, they accused Daniel of showing contempt for the king by willfully breaking it, for he had been observed praying to His God (vv. 12-13).

We pause to consider four marks of carnality in self-seeking people: First, motived by pride and envy, they accuse the righteous of wrongdoing. Second, they are mastered by a critical fault-finding spirit which ignores the good of the righteous. Third, they seek to create an authoritative environment to ensure that the righteous are falsely indicted. Fourth, they then appeal to civil authority in order to oppress the innocent and accomplish their selfish agenda. The evil entourage opposing Daniel was guilty of all four of these base tactics.

Darius was displeased with himself after hearing the indictment against Daniel; he knew that he had been tricked by a ploy that appealed to his ego (v. 14). The king sought to release Daniel, but apparently there were no loopholes in the statute and Daniel's accusers were insistent that Darius uphold the law (v. 15). Having exhausted his options, the king regretfully commanded that Daniel be cast in the den of lions as his edict demanded (v. 16). Nevertheless, this pagan king encouraged Daniel that "his" God whom he served continually would deliver him. William MacDonald comments on the effect that the life and convictions of a dedicated believer like Daniel have on an unregenerate soul:

> It is beautiful to see how even unbelievers will sometimes pick up on the faith and morals of consistent believers whom they observe at close hand. Only too often Christians fail their unsaved friends and relatives by not having as high standards of faith and practice as the world expects from God's people.[125]

Daniel was not such a person; he was willing to suffer loss, even to die, rather than to compromise his God-honoring convictions, and that testimony spoke volumes to the king. Religious hypocrites uttering "sweet Jesus" endearments do more harm to the cause of Christ than anything else; the lost need to witness men and women with unwavering devotion to the Lord Jesus as shown by obedience to His expressed will without reservation. Normally, when Scripture speaks of the will of God, it explicitly states what it is. There is no mystery about it, for God has declared to us His general will for our lives. Consequently, the more pertinent question becomes, not what is the will of God for my life, but will I obey the revealed will of God for my life? If you are a believer in Christ, there is only one right answer to this question. The Lord Jesus said, *"But why do you call Me 'Lord, Lord,' and not do the things which I say?"* (Luke 6:46), and *"If you love Me, keep My commandments"* (John 14:15). Do not call Jesus Christ "Lord" if you are not going to do what He says.

To walk out of God's will is to walk into nowhere.

— C. S. Lewis

Obedience to the Lord Jesus proves our love for Him. A lack of love for the Lord will be shown through an unyielding spirit and through disobedience. There is such an intimate tie between genuine love for the Lord and obedience to the Lord that Paul bluntly states, *"If any man love not the Lord Jesus Christ, let him be Anathema* [eternally condemned]" (1 Cor. 16:22). Daniel loved the Lord and was willing to demonstrate his love through conviction and consecration.

The entire language of the narrative paints a picture of the den of lions as being a cave-like enclosure with a single entrance, a hole in the ground, over the top of the cave or crevice. It was deep enough that no lions could jump or climb out, and the entrance was small enough that a rock could be pulled over the opening to secure it (v. 17). The Hebrew word *remah* translated "cast" in verse 16, literally means "to throw" and the language throughout the narrative speaks of falling down "to the bottom" and "up out of" the lion's den (vv. 23-24). It had to greatly grieve the king to see a righteous man in his eighties being thrown down into a cold, dark enclosure with hungry lions – the fall alone could have easily killed Daniel. The king and his lords sealed the stone that secured the mouth of the den with their own signets. Daniel's execution was approved by a plurality of authority, ensuring that no person, including the king, could tamper with the stone until morning without violating Persian law (v. 17).

Darius was grievously exasperated over the entire affair. The king did not eat or sleep until he knew how Daniel fared in the morning. He also did not seek entertainment or musicians to cause the night to pass more quickly (v. 18). His conscience smote him, for he knew that his own pride had sentenced Daniel to a terrible fate. On the other hand, Matthew Henry reminds us that innocent Daniel was not miserable in the den of lions because he trusted in his God:

We are sure of what the king doubted: that the servants of the living God have a Master well able to protect them. See the power of God over the fiercest creatures, and believe His power to restrain the roaring lion that goes about continually seeking to devour. Daniel was kept perfectly safe, because he believed in his God. Those who boldly and cheerfully trust in God to protect them in the way of duty shall always find Him a present help.[126]

The king suffered a sleepless night because he had offended his conscience, the benefit of which enabled him to be at the den of lions at first light (v. 19). After the stone was removed, Darius cried out with a lamenting voice, *"Daniel, servant of the living God, has your God, whom you serve continually, been able to deliver you from the lions?"* (v. 20). Everyone with the king waited in eerie silence for a response. Daniel replied to the king's question:

> *O king, live forever! My God sent His angel and shut the lions' mouths, so that they have not hurt me, because I was found innocent before Him; and also, O king, I have done no wrong before you* (vv. 21-22).

As Daniel stated, the miracle absolutely proved his innocence and that his God had sought fit to protect His prophet from being harmed by jealous men who contrived evil. The king was ecstatic and commanded that Daniel be lifted up out of the den (v. 23). He was examined and found to have no injuries; neither the lions, nor the fall, nor even the cold had harmed Daniel in anyway. Why was Daniel unharmed? Daniel was preserved because he was an innocent man who *"believed in his God"* (v. 23). Hence, the very snare that Daniel's conspirators had set to extinguish his life ultimately proved his innocence; this meant that his accusers were the ones guilty of corruption. Darius commanded that they and their families be thrown into the den of lions. The wild beasts made mastery of them even before they reached the bottom of the den (v. 24). This detail indicates that there must have been a lot of lions in the den to wreak such carnage on so many people. Daniel's God did not protect them from harm, which was further proof that Daniel was a just man.

The chapter closes with Darius making a decree throughout the empire – a decree that exalted Daniel's God, the God of the Jews, as the living, eternal, and powerful God, who should be feared by all. He does marvelous signs and wonders and even delivered His servant Daniel from powerful lions (v. 27). Daniel also enjoyed stately honor and prosperity during the reigns of Darius and Cyrus (v. 28). As previously mentioned, the Lord has vowed: *"Those who honor Me I will honor"* (1 Sam. 2:30) and through faithfulness and a commitment to prayer, Daniel experienced the full victory of God's promise!

Meditation

The greatest blunder Christians commit upon experiencing victory over sin lies in not using the way of victory to sustain it; instead, they try to perpetuate the victory by their works and determination.

— Watchman Nee

Prayer is life passionately wanting, wishing, desiring God's triumph. Prayer is life striving and toiling everywhere and always for that ultimate victory.

— G. Campbell Morgan

Kingdom Visions
Daniel 7

A Beastly Overview

The kingdom representation of the image in Nebuchadnezzar's dream (chp. 2) correlates nicely with the vision of beasts rising out of a turbulent sea in this chapter and also with John's visions in the Apocalypse. According to chapters 2 and 7, Daniel tells us that there would be five world kingdoms after the Egyptian and Assyrian empires. The Babylonian empire was ruling in Daniel's day and would be followed by the Medo-Persian, Greek, Roman, and Revived Roman empires. These various world systems in which Satan has reigned or will reign are also depicted in the seven heads of two beasts described by John in the book of Revelation:

- A terrible red dragon having seven heads, ten horns, and seven crowns (one for each of its heads) is used to represent Satan (Rev. 12:3). He is identified as Satan, the devil, and the serpent of old (Rev. 12:9).
- A beast rising up out of the sea (i.e., the nations) with seven heads and ten horns on one head, each horn having a crown representing the Antichrist who speaks for the dragon (Rev. 13:1, 17:9-14).

John also describes a third beast coming up out of the land (i.e. the land likely representing Israel) and having two horns, like a lamb; this beast represents the false prophet who talks like the dragon and causes people to worship the Antichrist (Rev. 13:11). These three beasts of Revelation 12 and 13 form an unholy trio that clearly mocks the Holy Trinity in form and operation: God the Father directs, the Son does the Father's will, and the Holy Spirit enables the Son to do the Father's will. Satan directs the affairs of the unholy trio. The Antichrist is the devil's human representative on earth and does his will – he is represented as "the little horn" that rises up in the head of the final, fierce beast in this chapter and who pulls three of the ten horns out. The false prophet gives honor to the beast through miracles and deceives many into worshiping the beast, and thus honoring Satan (Rev. 13:14-15). These similarities between the unholy trio and the Holy Trinity are profound and show the devil's attempts to honor himself by mimicking and mocking God's character, attributes, and doings.

John again describes the Antichrist in Revelation 17 and there identifies the heads of the beast as being kingdoms. At the time of John's writing, approximately A.D. 95, five of these kingdoms had fallen: the Egyptian, the Assyrian, the Babylonian, the Medo-Persian, and the Greek empires. The sixth kingdom, the Roman Empire, ruled in John's day. One world government had yet to be established, but Daniel identifies it as a Revived Roman Empire in which the Antichrist would rule with ten kings initially and then with seven (8:8, 24; Rev. 17:9-14). Human history has shown Daniel's prophecy to be true thus far. Though many nations have tried, there has not been a world empire since the fall of Roman rule in the fifth century A.D.

Daniel precisely named the Medo-Persian empire and then the Greek empire long before they were established (8:20-21). Understanding that the heads of the beasts represent kingdoms, and that the horns represent kings within the final kingdom explains why the crowns were on each of the seven heads of the dragon (depicting Satan's control of seven world empires), but were only on the ten horns of the seventh head, the final empire, when speaking of the beast rising out of the sea, the Antichrist. Paul identifies Satan as *"the god of this age"* (2 Cor. 4:4), and *"the prince of the power of the air"* (Eph. 2:2). On three occasions, the Lord Jesus said that Satan is *"the prince of this world"* (John 12:31, 14:30, 16:11). The world is presently Satan's delegated domain; he is the ruler of all seven world empires that span time leading up to the reign of Christ. The revived Roman Empire must be in place prior to the abomination of desolation which occurs at the midpoint in the Tribulation Period, since that is when the harlot, the one-world religious system, is destroyed by the Antichrist (Rev. 17:16).

The Night Visions

Daniel's first vision (which actually is three separate visions) occurred in the first year of Belshazzar's reign in Babylon, that is, just after he became a coregent with his father Nabonidus (v. 1). The year would be 553 B.C., meaning that Daniel would be in his late sixties (v. 1).

Before studying the specific prophecies of Daniel in the next six chapters, notice that the revelation is addressed to righteous Daniel and not to God's covenant people. At this particular moment, God is not in fellowship with His people who are dispersed; He is not publicly recognizing the Jewish nation. Through visions and angelic messengers, God speaks directly and personally to Daniel only.

The first set of visions occurred during a night dream while Daniel was in his bed; he immediately wrote down what he had seen, so that none of the details would be lost. He vividly describes what he saw: *"the four winds of heaven were stirring up the Great Sea"* (v. 2). The number four occurs again in verse 3 to describe the sum of beasts sequentially rising up out of the aquatic turbulence. What do the four winds, the four beasts, and the sea symbolize?

Metaphorically speaking, "the sea" repeatedly symbolizes the Gentile nations (Matt. 13:47; Rev. 13:1, 17:1, 15). Before addressing the meaning of the number "four," it should be understood that *numerology* forms a portion of the broader study called *biblical typology*. In Scripture, most numbers have a literal meaning (e.g. Christ arose from the grave on the *third* day), but some numbers serve a figurative purpose. We understand that the Lamb with *seven* horns in Revelation 5:6 symbolically represents the omnipotence of the Lamb of God, because in Scripture seven is the number of perfection, and a horn represents power as shown later in this chapter. Sometimes both a figurative and a literal meaning may be intended, especially when the obvious literal sense is within a personal narrative and the figurative sense conveys a future meaning verified elsewhere in Scripture. For example, the seven-year famine in Joseph's day was both an actual devastating famine that affected the whole land and also a forewarning of a yet future seven-year Tribulation Period that will devastate the entire planet.

Numbers one through forty, as well as many numbers above forty, are each used in a specific, and consistent, figurative manner throughout the Bible to show a particular meaning. This figurative repetition is one of many evidences which demonstrate that all Scripture comes from one Mind – it is God-breathed (2 Tim. 3:16). In Scripture, the number four represents *earthly order*: in the earth there are four directions, four seasons, and four realms in which life exists in the world (the sea, the air, on the ground, and below the ground). What the number represents and how it is applied here is similar to its use in Revelation 7:1 when the Lord suspended worldwide judgments to mark 144,000 Jewish witnesses during the Tribulation Period: *"I saw four angels standing at the four corners of the earth, holding the four winds of the earth, that the wind should not blow on the earth, on the sea, or on any tree."* This passage is not implying that the earth is flat, or has corners, but rather that a worldwide angelic influence resulted in a brief calm during the most destructive era of human history.

In Daniel's case the opposite is true; there was no rest, but rather angelic activities were stirring up worldwide turbulence. The Lord Jesus likens the invisible and unimpeded power of the Holy Spirit to wind in John 3:8 and Jeremiah speaks of angelic activities being as powerful as the wind (Jer. 23:19). This probably reflects the intense battle in the spiritual realm over the unfolding of God's predetermined counsel on earth, a reality more plainly addressed in Daniel 10. This understanding explains the number of the beasts and of the wind and the tempestuous sea (i.e., the devil is aggressively opposing the things of God).

Daniel then describes the first beast to rise out of the sea: *"The first was like a lion, and had eagle's wings. I watched till its wings were plucked off; and it was lifted up from the earth and made to stand on two feet like a man, and a man's heart was given to it"* (v. 4). Who does the lion represent? Scripture interprets itself and thankfully Jeremiah speaks of Nebuchadnezzar as a lion (Jer. 4:7) and Ezekiel compares him to an eagle (Ezek. 17:3). Furthermore, Daniel specifically told Nebuchadnezzar that he was the "head of gold" in the image of the kingdoms in chapter 2; thus, the king of the beasts, the powerful lion, is depicted to us first to represent the Babylonian Empire. The number of wings is not mentioned, but since at least two wings are needed to fly and eagles only have two wings, it would seem appropriate to assume the first beast initially had two wings, but then his wings were removed to humble him. This would agree with the narrative in chapter 4: Nebuchadnezzar, the proud, self-sufficient king, was punished with seven years of insanity, and when his reason was restored, he became a self-effacing Jehovah worshipper. This outcome is depicted in the posture of the beast: it stood upright on its two hind feet (more like a man than a lion) to demonstrate that this individual had lost his beastly nature and had adopted a more humane disposition.

Suddenly, a second beast emerged from the sea. It is described as a bear, which was raised up higher on one side than the other and has three ribs in its mouth (v. 5). A plurality of voices commanded the bear to *"devour much flesh."* Whether the order initiated from the Godhead or from angelic voices directing the affairs of God on earth is unknown, but the scenario does show that kingdoms of the earth are divinely appointed to accomplish God's sovereign purposes. The bear is a formidable beast; it is both strong and fierce. It is used here to symbolize the Medo-Persian Empire. The bear, raised up higher on one side indicates that Persia was the more powerful ally in the co-alliance. The three ribs in the bear's mouth may symbolize the three previous earthly kingdoms (i.e., the Egyptian, the Assyrian, and the Babylonian Empires) or they may reflect the three main regions of the Babylonian Empire which were conquered by the Medes and the Persians under Cyrus: Babylon in the east, Egypt in the south, and Lydia to the east in Asia Minor.

A third beast appearing from the sea was described as a leopard having four heads and four wings. The leopard is a swift animal (Hab. 1:8), known for its keen perception and agility in pursuing its prey (Jer. 5:6). The Medo-Persian kingdom was swiftly conquered by the Greeks, led by a young Alexander the Great, in only four years (334 to 330 B.C.). His agile, battle-hardened army then moved eastward and conquered much of India in the following six years (330 to 324 B.C.). However, Alexander's life ended in Nebuchadnezzar's palace in Babylon in 323 B.C.; he was only 32 years old. Alcoholism had weakened his body and he contracted an illness, perhaps malaria or typhoid fever, which after two weeks resulted in his death. A few years later, his four generals divided up the Greek Empire into four regions and each general ruled over his portion. As in verse 6, a *head* represents the conveyance of *authority*. John applies the same metaphor to describe the divine authority given the devil over the earth in Revelation 12:3 and that which he confers on the Antichrist during the Tribulation Period (Rev. 13:1-5, 17:9-10).

Daniel then describes a fourth beast as more ferocious than the previous three in its conquering escapades. It is described only as having iron teeth, bronze claws, and ten horns (vv. 8, 19). The iron teeth link this beast with the Roman Empire identified in Nebuchadnezzar's image in chapter 2 (the iron legs). When used symbolically in Scripture, the word "horn" represents power or strength, which is typically associated with authority. An animal uses its horns (or antlers) to protect itself or to demarcate its territory in the wild, either by fighting or by making rubbings. The Antichrist is described by Daniel as being a "little horn" who is granted dominion to rule the world for seven years (vv. 8-27). As before mentioned, the Lord Jesus is described as a Lamb with seven horns (Rev. 5). Since seven is the number of perfection and completeness in Scripture, we understand that these seven horns figuratively represent the Lord's omnipotence, or perfect power. Daniel does not picture the fourth beast as any particular animal, but John speaks of it as a mongrel with aspects of each of the three previous Empires:

> *And I saw a beast rising up out of the sea, having seven heads and ten horns, and on his horns ten crowns, and on his heads a blasphemous name. Now the beast which I saw was like a leopard, his feet were like the feet of a bear, and his mouth like the mouth of a lion. The dragon gave him his power, his throne, and great authority* (Rev. 13:1-2).

The Revived Roman Empire under the rule of the Antichrist is described here with the distinctive aspects of the previous world empires seeming to culminate in the Roman Kingdom, especially in its final stage during the Tribulation Period. What regions within the Roman Empire the ten kings represent is unknown, but Daniel tells us that when the Antichrist, "the little horn," rises to power, "he" (as identified in v. 24) will eliminate three of the ten kings (v. 8). The little horn has eyes like a man and a human voice which utters great blasphemies against God. While not apparent during the first half of the Tribulation Period, after the Abomination of Desolation (9:27), John states that what Daniel prophesied will be fulfilled concerning the Antichrist:

> *And he was given a mouth speaking great things and blasphemies, and he was given authority to continue for forty-two months. Then he opened his mouth in blasphemy against God, to blaspheme His name, His tabernacle, and those who dwell in heaven* (Rev. 13:5-6).

During the last three and half years of the Tribulation Period, much of the world population will be slaughtered and many will vow allegiance to the Antichrist by taking his mark. He will then lead the Gentile armies of the nations against the Jewish nation (Joel 2; Zech. 14; Rev. 19).

The Ancient of Days

Before speaking of Christ's Second Advent to war against the little horn, Daniel is first transported into the throne room of heaven, in the same way John will be to receive the vision of the Apocalypse (Rev. 4-5). Interestingly, like John, Daniel first describes the glory of God the Father (referred to as the Ancient of Days) before honoring God's Son, the Lamb:

> *I watched till thrones were put in place, and the Ancient of Days was seated; His garment was white as snow, and the hair of His head was like pure wool. His throne was a fiery flame, its wheels a burning fire; a fiery stream issued and came forth from before Him. A thousand thousands ministered to Him; ten thousand times ten thousand stood before Him. The court was seated, and the books were opened* (vv. 9-10).

Both God's brilliant attire and white hair portray His purity and holiness. John describes the glory of Christ in a similar majestic fashion (Rev. 1:13-15) and also God the Father's regal presence on His heavenly throne (Rev. 4:2-3). The description of the fire and wheels are reminiscent of Ezekiel's description of God's mobile throne (Ezek. 1). The wheels connected God's throne to the earth, and fire speaks of judgment throughout Scripture. Thus this scene conveys God poised to judge the wicked residing on the earth.

Like Daniel, John also acknowledges an innumerable host of attendants about God's throne, except John includes redeemed saints among the throng of angelic beings, who are also praising God and His Lamb (Rev. 5:11-12). It is likely that Daniel is referring only to angels as God's servants, as the Lamb had not yet come to the earth to shed His blood to redeem sinners.

John informs us that the Tribulation Period commences when the Son of God, the Lamb, takes a sealed scroll from the hand of His Father and opens its first seal (Rev. 5:1-17). The scroll is the title deed to the earth, and the Lord then oversees twenty-one specific judgments on the earth before His Second Advent. Presently, the Lord Jesus is on His

Father's throne (Rev. 3:21), but at the end of the Tribulation, after the last bowl judgment, He will establish His own everlasting kingdom of righteousness on the earth. Hence, Daniel is describing the Lord Jesus returning to the earth to vindicate Himself before His enemies (vv. 13-14).

Christ's Second Coming

Daniel confirms that heaven's courtroom is acutely aware of what is happening on the earth during the Tribulation Period, especially noting the pompous words and blasphemous doings of the Antichrist (v. 11). At the set time of his judgment, Christ will return to the earth to execute vengeance. The prophet Zechariah informs us that this will occur when the beast attacks God's covenant people and half the city of Jerusalem has been taken (Zech. 14:1-3). At that time, the Battle of Armageddon will occur and the Antichrist and his armies will be destroyed (Rev. 19:11-19); the Antichrist and the False Prophet will be then thrown into the Lake of Fire (Rev. 19:20). Daniel specifically mentions this outcome in verse 11. All who followed the Antichrist and persecuted the Jews will be eliminated from the earth prior to the Kingdom Age; this is called *The Judgment of Nations.*

The Lord Jesus taught about this judgment in the seventh of the Kingdom Parables found in Matthew 13:47-50. In that parable, the Lord casts a net into the sea (depicting the nations – Rev. 17:1, 15) and He sorts through what is caught. Those who did not follow the Antichrist are separated from those who did. The "good" are permitted into His kingdom; the "bad" are committed to eternal judgment. The net represents the influence of the kingdom gospel message that will be preached worldwide during the Tribulation Period (Matt. 24:14). This message consists of a warning not to worship the Antichrist and a declaration that judgment of the wicked and Christ's kingdom are coming soon (Rev. 14:6-12). The fish represent the living Gentiles who are saved during the Tribulation Period.

The Judgment of Nations is more specifically spoken of in Matthew 25:31-46 when the Lord separates the sheep (i.e., those who are allowed into the kingdom) and the goats (those who are eternally judged). Christ will punish all those who followed the Antichrist and who persecuted the Jews during the Tribulation Period (Matt. 25:40). This judgment will occur just after Christ's return to the earth at the end of the Great Tribulation (Matt. 24:21, 29, 36-41) and will not be expected by the general populace. The Judgment of Nations is carried out suddenly and those unfit for the kingdom will be abruptly removed from the earth. Daniel also previously alluded to this judgment (2:35, 44-45).

Those Gentiles who did not follow the beast will be permitted to enter into the Millennial Kingdom of Christ. Daniel speaks of this in verse 12; the dominion of the nations was taken away, but *"their lives were prolonged for a season and a time."* According to Revelation 20, that time is one thousand years. Christ's established kingdom will be over all peoples, nations, and languages of the earth and though the earth will pass away, His kingdom will last forever (v. 14).

The Interpretation

Daniel was disturbed and perplexed by the vision in his dream (v. 15). Perhaps he could better relate to the turmoil Nebuchadnezzar experienced in chapter 2 over the vivid nature of his recurring dream. God had bestowed on Daniel knowledge, wisdom, and *"understanding in all visions and dreams"* (1:17), yet on this particular occasion (and for the vision in the next chapter) Daniel was not able to make sense of what he had witnessed.

There was a throng of angels about God's throne, so Daniel asked one of them what the meaning of the vision was (v. 16). The man confirmed that each beast represented a kingdom that would rule over humanity (v. 17), but that ultimately the saints of the Most High would inherit an eternal kingdom under God's rule (v. 18). In fact, the interpretation given connects these world empires directly with the people of God, for the saints are repeatedly mentioned in the explanation (vv. 18, 21, 22, 25, and 27). This is probably the reason the interpretation of the first three beasts is not paramount – for the first and second advents of Christ would be during the rule of the dreadful and fierce beast.

The final outcome of Christ's Second Advent will be that all the saints associated with *"the Most High"* will inherit an eternal kingdom with Christ. Paul repeatedly speaks of Christians being positionally unified with the Lord in *"heavenly places"* or *"high places"* in his epistle to the Ephesians. The saints that Daniel is speaking of in verse 27 will not only include God's covenant people, but the saints from all ages, including the Tribulation saints whom the Antichrist temporarily overcomes (v. 25; Rev. 20:4): Thus, when Christ returns to the earth to establish His kingdom, He will do so *"with ten thousands of His saints"* (Jude 14). The Greek word *murias* or "myriad" is used here in the hyperbolic sense to imply an innumerable quantity. This vast host of saints, having already experienced the first resurrection, will rule and reign with the Lord in glorified bodies.

We are left to speculate as to why the Lord initially withheld the vision's meaning from Daniel. Perhaps the Lord wanted Daniel to interact with one standing near the throne to reinforce the idea that what Daniel was seeing was more than a mere dream. In the practical sense, this narrative shows us the importance of each believer in the body of Christ working together for the greater good. Even though God has equipped and gifted each member of the body and given them a calling to guide their service, this does not mean that we do not need others to broaden our understanding and assist us in the journey.

> If the Church is a living body united to the same head, governed by the same laws, and pervaded by the same Spirit, it is impossible that one part should be independent of all the rest.
>
> — Charles Hodge

Daniel was especially interested in the most vicious of the four beasts. It had ten horns, iron teeth, and bronze claws, and it broke and trampled whatever was in its way (v. 19). In posing his question, he specifically inquired about the little horn that had risen from the head of the fourth beast. This horn spoke pompous words, pulled out three of the ten existing horns, and also made war and prevailed against the saints (vv. 20-21). In the dispensation of the Law, Daniel would have understood the saints to be God's covenant people, thus referring to the nation of Israel. However, John (being in the dispensation of the Church Age) was provided further clarification: the Antichrist will oppress not only the Jews during the Tribulation Period, but also all those Gentiles who will not take his mark (Rev. 7:9-14; 13:7). We often refer to those who will not serve the ambitions of the Antichrist as Tribulation saints. This slaughter will continue until the Ancient of Days puts down his rebellion and establishes an everlasting kingdom for His people (v. 22).

The fact that the Beast is permitted to slaughter the saints during the Tribulation Period is a strong argument against the post-Tribulation rapture of the Church view (Rev. 13:7). Though the Church has been persecuted through the centuries, it has not been overcome to this degree. Speaking of the Church, the Lord promised that the *"gates of hell would not prevail against it"* (Matt. 16:18). There is no promise to protect the Church during the Tribulation Period, but only a remnant of Jews in a particular location (Rev. 12:12-17). Those Jews, not under God's protection in this specific location, will perish; Zechariah states that two-thirds of all Jews worldwide will die during *the Time of Jacob's Trouble* (Zech. 13:7-8).

The interpreter affirmed that the fourth beast would be the fourth kingdom to rule over the earth, that is, from Daniel's day forward (v. 23). However, sometime after this kingdom was established, it would be renovated by one speaking great blasphemies against the Most High. When "he" seizes control of the fourth kingdom, he will remove three of its governing authorities (as symbolized by the three horns; v. 24). In the last days of his kingdom, the Antichrist will be permitted to slaughter the saints (i.e., those who will not take his mark in the Tribulation Period); this will continue for *"a time, and times and half a time"* (three and a half years, which equals 1260 days or 42 months; v. 25). Immediately after this timeframe, the doom of the Antichrist and his followers will be executed and God will establish His own everlasting kingdom on earth in which all will obey and serve Him (vv. 26-27).

Although Daniel understood the meaning of the vision, he remained emotionally distressed by what he had witnessed (v. 28). The Jewish people had suffered much during the previous seventy years, but now Daniel knew they would face an even greater hardship in the future. Although he wrote down the vision and its meaning, he kept the revelation to himself. Apparently, it was not publicly shared until Daniel compiled his book some twenty years later. This meant that, no matter how hard the devil tried to serve Daniel as dinner to hungry lions, God would not permit his servant to perish until His purposes to be accomplished through Daniel were complete. In all these things we observe the mysterious foreknowledge of God. God is able to design the plan of salvation before time, with all the facts concerning possible permutations of events and outcomes unfolding in time. The failures of man and satanic opposition will not thwart the overall purposes of God;

rather, God's foreknowledge guarantees that faith-exercising individuals will receive His eternal blessings.

Meditation

Guidance, like all God's acts of blessing under the covenant of grace, is a sovereign act. Not merely does God will to guide us in the sense of showing us His way, that we may tread it; He wills also to guide us in the more fundamental sense of ensuring that, whatever happens, whatever mistakes we may make, we shall come safely home. Slippings and strayings there will be, no doubt, but the everlasting arms are beneath us; we shall be caught, rescued, restored. This is God's promise; this is how good He is.

— J. I. Packer

The Ram Subdues the Goat
Daniel 8

The Vision

The vision recorded in this chapter occurred two years after the one in chapter 7; it is the third year of Belshazzar's reign (v. 1). The previous vision occurred at night while Daniel was lying in his bed, presumably in his home in Babylon. We are not informed of his physical location or circumstances in this chapter, but rather that Daniel suddenly found himself in Shushan, standing by the River Ulai (v. 2).

Shushan was the winter headquarters of the Persian Empire and was located about two hundred miles east of Babylon on the Ulai Canal. This ancient city is within modern-day Iran and is sometimes referred to as Susa. In approximately sixty-six years, Esther, the wife of King Ahasuerus (Xerxes), would reside in the Shushan citadel (Est. 1:2) and forty years after that, Nehemiah would serve as King Artaxerxes' cupbearer at this same location (Neh. 1:1).

Daniel sees a ram with two long horns emerging from its head; however, the horn which appeared last grew longer than the first horn (v. 3). These two long horns gave the ram a tactical advantage as he sought to increase his dominion westward, northward, and southward (v. 4). We learn from the interpretation that the ram symbolizes the Medo-Persian Empire and that verse 4 describes the conquering strategy that it would employ. History shows that Cyrus did not seek to conquer the barbarians to the east (Alexander the Great would later defeat them), but rather his armies moved to the Black and Mediterranean Seas, and to the Persian Gulf to overcome all of western Asia and Egypt.

Indeed, the ram was invincible until a male goat with one notable, strong horn from the west suddenly appeared to challenge the ram's authority (v. 5). With tremendous speed and fury the goat quickly attacked the ram and broke off both its horns and trampled him on the ground; none had the strength or the desire to assist the ram (vv. 6-7). Until this time the cradle of humanity had been in the east: in the

Assyrian, Babylonian, and Medo-Persia Empires. The far west was thought to be a land of barbarians. Yet, for the first time in human history, a vanquishing army (portrayed by the stout male goat) suddenly appeared out of the west. Yet, as soon as this goat established his supremacy, its impressive horn was broken off and four smaller ones grew up in its place (v. 8).

The sight must have been startling to Daniel, who then witnessed the unusual event of yet another smaller horn jutting out of one of the four new horns, and then growing to prominence. The horn became powerful towards the south and the east, even to the "glorious land" of Israel (v. 9). In its wrath this horn even reached up as far as heaven to cast down some of the stars to the ground and trample them (v. 10). In contempt for God, the horn led his army to stop the Jewish sacrifices in Jerusalem by desecrating the temple (vv. 11-12). One of the "holy ones" (i.e., an angel; 4:17) explained to Daniel that the transgression of desolation would be permitted to occur for 2,300 mornings and evenings (v. 26) – after this the temple would be cleansed and proper offerings resumed (vv. 13-14).

The Interpretation

Daniel was baffled by the vision, but intensely desired to know its meaning (v. 15). The angel Gabriel appeared in human form near Daniel and was instructed by the Lord to give Daniel understanding of the vision (v. 16). Although Gabriel's visage is not described, there must have been a spectacular element to his outward manifestation to cause Daniel to fall to the ground in fear (i.e., Daniel knew that this was no ordinary man before him; v. 17). The first thing that Daniel was to realize was when the vision would be fulfilled: *"Understand, son of man, that the vision refers to the time of the end."* Although Daniel was conscious of what Gabriel was saying, he seemed to be in a deep slumber with his face to the ground (v. 18). Gabriel responded by touching Daniel and causing him to stand up so he would have Daniel's full attention, for Daniel was meant to understand what would happen during this time of indignation and when the appointed end of things shall come (v. 19).

Gabriel then identifies the Ram with the two horns (one being longer than the other) as Media and Persia, the coalition that defeated Babylon (v. 20). The representation of this alliance is also represented in the bear standing higher on one side in the previous chapter. This conveys the same meaning: the Persians became the stronger power (horn) in the coalition. The identity of the male goat is also stated: the kingdom of Greece and the large horn between its eyes represented its first king, Alexander the Great (v. 21). The leopard-like beast with four heads in the previous chapter aligns well with what is represented in the swift-moving male goat with four horns that rises up after the large horn (the first king) is broken off. Both suggest the quickness of the initial conqueror, whose kingdom would be divided in four parts after his death (v. 22). As stated in the previous chapter, this is exactly what happened to the Greek Empire. At the age of 32, Alexander the Great had conquered the known world, but died the following year; his four generals then divided his kingdom.

Then Gabriel informs Daniel of certain events that would surround a fierce king, having sinister schemes, in the latter days of the Greek Empire (v. 23). This king will powerfully destroy the mighty and then the holy people (i.e., the Jewish people; v. 24). He shall prosper through deceit, slaughter many, and exalt himself in his own heart (v. 25). His conceit and pride will cause him to challenge even the Prince of princes, who shall destroy the wicked king. Daniel was then told to seal up (to preserve in writing) the vision of the mornings and the evenings, which referred to events that would certainly unfold in a future time (v. 26). As in the previous vision, this revelation had an unnerving effect on Daniel; he felt sick for several days and could not fulfill his normal duties in the Babylonian court. He was astonished at the vision and its explanation, but no one could make sense of its meaning (v. 27).

Holocaust in Preview

Since both the Medo-Persian and Greek empires have passed away, one might wonder what possible benefit there is in considering this now fulfilled revelation. At least two benefits are suggested. First, the revelation of these world empires is obviously connected with God's estranged covenant people, and whatever concerns them touches His glory; this shows God's immense, ongoing care and concern for the Jewish people. Hamilton Smith explains a second important observation of the prophecies:

We have to remember that though these empires have *"had their dominion taken away: yet their lives were prolonged for a season and time"* (7:12). Thus, to the end of the times of the Gentiles, there will still exist nations that represent these once-powerful empires, and, at the time of the end, these nations will be found in opposition to the people of God – the Jews. This it is that gives such importance to the details of Daniel 8. It prophetically gives the history of these two empires in the day of their power, and their connection with the people of God – prophecies which have already been fulfilled. At the same time, their past history foreshadows their opposition to the people of God in the time of the end.[127]

As in most parables and prophecies within the Bible, much more is being foretold or foreshadowed than is immediately obvious. The Gentiles will continue to oppress God's covenant people long after the fall of the Medo-Persian and Greek empires. In fact, *war and desolation* are determined against them until the Second Advent of Christ (9:27).

In foretelling of the Antichrist and his endeavors during the Tribulation Period, the prophet Daniel provided a *predawn* prophecy of another evil man who would enter Israel under a banner of peace in order to slaughter the Jews (vv. 9-14, 23-27). Daniel prophesied Antiochus IV Epiphanes' assault on Israel nearly four centuries before it occurred. "Epiphanes" means "God made manifest" and Antiochus believed that he was the god Zeus.

In 168 B.C., Antiochus led a second attack on Egypt, where he had been successful two years earlier. Before Antiochus arrived in Alexandria, a Roman ambassador named Gaius Popillius Laenas blocked his path in order to deliver a message from the Roman Senate: Antiochus was warned to withdraw his army or consider himself at war with the Roman Republic. Humiliated, Antiochus capitulated and withdrew his Seleucid army. Israel, a region he governed, was on his direct route home.

Antiochus, full of rage, entered Israel in 167 BC. After learning that his appointed high priest, Menelaus, had been deposed by a small group of Jews, including Jason whom Antiochus had earlier removed from that office, he sought vengeance on the Jewish people. Pretending to come in peace, a force of 22,000 soldiers entered Jerusalem.[128] They attacked the city on the Sabbath, knowing that orthodox Jews would not fight on their holy day (1 Mac. 1:31-35; 2 Mac. 5:24-26). As predicted by Daniel, the false pretenses of peace, the immense slaughter, the temple desecration, and the sacrifices being stopped all took place (11:31-32). The Abomination of Desolation that Daniel foretold then commenced: pigs were offered to Zeus on an altar erected on the Bronze Altar of burnt offerings (1 Mac. 1:54-61). As Antiochus considered himself to be Zeus, these sacrifices were in his honor. Many women and children were captured and made slaves. Jerusalem was plundered and burned. Judas Maccabeus, a leader in the Jewish uprising, wrote of the heartbreaking incident:

> When these happenings were reported to the king, he thought that Judea was in revolt. Raging like a wild animal, he set out from Egypt and took Jerusalem by storm. He ordered his soldiers to cut down without mercy those whom they met and to slay those who took refuge in their houses. There was a massacre of young and old, a killing of women and children, a slaughter of virgins and infants. In the space of three days, eighty thousand were lost, forty thousand meeting a violent death, and the same number being sold into slavery (2 Mac. 5:11-14).

Daniel also prophesied that a remnant of Jews would rise up against Antiochus and drive him from their beloved city (11:32). It is likely that Antiochus departed and then returned to Jerusalem the following year to deal with the growing Jewish rebellion. Antiochus again left Jerusalem to deal with political unrest in Armenia and Persia. After hearing of yet another Jewish uprising, he sent Lysias to Jerusalem to exterminate the Jewish people, and to confiscate and redistribute their land (1 Mac. 3:32-36). Lysias was soundly defeated by Judas Maccabeus and his freedom fighters on several occasions during the next year (1 Mac. 4:1-28) and he finally withdrew from the region. After three years of intense fighting, the Jews won their liberation, recaptured Jerusalem, and regained control of the temple.

How does the prophecy of 2,300 "mornings and evenings" fit within the historical framework of this era? "Mornings and evenings" was a common Semitic idiom meaning days and nights or complete days. If the reference is to a literal full day, this period would span 6.3 years and refer to the entire situation in which Antiochus interfered with Jewish worship, beginning in 170 B.C. after returning to Israel from Egypt (after defeating Ptolemy VI) until he was defeated by

Jewish freedom fighters in late 164 B.C. Correlating the historical text from the books of First and Second Maccabees, Russell Earl Kelly supplies the following explanation supporting that the defilement pertains to 2,300 days, or six plus years:

1 Mac. 1:10	175 B.C.: 137th Seleucid year; Antiochus begins to reign
1 Mac. 1:10-15	171 B.C.: desolating covenant to worship Greek gods
2 Mac. 4:7-18	neglected sacrifices
1 Mac. 1:16-19	Antiochus plunders Egypt
1 Mac. 1:20-28	169 B.C.: plunders temple
1 Mac. 1:29-64	167 B.C.: plundered Jerusalem
1 Mac. 1:39	completely stopped sanctuary services
1 Mac. 1:43-53	sacrificed pig; death decree
1 Mac. 1:54-64	sets up a desolating sacrilege inside the temple
2 Mac. 6:1, 2	"compel the Jews to forsake the laws of their fathers and cease to live by the laws of God, and also to **pollute the temple** in Jerusalem and call it the temple of Olympian Zeus."
1 Mac. 4:42-58	164 B.C.: sanctuary cleansed; Antiochus died
2 Mac. 10:1-8	sanctuary purified[129]

The 2,300 literal day interpretation of the prophecy is hence supported by historical evidence; yet, many commentators believe the prophecy refers to the total cessation of morning and evening sacrifices over a period of 1,150 days. If this is what Daniel meant, this span of time aligns well with the record of the Jewish historian Josephus. He notes that there was exactly three years from the time when "their Divine worship was fallen off, and was reduced to a profane and common use," until the time when the lamps were lighted again, and the worship restored.[130] Yet, in his *Jewish Wars*, he says that Antiochus "spoiled the temple, and put a stop to the constant practice of offering a daily sacrifice of expiation for three years and six months."[131] The 1,150 days would fall within these two differing durations supplied by Josephus.

Albert Barnes favors the 2,300 literal day view and offers this general explanation for the slight disparity between the biblical duration (v. 14) and varying historical records:

The variety may be accounted for by the supposition that separate epochs are referred to at the starting point in the calculation. The truth was, there were several decisive acts in the history of Antiochus that led to the ultimate desolation of Jerusalem, and at one time a writer may have contemplated one, and at another time another. Thus, there was the act by which Jason, made high priest by Antiochus, was permitted to set up a gymnasium in Jerusalem after the manner of the pagan (Prideaux, iii. 216; Dan. 8:9), and the things which attracted the attention of Daniel were, that he "waxed great," and made war on "the host of heaven," and "cast some of the host and of the stars to the ground" (Dan. 8:10), and "magnified himself against the prince of the host" (Dan. 8:11) – acts which refer manifestly to his attack on the people of God, and the priests or ministers of religion, and on God himself as the "prince of the host" – unless this phrase should be understood as referring rather to the high priest. We are then rather to look to the whole series of events as included within the two thousand and three hundred days, than the period in which literally the daily sacrifice was forbidden by a solemn statute. It was practically suspended, and the worship of God interrupted during all that time.[132]

In summary, we have an idea of the approximate duration in which the Jewish offerings were suspended, but we cannot confirm, historically speaking, the exact number of days in which Antiochus interfered with proper temple worship in Jerusalem. It is generally asserted that on December 16, 164 B.C., about three years after its desecration, the temple was cleansed and rededicated to Jehovah (1 Mac. 4:52-58). This Jewish triumph was still being celebrated annually in the days of Christ as the Feast of Dedication (John 10:22); however, it is more often identified today by its Hebrew name *Hanukkah*.

Antiochus died of a sudden disease in 164 B.C., shortly after he withdrew from Jerusalem to engage invaders from the east. He challenged the Prince of princes (God's sovereignty) and was therefore *"broken without human means"* (v. 25). He is a type of the future Antichrist in that he desecrated the Jewish altar, stopped the Jewish sacrifices, sought to eradicate the Jewish people in a time of peace, and died shortly after. Likewise, Daniel is forecasting that a time of peace and safety will briefly exist in Israel just before the Antichrist strikes the Jewish nation. In the last half of the Tribulation Period, he will seemingly convince the world that the Jews are at the root of all the world's problems and they must be eliminated. Thus, the immense carnage during the Babylonian invasion of Jeremiah's day serves as a precursor to more devastating events yet to come upon the Jewish people during the Tribulation Period.

When the abomination of desolation occurs at the midpoint in the Tribulation Period, there will also be war in heaven. The archangel Michael, along with his angels, will war against the devil and his fallen angels in order to constrain them (all evil forces) to the earth (12:1; Rev. 12:7-10). Satan, knowing that his time is short, will be enraged and seek to exterminate the Jewish people (Rev. 12:12-15). However, the Lord will preserve and protect a remnant of His covenant people from harm (Rev. 12:16-17).

During the Tribulation, there will be 144,000 Jews who are actively testifying of Jehovah (Rev. 7:4-8) and there will also be angels heralding the gospel message as they fly over the earth (Rev. 14:6-12). The devil knows that salvation is possible only while an individual is alive to choose Christ: *"And as it is appointed for men to die once, but after this the judgment"* (Heb. 9:27). Accordingly, he will attempt to exterminate all those who honor Jehovah and those who might hear and trust the kingdom gospel message. Satan will spare only those willing to take the mark of the beast and to worship him. The Lord Jesus spoke of the horrific holocaust of life during this time:

> *For then there will be great tribulation, such as has not been since the beginning of the world until this time, no, nor ever shall be. And unless those days were shortened, no flesh would be saved; but for the elect's sake those days will be shortened* (Matt. 24:21-22).

If the Lord tarried longer than the appointed time to return to the earth, there would be no flesh left on the planet. Before the Tribulation Period concludes, the Antichrist will slaughter two-thirds of all Jews worldwide (Zech. 13:7-8). Daniel foretold that the Antichrist, as typified by evil Antiochus, would be defeated without human means – God would destroy him (v. 25). Indeed, the Lord Jesus Christ will descend at the end of the Tribulation Period to protect and deliver His covenant people. As mentioned earlier, Jerusalem will be partially conquered when the Lord descends to engage the Antichrist at the battle of Armageddon (Zech. 14). This conflict will occur in the Megiddo Valley where the armies of the world will have assembled against the Jewish nation. The Lord will completely obliterate them all with just an utterance from His mouth (Rev. 19:11-20). Spiritual wickedness in high places and the masses of humanity under demonic delusion are no match for the Creator and Sustainer of all things!

Meditation

Zion's King shall reign victorious,
All the earth shall own His sway;
He will make His kingdom glorious,
He will reign through endless day.

Nations now from God estranged,
Then shall see a glorious light,
Night to day shall then be changed,
Heaven shall triumph in the sight.

Then shall Israel, long dispersed,
Mourning seek the Lord their God,
Look on Him whom once they pierced,
Own and kiss the chastening rod.

— Thomas Kelly

Prayer and Answers
Daniel 9

We are for a third time introduced to King Darius, the Mede who conquered the city of Babylon under the authority of Cyrus the Persian. Therefore, the *"the first year of Darius"* in verse 1 is the same as *"the first year of Cyrus king of Persia"* (Ezra 1:1); both phrases relate to the year following the overthrow of Babylon in October of 539 B.C. In 538 B.C. Cyrus would fulfill the prophecies of both Isaiah and Jeremiah. For example, nearly two centuries prior to this, Isaiah had foretold that a king named Cyrus would be a great conqueror and would be used of God to rebuild His temple (Isa. 44:28-45:1). The prophecy was uttered during the days of the Assyrian Empire. This is an incredible prophecy in that it names both the individual and his future feats at a time when Solomon's Temple still stood and when Israel was still an autonomous Jewish state.

Later, but just prior to the time of the Jewish exile, Jeremiah prophesied that the Jewish captivity in Babylon would last only seventy years (Jer. 25:11-12, 29:10); with the overthrow of the Babylonian empire the Jews would be liberated and be permitted to return to their homeland. We learn in this chapter that Daniel, now likely in his early eighties, had lived through the sixty-six-year Babylonian Empire. Furthermore, Daniel now understood that Jeremiah's prophesied seventy-year exile period was being fulfilled by the Persian victory (v. 2). God had severely chastened the Jews for their idolatry, but He had also kept His promise to *"not make an end of them"* (Jer. 30:11) and He would bring them home again.

The number seventy is associated with the nation of Israel in a special way throughout Scripture. Genesis 46 provides the first roster of the nation, which included the names of those in Jacob's family who traveled with him to Egypt. In all, sixty-six sons and grandsons are named. Counting Joseph and his two sons, who were already in Egypt, and Jacob himself, the total number of males composing the nation of

Israel at this time was seventy (Gen. 46:5). There were seventy elders of Israel (Num. 11:16). During New Testament times, there were seventy members of the Sanhedrin and seventy witnesses sent out to Israel by Christ (Luke 10:1). As already mentioned, this thread of seventy and Israel can also be seen in the books of Jeremiah and Daniel where it is related to the regathering of the Jewish people to their homeland.

After comprehending the meaning of Jeremiah's prophecy, Daniel was burdened to fast and pray for the restoration of his people; he did so in sackcloth and ashes to demonstrate his shame and humility before the Lord (v. 3). He now understood that God had fulfilled Jeremiah's prophecy, but beyond the intellectual assessment, the prophecy was exercising his heart and conscience. H. A. Ironside explains:

> Daniel was not merely interested in the prophecy from an intellectual standpoint. The mere computing of times and seasons could not satisfy this devout man of God; but when he learned from his Bible that the time had almost drawn near for the people of Judah to be restored to their land, it stirred him to the very depths of his soul, and brought him down to his knees. He might have said, "If it is God's purpose to restore His people, He will carry that purpose out, whatever their condition, and I need not concern myself about this matter." But no, Daniel realized that when God is about to work, He begins by exercising His people that they may be restored in soul if they have wandered from Him and thus blessing would result upon their being brought into the place of self-judgment and humiliation before Him.[133]

God forbid that we explore His Word to merely gain knowledge of facts and historical information and miss His grander prerogatives of displaying His goodness and of confronting our sin, wrong attitudes, and lack of consecration! It is quite possible for believers to become focused on, and even argue about, meaningless things, such as dates, genealogies, names, historical customs, etc. and in the process to obscure the important message God has for us. *The Word of God is living and powerful ... is a Discerner of the thoughts and intents of the heart"* (Heb. 4:12), meaning that we want God's Word to have its way with us, just as it did with Daniel.

Daniel was moved to pray after understanding God's Word in the prophecy of Jeremiah. His prayer has three main segments: First, an upright Daniel identified with his unrighteous countrymen and acknowledged *their* sins against the Lord: sins of envy, pride, rebellion, and disobedience (vv. 3-7). Second, he affirms that God righteously vindicated His name by severely chastening His wayward people (vv. 8-15). Third, Daniel pleads for mercy on behalf of his countrymen (vv. 16-19). The answer to Daniel's prayers was a manifestation of God's grace – divine understanding of the mind of God was afforded to him through Gabriel (vv. 20-27).

In assessing the sorrowful history of his people, Daniel could have commenced his prayer by accusing his forefathers and the leaders in his day of negligence and failure. If anyone could argue that they were suffering in a foreign land because of the sins of others, it would be Daniel. But we do not see Daniel praying as the proud Pharisee did: *"God, I thank You that I am not like other men – extortioners, unjust, adulterers..."* (Luke 18:11). Rather, because Israel's sins were known among the nations, Daniel personally owns the sin of his countrymen and pleads with God on the basis of what the nations knew nothing about – the longsuffering and covenant-keeping nature of Israel's God. Hence, Daniel pleads for mercy and forgiveness for Israel (vv. 8-9). They had failed as a people to represent Jehovah properly among the nations (v. 10). Hence, Daniel openly confesses *their* sin to the Lord, stating He was righteous in chastening *them* for *their* disobedience:

Yes, all Israel has transgressed Your law, and has departed so as not to obey Your voice; therefore the curse and the oath written in the Law of Moses the servant of God have been poured out on us, because we have sinned against Him (v. 11).

Knowing the greatness of the Lord provides a believer with a better perspective in discerning the spiritual state of His people. Daniel is therefore able to properly discern the pitiful moral and spiritual condition of his countrymen. On this point Hamilton Smith writes:

Daniel recognizes that this low moral condition lies at the root of all the division and scattering that have come in among the people of God. He does not seek to place the blame for the division and scattering upon certain individuals, who may indeed have acted in a high-handed manner and perverted the truth and led many into error. This, we know, was the case with the kings, priests and false prophets. But, looking beyond the failure of individuals, he sees, and owns, the failure of God's people as a whole.[134]

Daniel's behavior is a sign of deep brokenness before the Lord, says William MacDonald:

> We need to be so broken that we will confess the sins of God's people as our own. This is what Daniel did (9:3-19). He was not personally guilty of most of the sins he catalogued. But he identified himself so closely with the nation of Israel that their sins became his sin. In this he reminds us, of course, of the One who "took our sins and our sorrows and made them His very own." And the lesson for us is that instead of criticizing other believers and pointing the accusing finger, we should confess their sins as if they were our own.[135]

About a century into the future, the honorable scribe Ezra will likewise identify with God's wayward covenant people and plead for mercy, though the Jewish nation was undeserving of it. Neither Ezra nor Daniel was personally guilty of moral or religious failure, but they realized that as part of Jehovah's covenant people, they had failed to obey God's law and to declare His glory to the Gentiles. We can learn a lot from Daniel's example of prayer, says H. A. Ironside:

> When we look around, and see the failure in the Church, the fleshliness and the worldliness that prevail on every hand, let us not be content to pass our judgment upon them, and lift up our hearts in spiritual pride...but oh, let us remember that we too are part of that Church which has failed. We cannot dissociate ourselves from other Christians; we have to take our place with them, and bow our heads in the presence of God and own that we have sinned. If we could remember this always, it would cure us of railing against the people of God who have less light than we have, or than we fancy we have.[136]

Daniel then affirms that God's extensive destruction of Jerusalem and of the temple was fully justified because He was honoring His own word – He did what He said He would do (v. 12)! To humbly agree with God that our sin must be punished to uphold the integrity of His name, and that we must turn away from our sin to receive His forgiveness and blessing is a sign of spiritual maturity (vv. 13-15). We choose our sin, but God chooses the consequences of our sin. Daniel understood that it is always best to accept God's chastening as an expression of His parental love, rather than further stiffening our necks against Him and going our own way (Heb. 12:6).

Come to the Savior now, He gently calls thee;
In true repentance bow, before Him bend the knee.
Come to the Savior now, you who have wandered far;
Renew your solemn vow, for His by right you are;
Come, like poor, wandering sheep returning to His fold;
His arm will safely keep, His love will never grow cold.

— John Wigner

After acknowledging Israel's sins and their deserved judgment, Daniel earnestly pled on behalf of the nation for God to turn away His righteous indignation and again bless His people:

O Lord, according to all Your righteousness, I pray, let Your anger and Your fury be turned away from Your city Jerusalem, Your holy mountain; because for our sins, and for the iniquities of our fathers, Jerusalem and Your people are a reproach to all those around us. Now therefore, our God, hear the prayer of Your servant, and his supplications, and for the Lord's sake cause Your face to shine on Your sanctuary, which is desolate. O my God, incline Your ear and hear; open Your eyes and see our desolations, and the city which is called by Your name; for we do not present our supplications before You because of our righteous deeds, but because of Your great mercies. O Lord, hear! O Lord, forgive! O Lord, listen and act! Do not delay for Your own sake, my God, for Your city and Your people are called by Your name (vv. 16-19).

It is a heart-wrenching prayer that boldly approaches God in the confidence of His own character and attributes as revealed in Scripture: *"We do not present our supplications before You because of our righteous deeds, but because of Your great mercies"* (v. 18). Amen! The patient and merciful nature of God is a good reminder to us to continue to plead with those who have stumbled morally or who have displaced God with vain things. Understanding this wonderful truth, Daniel pleads for the city, the holy mountain, the sanctuary and the people in relationship to God's ownership, not his or the nation's association with each; forgive for the sake of *"Your city," "Your holy mountain," "Your sanctuary,"* and *"Your people."* Daniel rises above all the failures of the people and pleads with God to esteem again what is His and what is associated with His name and glory! Daniel wanted to see God's great name receive all the honor it deserved from what God had deemed special to Him, and to no one else!

The content of Daniel's prayer can be summarized by the three occurrences of the word "face" in this chapter:

First, Daniel, a righteous man, set his *"face toward the Lord God to make request by prayer and supplications, with fasting, sackcloth, and ashes"* (v. 3). Daniel epitomizes what James will later exhort believers to do: *"Confess your trespasses to one another, and pray for one another, that you may be healed. The effective, fervent prayer of a righteous man avails much"* (Jas. 5:16).

Second, Daniel acknowledges the sins of the Jewish nation which have resulted in *"shame of face"* (v. 8). God had chosen the Jews to stand forth as *"a light to the nations"* (Isa. 49:6), that is, as a witness to the entire world of God's faithfulness, mercy, and patience. However, in their rebellious condition, the Jews did not represent God as a holy people – the outcome of which was shame.

Third, Daniel requested that God would shine His face on His sanctuary again (v. 17). Otherwise stated, Daniel was anticipating that through genuine repentance, God would indeed forgive and again bless His covenant people with His presence (vv. 18-19). Daniel was comforted by the fact that God would certainly glorify Himself, despite Israel's ruined testimony, because of His longsuffering and forgiving nature. Indeed, in a future day, when God's covenant people are restored to Him once and for all, the entire world will marvel at God's patient, forgiving nature and His steadfast faithfulness to His word.

Daniel's Seventy-Week Prophecy

As is often the case in Scripture, those devoted to God's Word are blessed with more divine revelation and understanding. Daniel continued in steadfast prayer, but, around 3 o'clock in the afternoon (the time of the evening sacrifice), he noticed the angel Gabriel flying towards him with great speed (vv. 20-21). Although it had been about twelve years since their previous encounter (chp. 8), Daniel immediately recognized Gabriel. Gabriel confirmed four things to Daniel (vv. 22-23): First, God had heard his prayers. Second, he had been sent in response to Daniel's petitions. Third, Gabriel was to provide Daniel with further understanding of the visions he had seen. Fourth, Gabriel confirmed that Daniel was "greatly beloved" by the Lord – a declaration that would thrill the heart of any saint.

Daniel had already been blessed by studying the prophecies of Jeremiah. He had come to understand that Jeremiah's dual seventy-year prophecies related to the timetable for the end of Jewish exile in Babylon and the renewal of agricultural blessing in Israel. Now God, through Gabriel, would share with Daniel His ultimate timetable (a seventy-week prophecy) which revealed God's plan for Israel's ultimate restoration and blessing:

Know therefore and understand, that from the going forth of the command to restore and build Jerusalem until Messiah the Prince, there shall be seven weeks and sixty-two weeks; the street shall be built again, and the wall, even in troublesome times. And after the sixty-two weeks Messiah shall be cut off, but not for Himself; and the people of the prince who is to come shall destroy the city and the sanctuary. The end of it shall be with a flood, and till the end of the war desolations are determined. Then he shall confirm a covenant with many for one week; but in the middle of the week he shall bring an end to sacrifice and offering and on the wing of abominations shall be one who makes desolate, even until the consummation, which is determined, is poured out on the desolate (vv. 24-27).

The foundational prophecy is broken into two major parts: sixty-nine weeks, which consists of two portions of seven weeks and sixty-two weeks, and then the final section of one week. The Hebrew word *shabua* is translated "week," but literally means "seven," much like our English word dozen means twelve of something. The "something" is determined by the context. What seven of something is Daniel speaking of? Based on how the final week is described elsewhere in Scripture, we are able to conclude that a week is speaking of seven years. The abomination of desolation committed by the Antichrist (the one who will make a peace covenant with the Jewish nation for one week) occurs in the middle of the week (Dan. 8:25; 9:27; Matt. 24:15; 2 Thess. 2:4). But Scripture elsewhere provides the exact timing of this event. It occurs "a time (1), times (2), and half a time (1/2)" after the start of the week of years (Dan. 7:25; 12:7; Rev. 12:14). This three and a half times is also equal to 1260 days (Rev. 12:6) or 42 months (Rev. 13:5). As just witnessed in the fulfillment of Jeremiah's seventy-year prophecy, a Jewish prophetic year in Scripture is consistently 360 days (12 months x 30 days/month = 360 days). Three and a half years would then be equal to 1260 days (3.5 years x 360 days/year = 1260 days). Thus, Daniel's prophecy is unmistakably speaking of seventy weeks of years or, literally, "seventy sevens."

Only Calvary could be referred to by the phrases *"to make an end of sin"* and *"to make reconciliation for iniquity."* The passage is thus Messianic in nature since it speaks of Christ being cut off and establishing everlasting righteousness among His people. Daniel's first sixty-nine weeks of years (or 173,880 days) spans the time from the command to rebuild Jerusalem (given to Nehemiah by Persian king Artaxeres Longimanus) to the time of Christ's death ("Messiah shall be cut off"). Included in this period were the seven sevens or forty-nine years to fully rebuild the walls and the city of Jerusalem (i.e., in fifth century B.C.).

It is obvious that this prophetic clock pertaining to the Jews stopped temporarily after their Messiah was cut off. The evidence for this is within the prophecy itself. The destruction of Jerusalem by the Romans occurred in A.D. 70, some thirty-eight years after Messiah was cut off, yet there is only one week (seven years) left in the prophecy after the death of Messiah. Also, the prophecy speaks of the destruction of Jerusalem as occurring after the cutting off of Messiah but before Antichrist's covenant with Israel. When Israel rejected her Messiah, her prophetic clock was temporarily stopped. Once the Antichrist signs the peace treaty with Israel, the prophetic clock will begin its final seven-year countdown and the Tribulation Period will start.

Both the starting point and the ending point of Daniel's prophecy are fixed. There would be sixty-nine weeks of years or 173,880 days (69 weeks x 7 years/week x 360 days/Jewish year = 173,880 days) from the command of Artaxerxes Longimanus to Nehemiah to rebuild the wall about Jerusalem (March 14, 445 B.C.) until Messiah's final presentation in Jerusalem (April 6, AD 32) and subsequent death.[137] The exact date will vary depending on the chronology used to date the command to rebuild. But like Jeremiah's seventy-week prophecies, the sixty-nine-week portion of Daniel's prophecy has been precisely fulfilled. The final week, associated with the Jewish nation, will begin with the signing of a covenant with the Antichrist. Since Daniel's seventieth week (v. 27) is associated with a seven-year period in which the Antichrist will rule the world (this period begins with a peace treaty with Israel), the time of tribulation in Matthew 24 must be the same as Daniel's seventieth week (the time of Jacob's trouble; Jer. 30:7).

The following diagram provides an overview of major prophetic events in relationship to Daniel's seventy-week prophecy.

BIBLE PROPHECY OVERVIEW

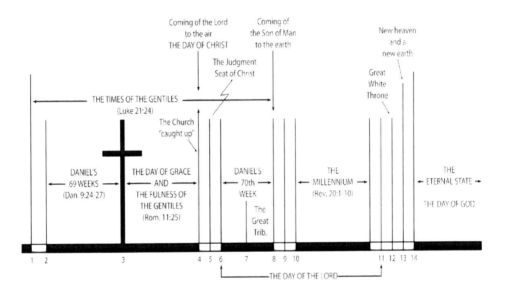

1. The Times of the Gentiles (Jer. 25:1)
2. Decree to rebuild Jerusalem (Neh. 2:1-8)
3. The cross of our Lord Jesus Christ (Luke 23:33)
4. The coming of the Lord to the air (1 Thess. 4:16-17)
5. The Judgment Seat of Christ (2 Cor. 5:10)
6. The 70th week of Daniel's prophecy (Dan. 9:26-27)
7. The Great Tribulation (Matt. 24:21)
8. The coming of the Son of Man (2 Thess. 2:7-8; Matt. 24:30)
9. The judgment of the living nations (Matt. 25:31-33)
10. The Millennium (Rev. 20:4-6)
11. The final rebellion (Rev. 20:7-9)
12. The judgment of the Great White Throne (Rev. 20:11-15)
13. The new heaven and the new earth (Rev. 21:1-5)
14. The eternal state (2 Pet. 1:11; 3:11-12)

Daniel's Seventy-Week prophecy also shows that God is maintaining a clear theological distinction between the Jewish nation and the Church, at least through the Millennial Kingdom (i.e., Rev. 20). The following figure graphically portrays God's plan of salvation for Israel (in the seventy-week prophecy) and the Church (which Christ builds after the 69th week concludes, but before the 70th week commences).

**GOD'S SALVATION FOR
ISRAEL AND THE CHURCH**

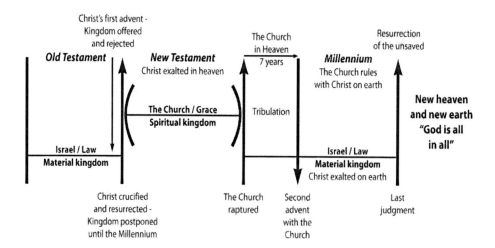

The broadest spiritual division among people living on the earth at any time would be saints and the lost – those who have been justified in Christ and those who have not. Yet the New Testament clearly identifies three human subcategories which anticipate the future working of God. Paul instructs believers to *"give no offense, either to the Jews or the Gentiles or to the Church of God"* (1 Cor. 10:32). The unconverted nation of Israel and unregenerate Gentiles were not to be stumbled from hearing the gospel. Quoting Amos and Peter, James explains that God has a different plan for saving Gentiles than He does for restoring the Jewish nation:

> *Simon has declared how God at the first visited the Gentiles to take out of them a people for His name. And with this the words of the prophets agree, just as it is written: "After this I will return and will rebuild the tabernacle of David, which has fallen down; I will rebuild its ruins, and I will set it up; so that the rest of mankind may seek the Lord, even all the Gentiles who are called by My name, says the Lord who does all these things"* (Acts 15:14-17).

Jehovah would call a people His children that were not His people (Hos. 2:23), and then He would rebuild the Jewish nation to become a beacon of divine truth among the nations (Amos 9:11-12). This is why Paul was so zealous to share the gospel with his fellow countrymen: *"Brethren, my heart's desire and prayer to God for Israel is that they may be saved"* (Rom. 10:1). He knew Israel's future, but it was not to be in his lifetime.

Presently, God is calling to Himself a people (Gentiles) that had no hope and no God (Eph. 2:11). When the Church is complete, the Lord Jesus shall descend to the clouds and with a trump and a shout gather all who are His from the earth. This will happen in the twinkling of an eye (1 Thess. 4:13-18; 1 Cor. 15:51-52). Then He shall begin to spiritually refine and awaken the Jewish nation and, after their conversion, establish the throne of David forever. While the Church is raptured vertically to meet Christ in the clouds prior to the Tribulation (1 Thess. 4:13-18), all Jews worldwide will be gathered horizontally back to the land of Israel to worship Him there at the end of the Tribulation Period (Ezek. 39:28-29).

Summary

After the Church Age is complete, the Lord will again refine and restore His covenant people, the Jews (Rom. 11:25). This time period correlates with the Tribulation Period which concludes with the Second Advent of Christ to the earth. This will be a visible coming in which the entire world will see the glory of Christ (Matt. 24:30; Luke 17:24). This timeframe corresponds to the final week (i.e., seven years) in Daniel's seventy-week prophecy (vv. 25-27). Jehovah is not finished with the Jewish nation, for He decreed an everlasting covenant with Abraham's descendants through Jacob. Jehovah is a covenant-keeping God and He has established irrevocable promises that He must fulfill.

Meditation

The first time [Christ] came to slay sin in men. The second time He will come to slay men in sin.

— Arthur Pink

Infidelity and Loyalty

The second coming of Christ will be so revolutionary that it will change every aspect of life on this planet. Christ will reign in righteousness. Disease will be arrested. Death will be modified. War will be abolished. Nature will be changed. Man will live as it was originally intended he should live.

— Billy Graham

Glory and Warfare
Daniel 10

To understand the ramifications of this chapter we must first be aware of what was happening in Jerusalem (Ezra 3) while Daniel is first praying and then dialoging with an angel in Babylon. The amnesty edict of Cyrus was issued in 538 B.C. and sometime afterwards the Jews departed in several groups, many arriving in their homeland during the first half of 536 B.C. A few months after reoccupying various cities throughout Judah, the Jewish returnees *"gathered together as one man to Jerusalem"* to set up an altar on the first day of the seventh month of the same year (Ezra 3:1). This would be early September 536 B.C. or as Daniel reckons, *"the third year of Cyrus"* (v. 1). The altar was erected among the remains of the previous temple.

Some 50,000 Jews had responded to Cyrus' amnesty decree and had returned to Israel. Cyrus had tasked these Jews with rebuilding the temple, but, before the work on the temple could commence, God's sacrificial system for atoning for His people's sins had to be reinstated. The altar and its sacrifices at Jerusalem marked the Jews as a distinctive people among the nations. Although the Jews were surrounded by opposition in their own homeland, they bravely erected an altar among the debris on the temple mount and began sacrificing on it. It had been fifty years since worship and sacrifices had been offered to Jehovah in Jerusalem. Militarily speaking, they were unarmed and outnumbered; their only defense was Jehovah. They were desperate and their only course of action was to obey God's Word which required morning and evening sacrifices to be offered, and to put themselves under the efficacy of those sacrifices, wholly trusting in their God. It is during this timeframe that Daniel is made aware of the intense angelic battle raging beyond what is seen, the outcome of which would determine the affairs of men.

Like his predecessor Moses (Ex. 34:9), Daniel owns the sins of the nation and, as we saw in the previous chapter, he confesses them as his own. The horrific conditions in Jerusalem were not the fallout from the Babylonian Empire, but rather of their own disobedience to God's Word. This realization and the further revelation that Daniel had received previously concerning the future suffering of his people prompted him to fast and mourn before the Lord for twenty-one days (vv. 2-3).

Daniel knew that his God was a covenant-keeping God and that, despite Jewish failure, God was obligated to keep His Word: *"For what if some did not believe? Will their unbelief make the faithfulness of God without effect? Certainly not! Indeed, let God be true but every man a liar"* (Rom. 3:3-4). Consequently, in times of persecution and failure, it would be profitable for Christians to mourn and weep before the Lord and then to remember and proclaim His promises, such as: *"I will build My church, and the gates of Hades shall not prevail against it"* (Matt. 16:18). Grief and fear often walk together, but fear staggers behind when genuine brokenness and faith join to bear up grief. Then mourning is displaced by joy and the hand of God prevails in our circumstances.

> With one consent we meekly bow beneath Thy chastening hand,
> And, pouring forth confession meet, mourn with our mourning land;
> With pitying eye behold our need, as thus we lift our prayer;
> Correct us with Thy judgments, Lord, then let Thy mercy spare.

> — John Hampden Gurney

The Heavenly Visitor

The narrative continues by providing an exact date for the events of the final three chapters: *"the twenty-fourth day of the first month"* (v. 4). However, we do not know if Daniel is referring to the Jewish calendar or Babylonian. Being in Babylon, it is more likely that he is referring to Tishri as the first month (which is the seventh month in the Jewish calendar). If that assumption is correct, Daniel's prayers would have coincided with the erection and cleaning of the altar in Jerusalem by the post-exilic Jews (Ezra 3:8).

After three weeks of mourning in prayer and fasting, Daniel and a few companions journeyed to the bank of the Tigris River, where they were met by a heavenly visitor (vv. 2-4). After seeing a brilliant light, the men with Daniel fled and hid themselves, but Daniel remained and he alone saw the vision (v. 7). Daniel provides a description of the man who was suddenly standing before him: he was wearing a white linen robe which was girded about the waist with gold; his countenance was as bright as lightning, his body like beryl, his eyes like torches of fire, and his arms and feet shone like burnished bronze (v. 5). The words of this individual sounded like the voice of a multitude of people speaking in unison (v. 6).

No doubt Daniel was debilitated because of three weeks of fasting, but the sight of this man was so overpowering that his remaining strength instantly dissipated (v. 8). Since Daniel had interacted with the angel Gabriel on two previous occasions, it would seem that the glorious figure before him was not Gabriel. Whether the eighty-plus-year-old Daniel fell down during this ordeal is unknown, but he apparently passed out and was face down on the ground. Although drowsy, Daniel could still discern the majestic sound of the words being uttered; however, none of these were recorded (v. 9).

The description of the heavenly visitor is nearly identical to John's description of Christ when He suddenly appeared to John (Rev. 1). The elderly John was also overwhelmed by the magnificent sight and fell to the ground as a dead man (Rev. 1:17). Commentators are divided as to whom Daniel initially saw in his vision. There are two suitable explanations. First, Daniel was privileged to see a theophany of Christ (vv. 5-9, 16-17), but it is an angelic messenger (perhaps Gabriel) who later arouses Daniel from his near-comatose state in verse 10. Obviously, Christ as the Son of God could not be hindered by the prince (demon) of Persia (v. 13; Jude 9), but a holy angel of lesser power could be, as verified by the text. The second option is that the person described in verses 5-9 is actually an angel who is permitted to reflect the glories of Christ, as is the case in Revelation 10:1.

The grammatical construction of verses 10-15 seems to favor the second understanding, until verse 16, when Daniel and the original angelic messenger are joined by another being of a yet more glorious countenance (perhaps the one described in verses 5-9). It is also evident from chapter 12 that there are actually two other heavenly beings with the original angelic messenger. H. A. Ironside and Albert Barnes hold the view that there is a single angelic messenger throughout, while other commentators, such as William Kelly, C. I. Scofield, James Vernon McGee, and Matthew Henry hold the two-person view (i.e., Christ and an angel). The latter writes:

399

> Christ appeared to Daniel in a glorious form, and it should engage us to think highly and honorably of Him … When the angel had told the prophet of the things to come, he was to return, and oppose the decrees of the Persian kings against the Jews."[138]

This conclusion does seem to be the better of the two opinions. Regardless of which view is correct, the sudden and spectacular appearance of this heavenly visitor displaying the character and glory of God dazed and incapacitated an already frail Daniel.

The Heavenly Messenger

The unnamed angel first touched the trembling Daniel, strengthening him to stand upright. He then told Daniel not to be fearful, for he was greatly beloved. Furthermore, he had been sent to give Daniel understanding of the vision he had seen concerning his people (vv. 10-11). The angel explained to Daniel that he had been dispatched by the Lord twenty-one days previously (i.e., the very day that Daniel had chosen to humble himself in prayer before the Lord), but he had been hindered by a more powerful fallen angel identified as *"the prince of Persia"* (v. 12). The mighty archangel Michael intervened to permit him to complete his mission and to deliver God's message to Daniel (v. 13).

When Lucifer led a rebellion in heaven and was cast out of God's presence, he likely took a third of the angels with him (Isa. 14:12-15; Rev. 12:3-4, 9). These fallen angels have various biblical distinctions and evil agencies: demons, spirits of divination, foul spirits, unclean spirits, and familiar spirits. Like the holy angels, fallen angels have ranks of differing authority and power (Eph. 6:12). Apparently, the angel sent to Daniel was opposed by a fallen angel of greater authority – one that Satan had assigned to manage his agenda in the Persian Empire. We cannot really imagine the spiritual warfare behind world affairs, especially in the dealings of God's covenant people, whom the devil hates.

The messenger had been sent to assist Daniel to understand what God would accomplish for His covenant people in the latter days (v. 14). After learning of the spiritual battle raging about him, an overwhelmed Daniel further regressed into a state of silent despondence (v. 15). However, when *"one having the likeness of the sons of men"* touched Daniel's lips, he found that he had the strength to audibly express how sorrowful and weary he felt (vv. 16-17). Daniel was then further invigorated by a second touch from *"the one having the likeness of men"* (v. 18). According to verse 19, the individual touching Daniel is also the angel speaking to Daniel.

The angel affirms to Daniel God's love and peace and instructs him to be strong. Daniel realizes that he now has the physical and emotional wherewithal to receive the details of the message: *"Speak, for you have strengthened me"* (v. 19). Before expounding his message to Daniel (the contents of the next two chapters), the angel affirms the urgent nature of his mission:

> I must return to fight with the prince of Persia; and when I have gone forth, indeed the prince of Greece will come. But I will tell you what is noted in the Scripture of Truth. (No one upholds me against these, except Michael your prince) (vv. 20-21).

"The Scripture of Truth" likely refers to God's predetermined plan for the nation of Israel. Satan was using powerful fallen angels to sway the governments of men to pursue evil and to oppose God's covenant people. But despite the enemies' efforts, Daniel was to be made aware of God's providential care for the Jews during the Persian and Greek Empires (11:2-35), the Tribulation Period (11:36-45), and the Kingdom Age (chp. 12). The angelic messenger confirmed that he had already strengthened Darius the Mede, which may explain why the king viewed Daniel so favorably back in chapter 6. God is always at work behind the visible domain of men to accomplish His sovereign will. Daniel, still having prophetic ministry to be made aware of and to record, was clearly a part of those purposes.

We learn from verse 21 that Michael the Archangel is especially connected with the care of the Jewish nation. Gabriel is also an angelic messenger associated with Israel (Dan. 8, 9; Luke 1:19). Besides Michael the archangel (Jude 9), Scripture reveals the existence of several types of heavenly beings: the four living creatures (Rev. 4), the cherubim (Gen. 3:24; Ezek. 1:5-14, 10:7), the seraphim (Isa. 6:1-7), and a host of innumerable angels having various ranks and authorities (Ps. 103:20-22; Eph. 1:21; Col. 1:16; Rev. 5:11).

Lucifer is likely the most powerful created being. Not even Michael the archangel would venture out of creation order to rebuke Satan, but rather he wisely said, *"The Lord rebuke you"* (Jude 9). We are much less powerful than angels. How can we possibly confront the evil power and deception of Satan on our own? Paul tells believers that we do not war against flesh and blood, but rather against spiritual wickedness in high places which are beyond the earthly scene:

Finally, my brethren, be strong in the Lord and in the power of His might. Put on the whole armor of God, that you may be able to stand against the wiles of the devil. For we do not wrestle against flesh and blood, but against principalities, against powers, against the rulers of the darkness of this age, against spiritual hosts of wickedness in the heavenly places (Eph. 6:10-12).

Victory is possible only when believers venture into heavenly places on their knees to receive power and wisdom from Him who is above all principalities and powers. Christians can do nothing without Christ (John 15:5), but can accomplish all that is approved of God through Him (Phil. 4:12). To war against spiritual wickedness in heavenly places, we must rely on a higher authority than the enemy's – thus, the paramount importance of Christ's priestly ministry. This means that believers must boldly approach Christ in heavenly places to receive resources to engage the darkness of this world and the wickedness in high places (Eph. 1:3, 3:10, 6:12). Only then can we *"be strong in the Lord and in the power of His might"* (Eph. 6:10). Only by employing the spiritual armor that God supplies and by getting on our knees before the throne of grace can believers effectively wrestle *"against principalities, against powers, against the rulers of the darkness of this age, against spiritual hosts of wickedness in the heavenly places"* (Eph. 6:12). Only God can fight our battles against wickedness in high places.

Peter, outside of God's will, drew a sword to protect Christ from being arrested, and consequently was defeated (John 18). Believers cannot use carnal weapons to win spiritual battles, and what is done in our strength is for our glory, not God's (2 Cor. 10:4-5). The real enemy is not the mocking atheist who lives next door, but spiritual *ranks* of wickedness in heavenly places. A soldier must be energized through prayer, clad with spiritual armor, and able to wield the sword of truth with precision, remembering that the more effective you are the more opposition there will be.

As witnessed in Daniel 10, the intense battle for the control of Jerusalem, the place where Jehovah had chosen to place His name, commenced when the Jews obeyed His word and began offering sacrifices to Him again. Satan understood that once God's people were again obedient to His revealed will, they would be unbeatable. In other words, the Jews were safer then than when Jerusalem was in her glory and surrounded by fortified walls. In the Church Age, believers in holy fellowship with God are safer on their knees than in any courtroom, or congressional house, or defending themselves with carnal weapons.

What we learn from Ezra 3 and Daniel 10 is that when God's people become desperate for Him, the spiritual warfare associated with their obedience becomes intense. Christians, therefore, would be wise to remain in the intimate presence of the Almighty by committing themselves to knowing and obeying God's Word, rather than deserting that privileged place of communion and blessing to hold hands with the devil (1 Cor. 10:20-21). There is a personal cost associated with obedience, but those who sow tears in God's presence shall ultimately reap joy (Ps. 126:5). Regrettably, many Christians are being ignorantly duped into a satanic agenda which hinders the work of God, damages the Church, and brings disdain on the name of the Lord Jesus Christ.

Meditation

Pray often, for prayer is a shield to the soul, a sacrifice to God and a scourge for Satan. ... The devil is nimble; he can run apace; he is light of foot; he hath overtaken many. They that would have heaven must run for it.

— John Bunyan

Darius to the Man of Sin
Daniel 11

The revelation of Gentile rule over the Jewish people has been intensifying with detail since the overall blueprint of five future world empires was revealed in chapter 7. In chapter 8, the prophecy focused on only two of the five kingdoms, the Persian and Greek Empires. In chapter 11, the prophetic emphasis is mainly placed on two of Alexander the Great's four generals and the portion of the Greek Empire they assumed control over after his death. The revelation conveyed to Daniel by the angelic messenger in this chapter is specific and has led some to assume that the chapter was written after the fact, perhaps in second century B.C. This thinking is refuted in "The Date" section of the *Overview*.

At the close of the previous chapter, Daniel's angelic messenger informed him of the spiritual warfare behind the visible scene of human endeavors. God chooses to use His angels to ensure that all His marvelous purposes for His people are accomplished. The angel with Daniel (probably with the support of Michael) had strengthened Darius the Mede to conquer the city of Babylon (v. 1).

Throughout Scripture we find God accomplishing His will for Israel and protecting His servants by His angels. For example, one angel slew 185,000 Syrian soldiers in one night in defense of a humble King Hezekiah who had cast himself completely on the Lord to protect the Jewish nation (2 Kgs. 19:35). When wicked men surrounded Lot's house and would have forced their way in, two angels smote the would-be intruders with blindness. This type of disorienting blindness was the same as that inflicted by God upon an invading Syrian army that had besieged His prophet Elisha at Dothan to kill him (2 Kgs. 6). Just moments earlier, Elisha asked the Lord to open the eyes of his fearful servant to see the angelic hosts protecting them from harm. The servant then saw a host of horses and chariots of fire throughout the surrounding mountains (2 Kgs. 6:17).

Dear believer, may we remember John's solemn words concerning the enemy that lurks about and threatens to devour, *"greater is He that is in you, than he that is in the world"* (1 Jn. 4:4). The Lord with anyone is a majority. Actually, the Lord alone is a majority! Hence, Elisha did not fear the enemy; he was just concerned about performing the will of God. And there is the lesson for us to follow: do His will, and don't be anxious about the rest. Believers are immortal and invincible until their earthly work is finished!

The angel then foretells the drama that will unfold concerning the next four emperors of the Persian Empire, the fourth being wealthier than the previous kings (v. 2). Cyrus' son Cambyses became ruler of Persia in 530 B.C.; he was followed by Pseudo-Smerdis, then Darius I Hystaspes, and the king of emphasis, Xerxes (also called Ahasuerus). Xerxes held the throne from 485 to 465 B.C. and was more influential and wealthy than his predecessors, often engaging Greece in warfare during his tenure.

Daniel's messenger then foretells that *"a mighty king shall arise, who shall rule with great dominion, and do according to his will"* (v. 3), but as soon as his kingdom is established it will be divided into four parts and others will rule it (v. 4). This, of course, is Alexander the Great, whose Greek Empire has already been represented in the bronze belly of Nebuchadnezzar's image (chp. 2), the winged leopard with four heads (chp. 7), and the male goat that sprouted four horns after the first powerful horn was broken off (chp. 8). As previously mentioned, Alexander conquered the Medo-Persian Empire (including Egypt) from 334 to 330 B.C. and then moved eastward to take much of India by 324 B.C. He died in Babylon the following year at the age of 32. Alexander had two sons, Hercules and Alexander who were both slain, one before and one after his death. This meant that there was no legitimate heir to Alexander's throne. Thus Daniel's prophecy was directly fulfilled concerning Alexander's four successors, who would not be of his posterity (v. 4).

His four generals then divided the kingdom and each ruled over their portion of it: Seleucus ruled Syria and Mesopotamia, Ptolemy governed Egypt, Lysimacus ruled Thrace and much of Asia Minor, and Cassander controlled Greece and Macedonia. Much of Daniel's prophecies pertain to the first two generals mentioned and their descendants who ruled over Egypt and Syria; hence, the Ptolemies are referred to as the kings of the south and the Seleucids as the kings of the north (vv. 5-32).

The following table correlates Daniel's prophecies with known history:

	Lines of Nobility: Ptolemies and Seleucids (vv. 5-35)		
B.C.	**The Ptolemies (Egypt)**	**B.C.**	**The Seleucids (Syria)**
323	Ptolemy I Soter (v. 5): son of Ptolemy Lagus, governor of Egypt. Assumes title "King of Egypt" in 304 B.C.	321	Seleucus I Nicator (v. 5): governor of Babylon; defeated an invasion by Antigonus in 316-312 B.C. with help of Ptolemy I Soter and became the uncontested ruler of Babylon in 312 B.C. – commencing the era of the Seleucids. Assumed the title of "king" in 305 B.C. and was murdered in 281 B.C.
285	Ptolemy II Philadelphus (v. 6): Responsible for the Septuagint. Gave daughter Berenice to Antiochus II in marriage to secure peace after years of war.		
		281	Antiochus I Soter
		262	Antiochus II Theus (v. 6): Divorced his wife Laodice to marry Berenice. Laodice poisoned both Berenice and Antiochus II and placed her son Callinicus on the throne.
246	Ptolemy III Euergetes (vv. 7-8): Invaded and despoiled Syria, and killed Laodice to avenge his sister Berenice's death.	246	Seleucus II Callinicus (vv. 7-9): Tried to invade Egypt after humiliating defeat, but failed. Fell from a horse and died.
		227	Seleucus III Ceraunus/II Soter (v. 10): Murdered by conspirators while warring in Asia Minor.

Lines of Nobility: Ptolemies and Seleucids (vv. 5-35)			
B.C.	**The Ptolemies (Egypt)**	**B.C.**	**The Seleucids (Syria)**
		223	Antiochus III the Great (vv. 10-11, 13, 15-19): younger brother of Seleucus III, was successful in campaigning against Egypt (219-217 B. C.) and establishing control over Palestine. The fortified city in this region is likely Sidon captured in 203 B.C. He then warred against Asia Minor (197 B.C.) and Greece (192 B.C.), but was not successful as Roman commander Cornelius Scipio was dispatched to intervene. Antiochus returned to Syria in 188 B.C. and died the next year.
221	Ptolemy IV Philopator (vv. 11-12, 14-15): Was initially successful against the invasion of Antiochus III (slaughtered many), but was defeated when Antiochus returned with a larger army comprised of Macedonians under Philip V's leadership and many Jews who were hoping the Egyptians would be driven from Palestine and they would achieve independence from Syria and Egypt. But this did not occur.		
204	Ptolemy V Epiphanes (v. 17): Was given Antiochus III's daughter in marriage in a failed attempt to bring peace between Egypt and Syria.		
		187	Seleucus IV Philopator (v. 20): the son of Antiochus III, heavily taxed the people to pay Roman tribute. He was poisoned and did not die in battle.

Lines of Nobility: Ptolemies and Seleucids (vv. 5-35)

B.C.	The Ptolemies (Egypt)	B.C.	The Seleucids (Syria)
181	Ptolemy VI Philometor (v. 25): Was attacked and defeated by Antiochus IV's smaller army at Pelusium (170 B.C.).		
		175	Antiochus IV Epiphanes (vv. 21-32): He is the "little horn" (8:9-12, 23-25) who invaded Israel under the promise of peace but murdered tens of thousands of Jews. He foreshadows the Antichrist, the "little horn" (7:8). Antiochus IV took the throne from its rightful heir, Demetrius Soter, the son of Seleucus IV. The people accepted him as king because he defeated an invading army and deposed Onias III, the high priest (the "prince of the covenant"). He moved against Egypt's larger army in the Nile Delta in 170 B.C. and won. He then hosted a feast to promote peace (both the victor and the vanquished ate at the same table). He returned through Israel with much wealth, but was frustrated because he had failed to secure all of Egypt – he took out his anger on the Jews by desecrating the temple. In 168 B.C. he again sought to invade Egypt, but was opposed by a Roman army that arrived by sea, led by Popillus Laenas. Antiochus decided not to engage the Romans in battle and returned to Israel enraged. In 167 B.C., 22,000 soldiers entered Jerusalem in peace, but attacked the Jews on the Sabbath day when they would not defend themselves. Over the next 3 years, thousands of Jews were slaughtered and enslaved), the temple was desecrated and sacrifices abolished.

Antiochus V Eupator ruled after Antiochus IV, but submitted to Roman guardianship in 163 B.C. There were fourteen more Syrian kings (each having brief reigns of lesser power) until Syria was formed into a Roman province under Pompey.

After Ptolemy VI Philometor there were six more Egyptian kings, the last being Ptolemy Auletes, who died in 51 B.C. By 30 B.C. his sons and daughter Cleopatra (who had a son by Julius Caesar and two sons and a daughter with Mark Antony in an attempt to hold power in Egypt) would all be dead and Egypt would be ruled by Rome. The Ptolemy dynasty was over.

The Atrocities of Antiochus IV in Judea

In chapter 8, the animal-like conduct of Antiochus IV in Judea from 167-164 B.C. was described by Judas Maccabeus. Jewish historian Josephus also records Antiochus IV's brutal and blasphemous conduct during his earlier intrusions into Jerusalem in 170 to 167 B.C.:

(246) King Antiochus, then, returning from Egypt through fear of the Romans, marched against the city of Jerusalem, and entering it in the 143rd year of the Seleucid reign, took the city without a battle, for the gates were opened to him by those who were of his party. (247) And having become master of Jerusalem in this way, he killed many of those who were in opposition, and taking large sums of money as spoil, he returned to Antioch. (248) Two years later, as it happened, in the 145th year...the king went up to Jerusalem, and by pretending to offer peace, overcame the city by treachery. (249) But on this occasion he did not spare even those who admitted him, because of the wealth of the temple, but through greed – for he saw much gold in the temple and an array of very costly dedicatory-offerings of other kinds, and for the sake of taking this as spoil, he went so far as to violate the treaty which he had made with them. (250) And so he stripped the temple, carrying off the vessels of God, the golden lampstands and the golden altar and table and the other altars, and not even forbearing to take the curtains, which were made of fine linen and scarlet, and he also emptied the temple of its hidden treasures, and left nothing at all behind, thereby throwing the Jews into deep mourning. (251) Moreover he forbade them to offer the daily sacrifices...and after plundering the entire city, he killed some of the people, and some he took captive together with their wives and

children, so that the number of those taken alive came to some ten thousand.[139]

(255) And many of the Jews followed the things the (Syrian) king ordered, some voluntarily but also through fear of paying the proclaimed penalty. But the noblest and best-born persons did not heed him but held their native customs to count more than the penalty he threatened for those who did not obey. And because of this they were abused each day. And they died, subject to bitter tortures. (256) For with bodies whipped and abused they were crucified while still alive and breathing. But their wives and the children whom they had circumcised in spite of the king's policy were strangled, by hanging from the necks of their crucified fathers.[140]

It is noted that the above accounts of Josephus agree with the historical record in 1 Maccabees 1:20-24. After three years of intense fighting, Jewish freedom fighters were victorious over Lysias, whom Antiochus IV had left to deal with the rebel Jews, while he engaged the invading Parthians in the east. Antiochus IV died suddenly during this campaign (in Iran) of a disease in 164 B.C.

The Seventieth Week

All of the detailed prophecies pertaining to the conflicts between the Ptolemies and the Seleucids in the preceding thirty-five verses have been fulfilled. Much of the previous narrative focused on Antiochus IV; the remainder of the chapter relates to a more brutal king that Antiochus merely foreshadowed – the Antichrist during the Tribulation Period. He is the second "little horn" in the book of Daniel (7:8); Antiochus IV, being the first, typifies the Antichrist (8:9-12, 23-25).

The remainder of this chapter contains prophecies pertaining to the future Tribulation Period, Daniel's seventieth week, which begins when the Antichrist signs a peace treaty with Israel to secure worldwide peace. The revived Roman Empire foretold by Daniel in chapter 7 must be in place prior to the abomination of desolation which occurs at the midpoint in the Tribulation Period, since that is when the one-world religious system is destroyed by the Antichrist (Rev. 17). This religious system is the culmination of the anti-god movement which first originated with Nimrod in Babylon long ago and is responsible for the death of millions of God's people throughout the course of human history; the harlot, as John describes her, is *"drunk with the blood of the saints"* (Rev. 17:5-6).

The peace of the Antichrist is a temporary, false peace which will engulf the world and allow him time to secure a political and economic system with himself at its head. Once in control, he will rid himself of the harlot, which served his worldwide agenda, and then he will claim to be god (Rev. 17:15-16). Anyone not pledging allegiance to him by taking his special mark, likely a technological means of economic transfer and global tracking, will be exterminated (Rev. 13:15-18). Indeed, a great many will not bow to him and will therefore be slaughtered (Rev. 7:9-14). From accumulated wealth the Antichrist is able to fortify his empire with great military strength (v. 38).

The angel told Daniel that this future "king" will rule the world, supported by ten influential kings (Rev. 17:12-13) who permit the Antichrist to do as he pleases. In the middle of the Tribulation Period, he will *"magnify himself above every god, shall speak blasphemies against the God of gods,"* referring to Jehovah (v. 36, 7:25; 2 Thess. 2:4-7). The angel foretold that the Antichrist *"shall regard neither the God of his fathers nor the desire of women, nor regard any god; for he shall exalt himself above them all"* (v. 37). In Revelation 13 we learn that a False Prophet, who works great wonders, will cause much of the world to worship the Antichrist. The False Prophet is depicted as a beast rising out of the land (speaking of Israel proper), whereas the Antichrist is described as a beast rising out of the sea (representing the nations).

The phrase in verse 37: *"the God of his fathers"* (speaking of Jehovah) provides a strong indication that the Antichrist will be a Jew incognito residing in the nations. The phrase *"nor the desire of women"* in the same verse is more difficult to discern. Some believe that it refers to the long-standing desire of Jewish women to give birth to the coming Messiah. If this is the meaning of the phrase, that would provide further evidence that the Antichrist will be of Jewish descent. However, some believe that it indicates that the Antichrist will be a homosexual, thus demonstrating further rebellion against God by rejecting His order for marriage. At the midpoint of the Tribulation Period he will openly defy Jehovah and the gods of the nations, and relentlessly enforce his insatiable desire to be worshipped by all the inhabitants of earth. Those who will not honor the Antichrist will be beheaded (Rev. 20:4). This test of allegiance and holocaust of life will be permitted by God until the Lord Jesus returns to the earth to destroy the Antichrist (Rev. 17:17, 19:19-20).

How does the Antichrist obtain global domination in just three and a half years? This feat is accomplished because he is helped by the *"god which his fathers did not know"* (v. 38), *"a foreign god"* which he serves (v. 39). This is none other than Satan himself, whom the Lord Jesus referred to three times as *"the prince of this world."* Those who pledge their alliance to this king will be rewarded with positions of authority and the land of those not complying at a bargain price (v. 39). The Antichrist, the evil king, is referred to exclusively in this section as "he," "him," and "his."

Verses 40 through 45 refer to events in the last half of the Tribulation Period. This section begins with the Antichrist mobilizing his army in Europe and quickly sweeping across and conquering many nations en route to the *"Glorious Land"* (i.e., Israel; vv. 40-41). He has come into the Mideast to confront an invading force from the south composed of Egyptians, Libyans, and Ethiopians. He defeats and despoils them (vv. 42-43). The king chooses not to conquer the territories of Edom, Moab, and Ammon at this time (v. 41), possibly because other invaders are approaching from the north and east. He also destroys these armies (v. 44). The Millennial Kingdom prophecies of Isaiah 11 may explain why Edom, Moab, and Ammon were spared destruction:

> *Ephraim shall not envy Judah, and Judah shall not harass Ephraim. But they shall fly down upon the shoulder of the Philistines toward the west; together they shall plunder the people of the East; they shall lay their hand on Edom and Moab; and the people of Ammon shall obey them* (Isa. 11:13-14).

Divine judgment of these three nations is to be executed by Israel; hence, these three nations escape the wrath of the willful king in the Tribulation Period. In the aftermath of the two battles, the Antichrist takes up residence in Jerusalem (on the holy mountain) located between the Mediterranean Sea and the Dead Sea (v. 45). He likely does so in order to proclaim that he is the long-awaited Jewish Messiah, for he has twice delivered Israel from invasion. The section then closes with the defeat of the Antichrist at the Battle of Armageddon – Christ's Second Coming.

The prophecies pertaining to the Antichrist being in Jerusalem and his ultimate defeat easily align with many other Scriptures; however, his battles to fend off would-be invaders of the Holy Land from the south and north early in the Tribulation Period are admittedly more obscure. J. Dwight Pentecost suggests that these two battles occur in the last half of the Tribulation Period,[141] but it seems more likely that it is towards the latter portion of the first half of the Tribulation Period and that a full-scale follow-up invasion (i.e., the Battle of Gog and Magog) occurs shortly after the Antichrist's battles (vv. 40-43). If this assumption is correct, the Battle of Gog and Magog would be immediately followed by the Abomination of Desolation and the last half of the Tribulation Period. J. Dwight Pentecost describes the Antichrist's victory in verses 40-43:

> The king of the South and the king of the North will fight against the Antichrist. ... When the Antichrist hears of this invasion, he will move his army from Europe into the Middle East, sweeping through many countries like a flood (v. 40). He will move quickly into the land of Israel, the Beautiful Land (v. 41). His first strike will be against Egypt (11:42-43a), for Egypt and her Arab allies (Libyans and Nubians, v. 43) are the ones who will initiate the invasion on Israel. ...The Antichrist will hear alarming reports from the east ... and from the north. Enraged, the Antichrist will set out to destroy many of the invaders. Then he will occupy Israel and will pitch his royal tents between the seas, that is, between the Dead Sea and the Mediterranean Sea, at the beautiful holy mount, probably Jerusalem. Posing as Christ, the Antichrist will set up his headquarters in Jerusalem, the same city from which Christ will rule the world in the Millennium (Zech. 14:1).[142]

This explanation seems reasonable. By the beginning of the Tribulation Period, we know that the Jews will have taken back their land through war (Ezek. 38:8) and then they will sign a seven-year peace treaty with the Antichrist (9:27). The Jewish people will enjoy a short season of false peace just before suffering a terrible holocaust in the last half of the Tribulation Period. Before the Tribulation Period is over, two-thirds of the Jews in the world will be slaughtered (Zech. 13:7-8). It is the author's opinion that the events of verses 40-44 occur in the first half of the Tribulation Period, as the Antichrist will not have fully solidified global rule, nor has he yet claimed to be God in the temple. His defense of Israel at this time will prove his willingness and ability to enforce his peace treaty with Israel.

The Antichrist's peace covenant will initially allow the Jews to dwell safely in unprotected villages in Israel, a land which they took back with a sword. However, his protection of Israel suddenly dissipates with the battle of Gog and Magog (Ezek. 38:11), which will likely occur just prior to the midpoint of the Tribulation Period. This battle should not be confused with the Battle of Armageddon at the end of the Tribulation Period (Rev. 19). In that confrontation the Lord descends from heaven to the earth, completely defeats all opposing armies, and every eye shall see Him (Matt. 24:30; Rev. 1:7). None of these factors are evident in the Battle of Gog and Magog.

It does not seem likely that the battles of the Antichrist (vv. 40-44) are directly associated with the Battle of Gog and Magog either, though many commentators hold that view. Jeremiah (Jer. 31), Ezekiel (chps. 38-39), and Joel (Joel 2) provide prophetic details of the Battle of Gog and Magog. Ezekiel identifies *Rosh* with the land of Magog (likely Russia), Togarmah (eastern Turkey), Gomer (Armenia), Persia (Iran), Ethiopia, and Libya as siding with Gog. While it is true that the list of those invading Israel is similar, it is the Antichrist who defeats the invaders in the preceding verses to accomplish his wicked agenda, not the Lord. The Jews will have rebuilt their temple and resumed their sacrifices when this invasion from the south and then from the north and east occurs. Having rejected their true King, the Jewish nation will accept the Antichrist (the one who protected them), thus fulfilling the Lord's own words: *"I have come in My Father's name, and you do not receive Me; if another comes in his own name, him you will receive"* (John 5:43).

Ezekiel tells us that it is the Lord who defeats Gog and his armies, not the Antichrist (Ezek. 39). This is accomplished by causing delusion among horses and riders, betrayal among allies, and supernaturally casting gigantic hailstones down on the invaders. Regardless of the Antichrist's agenda and his celebrated victories, he will be no match for the Lord of Glory when He appears for the Battle of Armageddon. While it is possible that the helpless man in verse 45 is the king of the north who is defeated by the Antichrist, this author favors that it is speaking of the Antichrist. When the Lord appears to destroy him, it will be as the angel says, *"no one can help him"* (v. 45).

Meditation

Look, ye saints! The sight is glorious: see the Man of Sorrows now;
From the fight returned victorious, every knee to Him shall bow:
Crown Him, crown Him, crown Him, crown Him, crown Him, crown
   Him.
Crowns become the Victor's brow, crowns become the Victor's brow.

— Thomas Kelly

Names and Resurrections
Daniel 12:1-3

The subject matter of Daniel's seventieth week, including the destruction of the Antichrist, continues from the previous chapter. The angel informed Daniel that a terrible period of distress (worse than any previous time of suffering) was ahead for the Jewish nation, but that Michael would intervene to preserve those whose names were written in God's book (v. 1). Michael is the archangel who is assigned to watch over God's covenant people.

The prophet Jeremiah wrote of this future timeframe: *"Alas! For that day is great, so that none is like it; and it is the time of Jacob's trouble, but he shall be saved out of it"* (Jer. 30:7). When the abomination of desolation occurs at the midpoint in the Tribulation Period, there will also be war in heaven. The archangel Michael, along with his angels, will war against the devil and his fallen angels in order to restrict evil to the earth (v. 1; Rev. 12:7-10). Satan, knowing that his time is short, will be enraged and will seek to exterminate the Jewish people (Rev. 12:12-15). However, the Lord will preserve from harm a remnant of His covenant people (Rev. 12:16-17).

During the Tribulation, there will be 144,000 Jews who are actively testifying of Jehovah (Rev. 7:4-8) and there will also be angels heralding the gospel message as they fly over the earth (Rev. 14:6-12). The devil knows that salvation is possible only while an individual is alive to choose Christ: *"And as it is appointed for men to die once, but after this the judgment"* (Heb. 9:27). Accordingly, he will attempt to exterminate all those who honor Jehovah or those who might hear and trust the kingdom gospel message. Satan will spare only those willing to take the mark of the beast and worship him. The Lord Jesus spoke of the horrific holocaust during this timeframe:

For then there will be great tribulation, such as has not been since the beginning of the world until this time, no, nor ever shall be. And

416

unless those days were shortened, no flesh would be saved; but for the elect's sake those days will be shortened (Matt. 24:21-22).

If the Lord tarried longer than the appointed time to return to the earth, there would be no flesh left on the planet. Before the Tribulation Period concludes, the Antichrist will slaughter two-thirds of all Jews worldwide (Zech. 13:7-8). However, the Lord Jesus Christ will descend at the end of the Tribulation Period to protect and deliver His covenant people (i.e., those Jews whose names are written in His book). But to what book is the angel referring?

God's Books

John affirms that no human will be able to enter through any of New Jerusalem's twelve gates unless their names are written in *The Lamb's Book of life* (Rev. 21:27). Moses also refers to a book of names in God's possession shortly after the Israelites had angered God by creating and worshipping a golden calf at Mt. Sinai (Ex. 32). Moses, who had been with the Lord for forty days on the mountain, descended its slopes to confront the people. The calf was destroyed and 3,000 people perished that day in judgment. The next day, Moses reminded the people that they had committed a great trespass against God, and said he would return to Mount Sinai to intercede on their behalf and to learn from the Lord how atonement could be offered for their sin (Ex. 32:30-35).

Then Moses asked the Lord to blot his own name out of His book if the nation as a whole could be spared judgment. Like Paul centuries later (Rom. 9:3), he pled for God to condemn him so that mercy could be granted to the Israelites. These were hypothetical prayers, for both men knew their divine callings and that God could not condemn those He had declared righteous, but they do demonstrate the supernatural compassion of these men for their countrymen. Evidently, Moses knew that God kept a roster of the names of everyone He would create (including those who perish in the womb) in a book entitled the *Book of the Living* (Ex. 32:32-33). David refers to this same book in Psalm 69:28, and then again in Psalm 139:15-16, which confirms that this book contains the specific details of each person prior to that individual's conception.

Moreover, Revelation 3:5 also speaks of the *Book of the Living* and assures us that the names of the faithful (true believers) are not blotted out of this book. On the other hand, unbelievers' names are blotted out of the *Book of the Living* as they die because they did not receive God's forgiveness for their sins while they were living (Heb. 9:27). This means that when The Book of the Living is reviewed at the Great White Throne judgment (after the earth's destruction), it will contain the names of only the righteous. The Lord Jesus told His disciples (see Matt. 10:20) to rejoice because their names were written in heaven. The Greek verb translated *"written"* in this passage of Matthew is in the perfect tense, which means it can be rendered, as Kenneth Wuest does in his expanded translation: *"your names have been written in heaven and are on permanent record up there."* This statement may refer either to the *Book of the Living* or to *The Lamb's Book of Life*, which is a timeless roster of all the redeemed – all who will be saved throughout time (Rev. 21:27). Revelation 13:8 and 17:8 also speak of *The Lamb's Book of Life*. It is my opinion that the Lord was referring to this book while speaking to His disciples.

The *Book of the Living*, though written before time began, has its fulfillment in time. *The Lamb's Book of Life*, also written before creation, has its verification at the Great White Throne judgment. The former book has names blotted out of it as the lost die, while the latter remains unaltered – only the names of those who would come to salvation are written in it. The *Book of Life* (or the *Book of the Living*) initially contained the names of all those who would ever live, but those not coming to salvation never had their names written in *The Lamb's Book of Life*. Because the names of the lost, when they die, are blotted out of the former book, both books will match at the Great White Throne judgment; their records will be in perfect agreement. The one shows God's foreknowledge; the other, His record of human responsibility.

Because of Moses' great love for God's people, he was willing to be blotted out of the *Book of the Living* in order to secure forgiveness for the Israelites. Moses was willing to suffer in the place of sinners. God's later working in human affairs would be characterized by a similar message: the Lord Jesus willingly took the place of condemned sinners at Calvary in order to secure the opportunity for them to be forgiven and restored to God. Accordingly, it is only Christ's intercession and judgment at Calvary on our behalf as our substitute which keeps anyone's name eternally imprinted in the *Book of the Living*.

Every human ever conceived has their name written in the *Book of the Living*, whether they were born or not. The *Book of the Living* is a ledger of everyone that God has created through the process of procreation since He formed our first parents. If one dies without exercising faith in God's revealed plan of salvation, that person's name is blotted out of this book.

Two Resurrections

The angel then explains that having one's name written in God's book ensures a bodily resurrection to enjoy everlasting life and that anyone not having his or her name written in God's book ensures a bodily resurrection to experience everlasting shame and contempt:

> *And many of those who sleep in the dust of the earth shall awake, some to everlasting life, some to shame and everlasting contempt. Those who are wise shall shine like the brightness of the firmament, and those who turn many to righteousness like the stars forever and ever* (vv. 2-3).

Natural law governs us while we sojourn on earth, but that is not true in the spiritual realm of the afterlife. Whether one spends eternity in heaven or in hell, everyone will undergo a spiritual resurrection. This ensures that all individuals will have a body suited for their final destination. The Lord Jesus taught that He, as the Son of God, created all life and that all life was in Him (John 1:3-4). He also stated that, at His command, all the deceased would be resurrected (i.e., every disembodied soul would be joined to an immortal body that can never die):

> *Most assuredly, I say to you, he who hears My word and believes in Him who sent Me has everlasting life, and shall not come into judgment, but has passed from death into life. Most assuredly, I say to you, the hour is coming, and now is, when the dead will hear the voice of the Son of God; and those who hear will live. For as the Father has life in Himself, so He has granted the Son to have life in Himself, and has given Him authority to execute judgment also, because He is the Son of Man. Do not marvel at this; for the hour is coming in which all who are in the graves will hear His voice and come forth – those who have done good, to the resurrection of life, and those who have done evil, to the resurrection of condemnation* (John 5:24-29).

From this passage we learn that there will be two types of resurrection: a resurrection of the just to eternal residence in heaven, and a resurrection of the condemned to be punished for eternity in the Lake of Fire (Rev. 20:10, 15). The Lord Jesus has received authority from His Father to initiate both of these resurrections, but Scripture informs us that the first resurrection (i.e., of the just) occurs in several stages, while the resurrection of the condemned happens all at once.

The First Resurrection

Though the resurrection of the condemned occurs all at once at the Great White Throne judgment (Rev. 20:11-15), the *resurrection of life*, also called the *first resurrection* (Rev. 20:5-6), occurs for the righteous at several distinct points in time prior to the Great White Throne judgment. The Eternal State, the everlasting reality of a new heaven and new earth without sin, follows this final judgment. Time ceases to have meaning after this. Christ was raised from the dead three days after He gave His life as a ransom for humanity at Calvary. Though there had been six bodily resurrections recorded in the Bible previously, Christ was the first individual to experience glorification (to receive a glorified body which would be suitable for the dynamics of heaven). The number seven is used in the Bible to symbolize completeness and perfection and Christ, the seventh human raised from the dead, was the first to experience perfect resurrection. As Paul puts it, the Lord Jesus was *"the first fruits of the dead"* to appear before God in heaven (1 Cor. 15:20-23).

Shortly after Christ's resurrection, some deceased believers were also raised from the dead, probably as further validation of Christ's own resurrection. They either underwent a bodily resurrection (like Lazarus' resurrection recorded in John 12) or glorification (the same type of resurrection that Christ experienced) – Scripture does not specify which type. If this were only a bodily resurrection, those saints would have had to die a second time. It seems unlikely that God would have allowed these saints to enjoy fellowship with Christ in paradise and then put them back on the earth again to live a normal human existence in a sin-cursed world.

The next stage of the first resurrection will be when Christ returns for His Church. He will descend to the clouds and all true believers (both those who have died and also those still alive) will be quickly caught up from the earth to experience glorification (1 Thess. 4:13-18; 1 Cor. 15:51-52). At that moment, all Christians (and perhaps Old Testament saints as well, per Heb. 11:39-40) will receive the same kind of perfect body that the Lord did after His resurrection (Phil. 3:21; 1 Jn. 3:2). This spectacular event ends the Church Age and will be followed by a devastating period on earth called the Tribulation.

After all true Christians (i.e., those who had been born again and are indwelt by God) have been removed from the earth, the Antichrist will be allowed to rule the world for seven years (2 Thess. 2:4-7; Dan. 9:27). God will pour out great wrath upon the earth at this time and Satan will attempt to gain as many followers as possible and slaughter those who will not take his mark and pledge allegiance to the Antichrist (Rev. 12:12; 13:11-18). The holocaust during this time will be horrendous; the Lord Jesus said that if He should tarry longer than the appointed time for His return to the earth, humanity would be wiped out (Matt. 24:21-22). Considering the twenty-one specific divine judgments which occur at this time (Rev. 6-17), the Battle of Gog and Magog (Ezek. 38 - 39), the chastening of Israel (Rom. 9:27), and the Battle of Armageddon (Rev. 19), it is quite conceivable that seventy-five percent of the world population will die during this epoch. Two-thirds of all Jews will be murdered during the Tribulation Period (Zech. 13:7-8), but God will protect a remnant of His covenant people from the Antichrist (Rev. 12:13-17) in order to fulfill remaining promises to Abraham and David (Gen. 15:18-21; Ps. 89:3-4; Luke 1:32-33, 67-79).

The good news is that many during the Tribulation Period will choose to be beheaded by the Antichrist (Rev. 20:4) rather than to take his mark of identification and worship him (Rev. 7:9-14). Those who heard the gospel message of Jesus Christ during the Church Age will not be given the opportunity to receive salvation during the Tribulation Period – they will take *"the mark of the beast"* and follow him into destruction (2 Thess. 2:10-12). Because they rejected God's Son's offer of salvation and opted instead to pursue pleasure in unrighteousness, God will not allow them to understand the truth in order to be saved. On the other hand, those martyred for choosing to worship God rather than the Antichrist will experience the first resurrection at the end of the Tribulation Period (Rev. 20:4). This miraculous event coincides with Christ's physical return to the earth to destroy the Antichrist, to judge and remove wickedness from the earth, and to establish His earthly kingdom, which will last one thousand years (Rev. 20:4-6).

Revelation 20:1-8 informs us that Satan will be bound in the bottomless pit during Christ's reign on earth. However, at the end of that time he will be released to again test man's resolve to follow God. Even after one thousand years of peace and prosperity, the devil will successfully convince the nations of the earth to rebel against Christ. One might ask, "Why would God allow Satan to lead such a rebellion against His own Son? Why not just destroy Satan and be done with wickedness?" Unfortunately, wickedness would not expire with the end of Satan, for his rebel spirit entered into the world in Eden and intruded into humanity (1 Jn. 2:16). Death and rebellion have been passed down to every generation since that time (Rom. 5:12). Summarizing the state of the human heart, the prophet Jeremiah wrote, *"The heart is deceitful above all things, and desperately wicked; who can know it? I, the Lord, search the heart, I test the mind, even to give every man according to his ways, according to the fruit of his doings"* (Jer. 17:9-10). Before destroying Satan, God will allow him to test the human heart's fortitude for godliness, and find it lacking. While enjoying God's fellowship in a perfect environment, both the first man (Adam) and the last humans on earth before it is destroyed (Rev. 20:11; 21:1; 1 Pet. 3:10) are shown to be incapable of pleasing God when tempted to sin against Him.

Man, left to himself, will always go his own way; he will turn away from God (Isa. 53:6). God provided a righteous solution for human rebellion by judging His Son Jesus Christ in our place and by giving those who would trust in Him eternal life. Those who will not trust in God's means of salvation in Christ will experience eternal death in hell. So, no matter when individuals live, no matter what dispensation of accountability is present when they lived, all the redeemed (those justified by faith) will experience the first resurrection and enter into the Eternal State; all others will receive resurrected bodies before being cast into the Lake of Fire. These are the only two types of eternal resurrections that the Bible identifies – one to everlasting life and one to everlasting torment and separation from God.

The Second and Final Resurrection

Satan's final rebellion will end when the earth is destroyed at the conclusion of Christ's Millennial Kingdom. At that time, God will judge the wicked and cast them into the Lake of Fire. This spiritual abode is often referred to as "hell," and was originally created for the purpose of punishing Satan and his fallen angels (Matt. 25:41). Before God creates a new heaven and earth, He will resurrect those who would not receive the truth of salvation by faith. God is a good record-keeper and is faithful to uphold His Word. A number of books will be opened at this divine trial to demonstrate that God is fully cognizant of sin and completely just in punishing the wicked for their sins. In fact, the wicked, knowing their own guilt, will not attempt to plead their case before Him (Ps. 64:1; Rom. 3:19). Consequently, all who are tried at the Great White Throne judgment are found guilty of violating God's perfect, righteous standard.

God's minimum requirement to enter into heaven is sinless perfection. Committing just one sin during one's entire life will prevent entrance into God's presence, that is, unless one has been declared righteous in Christ. Though the Christian is not sinless, he or she has a position of sinless perfection in Christ, and indeed, because of that union, should sin less (Rom. 6:1-4). As no one can undo one morally wrong act through the performance of many good ones, it is impossible to enter heaven by doing good works (Rom. 4:3-4; Eph. 2:8-9).

To believe that one is deserving of heaven through doing good deeds is offensive to God, for that would mean that His judgment of His own Son on our behalf did not sufficiently satisfy His righteous demand for justice. This mindset means that individuals are really trusting in themselves, and not in Christ alone, for salvation. It is the erroneous message of world religion that you can improve your own spiritual essence or position through personal effort – essentially, you don't need a Savior. World religion says, "do, do, do," while biblical Christianity proclaims, "done, done, done." The former promotes personal effort for salvation, while the latter acknowledges that only personal faith in a Savior can save.

At the Great White Throne judgment, which occurs just prior to the Eternal State, everyone who has not experienced bodily resurrection will. Hades, the holding place of disembodied souls of the wicked, will be cleared out and these individuals, in resurrected bodies, will stand before the Lord to be judged. Some think that religion will save them and earn them an eternal place in the *Book of Life*; this will be the moment that they will learn otherwise. Everyone resurrected to stand before God at the Great White Throne judgment will be found guilty and will be cast into the Lake of Fire (Rev. 20:11-15). In summary, the first resurrection occurs in stages and is unto everlasting life with the

Lord, and the second resurrection is unto everlasting death in the Lake of Fire.

Reflecting Christ's Glory

The angel informed Daniel that glorified saints in heaven will shine like the brightness of the firmament, and those turning others to the Lord will shine like the stars forever (v. 3). Have you ever wondered how people will be attired in heaven or how they will appear? The Lord Jesus rebuked the Church at Laodicea with these words: *"You are wretched, miserable, poor, blind, and naked – I counsel you to buy from Me gold refined in the fire, that you may be rich; and white garments, that you may be clothed, that the shame of your nakedness may not be revealed; and anoint your eyes with eye salve, that you may see"* (Rev. 3:17-18). Those in the Church at Laodicea were not living for Christ; consequently, God's righteousness was not displayed in their lives. While all believers in the Church have been declared positionally righteous in Christ, each believer has the opportunity to labor in righteousness for Christ. Those things which are done in accordance with revealed truth and in the power of the Holy Spirit have eternal value; these righteous acts are what the believer is adorned with throughout eternity. In heaven, the bride of Christ must have righteous attire; she is *"arrayed in fine linen, clean and bright, for the fine linen is the righteous acts of the saints"* (Rev. 19:8).

Paul explains in 1 Corinthians 15:40-42 that, after the resurrection, some saints will shine with the glory of God more brightly than others, just as some stars in the nighttime sky are brighter than other stars. This acquired glory directly reflects the righteous acts (good works) that are done for Christ by His strength in this present life. Eternal glory, evidently, has a weight to it; in other words, its quality is measurable (2 Cor. 4:17) and can be earned by believers through selfless service for Christ now. Thus, to be appropriately dressed for eternity, believers should secure for themselves a covering of eternal glory, which consists of righteous acts. Though saved, a believer may still appear to be spiritually naked in heaven (i.e. personal acts of righteousness on earth provide believers with varying reflections of God's glory in heaven: Rev. 3:18; 1 Cor. 15:41-42; 2 Cor. 4:17). Without being justified in Christ, no one can enter heaven, and only by doing righteous acts for

Him and by His power do believers contribute to their eternal attire of glory.

Though believers in heaven will reflect the glory of God in varying degrees, all the redeemed will be wearing white robes and will have human form (Rev. 4:4, 19:14). Even before the martyred Tribulation saints experience glorification after the Tribulation Period (Rev. 20:4), they are described as wearing white robes in heaven (Rev. 6:11, 7:9, 13). The white robes represent divine purity and righteous position in Christ. All will be wearing the same thing; there will be no unusual outward qualities to attract attention, nor will we have the wherewithal to respond to such things anyway.

What is delightful and precious about everyone in heaven is that they will shine with the glory of God and will desire to worship and to honor Him in everything they do. What makes heaven heaven is that the One who suffered and died for you and for me will be there – anything that draws attention from Him will be an intolerable distraction. Every believer will enjoy the same blessed reality: *"My Beloved is mine, and I am His"* (SOS 2:16).

Meditation

> Immanuel, God with us in our nature, in our sorrow, in our lifework, in our punishment, in our grave, and now with us, or rather we with Him, in resurrection, ascension, triumph, and Second Advent splendor.
>
> — Charles Spurgeon

> The Word of truth teaches in the clearest and most positive terms that all of the dead will be raised. No doctrine of the faith rests upon a more literal and emphatic body of Scripture authority than this, nor is any more vital to Christianity.
>
> — C. I. Scofield

Tribulation Woes and Kingdom Blessings
Daniel 12:4-13

The angel concludes God's message to Daniel in verse 4: *"But you, Daniel, shut up the words, and seal the book until the time of the end; many shall run to and fro, and knowledge shall increase"* (v. 4). There would be no more divine messages for the elderly Daniel to record; he was to finish and secure his writings. His book would preserve the revelation that God intended Israel to benefit from as they neared the time of Jacob's Trouble.

From God's perspective, Israel is now between the 69th and the 70th prophetic weeks: Messiah came, was rejected, and was *"cut off"* (9:24-26), and the only thing remaining is *"the time of the end"* (9:27). Consequently, in respect to Israel, Daniel's book will be shut up until the end because the nation will continue in spiritual blindness until that time (Rom. 11:25). However, for those in the Church Age, these things are not sealed up, but rather are available for our understanding (Rev. 22:10, 16). After His resurrection, the Lord gave His Jewish disciples, His apostles for the Church, understanding of Old Testament Scripture, to better convey to us the mysteries of God's grace in New Testament Scripture (Luke 24:45).

Those believers in Daniel's day could not possibly have understood what Daniel wrote, but as the centuries continue to progress down the corridors of time, saints in the Church Age are able to understand with increased clarity what Daniel wrote, for we have God's Word and the Holy Spirit to enlighten our understanding. So the period directly prior to "the end times" (i.e., the Tribulation Period) will be characterized by Christians having a greater awareness of Daniel's prophecies, and also greater opportunity and an excitement to share its meaning – *"they will run to and fro."* Albert Barnes explains how this phrase relates to *"knowledge shall increase"* in the proper context of the passage:

Many shall run to and fro - Shall pass up and down in the world, or shall go from place to place. The reference is clearly to those who should thus go to impart knowledge; to give information; to call the attention of men to great and important matters. The language is applicable to any methods of imparting important knowledge, and it refers to a time when this would be the characteristic of the age. There is nothing else to which it can be so well applied as to the labors of Christian missionaries, and ministers of the gospel, and others who, in the cause of Christian truth, go about to rouse the attention of men to the great subjects of religion; and the natural application of the language is to refer it to the times when the gospel would be preached to the world at large.

And knowledge shall be increased - To wit, by this method. The angel seems to mean that in this way there would be an advance in knowledge on all the subjects of religion, and particularly on the points to which he had referred. This would be one of the characteristics of these times, and this would be the means by which it would be accomplished. Our own age has furnished a good illustration of the meaning of this language, and it will be still more fully and strikingly illustrated as the time approaches when the knowledge of the Lord shall fill the whole world.[143]

Some commentators suggest the phrases "many shall run to and fro" and "knowledge shall be increased" primarily relate to the swifter modes of transportation and an exponential increase in knowledge. While it is possible that these technological advances may occur simultaneously with the propagation of spiritual knowledge, the primary interpretation is likely that as the Tribulation Period nears, the meaning of Daniel's prophecies would become more evident. Those enduring the harsh reality of the Tribulation Period will perfectly understand their fulfillment.

The remainder of the chapter records two questions and two responses. The first question is by one of two escorting angels and the second is from Daniel; the angelic messenger with Daniel responds to both inquiries.

Apparently, when the angelic messenger (perhaps Gabriel) arrived at Daniel's location at the Tigris River (10:4), he was escorted by two other angels, under Michael's authority, who are now mentioned (v. 5). Both are clothed in white linen and one of these two angels took up a position on the opposite river bank and called out to the other escorting angel: *"How long shall the fulfillment of these wonders be?"* (v. 6). Which wonders was the angel referring to? Given the angelic messenger's response to the question, the answer is obviously that which pertains to the Tribulation Period (11:36-45). The angel standing next to Daniel responded by lifting both hands upward and swearing in the name of the One who lives forever (i.e., the One who possesses all life, which is God): *"It shall be for a time, times, and half a time; and when the power of the holy people has been completely shattered, all these things shall be finished"* (v. 7). During the last half of the Tribulation Period, the Antichrist will be permitted to slaughter the saints (except for a remnant of the nation of Israel; Rev. 12). As previously explained in chapters 7 and 9, this will continue for *"a time, and times and half a time"* (three and a half years, which equals 1,260 days or 42 months).

Daniel asks the angelic messenger the second question: *"My lord* [a word meaning "sir"], *what shall be the end of these things?"* The angel responds by telling Daniel to seal up his writing, for its revelation was not for his time, but others, those who are wise, would understand it in a future day (vv. 9-10). The angel then provides two additional periods of time relating to the 1,260-day abomination prophecy which will conclude the Tribulation Period: First there would be 1,290 days from the abomination of desolation (including the prohibition of proper daily sacrifices) until the end. Second, there would be great blessing for those surviving the Tribulation Period after an additional 45 days (1,335 days from the abomination of desolation).

We are not told specifically why there is an additional thirty days to the time, times, and half a time duration, which relates to the destruction of the Antichrist. This extra thirty days may relate to the total period of time that the beast's image is permitted to be displayed in the temple of Jerusalem (perhaps after the death of the Antichrist) or it may speak of the period between the taking away of the Jewish offerings before the Antichrist commits the Abomination of Desolation (i.e., demands worship in the temple as God). H. A. Ironside suggests a general meaning of the thirty-day interim:

> The extra thirty days will doubtless be devoted to the purging out of the kingdom of all things that offend and do iniquity, though the Lord will appear, on behalf of the remnant and for the destruction of the

Beast and Antichrist, at the expiration of the twelve hundred and sixty days.[144]

It is the author's opinion that *The Judgment of Nations* (see chapter 7 for a detailed explanation) will be completed within thirty days after the death of the Antichrist. All on the earth who took his mark will be executed and those who did not will be permitted to enter Christ's kingdom (Rev. 19:21). All those deemed unfit for Christ's kingdom will be abruptly removed from the earth.

Daniel is the only prophet to inform us that there will be a 75-day interval between the destruction of the Antichrist at the battle of Armageddon and the beginning of the blessings of the Kingdom Age (Dan. 12:7-13; Rev. 17-21). This time period is necessary to accomplish the Judgment of Nations, to cleanse the earth of the defilement and the devastation of the previous seven years, and to regather all Jews back to the Promised Land (Ezek. 39:28).

This truth has already been illustrated for us in Nebuchadnezzar's dream in chapter 2 when the stone from heaven (Christ) falls to the earth and smashes the image representing all Gentile dominion throughout the ages. The debris is then blown away by the wind and, afterwards, the stone grows into a great mountain. The Spirit of God is pictured in the wind (John 3:8), and mountains in Scripture are used to symbolize kingdoms (Isa. 2:2-3; Mic. 4:1; Rev. 17:9-10). But after all wickedness has been purged from the planet and it has been supernaturally rejuvenated to nullify the effects of sin, Jerusalem will be the seat of God's glory on the earth.

Conclusion

The Lord's Second Advent to the earth will conclude the period of time that the Gentiles were allowed to rule over Israel (Rom. 11:25). This event also coincides with the end of Israel's spiritual blindness (Rom. 11:7-14). When Christ came to the earth two thousand years ago, He removed the veil God had put over the Law (i.e., its full purpose was not disclosed until after Christ's ascension to heaven), but the Jews picked the veil back up and blindfolded themselves to the truth (2 Cor. 3:6-18). The purpose of the Mosaic Law was to show the Jews their sin (Rom. 3:20) and to point them to the solution: Christ (Gal. 3:24). At Calvary, Christ satisfied all of the judicial claims of the Law by substitutionally dying in the place of sinners. By rejecting His kingdom gospel message, the Jews became locked into a state of blindness, a condition that Satan works hard to maintain (2 Cor. 4:4).

However, during the Tribulation Period, the Jewish nation will be refined and then restored to God at its conclusion (Rom. 9:27; 11:26-32). They will recognize Jesus Christ as their Messiah (Zech. 12:10). Until then, the Lord Jesus Christ is building His Church which, although it includes both Jews and Gentiles, is chiefly composed of Gentiles. Moreover, God is bestowing blessings on Gentile believers to provoke the Jews to jealousy; this will ultimately result in their return to Him (Rom. 11:11-15). The Jews stumbled over Christ at His first advent and the blessing He offered them instead fell into the laps of the Gentiles, who were not even expecting it (Luke 20:9-16; Rom. 9:32). Thus, God is calling a people that were not His people by covenant to be His children (Hos. 2:23; Eph. 2:11-16). Gentiles are being brought into the good of the New Covenant (Hos. 1:10; Rom. 9:25-26).

There are those who teach that God is finished with the nation of Israel and that the Church has replaced the nation of Israel in God's plan of blessing. However, it should be emphasized that the New Covenant, sealed by Christ's own blood, was not confirmed with Gentiles, but with the houses of Israel and Judah (Heb. 8:8). God has sworn by His own name to complete what He promised to Abraham, Isaac, Jacob, and David. *"My covenant I will not break, nor alter the word that has gone out of My lips"* (Ps. 89:34). Jehovah is a covenant-keeping God and through the two earthly advents of Christ, God will fulfill all that He has promised to do! Who but God could have ever devised a plan to show so much grace to rebels? Thankfully, Jew and Gentile can benefit from the New Covenant, which is sealed with the blood of the Lord Jesus Christ, at this very moment.

The angel's final instructions to Daniel also confirm that God is not finished with the Jewish nation. Daniel was about to go the way of men (i.e., experience death), but in the latter days, when Israel was restored to Jehovah, he would be raised from the grave, with his fellow countrymen, to enjoy their promised inheritance (v. 13). It is at this moment that all saints who have previously died (i.e., Old Testament and tribulation saints) will experience glorification, says James Vernon McGee:

> Daniel is told (as the Lord Jesus told Simon Peter) that he would die. He would not live to see the return of Christ, but he would be raised

from the dead to enter the Millennium. "In thy lot" means that Daniel will be raised with the Old Testament saints at the beginning of the Millennium. "At the end of the days" brings us to the abundant entrance into Christ's kingdom.[145]

All those who have trusted the Lord and faithfully serve Him will rule and reign with the Lord Jesus in His kingdom to some degree (Rev. 21:7). The nation of Israel has a specific earthly inheritance which is described in the last two chapters of Ezekiel and they will receive it. The Tribulation martyrs who would not receive the mark of the beast will rule and reign with Christ (Rev. 20:4). And the Church will obtain her eternal heavenly inheritance with her head – the Lord Jesus Christ (2 Tim. 2:12)! The prophetic promise of God spoken by John will then be fulfilled: *"He who overcomes shall inherit all things, and I will be his God and he shall be My son"* (Rev. 21:7-8).

Meditation

And whatever you do, do it heartily, as to the Lord and not to men, knowing that from the Lord you will receive the reward of the inheritance; for you serve the Lord Christ (Col. 3:23-24).

Blessed be the God and Father of our Lord Jesus Christ, who according to His abundant mercy has begotten us again to a living hope through the resurrection of Jesus Christ from the dead, to an inheritance incorruptible and undefiled and that does not fade away, reserved in heaven for you, who are kept by the power of God through faith for salvation ready to be revealed in the last time (1 Pet. 1:3-5).

Endnotes

[1] P. C. Craigie, *Ezekiel* (Westminster, Philadelphia, PA; 1983), p. 22

[2] H. A. Ironside, *An Ironside Expository Commentary: Ezekiel* (Loizeaux Brothers, Inc. Bible Truth Depot, Neptune, NJ; 1949), p. xii

[3] William MacDonald, *Believer's Bible Commentary* (Thomas Nelson Publishers, Nashville, TN; 1989), p. 1041

[4] J. N. Darby, *Synopsis of the Books of the Bible Vol. 4* (Stow Hill Bible and Tract Depot, Kingston, ON: 1948), p. 279

[5] F. C. Cook, *Barnes' Notes Bible Commentary Vol. 5 – Proverbs to Ezekiel* (Baker Book House, Grand Rapids, MI; 1981), p. 312

[6] Kyle M. Yates, *Preaching From the Prophets* (Baptist Sunday School Board; June 1953), p. 181

[7] P. L. Tan, *Encyclopedia of 7700 illustrations* (Bible Communications, Garland TX; 1996, c1979)

[8] L. E. Cooper, *The New American Commentary – Ezekiel* (Broadman & Holman Publishers; 1994), p. 94

[9] Charles H. Dyer & Dallas Theological Seminary, *The Bible Knowledge Commentary: An Exposition of the Scriptures* (Victor Books, Wheaton, IL; 1983-1985), p. 1235

[10] F. C. Cook, op. cit., p. 315

[11] William Kelly, *Notes on Ezekiel*, STEM Publishing; chp. 4: http://stempublishing.com/authors/kelly/1Oldtest/EZEKIEL.html#a0

[12] H. A. Ironside, *An Ironside Expository Commentary: Jeremiah and Lamentations* (Shiloh Christian Library), p. 38

[13] William Kelly, op. cit.; chp. 7

[14] Charles H. Dyer & Dallas Theological Seminary, *The Bible Knowledge Commentary: An Exposition of the Scriptures* (Victor Books, Wheaton, IL; 1983-1985), p. 1163

[15] Alexander Hislop, *The Two Babylons* (Loizeaux Brothers, Neptune, NJ; 2nd ed. - 1959), p. 21

[16] Ibid., p. 22

[17] Ibid., p. 70

[18] Ibid., p. 88

[19] Ibid., p. 69

[20] Ibid., p. 21

[21] Ibid., p. 87

22 Walter J. Veith, PhD, *Paganism and Catholicism: The Mother-Son Sun Worship System* (Amazing Discoveries) [last accessed March 28, 2017] http://amazingdiscoveries.org/S-deception_paganism_Catholic_Nimrod_Mary
23 F. C. Cook, op. cit., p. 324
24 D. L. Moody, *A Jealous God* Sermon 502; March 29, 1863
25 L. E. Cooper, op. cit., p. 127
26 William MacDonald, op. cit., p. 852
27 H. A. Ironside, *Notes on the Book of Ezra* (Shiloh Christian Library, no date), pp. 5-6
28 Hamilton Smith, *The Psalms*, STEM Publishing: http://stempublishing.com/authors/smith/PSALMS.html
29 William Kelly, op. cit.; chp. 11
30 L. E. Cooper, op. cit., p. 149
31 H. A. Ironside, *An Ironside Expository Commentary: Ezekiel*, op. cit., p. 82
32 Ibid, p. 98
33 F. C. Cook, op. cit., p. 338
34 J. B. Taylor, *Ezekiel* (InterVarsity Press, Downers Grove, IL; 1969), p. 147
35 H. A. Ironside, *An Ironside Expository Commentary: Ezekiel*, op. cit., p. 116
36 William MacDonald, op. cit., pp. 1051-1052
37 W. T. P. Wolston, *Ezekiel's Forty Days*, STEM Publishing; chp. 18 http://stempublishing.com/authors/wolston/40DAYS08.html
38 Charles H. Dyer, op. cit., p. 1262
39 William MacDonald, op. cit., p. 1052
40 William Kelly, op. cit.; chp. 20
41 Charles H. Dyer, op. cit., p. 1268
42 W. Graham Scroggie, *The Land and the Life of Rest* (Harvey Christian Pub., Hampton, TN; 1950), p. 48
43 A. W. Pink, *Gleanings in Genesis* (Moody Press, Chicago: 1922), p. 274
44 Charles H. Dyer, op. cit., p. 1271
45 Jeremy Hughes, *Secrets of the Times* (Sheffield Academic Press, Sheffield; 1990), p. 229
46 Sir Robert Anderson, *The Coming Prince*: Chapter 5 – The Prophetic Year http://www.WhatSaithTheScripture.com
47 Ibid., Preface to the Tenth Edition [last accessed March 28, 2017]
48 L. E. Cooper, op. cit., p. 239
49 Matthew Henry, *Commentary on the Whole Bible, Vol. 3* (MacDonald Pub. Co., Mclean, VA; 1985), Eccl. 7:7
50 Ibid., 1 Cor. 3:18
51 Quintus Curtius Rufus, *History of Alexander the Great of Macedonia*; Section 4.4.10-21
52 H. A. Ironside, *Proverbs* (Loizeaux Brothers, Neptune, NJ; 1995), p. 67
53 Matthew Henry, *Commentary on the Whole Bible, Vol. 4* (MacDonald Pub. Co., Mclean, VA; 1985), Isa. 6

54 Albert Barnes, *Barnes Notes – 1 Cor. 11:6* (Baker Book House, Grand Rapids, MI; reprinted from 1884 edition published by Blackie and Son, London), Isa. 6

55 William MacDonald, op. cit., p. 944

56 Warren Wiersbe, *Wiersbe's Expository Outlines on the Old Testament* (Victor Books, Wheaton, IL; 1993), electronic copy

57 Warren Wiersbe, *The Bible Exposition Commentary, Vol. 2* (Victor Books, Wheaton, IL; 1989), p. 582

58 Enns, P. P., *The Moody Handbook of Theology* (Moody Press, Chicago, IL; 1997, c1989), electronic copy: *Attributes of God* section

59 Watchman Nee, *Love One Another* (reprinted by Christian Fellowship Publishers; Richmond, VA; 1975)

60 Charles H. Dyer, op. cit., p. 1289

61 William Kelly, op. cit.; chp. 32

62 H. A. Ironside, *An Ironside Expository Commentary: Ezekiel*, op. cit., p. 225

63 Matthew Henry, *Commentary on the Whole Bible, Vol. 4* (MacDonald Pub. Co., Mclean, VA; 1985), p. 949

64 Ibid. p. 950

65 H. A. Ironside, *An Ironside Expository Commentary: Ezekiel*, op. cit., p. 238

66 James Vernon McGee, *Thru The Bible Commentary Vol. 3* (Thomas Nelson Publishers, Nashville, TN; 1983), p. 505

67 David Baron, *The Shepherd of Israel and His Scattered Flock* (Morgan and Scott; 1910), pp. 8-9

68 L. E. Cooper, op. cit., pp. 304-305

69 William Kelly, *Notes on Jeremiah and Lamentations* (Jer. 31) http://www.stempublishing.com/authors/kelly/1Oldtest/jeremiah.html

70 *Oxford English Dictionary* (Oxford University Press, NY); 1989

71 William Kelly, op. cit.; chp. 36

72 L. E. Cooper, op. cit., p. 314

73 Kyle M. Yates, op. cit., p. 184

74 Rabbi David E. Lipman, *The Birth of Israel,* [last accessed on March 28, 2017] http://www.myjewishlearning.com/israel/History/1948-1967/Birth_of_Israel.shtml

75 L. E. Cooper, op. cit., p. 329

76 William Kelly, op. cit.; chp. 38

77 Barry Cunliffe, *The Oxford History of Prehistoric Europe* (Oxford University Press; 1994), pp. 381–382

78 Josephus, *Antiquities of the Jews*, I:6.

79 L. E. Cooper, op. cit., p. 334

80 H. A. Ironside, *An Ironside Expository Commentary: Ezekiel*, op. cit., p. 269

81 Jewish Virtual Library – Vital Statistic: Population of Israel [last accessed March 28, 2017]: http://www.jewishvirtuallibrary.org/jsource/Society_&_Culture/Population_of_Israel.html

82 Donald Barnhouse, *The Invisible War* (Zondervan Pub. House, Grand Rapids, MI; 1965), p. 107).

83   Lambert Dolphin, The Temple Of Ezekiel [last accessed on March 28, 2017]: http://www.templemount.org/ezektmp.html (diagram digitally enhanced for clarity)

84   Original concept from Iain M. Duguid, *Ezekiel*, NIVAC, p. 473 (diagram modified with additional information) [last accessed on March 28, 2017]: http://www.members.optusnet.com.au/futurewatch/id103.htm

85   Charles H. Dyer, op. cit., p. 1303 (diagram digitally enhanced for clarity)

86   Original template from Charles H. Dyer, op. cit., p. 1303

87   Charles H. Dyer, op. cit., p. 1308

88   William Kelly, op. cit.; chp. 44

89   H. A. Ironside, *An Ironside Expository Commentary: Jeremiah and Lamentations* (Shiloh Christian Library), p. 153

90   F. B. Hole, http://stempublishing.com/authors/hole/Pent/LEVITICUS.html

91   William Kelly, op. cit.; chp. 40

92   Charles C. Ryrie, *Dispensationalism,* revised edition (Moody Press, Chicago, IL; 1995), p. 115

93   J. N. Darby, op. cit., p. 307

94   Matthew Henry, op. cit., p. 1005

95   F. C. Cook, op. cit., p. 421

96   Mark Perry, *An Introduction to Ezekiel 40-48* [last accessed on March 28, 2017] http://mkperry.blogspot.com/2005/07/introduction-to-ezekiel-40-48.html

97   William Kelly, op. cit.; chp. 48

98   F. M. Cross Jr., *The Ancient Library of Qumran*, 2nd ed. (Doubleday, Garden City NY; 1961), p. 43

99   *Bible and the Spade* Vol. 24; No. 2 (Spring 2011): "New Light on the Book of Daniel from the Dead Sea Scrolls"

100   E. Ulrich, (Daniel Manuscripts from Qumran, Part 2: Preliminary Editions of 4QDanb and 4QDanc. *Bulletin of the American Schools of Oriental Research* 274:3–26; 1989), p. 3

101   Hamilton Smith, *The Book of Daniel*, STEM Publishing: http://stempublishing.com/authors/smith/DANIEL.html

102   Albert Barnes, *The Bible Commentary – Daniel Vol.1* (Baker Book House, Grand Rapids, MI; reprinted 1879), p. 3

103   Hamilton Smith, op. cit., chp. 1

104   Albert Barnes, op. cit., p. 108

105   Matthew Henry, *Commentary on the Whole Bible, Vol. 4* (MacDonald Pub. Co., Mclean, VA; 1985), Dan. 1

106   H. A. Ironside, *Daniel the Prophet* (Loizeaux Brothers, New York, NY; 1960), p. 19

107   H. A. Ironside, *Notes on the Book of Ezra* (Shiloh Christian Library, no date), pp. 5-6

108   Hamilton Smith, op. cit., chp. 2

109   V. Raymond Edman, *They Found the Secret* (Zondervan Publishing House, Grand Rapids, MI; 1984), p. 19

110 Hamilton Smith, op. cit., chp. 3
111 J. N. Darby, *Studies on the Book of Daniel*, STEM Publishing:
http://stempublishing.com/authors/darby/PROPHET/05023_31E.html#a1
112 Jim Elliot, quoted by wife Elisabeth Elliot in *Shadow of the Almighty* (Harper and Row, New York, NY; 1958), p. 108
113 Matthew Henry, op. cit., Dan. 3
114 William Kelly, *Notes on the Book of Daniel*, STEM Publishing:
http://stempublishing.com/authors/kelly/1Oldtest/Daniel.html
115 William Kelly, *Proverbs*, STEM Publishing:
http://stempublishing.com/authors/kelly/1Oldtest/proverbs.html
116 H. A. Ironside, *Proverbs* (Loizeaux Brothers, Neptune, NJ; 1995), p. 67
117 R. C. Chapman, *Robert Cleaver Chapman of Barnstaple*, by W. H. Bennet (Pickering & Inglis, Glasgow, Scotland; no date – 1st ed.), pp. 125-126
118 Herodotus, *Histories*, 1.178-186
119 Ibid., 1.191
120 James B. Pritchard, *Ancient Near Eastern Texts Relating to the Old Testament* (Princeton University Press, Princeton, NJ; 1955), p. 306
121 Ibid., p. 313
122 H. A. Ironside, *Daniel the Prophet*, op. cit., pp. 79-80
123 Leon J. Wood, *A Commentary on Daniel* (Zondervan, Grand Rapids, MI; 1973), p. 154
124 Hamilton Smith, op. cit., chp. 6
125 William MacDonald, *Believer's Bible Commentary* (Thomas Nelson Publishers, Nashville, TN; 1989), p. 1082
126 Matthew Henry, op. cit., Dan. 6
127 Hamilton Smith, op. cit., chp. 8
128 F. F. Bruce, *Israel and the Nations* (Paternoster Press, UK; 1963), pp. 134-154
129 Russell Earl Kelly, *Exposing Seventh-day Adventism*, chp. 16
http://www.tithing-russkelly.com/sda/id29.html
130 Josephus, *Antiquities* b. xii. ch. vii. Section 6
131 Josephus, *Jewish Wars*. b. i. ch. i. Section 1
132 Albert Barnes, *The Bible Commentary – Daniel Vol. 2* (Baker Book House, Grand Rapids, MI; reprinted 1879), p. 115
133 H. A. Ironside, *Daniel the Prophet*, op. cit., p. 157
134 Hamilton Smith, op. cit., chp. 9
135 William MacDonald, *True Discipleship* (Gospel Folio Press, Port Colborne, ON; 2003), p. 159
136 H. A. Ironside, *Daniel the Prophet*, op. cit., p. 159
137 Sir Robert Anderson, *The Coming Prince* (Hodder & Stoughton, London; 1881, reprinted by Kregel, Grand Rapids, MI; 1975)
138 Matthew Henry, op. cit., Dan. 10
139 Josephus, Antiquities 12.246-251
140 Ibid., 12.255-256

[141] J. Dwight Pentecost, *The Bible Knowledge Commentary: An Exposition of the Scriptures* (Victor Books, Wheaton, IL; 1983-1985), p. 1371

[142] Ibid., p. 1372

[143] Albert Barnes, *The Bible Commentary – Daniel Vol. 2, op. cit.,* p. 262

[144] H. A. Ironside, *Daniel the Prophet*, op. cit., p. 236

[145] James Vernon McGee, *Thru the Bible* Vol. III (Thomas Nelson Publishers, Nashville, TN; 1981), p. 606

CPSIA information can be obtained
at www.ICGtesting.com
Printed in the USA
LVOW10s2138170417

531055LV00066B/1698/P